C++ Standard Library
Practical Tips

D1500978

C++ STANDARD LIBRARY
PRACTICAL TIPS

GREG REESE

CHARLES RIVER MEDIA, INC.
Hingham, Massachusetts

Acquisitions Editor: James Walsh
Cover Design: Tyler Creative

CHARLES RIVER MEDIA, INC.
10 Downer Avenue
Hingham, Massachusetts 02043
781-740-0400
781-740-8816 (FAX)
info@charlesriver.com
www.charlesriver.com

This book is printed on acid-free paper.

Greg Reese. *C++ Standard Library Practical Tips.*
ISBN: 1-58450-400-5

Library of Congress Cataloging-in-Publication Data
Reese, Greg, 1959-
  C++ standard library practical tips / Greg Reese.
    p. cm.
  Includes bibliographical references and index.
  ISBN 1-58450-400-5 (pbk. with cd-rom : alk. paper)
  1. C++ (Computer program language) I. Title.
  QA76.73.C153R44 2005
  005.13'3--dc22

                    2005015845

Printed in the United States of America
05 7 6 5 4 3 2 First Edition

To Katie,

who gave me the time to write this book

Contents

Acknowledgments   xv
Preface   xvii

Chapter 1 The C++ Standard Library   1

Introduction and History   1
Overview   3
  Language Support   5
  Diagnostics   6
  General Utilities   7
  Strings   7
  Locales   8
  Containers   9
  Iterators   9
  Algorithms   10
  Numerics   10
  Input / Output   11
Error Handling   12
  Exception Handling   13
  Exception Handling in the Standard Library   18
Namespaces   21

Chapter 2 Review of the Standard Template Library   27

History   29
Iterators   30
  Iterator Categories   30
  Ranges   36

Iterator Adaptors	38
Reverse Iterators	38
Insert Iterators	44
Stream Iterators	47
Containers	49
Sequence Containers	49
Associative Containers	53
Container Adaptors	56
Miscellaneous Containers	58
Functors	60
Predefined Function Objects	63
Algorithms	70
Nonmodifying Algorithms	72
Modifying Algorithms	73
Mutating Algorithms	73
Partitioning and Sorting Algorithms	74
Sorted Range Algorithms	75
Heap Algorithms	76
Numeric Algorithms	76
Binary Algorithms	77
Error Handling	77
Endnotes	80
Chapter 3 Tips on Containers in General	**81**
Tip 0 Sample Tip—Display the Elements of a Container	82
Tip 1 Use the Right Container	85
Tip 2 Requirements on Container Elements	87
Tip 3 C-Style Arrays Have Beginning and End Iterators	90
Tip 4 Construct a Container Filled with the Same Value	93
Tip 5 Construct a Container Filled with Specified Values	94
Tip 6 Construct One Container from Another	96

Tip 7   Construct a Container from Standard Input   98

Tip 8   Store Specified Values in an Existing Container   100

Tip 9   Store Contents of One Container in Another   102

Tip 10   Append One Container to Another   104

Tip 11   Exchange Containers   106

Tip 12   Get a Container's Size and Maximum Size   109

Tip 13   Is One Container Greater Than Another?   111

Tip 14   Are Two Containers Equal?   114

Tip 15   Access a Container in Reverse   116

Tip 16   Display a Container on Standard Output   120

Chapter 4 Tips on Vectors   123

Tip 17   Reserve Space for Elements   123

Tip 18   Remove Excess Memory   125

Tip 19   Use an Index   128

Tip 20   Convert Between Iterators and Indexes   131

Tip 21   Be Careful of Invalidated Iterators   134

Tip 22   Classes Should Have Constructors, Destructors, and an Assignment Operator   136

Tip 23   Fast Access at the Back   140

Tip 24   Checked and Unchecked Access   144

Tip 25   Get a C-Style Array from a Vector   147

Tip 26   Use a Vector of Booleans to Manipulate Bits   149

Chapter 5 Tips on Deques   153

Tip 27   Operations at Front   153

Tip 28   Alternative to a Vector of Booleans   156

Chapter 6 Tips on Lists   161

Tip 29   Use the Front and Back   161

Tip 30   Sort   164

Tip 31   Splice   169

Tip 32   Merge   176

Tip 33   Remove Duplicates   182

Chapter 7 Tips on Associative Containers   **187**

Tip 34   Initialize with Specified Values   189

Tip 35   Use a Map or Multimap as a Dictionary   193

Tip 36   Search in Sets and Multisets   197

Tip 37   Search in Maps and Multimaps   207

Tip 38   Modify or Remove Elements in a Set or Multiset   218

Tip 39   Modify or Remove Elements in a Map or Multimap   222

Tip 40   Use the Sorted Range Algorithms with Sets and Multisets   233

Chapter 8 Tips on Other Containers   **241**

Tip 41   Using a Stack Data Structure   241

Tip 42   A First-In, First-Out Data Structure and Buffering   244

Tip 43   Buffering with Priority Removal   248

Tip 44   Using a Fixed-Size Collection of Bits   252

Tip 45   Using a Pair of the Same or Different Data Types   256

Chapter 9 Tips on Algorithms   **261**

Tip 46   Use the Most Specific Algorithm   261

Tip 47   Use a Function in Algorithms   264

Tip 48   Use a Class Member Function in an Algorithm   271

Tip 49   Use a Pointer to a Class Member Function in an Algorithm   276

Tip 50   Freeze an Argument to a Function Object   283

Tip 51   Find and Erase the First or Last Matching Element   287

Tip 52   Remove All Matching Elements   294

Tip 53   Really Remove All Matching Elements   297

Tip 54   Sort Before Performing Set Operations   302

Tip 55   Sort on One of Many Fields   310

Tip 56   Sort with Multiple Criteria   314

Tip 57   Sort Without Copying   322

Tip 58   Copy if a Condition Is Met   327

Tip 59   Operate on Each Element of a Container   330

Chapter 10   Tips on Text Processing   339

Tip 60   Copy Strings and Substrings   341

Tip 61   Concatenate Strings and Substrings   343

Tip 62   Search Strings   345

Tip 63   Replace Characters by a Given Character   349

Tip 64   Reverse Strings and Get Their Length   351

Tip 65   Compare Strings with Case-Sensitivity   353

Tip 66   Compare Substrings with Case-Sensitivity   355

Tip 67   Compare Strings without Case-Sensitivity   359

Tip 68   Compare Substrings without Case-Sensitivity   364

Tip 69   Read Formatted Strings   370

Tip 70   Write Formatted Strings   373

Tip 71   Get a C String from a C++ string   376

Tip 72   Strip Whitespace   378

Tip 73   Convert to Upper or Lower Case   382

Tip 74   Extract Words Delimited by Whitespace   384

Tip 75   Extract Tokens That Are Between Delimiters   386

Chapter 11   Tips on Numerical Processing   391

Tip 76   Perform Arithmetic on Containers   391

Tip 77   Complex Numbers   394

Tip 78   Differences Between a Container's Elements   398

Tip 79   Make Consecutive, Evenly Spaced Numbers   402

Tip 80   Make a Sequence of Random Numbers   405

Tip 81   Evaluate a Mathematical Function   407

Tip 82   Compute the Dot Product   411

Tip 83   Find the Minimum and Maximum in a Container   415

Tip 84   Minimum and Maximum of Two Values Using
          Custom Criterion   417

Tip 85   Minimum and Maximum of Data Types   419

Tip 86   Compute the Mean   423

Tip 87   Compute the Median   424

Tip 88   Compute the Mode   427

Tip 89   Compute the Percentile   430

Tip 90   Compute Statistics of Data   434

Tip 91   Input and Output in Binary Format   437

Tip 92   Input and Output in Octal Format   440

Tip 93   Input and Output in Hexadecimal Format   442

Tip 94   Display Leading Zeros of Integers   444

Tip 95   Display Precision of Floating-Point Numbers   446

Tip 96   Display a Thousands' Separator   449

Tip 97   Access Data in a File   452

Chapter 12 Final Tips   **457**

Tip 98   Get a Free, Portable STL   457

Tip 99   Get Free, High-Quality STL Code   458

Tip 100   Share the Wealth—Contribute Your Favorite Tip   460

Chapter 13 Image Processing   **461**

Image Class   463

Image Creation   472

   Block   473

   Vertical Bars   474

Image Magnification   477

   Shrinking   477

   Expanding   480

Image Arithmetic   483

Subtraction   487

Image Enhancement   488

  Clipping   489

  Look-Up Tables   495

  Convolution   500

Appendix A More Information on STL Algorithms   **513**

Appendix B About the CD-ROM   **523**

Contents   523

System Requirements   524

Installation   524

References   **527**

Bibliography   **529**

Books   529

  The C++ Standard Library and the STL   529

  General C++   529

Magazine Articles   530

Web Sites   531

Internet Usenet Groups   532

Index   **533**

Acknowledgments

Thanks to all the reviewers, who took the time out of their busy lives to read and critique the manuscript. They are Ian Long, Ronald van Loon, Jan Christiaan van Winkel, and Steve Vinoski, who reviewed an early version of the manuscript; Andrew Sterian, who read the half manuscript; and Randi Stern and Dietmar Kuhel, who made it through the entire manuscript. I am especially indebted to Dietmar, who went far and beyond the call of a reviewer's duty. This book, and especially Chapter 2, are much better for his thorough and knowledgeable comments.

Jim Walsh, my editor at Charles River Media, has been professional and courteous throughout this project, especially when under a barrage of my naïve questions on publishing. I would also like to thank the following people: Mike Uchic, for letting me use one of his material micrographs; Mark Cannon, for his picture of the Russian-style church in Alaska; Patty Jackson, Registered Dental Hygienist, for the X-ray of the tooth in the model jaw; and Chris Woodward, for the list of his many publications. Finally, I would like to thank all the authors of C++ books and all the C++ programmers from whose works I have learned so much.

Preface

For the last 10 or so years, I've been programming in C++. I really enjoy the language for its power, brevity, and accommodation of three major programming styles—structured programming, object-oriented programming, and generic programming. In addition, C++ has a powerful and concise library that comes with every compiler that conforms to the language standard. Unfortunately, the library is not the easiest thing in the world to learn and use. And, although there are many good C++ textbooks and some very good C++ Standard Library reference books (my copy of Nicolai Josuttis's excellent *The C++ Standard Library* is falling apart from use), I haven't found any works that provide quick, concise, Standard Library solutions to practical programming problems. So, necessity being the mother of invention, I wrote this book to fill that gap.

The book's primary audience is new and intermediate C++ Standard Library programmers. They can be in any application area that uses C++, such as graphics programming, multimedia development, scientific computation, or financial software. They often have titles like Programmer, Software Engineer, Software Developer, or Applications Developer. People in this target audience should have a moderate amount of experience programming C++. This might include a course in the language, studying any of the plethora of C++ textbooks or tutorials, and perhaps even a year or two of actual programming experience. These programmers should also have some experience, even if it is minimal, using the Standard Library. For example, they should be able to call the Standard Library functions and understand the rudiments of templates and Standard Library containers. However, they do not need to know what parts of the Standard Library they should use to solve their programming problems. After all, that's the point of this book!

The book is organized in a way that lets you quickly find the answer to your programming problem. The heart of the book is the 100 tips on using the C++ Standard Library. They're all short—about two to four pages each. Just look at the tip titles in the table of contents and flip to one you're interested in. You'll notice that each tip starts with a short solution. This is a very concise answer to the programming problem. If you're an experienced Standard Library user or you just need to jog your memory, this short paragraph or two will satisfy you.

Following the bare-bones answer is a detailed solution. This is useful if you've never used the tip's technique or if the short solution is just too concise. The detailed answer has a complete C++ program that illustrates the method in the tip. The text discusses the code and gives a thorough explanation of its key points. A few of the programs may seem longer than what is necessary solely to demonstrate a technique. I've done this on purpose, though. One of the things that bothers me about many technical books is that the examples are too simplistic to be of much help. Because object-oriented programming is so important to C++, quite a few of the programs use classes, and this causes the code to be longer. However, I find this makes the examples more realistic, helpful, and valuable. Deciding between brevity and practicality is subjective, however, and someone is certainly bound to be disappointed by my choice.

Nonetheless, you don't have to worry about having to slog through endless pages of pontification—the programs are only about a page or two long, and the explanations just slightly longer. You can quickly get a good understanding of your problem's solution and then get back to the fun stuff—writing code.

If you'd like to explore a tip in more detail, you have several options. First, each tip has references to other relevant tips. These tips may contain alternate techniques, related methods, or supplementary material. Second, the tips are grouped according to topic. Thus, for example, if you're about to start working with vectors and would like some background first, you can leaf through Chapter 4, "Tips on Vectors." It will give you some tips on the power and pitfalls of this container. Third, Chapter 13 has an application that uses some of the tips in a realistic setting. If the technique you're interested in is in this chapter, you get to see it in action. Finally, Chapters 1 and 2 contain an overview and review of the Standard Library and its main component, the Standard Template Library. This information helps you see how the tip fits into the general scheme of things and serves as a good review of some basic Standard Library concepts.

1 The C++ Standard Library

INTRODUCTION AND HISTORY

The power of modern computer languages lies not as much in the languages themselves as in their accompanying libraries. A *library* is a collection of software components used to make other pieces of software. Often you use it to make a whole program, but you can also use it to build other components such as functions or classes. Libraries have various advantages over custom code:

- They may deal with a specialized field such as finance or arcane subjects like non-uniform rational B-splines. Creating these libraries can require subject matter expertise or special programming techniques not available to the typical programmer.
- They can provide low-level access to the operating system, such as file attributes or the system time and date.
- They can provide high-level access to the operating system, for example, the encapsulation of detailed GUI (graphical user interface) calls into a more usable GUI framework.
- They can provide commonly used software. This helps prevent masses of programmers from creating their own versions of the code and thus continually reinventing the wheel.
- They allow more functionality to be added to a language without changing the core of the language itself.

The *standard library* of a language is a library that comes with the official version of the language. Besides the previously mentioned advantages of libraries, using a standard library can benefit programmers and organizations in the following ways:

1

- They will develop programs more quickly. A standard library usually contains a large amount of functionality that is commonly used in programming. This means that software developers won't have to take time to create this code.
- They will write programs that are more reliable because standard libraries tend to be extensively tested and used.
- They will write software that is more portable because a standard library is available on a wide variety of computers and operating systems—after all, it's the standard.
- They will have shorter development times because standard libraries are widely used and recognized. Programmers starting on a project with standard library code will not have to spend time learning that part of the software.
- They will have lower maintenance costs because a standard library is familiar to many programmers and this avoids costly learning time.

The C++ Standard Library provides many of these benefits. It has code that deals with specialized applications (complex numbers, numeric computations), low level file information, common functionality (searching, sorting, replacing, counting, etc.), and popular data structures (vector, list, deque, map, set). It also allows the language to change while keeping the core part of C++ the same. For example, many of the modifications currently being proposed to standard C++, such as tuples, special mathematical functions, regular expressions, and an extendable random number facility are purely additions to the Standard Library and not changes in the basic language itself.

Just as C++ evolved from C, the C++ Standard Library came from the Standard C Library. The latest version of the C++ Standard Library took ten years to develop and became part of the official, worldwide C++ language standard in 1998. One important design consideration was to specify and standardize the relationship between C++ and the Standard C Library, which was used ubiquitously in the C programming world. The result was that the Standard C Library, with minor changes, actually became part of its C++ counterpart. However, the library also has other goals [Stroustrup94]:

- It should be affordable and essential to all programmers.
- It should be efficient enough so that a programmer is not tempted to write his own version because he believes it will be faster.
- It should be reasonably convenient and safe.
- Any functionality it has should be reasonably complete. That is, if the library provides services in an area, you should be able to complete basic programs in that field without having to replace the library's code or create additional core software. Note, however, that the library does not cover some major areas of programming, such as GUI and Internet.

■ It should be type safe, support common programming styles, and work well with user defined types.

Unfortunately, clarity, consistency, and ease of use were not design goals. The library's style is not consistent because it evolved over time and different people designed different parts. For example, C++ text strings have extensive error checking whereas the Standard Template Library, the major component of the Standard Library, has virtually none. In addition, although the library is very powerful, it can also be cryptic. It's often not obvious how to accomplish even a routine task. The tips in this book are meant to fix that situation and let you use the C++ Standard Library to its fullest potential.

OVERVIEW

The components of the C++ Standard Library fit into a number of general categories, as Figure 1.1 shows. They are as follows: language support, diagnostics, general utilities, strings, locales, containers, iterators, algorithms, numerics, and input/output (I/O). Algorithms, containers, iterators, and numerics are, for historical reasons, often grouped together and referred to as the Standard Template Library (STL). The Standard C Library is also, with minor modifications, part of the C++ Standard Library. The C++ standard incorporates the C library by reference (see Figure 1.1) and doesn't discuss its details. This book will do the same.

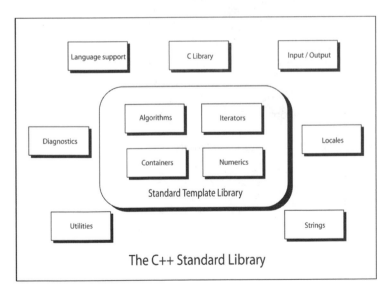

FIGURE 1.1 Components of the C++ Standard Library.

Briefly put, the categories provide the following:

Language support: Capabilities, such as memory allocation and exception processing, required by some parts of the core language

Diagnostics: A framework for reporting errors in C++ programs

General utilities: Components called by users and other parts of the Standard Library

Strings: Specialized classes for working with small amounts of text

Locales: Support for internationalization of text processing

Containers: Classic data structures, such as the list, vector, and map

Algorithms: Functions for basic processing such as searching, sorting, and replacing

Iterators: Generalized pointers that connect containers to algorithms

Numerics: Algorithms (functions) useful primarily in numerical computations

Input/Output: The primary C++ mechanism for input and output

Standard C library: The C-language standard library

All elements of the C++ Standard Library are declared or defined in a *header*. The compiler inserts this code into a translation unit, typically a file. To specify a header, use the preprocessing directive

```
#include <header_name>
```

where `header_name` is the name of the header that you need. To find what header or headers you need for a particular Standard Library component, check for that component's description in your compiler documentation or in a reference book. Table 1.1 lists the 32 headers that contain all of the Standard Library component declarations or definitions.

TABLE 1.1 The C++ Standard Library Headers

`<algorithm>`	`<bitset>`	`<complex>`	`<deque>`	`exception>`
`<fstream>`	`<functional>`	`<iomanip>`	`<ios>`	`<iosfwd>`
`<iostream>`	`<istream>`	`<iterator>`	`<limits>`	`<list>`
`<locale>`	`<map>`	`<memory>`	`<new>`	`<numeric>`
`<ostream>`	`<queue>`	`<set>`	`<sstream>`	`<stack>`
`<stdexcept>`	`<streambuf>`	`<string>`	`<typeinfo>`	`<utility>`
`<valarray>`	`<vector>`			

The parts of the Standard C Library that C++ uses are in 18 headers. Table 1.2 shows their C++ names. These are the same as the C names except the ".h" is dropped and a "c" prefix is added, for example, `<assert.h>` becomes `<cassert>`, `<stdio.h>` becomes `<cstdio>`; The chief difference between the two is that the C++ headers put all C library elements except macros into the `std` namespace, whereas the C headers (which can also be used in C++) place their elements in the global namespace. Because of this, unless your program needs strict C-compatibility, you should use the C++ headers. (For more information on namespaces, see "Namespaces" at the end of this chapter.)

TABLE 1.2   C++ Header Names for C Headers

`<cassert>`	`<cctype>`	`<cerrno>`	`<cfloat>`	`<ciso646>`	`<climits>`
`<clocale>`	`<cmath>`	`<csetjmp>`	`<csignal>`	`<cstdio>`	`<cstdlib>`
`<cstdarg>`	`<cstddef>`	`<cstring>`	`<ctime>`	`<cwchar>`	`<cwctype>`

Language Support

The language support section of the library contains headers that let you work with dynamic memory, exception handling, type identification, and some miscellaneous things. Table 1.3 shows how the Standard Library groups the headers. Table 1.4 lists the headers in Table 1.3 alphabetically and briefly describes their contents.

TABLE 1.3   Categories of Language Support Header

Category	Headers
Dynamic memory management	`<new>`
Exception handling	`<exception>`
Implementation properties	`<limits>`, `<climits>`, `<cfloat>`
Other runtime support	`<csetjmp>`, `<csignal>`, `<cstdarg>`,`<cstdlib>`, `<ctime>`
Start and termination	`<cstdlib>`
Type identification	`<typeinfo>`
Types	`<cstddef>`

TABLE 1.4 Language Support Headers

Header	Functionality
`<cfloat>`	Information about floating point data types, such as their minimum, maximum, number of digits in their exponent and mantissa, and so forth. Use `<limits>` instead
`<climits>`	Minimum and maximum values of all basic data types. Use `<limits>` instead
`<csetjmp>`	Nonlocal jumps. Use `<exception>` instead
`<csignal>`	Signal handling
`<cstdarg>`	Variable arguments
`<cstddef>`	NULL, `offsetof`, `ptrdiff_t`, and `size_t`
`<cstdlib>`	Exit routines and macros, runtime environment information
`<ctime>`	System time and date functions, such as `clock` and `time`
`<exception>`	`exception` class, `bad_exception` exception, exception handlers
`<limits>`	Information about properties of basic data types, such as their minimum and maximum, and the maximum amount of numerals in their representation
`<new>`	Operators `new` and `delete`, exceptions for dynamic memory allocation
`<typeinfo>`	Class to hold runtime information about an object's data type, exceptions for this class

The header `<limits>` expands on and replaces `<climits>` and `<cfloat>`. It contains a class template that provides information for all built-in data types that can represent numbers. It's better to use `<limits>` rather than the two older headers because it has the following advantages:

- Offers more type safety
- Lets you write templates that can evaluate these limits
- Contains more information
- Avoids the use of macros
- Allows you to easily write limits for your own data types

Diagnostics

The diagnostics section of the Standard Library describes library components used for detecting and reporting errors. Table 1.5 lists the headers and briefly describes their contents. "Error Handling" later in this chapter has an extensive discussion of error detection and reporting.

TABLE 1.5   Diagnostics Headers

Header	Functionality
`<cassert>`	`assert` macro
`<cerrno>`	Global error-number variable, numbers for common errors
`<stdexcept>`	Predefined exceptions for common errors

General Utilities

This section of the Standard Library contains utility components used by other parts of the library. C++ programs may use them also. Table 1.6 lists the headers and briefly describes their contents.

TABLE 1.6   General Utilities Headers

Header	Functionality
`<ctime>`	System time and date functions, such as `clock` and `time`
`<functional>`	Function objects (see "Functors" in Chapter 2)
`<memory>`	Allocators, raw memory, and autopointers
`<utility>`	Generic relational operators, `pair` data structure

Strings

The Strings section of the library contains headers that let you work with C-style strings (null-terminated character arrays) and the new C++ text strings. The latter are far superior, so you should use them if you can. Chapter 10 explains their advantages and shows you the C++ equivalents for the common C-string functions, such as `strlen` and `toupper`. Table 1.7 shows how the Standard groups the headers. Table 1.8 lists the headers in Table 1.7 alphabetically and briefly describes their contents.

TABLE 1.7   Categories of String Headers

Category	Headers
C-string utilities	`<cctype>`, `<cstdlib>`, `<cstring>`, `<cwchar>`, `<cwctype>`
Character traits	`<string>`
String classes	`<string>`

TABLE 1.8   String Headers

Header	Functionality
`<cctype>`	Test characteristics of single characters, convert C-string characters to upper or lower case
`<cstdlib>`	Conversion between numbers and C-strings
`<cstring>`	Functions to work on C-strings (null-terminated strings)
`<cwchar>`	Functions for working with multibyte characters
`<cwctype>`	Similar to `<cctype>` but operates on multibyte characters
`<string>`	Character traits and requirements, C++ string classes and functions

Locales

The locales section of the Standard Library has components that encapsulate cultural information and so make it easier to create international versions of C++ programs. Facilities include support for character classification and string collation of different languages; formatting and parsing of numbers, monetary amounts, and dates and times; and message retrieval. Table 1.9 lists the headers and briefly describes their contents.

TABLE 1.9   Locales Headers

Header	Functionality
`<clocale>`	Formatting of times, dates, monetary amounts, and numbers using the Standard C Library facilities
`<locale>`	Formatting of times, dates, monetary amounts, numbers, single characters, and message catalogs

Containers

This part of the library provides you with containers, that is, objects that hold other objects. The containers include a number of classic data structures such as the vector, list, and stack. Table 1.10 shows how the Standard Library groups the headers. Table 1.11 lists the headers in Table 1.10 alphabetically and briefly describes their contents. Containers are part of the STL and are intimately linked to algorithms and iterators. "Containers" in Chapter 2 reviews these objects. Chapters 3 through 8 have many tips on using containers.

TABLE 1.10   Categories of Container Headers

Category	Headers
Associative containers	`<map>`, `<set>`
Bitset	`<bitset>`
Sequence containers	`<deque>`, `<list>`, `<queue>`, `<stack>`, `<vector>`

TABLE 1.11   Container Headers

Header	Functionality
`<bitset>`	Fixed size container of Booleans
`<deque>`	Double-ended queue
`<list>`	Doubly linked list
`<map>`	Map and multimap
`<queue>`	Queue and priority queue
`<set>`	Set and multiset
`<stack>`	Stack
`<vector>`	Vector

Iterators

Iterators let you move among the elements of containers. They serve as the interface between containers and STL algorithms. The building blocks of iterators are in the header `<iterator>`. Table 1.12 lists the specific components that the header defines. You don't have to explicitly include `<iterator>` as often as you would think because container and algorithm headers include it. "Iterators" in Chapter 2 discusses these objects.

TABLE 1.12   Iterator Headers

Header	Functionality
`<iterator>`	Iterator tags, traits, operations (`advance` and `distance`), and base class, predefined iterators, reverse iterators, insert iterators, stream, and stream buffer iterators

Algorithms

The Standard Library algorithms are function templates that do common types of processing such as sorting, searching, copying, and removing. Although all algorithms are in the header `<algorithm>`, the Standard Library divides them into three groups, as Table 1.13 shows. (The Standard Library also includes the functions `bsearch` and `qsort` in the header `<cstdlib>` from the Standard C Library, but these aren't used very much in C++.) Algorithms are part of the STL and typically operate on containers via iterators. For a review of algorithms, see "Algorithms" in Chapter 2. Chapter 9 is filled with tips on using algorithms.

TABLE 1.13   Categories of Algorithms

Category	Operations
Mutating	Copying, exchanging, replacing, removing, filling, removing duplicates, reversing, rotating, shuffling
Nonmodifying	Finding first, last, adjacent match, and first mismatch. Testing for equality, reading each element of a container
Sorting and searching	Partial, stable, and copy sorting, binary searches, merging, set and heap operations, finding minimum and maximum, permuting

Numerics

This part of the library has components that are specially designed for numerical work. Table 1.14 shows how the Standard Library groups the headers. Table 1.15 lists the headers in Table 1.14 alphabetically and briefly describes their contents. Be careful about using `valarrays`. They are not well designed or tested and may be replaced by better methods. This book does not discuss them any further. Chapter 11, however, does provide several examples of using the numeric algorithms.

TABLE 1.14   Categories of Numerics Headers

Category	Headers
C library	`<cmath>`, `<cstdlib>`
Complex numbers	`<complex>`
Numeric arrays	`<valarray>`
Numeric operations	`<numeric>`

TABLE 1.15   Numerics Headers

Header	Functionality
`<cmath>`	Common mathematical functions (trigonometric, exponential, power, rounding, etc.), common numerical constants
`<complex>`	Floating-point complex numbers
`<cstdlib>`	Random number generator, conversion between numbers and C-strings
`<numeric>`	Inner product, sum of elements, running sum, adjacent difference
`<valarray>`	Arrays of numerical values

Input/Output

This part of the library provides the fundamental I/O system for the language, such as the standard input and output streams cin and cout. Because the stream system is so well designed, virtually identical code produces formatted input and output regardless of the source and destination of a stream. In other words, you read and write the same way with the standard output, a file, a memory stream, or a user-defined stream.

Table 1.16 shows how the Standard Library groups the headers. Table 1.17 lists the headers in Table 1.16 alphabetically and briefly describes their contents. Chapter 11 has a number of tips on I/O.

TABLE 1.16   Categories of I/O Headers

Category	Headers
File streams	`<fstream>`, `<cstdio>`, `<cwchar>`
Formatting and manipulators	`<istream>`, `<ostream>`, `<iomanip>`
Forward declarations	`<iosfwd>`
Iostreams base classes	`<ios>`
Standard iostream objects	`<iostream>`
Stream buffers	`<streambuf>`
String streams	`<sstream>`, `<cstdlib>`

TABLE 1.17   I/O Headers

Header	Functionality
`<cstdio>`	C-style I/O
`<cstdlib>`	Conversion between numbers and C-strings
`<cwchar>`	Multibyte character functions
`<fstream>`	File streams
`<iomanip>`	Manipulators with arguments
`<ios>`	I/O stream base classes, manipulators with no arguments, format flags, failure bits, open modes
`<iosfwd>`	Forward declarations for all stream classes
`<iostream>`	Standard I/O stream objects, such as `cin`, `cout`
`<istream>`	Basic input stream, input formatting
`<ostream>`	Basic output stream, output formatting
`<sstream>`	String based streams
`<streambuf>`	Stream buffers

ERROR HANDLING

Real-life programs are, or should be, composed of modules. In such programs, especially when different people write the modules, it's good to think of error handling as being divided into two major actions. One action is to report errors that cannot be handled locally to other parts of the program. The other action is to deal with those errors, that is, for a module to handle errors that occurred in other modules. For example, if you write a function that is to be used by others, your function can detect errors while it is running, but it wouldn't know what to do about them. This is because it doesn't know how, or in what context, it is being used. On the other hand, the calling code may know how to handle errors, but it can't reach down into your function to detect them.

In C and simple uses of C++, programmers typically report errors by returning an error object. This object can be a `struct` or a class, perhaps with detailed information on the error. However, it often is just an integer. The integer can simply relay binary information; for example, zero means failure and nonzero means success. Alternatively, the integer can represent success or types of failure. For example, zero may mean success and each number greater than zero represents a different kind of error. There can be even more information packed in the integer, such as groups of bits that represent the level of failure or success or a bit that indicates whether the returned error is from the operating system or the user.

There are a number of problems with this system of handling errors:

- Interfaces get cluttered because they have to report the error, either as a return value or as a reference.
- There is no standard representation of the error. It can be an integer with lots of different interpretations, a `struct`, or a class. These last two can of course have widely varying formats.
- The code must check every function call for errors. This can easily make the program much bigger.
- The most important deficiency of handling errors by returning error codes is that nothing forces the calling code to do something about a returned error. Too often, the caller doesn't process the returned value or, worse, doesn't even accept it. Unfortunately, in these cases, the program can often continue limping along, slowly deteriorating or suddenly crashing. It's very hard to debug problems like this because the symptoms occur much later than the cause.

Exception Handling

C++ provides an alternate method for dealing with errors called the *exception handling system*. It is a facility for transferring information and flow of control from the point where an error occurs to a place in the program that can respond to it. When using the exception handling system, you should restrict the errors you manipulate with it to those that are truly exceptional (hence, the name of the system). Often things that go wrong can be expected to go wrong and so should be handled locally. For example, your application might try to open a nonexistent file because the user may have misspelled the file name or entered the path incorrectly. If this is likely to happen, it would not be an exceptional event if it occurred, so using the exception handling system would not be appropriate in this case.

Exception handling returns errors in a separate path from the normal program execution flow. Its advantages are that it does the following:

- Provides a framework for using consistent error types
- Is used almost everywhere by the Standard Library
- Allows constructors (which can't return values) to signal an error
- Makes programs crash if the errors aren't handled

Although this last action may sound draconian, it's a clear and insistent reminder during development that errors should not be ignored.

In the C++ exception handling system, when a piece of code encounters a problem, the code reports it by *throwing an exception*. It does that by using the `throw` keyword followed by an object, for example, integer, literal constant, class, `struct`, and so on. Throwing an exception transfers control to an exception handler (described later).

As an example of throwing an exception, suppose you have a class called `Port` that lets you work with an I/O port. It has a constructor that accepts a port number. It also has the member function `ready` that tells whether the port can be used. The function

```
void activate_minicam_port()
{
   const int minicam_port_number = 54;
   Port minicam_port( minicam_port_number );
   //...
   if( !minicam_port.ready() )
      throw string( "Timeout on minicam port" );
   //...
}
```

attempts to activate a particular port, say one connected to a miniature camera (minicam). It makes a `Port` instance, does some processing (perhaps waiting a set amount of time to ensure that the port is active) and tests the port to see if it's ready. If it's not, the function throws an exception. In this case, the data type of the exception is a C++ text string.

The thrown exception starts a process called *stack unwinding*. First, C++ calls all the destructors of class instances that are in the same scope as the throw statement. Then, until the exception is handled (as described shortly), C++ calls all the destructors in the surrounding scope, then in the scope surrounding that, and so on. When the exception gets to the function (if any) that called the code with the throw statement, C++ executes all its destructors. C++ keeps the chain of calling functions on a call stack—hence, the term "unwinding the stack." Note that stack unwinding is separate and different from the normal execution of nested functions.

If the program has not handled the exception by the time the stack unwinding is through with the main program (function `main`), C++ shuts the program down by calling the predefined function `terminate`. This function then calls another built-in function, `abort`, which ends the program

Robust programs will not let an exception go far enough to crash the program. They will try to respond to all exceptions. To handle a thrown exception, the receiving code must first wrap the sending code in a *try block*. This is the keyword `try` followed by a pair of braces with the sending code in it. For example, suppose the function `take_pictures` calls `activate_minicam_port`. The coder knows that `activate_minicam_port` can throw an exception, so it puts the call of that function in a try block, that is,

```
void take_pictures( int frame_rate )
{
    try
    {
        activate_minicam_port();
    }
    //...
}
```

Immediately following the try block, you must put at least one *catch block*, also called an *exception handler*. (The only intervening lines must be comments or all whitespace.) The catch block is the keyword `catch` followed by a pair of parentheses with an argument and then followed by a pair of braces with statements. The argument specifies the data type that the exception handler can catch and optionally provides the name of a variable to which the thrown object is assigned. If there are no catch blocks that can accept the object thrown, C++ continues unwinding the stack until it gets to an enclosing catch block that can accept the exception's data type or it reaches `main`.

The only way for a program to enter a catch block is if the code in the immediately preceding try block throws an exception that the catch block can accept. If the catch block can't receive the exception, C++ continues unwinding the stack. If the try block doesn't throw an exception, the execution flow skips all immediately following catch blocks and continues at the code after them.

The statements in a catch block are the code that deals with the exception. For example,

```cpp
void take_pictures( int frame_rate )
{
    try
    {
        activate_minicam_port();
    }

    catch( const string& error )
    {
        cycle_minicam_power();
    }
}
```

In this case, the code cycles the minicam's power, that is, turns it off and back on. Sometimes an exception handler may do something with an exception (perhaps write it to an error log) but needs to pass it on to other code to actually resolve it. In other words, the catch block only partially handles the exception. To forward a caught exception, use a throw statement with no argument. For example,

```cpp
void take_pictures(int frame_rate)

{
    try
    {
        activate_minicam_port();
    }

    catch( const string& error )
    {
        cerr << "Error \"" << error << "\" from activate_minicam_port\n";
        throw;
    }
}
```

cerr is the standard error stream, which is often directed to a console or a file.

Here are some other things to be aware of when using the exception handling system:

- You can follow a try block with more than one catch block. Each catch block should handle a different exception. (If any of the items caught are derived classes, see the next item in this list.)
- Suppose you want to catch a class and its derived classes but handle some of the derived classes differently. If you're doing so by pointer or reference you must put exception handlers for the derived classes you want to treat differently first. After those, put an exception handler to the base class. This will catch the base class and any derived classes that you didn't catch separately. If you put the handler for the base class first, the handler will catch all exceptions of the base class and derived classes and your individual catch blocks will never be activated.
- If your catch block will be receiving classes, you should make the argument to the block be a reference or pointer to the class. This will prevent *slicing*, the removal of derived-class material when a derived-class object is assigned to a base-class object.
- To make an exception handler catch any exception, use three periods (...) as its argument, for example, `catch(...){ //code }`.

To document and enforce the types of exceptions that a global or member function can throw, attach an *exception specification* to its declaration and definition. Right before the terminating semicolon, put the keyword `throw` with the data types in parentheses. This indicates that the function can throw only those exceptions. The exception specification is not part of a function's signature. Thus, for example, if two functions have the same signatures but different exception specifications, the compiler will still consider the functions to be ambiguous and produce a compiler error.

The following code snippet illustrates various exception specifications:

```
void f( int a, int a_squared ) throw( int, const char* );

class Mailbox
{
    public:
    Mailbox( int zipcode ) throw( double );

    void deposit_letters( int num_letters );

    int capacity() const throw();
};
```

The global function `f` can only throw an integer or a pointer to constant characters. The `Mailbox` constructor can only throw a `double`. If a function doesn't have any exception specification (such as `deposit_letters`), it can throw any exception. If a function has an exception specification in which `throw` has no arguments, such as `capacity`, that function cannot throw exceptions at all.

If a function has an exception specification and throws an exception other than one listed, a series of events occurs. First, C++ changes the throw into a call to the Standard Library function `unexpected`. By default, `unexpected` calls another predefined function, `terminate`. This calls the built-in function `abort`, which shuts down the program. You can change these default actions. See a good C++ book, for example, *The C++ Programming Language* [Stroustrup97], for details.

Table 1.18 shows the exceptions used by the *core language*, that is, the part of C++ not in the Standard Library. (The library also uses them.) All these exceptions are derived from the base class `exception`. It and `bad_exception` are available through the header `<exception>`, `bad_alloc` is in `<new>`, and `bad_cast` and `bad_typeid` are in `<typeinfo>`. You rarely need to explicitly include these files directly because the major headers include them. However, the C++ standard does not mandate which headers a header needs to include. If you're planning to port your code, it's best to explicitly include all the headers that you need.

TABLE 1.18   Exceptions Used by Core Language

Exception	Use
bad_alloc	Can't allocate memory, that is, operator `new` fails
bad_cast	Type conversion on a reference type fails, that is, `dynamic_cast` fails
bad_exception	Function throws an exception not in its exception specification
bad_typeid	Zero or null pointer passed to operator `typeid`, that is, `typeid` fails

The class `exception` contains a constructor, copy constructor, destructor, and assignment operator. It also has the virtual member function `what` that returns a pointer to constant characters. This user-defined C-style text string describes the error.

Exception Handling in the Standard Library

The Standard Library is made up of software that comes from different sources, has different designs, and was developed at different times. The error and exception handling reflects this diversity. Some of the library, such as strings, has thorough error handling. Other parts, such as the STL, hardly check for errors at all. When a member of the Standard Library does throw an exception, though, it is always one derived from the base class exception.

The Standard Library can throw exceptions from the parts of the core language that it uses. (Table 1.18 lists these core language exceptions.) However, the library also throws other exceptions that are more closely related to it. The exceptions deal with two general categories of errors. Incorrect programming, such as indexes that are out of range, causes *logic errors*. They are in theory preventable. The program's environment causes *runtime errors*, and they are typically beyond the scope of the program's control, for example, a low-memory condition. In addition, they are often hard to predict.

All logic errors are derived from the exception class logic_error, which in turn is derived from exception. All runtime errors are derived from runtime_error, which also comes from exception. The header <stdexcept> defines all of these exception classes. Figure 1.2 shows the inheritance hierarchy and Table 1.19 lists the exceptions. The Standard Library itself can throw these exceptions and additional ones. This is because application code that is called or used in the Library may throw other exceptions. One exception from the STL that may appear in realistic programs is bad_alloc, which indicates a failure in allocating memory.

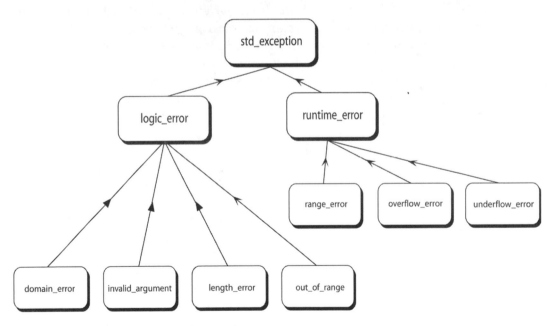

FIGURE 1.2 Hierarchy of exceptions in the Standard Library.

TABLE 1.19   Standard Library Exceptions

Exception	Use
domain_error	Value not in domain of a mathematical operation
invalid_argument	Argument to a function not in valid range
length_error	Attempt to create an object larger than the maximum allowable size
logic_error	Generic logic error
out_of_range	An argument out of the allowable range
overflow_error	Arithmetic overflow
range_error	Range error in internal computation
runtime_error	Generic runtime error
underflow_error	Arithmetic underflow

You can make your own exception classes by deriving directly from exception or the classes in Table 1.18, which are also derived from exception. Just override the virtual member function what to return the message you want.

You can also use the exception classes in the Standard Library to deliver custom error messages. One way to work with them is to derive your own classes from them, as explained in the preceding text. As a base class, you can use logic_error, runtime_error, or any of the standard exceptions derived from them. However, if you only need to change the message and not the exception class, you can use a standard exception. That's because logic_error, runtime_error, and all their child classes have a constructor that accepts a text string or, through a conversion, a C-style text string. To throw such an error in your own code, use a throw statement with the exception class and a string or string literal as its argument, for example,

```
throw range_error( "Exceeded maximum path length in compute_path()" );
```

Although it's convenient to use these predefined exception classes, be aware that catch blocks can't distinguish between a built-in error that your code throws and the same error thrown by the Standard Library. If this confusion is likely to happen, you may want to derive your own exception class from logic_error or runtime_error and catch it instead. As long as you provide it a constructor that accepts a string, as its parent class does, it will be as easy to use as the two built-in base classes for logic and runtime errors.

NAMESPACES

Suppose you're part of a group that is working on a large software project with other groups. You're careful about checking and reporting runtime errors and have written the function

```
void display_error( int error_number )
```

to display the error message associated with the passed error number. All goes well until you try to use another group's code with yours. You discover that they're also careful about reporting errors and have written a function with the same name and signature as `display_error`. When the linker tries to link all the modules, it sees two different functions with the same name and signature. The linker doesn't know which one to use, so it produces an error. A duplicate identifier like this is called a *name collision* or *name clash*.

C++ provides a method of preventing name collisions or name clashes—namespaces. A *namespace* is a scope that contains logically related objects. You can put functions, classes, and variables in a namespace. To do this, use the keyword `namespace` followed by the namespace's name and then insert all declarations enclosed in a pair of braces, such as

```
namespace G5
{
    void display_error( int error_number );
    class GUI_element
    {
        //...
    };
    void log_error( int error_number );
}
```

You can define classes and functions inside a namespace, but to separate the interface from the implementation, it's better to define such objects outside.

There are three ways to get access to an entity in a namespace. The first is to prefix the identifier with the name of the namespace followed by the scope operator (`::`). (A namespace member written this way is said to be *qualified*.) For example, to define the function `display_error` you would write

```
void G5::display_error( int error_number )
{
    // put code here
}
```

If you were to omit the namespace when defining the function, you would get a compiler error. Other sources of compiler errors are spelling the function differently in the declaration than in the definition and having different signatures in those places.

When calling a namespace member, make sure it is qualified, for example,

```
void compute()
{
   int result = do_compute();
   if( result != 0 )
      G5::display_error( result );
}
```

For convenience, you don't have to qualify nonmember functions in a namespace when calling them if an argument is in the same namespace. If the compiler can't find the function, it will look for it in the namespaces of the function's parameters. For example, in the code

```
namespace Megacorp
{
   class Transaction
   {
      // ...
   };

   void add_to_queue( const Transaction& t );
}

int main( )
{
   Megacorp::Transaction transaction;
   add_to_queue( transaction );
   // ...
```

Even though the program doesn't qualify add_to_queue with the namespace Megacorp when it calls the function, the compiler figures this out because the argument is in that namespace. (This rule is often called *argument-dependent lookup* or *Koenig lookup*.)

If you declare a name outside all named namespaces, blocks, and classes, C++ places it in a default namespace called the *global namespace*. You can access objects in this namespace by prefixing their names with just the scope operator (::), such as ::var or ::adjust(5). For example, the output of

```
namespace K
{
   int k = 9;
}

int k = 7;

int main( )
{
   int k = 5;
   cout << "k = " << k << "   ::k = " << ::k << "   K::k = " << K::k;
   // ...
```

is

```
k = 5   ::k = 7   K::k = 9
```

It can get tedious to type in the namespace and the double colon frequently. It certainly makes the code more cluttered. To make things easier you can use the second way of accessing a member of a namespace, which is to write a *using-declaration*. This tells the compiler to assume that a particular name is in a given namespace if the code doesn't explicitly specify a namespace. Make a using-declaration by writing the keyword using followed by the object's namespace, the scope operator, and name, for example,

```
using G5::display_error;
```

The usual scoping rules apply to a using-declaration. Anytime the declared name appears after the using-declaration and in its scope, the compiler assumes the name is in the specified namespace. For example, the code

```
using G5::display_error;

void compute()
{
   int result = do_compute();
   if( result != 0 )
      display_error( result );
}
```

compiles fine even though it does not explicitly specify the namespace G5 in the call of display_error. You have to be careful doing this because if there were another function with the same name and signature, the compiler wouldn't be able to distinguish the two and you'd be back to the original name-collision problem.

The third namespace access method is even more powerful and more hazardous. It is the *using-directive*. This is the statement using namespace followed by a namespace name, for example,

```
using namespace G5;
```

This makes all the names in the namespace G5 available. It's equivalent to writing a using-declaration for each member of the G5 namespace. The advantage of the directive is that it reduces the clutter in the code by letting you avoid specifically writing the namespace and scope operator for many objects. The disadvantage is that there are now many more objects that could cause a name collision.

Organizations usually have coding style guides that specify how and when using-declarations and using-directives should appear. Some groups may prohibit their use completely. Others may allow only a few specific names to be used in these declarations or directives, such as cin, cout, and endl, which are in the namespace std (see the text later in this section). In any case, you should never put using-declarations or using-directives at a global scope in a header. This will cause *global-namespace pollution*, that is, the addition of many new identifiers to the global namespace.

There's a lot more to namespaces than what is shown here. You can do the following:

- Nest namespaces, that is, have one inside another
- Have unnamed namespaces
- Make a namespace alias, for example, replace a long namespace name with a shorter one
- Compose a namespace from other namespaces
- Make a namespace from only some of the names in another namespace
- Add to an existing namespace

Stroustrup has a good discussion of all of these aspects of namespaces [Stroustrup97].

All entities in the C++ Standard Library, except for macros and the operators new and delete, are in the namespace std (standard) or a namespace nested in std. In addition, the Standard C Library is part of the C++ Standard Library. To use the Standard C Library headers with the entries in the namespace std, drop the ".h" from the file name and prepend a "c", for example, change <stdlib.h> to <cstdlib>, change `<math.h>` to `<cmath>`. The C headers work in C++, but they put all their contents into the global namespace. Unless you're trying to get strict C compatibility with your program, it's better to use the C++ versions of the headers.

A program is allowed to redefine the various versions of operators `new` and `delete`. However, except in a few circumstances, if a program adds things to the `std` namespace or a namespace in it, the resulting behavior is undefined. Even though application programmers shouldn't change `std`, compiler and library writers sometimes do add to it. This brings about another detriment to having a `using namespace std;` statement in your code. If your code compiles fine but a library writer adds some entities to `std`, when you recompile you could get a name clash even if you haven't changed anything in your code.

All code in this book, both full programs and snippets, assumes that there is a `using namespace std` using-directive placed (but not shown) so that none of the calls to Standard Library components must be qualified. Though this is not good style in real-life programming, it makes the code in this book more legible.

2 Review of the Standard Template Library

C++ supports three general styles of programming—structured, object-oriented, and generic. The *Standard Template Library (STL)* is an excellent example of generic programming. The library's name is actually quite descriptive. It's standard because it's officially part of the C++ language. The most commonly used components are templates, and it's a library, that is, a collection of components with which to make software and not an application in its own right.

One definition of *generic programming* is writing code in which the data type is a parameter. For example, you might write a function that copies a sequence of numbers from one array to another. The algorithm to do this is the same, regardless of the data type. Instead of writing a group of overloaded routines (one for each data type, such as `char`, `int`, `float`, or `double`), you write one template function. When a programmer passes an input and output array to your function, the compiler examines the data type of the arrays and creates the correct version of the function for you. This means you have much less code to write.

Another definition comes from Alexander Stepanov, the prime creator of the STL. He defines generic programming as finding the most abstract representations of efficient algorithms, that is, finding the most general set of requirements on an algorithm that still let it perform efficiently.

Three types of components form the heart of the STL—iterators, containers, and algorithms. Containers are structures that hold objects. The STL comes with seven containers that meet certain requirements and are commonly used. They are the vector, list, deque, set, multiset, map, and multimap. Algorithms are functions that operate principally on containers. They include sorting, copying, searching, replacing, and programmer-specified operations on each element. Iterators are a generalization of pointers. They allow movement through containers and access to the elements. They also form the interface between containers and algorithms, that is, the algorithms operate on a sequence of elements specified by two iterators. In general, the iterators can come from any container and, because the algorithms are templates, they can operate on any data type. This keeps the STL small and easier to use. For example, one STL algorithm (`copy`) can copy any data type from any part of any container to any part of any other container. (There are some restrictions on the data types, but they are very mild.)

The STL also has some other components:

Functors: Small, function-like objects that can be passed to algorithms to specify their functionality; for example, passing the functor `plus` to the `transform` algorithm causes it to add corresponding elements in a container.

Adaptors: Pieces of software that allow other STL components to operate more generally, for example, a stream adaptor makes iterators for a stream so that the stream can be used in algorithms. There are also container adaptors that specialize the standard containers to produce other useful containers such as the queue, priority queue, and stack.

Allocators: Generalized memory models.

Miscellaneous: `pair` (a data structure that holds two elements that may have different data types), convenient definitions of comparison operators, such as <, >=, and so on.

Figure 2.1 illustrates the basic parts of the STL and their relationship. Iterators serve as a link between containers and algorithms. The algorithms typically accept input via iterators from a container and send the output, again through iterators, to another container. However, there are variations on this theme that Figure 2.1 highlights by placing in dashed ovals. For example, some algorithms use functors to determine what operations to perform. Adaptors can modify the functors. In addition, adaptors can modify sources or destinations other than containers, for example, file or I/O streams, by making iterators for them so they can serve as inputs or outputs to algorithms.

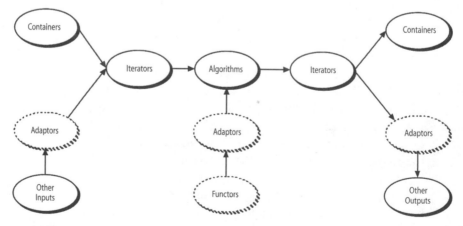

FIGURE 2.1   Basic components of the STL.

Before going on, you should be aware that—precisely speaking—the Standard Template Library doesn't exist anymore. It was merged into the C++ Standard as part of the C++ Standard Library. Actually, nowhere does the C++ Standard mention "STL" or "Standard Template Library." However, the term is still very much in common use, and this book will continue that tradition too.

HISTORY

Even though the STL is now part of the Standard Library, it has a different and interesting history. Alexander Stepanov created the STL. He was born in Moscow, Russia, and studied mathematics. It was too abstract for his taste, so he went into programming. One of his early jobs was working on a team that developed a mini-computer to control hydroelectric power stations. This gave him an eye-opening experience in software reliability (power stations are difficult to reboot) and software efficiency (water falls quickly). In 1976, Stepanov got a bad case of food poisoning from eating raw fish. While in the hospital and delirious, he realized that it's possible to add numbers in parallel only because addition is associative. He generalized this idea and put it in mathematical terms by stating that a parallel reduction algorithm is associated with a semigroup type. He developed the concept further to come up with a fundamental principle—algorithms are defined on algebraic structures. It took another couple of years to extend this tenet by adding complexity requirements. Then it took him 15 more years to make the theory work in practice.

Stepanov eventually went to the United States and worked at various industrial research laboratories and universities. He and Dave Musser developed the Ada Generic Library, a precursor of the STL. After working briefly at Bell Labs and developing a library of algorithms in C++, he moved to HP Labs in Palo Alto, California. This is where, in 1993, he returned to his research on generic programming, which resulted in the STL. In 1995, he moved to Silicon Graphics and, with Matt Austern and Hans Boehm, did further work on the Standard Template Library.

Other people also contributed to the STL. Andrew Koenig explained topics in the C programming language to Stepanov. Koenig and Bjarne Stroustrup (the inventor of C++) pushed hard to get the STL into the C++ Standard. Meng Lee put a tremendous amount of time and effort into coding the STL and documenting it. Starting in 1994, all these people shepherded the STL through the standardization process until it finally became part of the official language.

The STL fits in well with Stepanov's long-term vision for new directions in programming. He, and many other people, would like to change software development from a craft to a field of engineering. Stepanov believes that a collection of software components that are generic, efficient, and have documented complexities should be available to everyone. This will free programmers from having to continually reinvent the wheel. That is, they will no longer have to write a binary search algorithm, a sorting routine, and so forth. They can take the standardized components, use them in their programs, and get on with their work.

For more information on the history of the STL, see [LoRusso97] and [Stevens95]. Most of the historical information in this section comes from those two articles.

ITERATORS

An important concept that came out of the development of the STL is the use of iterators. "To iterate" means to do something repeatedly. In the STL, an iterator is an object that can move from one element in a sequence to another and another. Iterators are important for traversing a sequence and serving as bridges between containers (data structures that hold objects) and the STL algorithms (functions that operate on sequences). Having the algorithms operate only on iterators rather than the containers themselves enables the algorithms to be independent of the details of traversing any particular container's elements. Iterators also enable algorithms to work on other sources of elements such as I/O and file streams.

Iterator Categories

Besides being able to come from different sources, iterators themselves come in different categories. One convenient way to understand iterators is to think of them as generalized pointers. A pointer can move back and forth among elements in an array and read and write to them. An iterator is an object that can move among elements in a sequence. (A *sequence* is a collection of elements that can be traversed from beginning to end by using an operation that moves from one element to the next.) There are, however, important differences between a pointer and an iterator:

- There is no such thing as a NULL iterator.
- There are different categories of iterators. Most do not have all the abilities of a pointer, such as moving backward, having values added or subtracted to them, or overwriting an element.
- Iterators can be used with objects other than containers or arrays of elements. For example, they can operate on text strings or file and I/O streams.
- Although all pointers are iterators, not all iterators are pointers. Many are actually classes that move through memory by complicated routes.
- The objects that iterators point to do not have to be contiguous in memory.

The last point is of practical importance because many containers such as lists, sets, and maps do not store their elements contiguously or even in the order you put them into the container.

However, each container defines an iterator that can move through its elements. Sometimes the elements are contiguous (e.g., a vector) and sometimes not (e.g., a list). Sometimes the next element is the element that was inserted into the container after the current one, for example, in a vector. Sometimes the order of insertion is irrelevant and the next element is the one with the next highest value, as in a set. What's important is that the interface is always the same, that is, you move to the next element in a sequence by incrementing (++) an iterator.

Figures 2.2 and Figure 2.3 illustrate these ideas. Figure 2.2 shows that conceptually the iterator's increment operator always moves it forward (to the right in the figure) by one element. Figure 2.3 shows what the actual path of the iterator through memory might look like for a doubly linked list container. Notice that unlike a pointer being incremented in an array, incrementing an iterator might make it go between noncontiguous blocks of memory and even do so backward.

FIGURE 2.2   Moving through elements of a sequence by incrementing (++) an iterator.

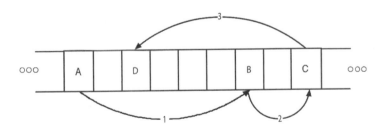

FIGURE 2.3   Iteration through elements of a list in memory.

A better view of an iterator is that it is a concept that defines certain requirements and behaviors. Any software component that satisfies these requirements and behaviors is, by definition, an iterator. Simply put, if it acts like an iterator, it *is* an iterator. The principal requirements of an iterator are that it be able to perform the following operations:

- Read and/or write to the element it is pointing to by using the dereferencing operators * or ->
- Go to the next element by using the increment operator ++
- See if it is equal to another iterator by using the operator ==

If you can access (dereference) an iterator, that iterator is *dereferenceable.* You can always increment an iterator once past the last element in a container. However, you can't dereference the iterator there.

There are actually five categories of iterators, as Figure 2.4 shows. Each category has all the abilities of the ones preceding it. You can also create your own iterator type that will work with the rest of the STL as long as it defines the appropriate operators.

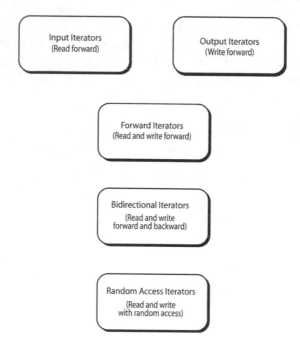

FIGURE 2.4   Iterator categories.

Regardless of what category an iterator is in, it can be const or non-const. A constant iterator (const_iterator in containers) is like a constant pointer—you can read the dereferenced value but you can't change it. However, the type of object the iterator points to is what ultimately determines the access; for example, even if you have a non-const iterator, it can't write to a const element.

Tables 2.1 through 2.5 list the requirements for the five categories of iterators. Algorithms are often implemented only through iterators, and to do so it's necessary to determine the value and difference type that correspond to an iterator type. The Standard Library defines iterator traits and tags to handle these and other requirements, but the tables that follow do not show them.

Table 2.1 lists the capabilities of input iterators. Their main function is to let you move forward through a sequence and read the elements. You can use any class or built-in data type that satisfies the requirements in Table 2.1 as an input iterator.

TABLE 2.1 Capabilities of Input Iterators. i, i1, i2 Are Iterators, I Is Iterator Type

Operation	Name	Action
`*i`	Dereferencing	Read access to the element.
`i->member`	Dereferencing	Read access to a member of element (if any exist).
`i1 == i2`	Equality	Test if two iterators are equal. Return value convertible to `bool`.
`i1 != i2`	Inequality	Test if two iterators are not equal. Return value convertible to `bool`.
`++i`	Preincrement	Step forward one element. Return new position.
`i++`	Postincrement	Step forward one element. Return old position.
`I i1( i2 )`	Copy constructor	Make a new iterator that is a copy of the old one.
`i1 = i2`	Assignment	Make one existing iterator be the same as another.

An input iterator has the strange property such that if you read it and move on (increment), you can't read the old position again. More specifically, if you read the old position again, there's no guarantee that the two values you read will be the same. Thus, any algorithm that uses input iterators should never access any iterator location more than once. In other words, it should be a *single-pass algorithm*. Another implication of only being able to read elements once is that if you make a copy of an input iterator and increment both it and the original, the two resulting iterators may point to different values.

Output iterators are the complement of input iterators, that is, you can only write with them. However, like input iterators, they are just able to move forward. Table 2.2 lists their capabilities. Their main function is to let you move forward through a sequence and write to the elements. You can use any class or built-in data type that satisfies the requirements in Table 2.2 as an output iterator.

TABLE 2.2 Capabilities of Output Iterators. o, o1, o2 Are Iterators, O Is Iterator Type

Operation	Name	Action
*o	Dereferencing	Write access to the element (left side of assignment statement only).
++o	Preincrement	Step forward one element. Return new position.
o++	Postincrement	Step forward one element. Return old position.
O o1(o2) O o1 = o2	Copy constructors	Make a new iterator that is a copy of the old one.

You can only write one time to an element that an output iterator points to. More specifically, if you write to the same iterator position twice, there is no guarantee that the second value will overwrite the first. This implies that output iterators should only be used in single-pass algorithms.

Table 2.3 lists the capabilities of forward iterators. These iterators are very useful because they let you move forward through a sequence and read from or write to its elements. You can use any class or built-in data type that satisfies the requirements in Table 2.3 as a forward iterator.

TABLE 2.3 Capabilities of Forward Iterators. i, i1, i2 Are Iterators, I Is Iterator Type

Operation	Name	Action
Any in Table 2.1		Actions for an input iterator.
Any in Table 2.2		Actions for an output iterator.
I i	Declaration	Declare a forward iterator.
I()	Default constructor	Make a forward iterator with default values.
i1 == i2	Equality	Test if two iterators are equal. Return value convertible to bool.
i1 != i2	Inequality	Test if two iterators are not equal. Return value convertible to bool.
++i	Preincrement	Step forward one element. Return new position.
i++	Postincrement	Step forward one element. Return old position.
I i1(i2)	Copy constructor	Make a new iterator that is a copy of the old one.
i1 = i2	Assignment	Make one existing iterator be the same as another.

A forward iterator is a combination of an input and output iterator and has all the capabilities of an input iterator and almost all of an output iterator. (The difference between the output capabilities of a forward iterator and that of the output iterator is that you can always write to an output iterator. To write to a forward iterator, you must make sure that the iterator is dereferenceable and that it doesn't refer to a constant element.)

You can access elements of a forward iterator more than once. Forward iterators are good for use with *multipass algorithms*, that is, algorithms that use iterators to pass through a sequence more than one time. You can use a forward iterator anywhere that requires an input or output iterator.

Table 2.4 lists the capabilities of bidirectional iterators. These iterators let you move forward or backward through a sequence and read from or write to its elements. You can use any class or built-in data type that satisfies the requirements in Table 2.4 as a bidirectional iterator. You can substitute a bidirectional iterator wherever a forward iterator is required.

TABLE 2.4   Capabilities of Bidirectional Iterators. `i`, `i1`, `i2` Are Iterators, `I` Is Iterator Type

Operation	Name	Action
Any in Table 2.3		Actions for a forward iterator.
`--i`	Predecrement	Step backward one element. Return new position.
`i--`	Postdecrement	Step backward one element. Return old position.

Table 2.5 lists the capabilities of random access iterators. These are the most powerful iterators. In addition to having all the capabilities of bidirectional iterators, random access iterators let you immediately access any element in a sequence by indexing. You can use any class or built-in data type that satisfies the requirements in Table 2.5 as a random access iterator. By design, pointers satisfy these requirements, that is, pointers are random access iterators. You can substitute a random access iterator wherever a bidirectional one is required.

TABLE 2.5 Capabilities of Random Access Iterators. `i`, `i1`, `i2` Are Iterators, `I` Is Iterator Type, `n` Is Difference Type

Operation	Name	Action
Any in Table 2.4		Actions for a bidirectional iterator.
`i += n`	Self-increment	Move forward or backward (n negative) n elements.
`i + n` `n + i`	Increment addition	Add or subtract (n negative) iterator and offset.
`i -= n`	Self-decrement	Move backward or forward (n negative) n elements.
`i - n` `n - i`	Increment subtraction	Subtract or add (n negative) iterator and offset.
`i[n]`	Indexing	Get value of nth element.
`i1 -- i2`	Distance	Number of steps (`++` or `--`) to get from `i1` to `i2`.
`i1 < i2`	Less than	Decide if `i1` comes before `i2`.
`i1 > i2`	Greater than	Decide if `i1` comes after `i2`.
`i1 <= i2`	Less than or equal	Decide if `i1` does not come after `i2`.
`i1 >= i2`	Greater than or equal	Decide if `i1` does not come before `i2`.

Ranges

One of the most important uses of iterators is specifying a range of elements. A *range* is a pair of iterators that marks the beginning and end of a sequence. This is one of the most ubiquitous concepts in the STL because almost all the algorithms accept a range to specify the elements to work on. The STL *always* uses half-open ranges, denoted by `[i,j)`. A *half-open* range includes the first iterator and goes up to the last iterator but does *not* include it, as Figure 2.5 shows. An *empty range* is one in which both iterators are the same, for example, `[i,i)`. Empty ranges are legal and convenient. If an algorithm receives an empty range, it doesn't do any processing on the sequence.

One advantage of half-open ranges is that loops that use them have a simple termination criterion, namely, to stop when the loop iterator is equal to the end of the range. For example, Listing 2.1 shows a simple template function that doubles every number in a range. You can see how clear the loop is. You can also see another advantage of using half-open ranges—there's no need for additional code that can handle an empty range. If the user passes an empty range (so that the two iterators are equal), the loop never executes.

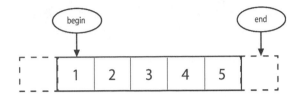

FIGURE 2.5 Beginning and end iterators of a range.

LISTING 2.1 A Template Function That Doubles Numbers

```
template< class ForwardIterator >
void doubler( ForwardIterator start, ForwardIterator stop )
{
    while( start != stop )
        *start++ *= 2;
}
```

The STL doesn't check ranges to see if they're legitimate, so you have to. You must make sure that every range you use is *valid*. This means that for the range [i,j), j must be *reachable* from i, that is, you can get to j by incrementing i (++i) a finite number of times. If j is not reachable from i that means that i and j are not in the same range or that j is behind i, that is, j is closer to the start of the range than i is. If you use an invalid range in an STL algorithm, what happens is not defined, but it's likely to cause bad problems.

All standard containers have member functions that provide access to the beginning (begin) and end (end) of their element range. The containers also provide iterators for traversing their elements. To declare an iterator that points into a container, specify the container type, the data type in angle brackets, the scope operator (::), and the word "iterator" (or "const_iterator" for constant containers), for example, vector<int>::iterator i; . The following code snippet illustrates some common ways that container iterators are used and misused:

```
vector<double> volume;
// ... put some numbers in the vector

// use an STL algorithm to sort the elements. The container provides the
// range
sort( volume.begin(), volume.end() );
```

```
// for efficiency in next loop, store end iterator
vector<double>::iterator volume_end = volume.end();

// multiply each element by 10 and add a random number between 0 and 50
for( vector<double>::iterator i = volume.begin(); i != volume_end;
   ++i )
   *i = *i * 10 + rand() % 51;

// try to sort
sort( volume.end(), volume.begin() ); // BAD — 1st iterator is past 2nd

vector<double> area;
// ... put in some numbers

// try to sort
sort( volume.begin(), area.end() ); // BAD — iterators from different
                                     // containers

sort( volume.begin(), volume.end() ); // GOOD
```

Notice also that before the for-loop, the code stores the end iterator of the vector. Making a local copy of a container's end iterator for use in a loop is helpful. Otherwise, the loop would call the container's member function end at each iteration, resulting in the construction and destruction of an iterator on every pass. You have to be sure that the end iterator won't change during the loop's execution. It's also a good idea to avoid mixing iterators and constant iterators. Thus, even though it would be safer for volume_end to be a const_iterator, the code declares it to be a regular iterator because it is compared to the iterator i, which can't be constant.

ITERATOR ADAPTORS

The most common source of iterators is containers. Iterator adaptors let you use STL algorithms with inputs and outputs other than containers. *Iterator adaptors* are special versions of iterators that let STL algorithms operate in reverse, or insert instead of overwrite (assign), or function with streams. The adaptors are easy to use, operating in almost the same way as regular iterators. To access any of the iterator adaptors, you must include the header <iterator>.

Reverse Iterators

One kind of iterator adaptor is the *reverse iterator*, which lets you traverse a range in reverse by defining the increment operator (++) to move backward and the decrement operator (`--`) to move forward. This may sound confusing, but fortunately that's an implementation detail and doesn't change how easy it is to use a reverse iterator.

All standard containers let you use reverse iterators on their elements. They have two member functions that specify the range of a reverse iteration. The first, `rbegin`, accesses the beginning of the reverse iteration range. The second, `rend`, accesses the end. Each standard container also provides a reverse iterator and a constant reverse iterator. The latter is like a constant pointer—you can read the dereferenced value, but you can't change it. To use reverse iterators, you don't need to include a header other than that for the container.

You use reverse iterators pretty much the same way as regular iterators. For example, suppose you have a vector of integers `v`, and you want to find the first element that is equal to five. You can do this with the STL algorithm `find`, for example,

```
vector<int>::iterator i = find( v.begin(), v.end(), 5 );
if( i != v.end() )
    cout << "Found the first five\n";
else
    cout << "Couldn't find a five\n";
```

There's no need for a different algorithm to locate the last five in the vector. You simply search in reverse, and the first value of five you come to is really the last one in the vector, for example,

```
vector<int>::reverse_iterator i = find( v.rbegin(), v.rend(), 5 );
if( i != v.rend() )
    cout << "Found the last five\n";
else
    cout << "Couldn't find a five\n";
```

The code is identical except for using the reverse versions of `begin`, `end`, and `iterator`, that is, `rbegin`, `rend` and `reverse_iterator`. Be careful not to mix the regular versions with the reverse ones because they don't work together. In particular, remember after the call to `find` to test against `rend`, not `end`.

The program in Listing 2.2 loads a vector with the numbers one through six, gets an iterator that points to the first element whose value is five, constructs a reverse iterator from the regular one, and displays the values of both.

LISTING 2.2   Iterator and Reverse Iterator Values

```
#include <algorithm>
#include <iostream>
#include <vector>
```

```
using namespace std;

int main( )
{
   vector<int> v( 6 );

   for( int i = 1; i <= 6; ++i )
      v[i-1] = i;

   vector<int>::iterator j = find( v.begin(), v.end(), 5 );
   vector<int>::reverse_iterator j_reverse( j );

   cout << "*j = " << *j << "\n*j_reverse = " << *j_reverse << endl;
}
```

The surprising output of the code is

```
*j = 5
*j_reverse = 4
```

Here's what's going on. Figure 2.6 shows what you might initially believe are the reverse beginning and end iterators. You can see that the reverse end iterator is one element past the start of the sequence. The problem with this is that containers aren't required to define an iterator that points to a location before their elements, even if that iterator is never dereferenced. However, the container iterators must be valid for one increment past the last element, although you can't dereference them there. These requirements on an iterator that points immediately before or after a container come from C, where pointers to arrays have the same restrictions.

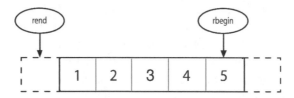

FIGURE 2.6   Desired (but incorrect) positions of the beginning and end reverse iterators.

Figure 2.7 shows the STL designers' clever solution to the problem. They made the location of the reverse beginning iterator be one past the end of the sequence, and they made the location of the reverse end iterator be the first element in the sequence. Then they overloaded the dereferencing operators (* and ->) to return the value of the *preceding* element. You can see from Figure 2.7 that this works very nicely. The reverse beginning iterator is located one element past the sequence, which is legal. However, when it's dereferenced, it actually returns the last element. The reverse end iterator is at the first element, so its location certainly exists. If it were to be dereferenced, it would have to provide the value of an element preceding the sequence, which doesn't exist. However, as with regular iterators, you're not allowed to dereference the end iterator, and this avoids accessing a nonexistent element.

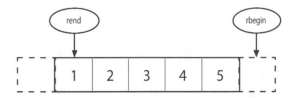

FIGURE 2.7 Correct positions of the beginning and end reverse iterators.

These definitions of reverse iterators allow them to work properly in the STL algorithms. Put another way, reverse iterators let the STL provide functionality that operates in the reverse direction, such as finding or replacing the last element, without adding any new algorithms.

You can get a reverse iterator from any bidirectional or random access iterator by passing the regular iterator to the reverse iterator's constructor, as Listing 2.2 shows. There's a problem with this—should the reverse iterator have the same position as the iterator or produce the same value? The STL designers chose the first course, which Figure 2.8 shows. The location stays the same, but the values are different because the reverse iterator returns the value of the preceding element. This explains the output of the program in Listing 2.2. Figure 2.8 also implies that if you're converting a *single* iterator to a reverse iterator and want the two to have the same value, you should increment (++) the reverse iterator once.

There's a big advantage to making the reverse iterator keep the same position as the regular iterator. If you make a *pair* of reverse iterators from a pair of forward iterators, you don't have to do anything more to the reverse pair when you use them as a range. That is, they will produce the same result as the regular pair but in reverse order. Listing 2.3 is an example of making a pair of reverse iterators from regular iterators.

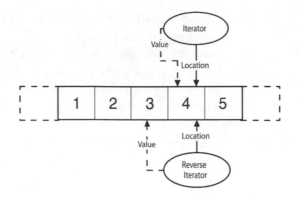

FIGURE 2.8 An iterator and its corresponding reverse iterator.

LISTING 2.3 Going from Regular Iterators to Reverse Iterators

```cpp
#include <algorithm>
#include <iostream>
#include <iterator>
#include <vector>

using namespace std;

int main( )
{
    vector<int> v( 5 );
    for( int i = 0; i < 5; ++i )
        v[i] = i + 1;

    vector<int>::iterator regular1 = v.begin() + 1;
    vector<int>::iterator regular2 = v.end() - 1;
    vector<int>::reverse_iterator reverse1( regular1 );
    vector<int>::reverse_iterator reverse2( regular2 );

    cout << "Regular range: ";
    copy( regular1, regular2, ostream_iterator<int>( cout, " " ) );
    cout << "\nReverse range: ";
    copy( reverse2, reverse1, ostream_iterator<int>( cout, " " ) );
}
```

The output of the program in Listing 2.3 is

```
Regular range: 2 3 4
Reverse range: 4 3 2
```

Figure 2.9 illustrates the code in Listing 2.3. The program displays all members of a vector except for the first and last one. Then it gets a reverse range from the regular range and makes the same display except in reverse. The code produces both displays with the STL algorithm copy and the iterator adaptor ostream_iterator, explained later in "Stream Iterators." For more details on this easy way of using copy to display a range on the standard output stream, see Tip 16.

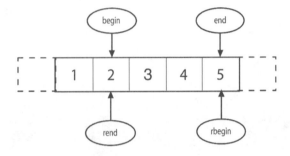

FIGURE 2.9 A regular range and its reverse equivalent.

If you have a reverse iterator and want to get an iterator from it, use the reverse iterator's base member function. If you get a pair of iterators from a pair of reverse iterators that make a reverse range, you can use the regular pair without modification as a normal range in STL algorithms. If you want to use a single iterator that comes from a reverse iterator, you'll have to decrement (--) once what base returns so the two iterators can refer to the same value. The code in Listing 2.4 provides examples of these ideas.

LISTING 2.4 Going from Reverse Iterators to Regular Iterators

```
int main( )
{
   vector<int> v( 5 );
   for( int i = 0; i < 5; ++i )
     v[i] = i + 1;

   vector<int>::reverse_iterator reverse1 =
      find( v.rbegin(), v.rend(), 4 );
   vector<int>::reverse_iterator reverse2 =
```

```
        find( v.rbegin(), v.rend(), 2 );

    cout << "Reverse range: ";
    copy( reverse1, reverse2, ostream_iterator<int>( cout, " " ) );
    cout << "\nRegular range: ";
    copy( reverse2.base(), reverse1.base(),
        ostream_iterator<int>( cout, " " ) );

    vector<int>::iterator regular2 = reverse2.base();
    cout << "\n*reverse2 = " << *reverse2
        << "    *regular2 = " << *regular2;
    --regular2;
    cout << "    *--regular2 = " << *regular2 << endl;
}
```

The output is

```
Reverse range: 4 3
Regular range: 3 4
*reverse2 = 2    *regular2 = 3    *--regular2 = 2
```

The output shows that when you use the `base` member functions of a pair of reverse iterators to get a pair of regular iterators you don't have to modify the latter to use them as a range in STL algorithms. However, if you get a regular iterator from a single reverse iterator via the base member function you must decrement the regular iterator in order to make the values obtained by dereferencing the iterators be the same. See Tip 39, Tip 51, and Tip 72 for examples of obtaining an iterator from a reverse iterator.

Insert Iterators

Reverse iterators are not the only kind of iterator adaptors. Another type of iterator adaptor is an *insert iterator*, also called an *inserter*. All insert iterators are in the output iterator category. You can only write to them—you can't read from them.

Normally, an iterator in an output range overwrites an element it is operating on by assigning the current iterator value to the output element. An insert iterator makes an iterator insert into a sequence instead of overwriting in it. In other words, an assignment to the value of the iterator becomes an insertion instead. Inserters are commonly used with algorithms to work with output ranges that may not be large enough. An algorithm just overwrites (assigns) old elements with new ones, so an output container must always have enough elements to accommodate those that the algorithm produces. For example, in the code snippet

```
vector<int> in;
// store some numbers in the vector...

vector<int> out( in.size() );
replace_copy( in.begin(), in.end(), out.begin(), 5, 10 );
```

the algorithm `replace_copy` replaces all values of five with ten as it's copying the input to the output. The output will end up receiving exactly the same number of elements that are in the input, so the code can set the size of the output vector ahead of time by passing the size of the input vector to the output vector's constructor. On the other hand, the code

```
vector<int> in;
// store some numbers in the vector...

vector<int> out;
remove_copy( in.begin(), in.end(), back_inserter( out ), 5 );
```

calls a different algorithm, `remove_copy`. As the algorithm is copying the input elements to the output, it removes all outgoing values of five. The program doesn't know in advance how many will be removed, so it can't determine the length of the output vector. The program could make that vector the same length as the input vector because there couldn't be more elements copied than are in the input. That, however, could be a big waste of space if the input range were large and many elements were removed. It would also necessitate calling the default constructor for all the elements, even those that are not eventually used by the algorithm.

A better solution is to use a *back inserter*, which appends elements to the back of a container. Thus, instead of assigning each element that is not equal to five to an output element, the algorithm now calls the output container's `push_back` member function to do the appending. This means that a back inserter can only accept containers that have a `push_back` member function. The standard containers that do are the vector, deque, and list. You can also use a back inserter with a string.

The second insert iterator is the front inserter, appropriately called `front_inserter`. It *prepends* elements, that is, adds them to the front of the output range. `front_inserter` is commonly used in algorithms for the same reason that the back inserter is used, namely, to handle cases in which you don't know how big the output container should be. You call it the same way as the back inserter, but it only works with containers that have a `push_front` member function. The standard containers that meet this requirement are the deque and list.

The third insert iterator is the *general inserter*, called `inserter`, which allows you to insert elements at a specified position in the output range. This iterator calls the `insert` member function, and you can use it with all standard containers and the string because they all have `insert`. Note, however, that for associative containers, the specified position is only a hint. An associative container orders its elements by value, so the inserted element may not end up at the desired location. The code in Listing 2.5 has an example of each of the three kinds of inserters. Tip 34 provides an additional example of a general inserter.

LISTING 2.5   Front, Back, and General Inserters

```
list<int> l( 3, 1 );
tips::print( l, "Original" );
list<int>::iterator middle = ++l.begin();
fill_n( front_inserter( l ), 3, 5 );   // prepend 3 5s
tips::print( l, "After front inserter" );

fill_n( inserter( l, middle ), 2, 7 );   // insert 2 7s in the middle
of original
tips::print( l, "After inserter" );

fill_n( back_inserter( l ), 1, 9 ); // append 1 9
tips::print( l, "After back inserter" );
```

The output is

```
Original: 1 1 1
After front inserter: 5 5 5 1 1 1
After inserter: 5 5 5 1 7 7 1 1
After back inserter: 5 5 5 1 7 7 1 1 9
```

The code in Listing 2.5 starts by declaring a list container with three ones in it. `tips::print`, a custom function that prints a text string and all elements in a container (see Tip 0) displays the container's initial state, as the first line of the output shows. To prepend copies of the same number to the list, you can use the STL algorithm `fill_n` and a front inserter as shown. To put the copies into the middle of the list, make an iterator as shown that points to the element in front of which you want to insert the numbers. Then call the general inserter as the code illustrates. Finally, to append numbers, call `fill_n` with a back inserter as the code in Listing 2.5 demonstrates.

Stream Iterators

In addition to reverse iterators and insert iterators, there's another kind of iterator adaptor—the stream iterator. The *stream iterator* lets you use an input or output stream in an algorithm. Just as an insert iterator changes an assignment to an insertion, a stream iterator changes an assignment to an output operation using operator<<. It also changes an input iterator to a read from an input stream using operator>>. To use stream iterators, include the <iterator> header.

An *output stream iterator* converts an assignment into a write to an output stream. Its constructor is

```
ostream_iterator<T> os( out_stream, const char* delimiter = 0 )
```

T is the data type of the input range in the algorithm, out_stream is an output stream (such as cout), and delimiter is an optional text string that gets written after each element that is sent to the output stream iterator. An example of using an output stream iterator is

```
vector<int> v( 3 );
v[0] = 1;
v[1] = 2;
v[2] = 3;

copy( v.begin(), v.end(), ostream_iterator<int>( cout, " " ) );
cout << endl;
copy( v.begin(), v.end(), ostream_iterator<int>( cout, "\n" ) );
```

The call to the STL algorithm copy would typically copy elements from an input range to an output range. In the preceding code, though, the output stream iterator makes the destination of the data be the standard output stream. What is displayed is

```
1 2 3

1
2
3
```

In the first use of ostream_iterator, the delimiter is the space, so all the vector elements appear on one row with a space between them. In the second use, the delimiter is the newline character, so the three elements appear in a column.

One thing you might find peculiar in the code is the expression `ostream_iter-ator<int>( cout, " " )`. This is an *unnamed, temporary variable*. In C++, you can make a class object (instance) by calling the class name followed by the signature of a constructor but no variable name. For example, if you have a class called `Message`, and it has the constructor `Message( const char* text )`, you can create an instance and push it on a list with the statements:

```
list<Message> l;

Message m1( "Fire!" );
l.push_back( m1 );
```

You can also do it with an unnamed, temporary variable like this:

```
list<Message> l;

l.push_back( Message( "Fire!" ) );
```

Many STL coders prefer the second way because it saves a line of typing and avoids creating a variable that is only used twice. Whether you want to use un-named, temporary variables or not, it's a common idiom, so it's good to be able to recognize it.

The complement of an output stream iterator is an *input stream iterator*. This iterator adaptor lets algorithms read from an input stream by using iterators. It converts the iterator's reading of an element to reading a stream by using `operator>>`. You can read from the standard input stream (Tip 7) or an input file stream (Tip 97).

The constructor for an input stream iterator is `istream_iterator<T>( instream )`, where `T` is the data type of the input range and `instream` is an input stream. There is also the default constructor `istream_iterator<T>()`, which interestingly enough acts as an end-of-stream iterator. If the stream is a file stream, this is equivalent to an end-of-file marker. Having the end-of-stream iterator allows you to read in a loop until you reach the end of the stream. It also provides the ending iterator for the input range in an algorithm. For example, suppose you have a text file with one column of integers. Once you've opened the file, you can read all the data and display it with one statement:

```
ifstream in( "numbers.txt" );
if( !in )
{
    cout << "Couldn't open numbers.txt\n";
    return 0;
}
```

```
copy( istream_iterator<int>( in ), istream_iterator<int>(),
    ostream_iterator<int>( cout, "\n" ) );
```

The STL algorithm `copy` takes an input range and the start of an output range. Here, the start of the input range is an input stream iterator made from the file input stream, the end of the input range is the input stream iterator's default constructor, and the start of the output range is an output iterator made from the standard output stream.

CONTAINERS

The main function of iterators is to connect containers to algorithms. *Containers* are data structures that store objects. The STL comes with seven *standard containers*, which are containers that meet certain requirements in the C++ standard. One of the mandated items is the specification (through `typedefs`) of the data types of the following: elements, references to elements, iterators, and the *size* of the container (the number of elements it has). Another item is the constructors, destructors, and assignment operators that are necessary. There are also mandatory comparison operators and member functions that provide information about the number of elements. Finally, every standard container has member functions that mark the beginning and end of the range of elements inside it, appropriately called `begin` and `end`. To have an algorithm process all elements in a container, simply pass the algorithm `begin` and `end`.

Each functional requirement comes with a complexity requirement that describes the number of operations or the amount of time that the functionality can take to run. Typically, these are stated in terms of the number of elements in the container. For example, inserting an element in the middle of a list (or anywhere, for that matter) takes the same amount of time regardless of how many elements there are. However, inserting an element into the middle of a vector takes an amount of time proportional to the number of elements that come after the one inserted.

All the standard containers are *homogeneous*. This means that all the elements must have the same data type. The standard containers are also divided into two groups—sequence containers and associative containers.

Sequence Containers

The first of the two general types of containers is a *sequence container*. This container maintains its elements in linear order. The order depends on the time and place the elements are inserted into the container rather than on the elements' values. For example, if you insert three elements onto the back of a sequence container, they will stay in that order, even if the first element has a higher value than the third. The elements are not necessarily stored in order in memory. Actually, the elements in a list container are usually not even contiguous in memory. What is true, though, is that when traversing the container, the elements will appear in order regardless of where they are in memory.

There are three standard sequence containers. They each have advantages and disadvantages. Some are good for random access and others are not. Some are great for inserting and deleting, but their performance depends on where you insert or delete. Tip 1 provides a chart that can help you choose the right container to use for your application.

One standard sequence container is a vector. A *vector* is a one-dimensional dynamic array. To use a vector, you must include the header <vector>. A vector is like a C-style array in that you can access its elements by indexing ([ ]), and such access is fast. However, its big advantage is that it automatically increases its size if it needs to. The vector is the workhorse of the standard containers. It performs well in many situations and is a good choice if you have no reason to prefer another container.

Figure 2.10 shows the arrangement of a vector's elements in memory. The elements, marked A, B, C, and D in the figure, are contiguous in memory.[1] In addition, a vector often allocates a bigger block of memory than it needs for holding the elements it currently has. (Figure 2.10 shows these as shaded blocks.) From this arrangement, you can infer a number of things:

- Random access is fast because to get to any element, the vector takes the product of the element's size (in bytes) and its index and moves forward that amount in memory from the location of the first element.
- Inserting an element at the end is fast if the vector contains unused memory.
- Inserting an element anywhere but at the end is slow. The vector must keep the elements contiguous in memory. To do this, it moves in memory all elements that follow the point of insertion (to the right in Figure 2.10) to make room for the newcomer. This movement takes time.
- Similarly, deleting an element anywhere but at the end is slow, as inserting an element is.
- All iterators, pointers, and references to elements after a point of insertion or deletion are invalidated because those elements have been moved in memory.
- If the vector does not have enough unused room to put inserted elements, it must reallocate memory. It has to allocate new memory, call copy constructors to make the new elements from the old ones, call the destructors of the old elements, and deallocate the old memory. This takes a lot of time. Fortunately, it shouldn't happen that often, and sometimes there are things you can do (see Tip 17) to make reallocation unnecessary.

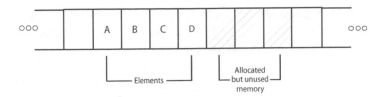

FIGURE 2.10   Arrangement of a vector in memory.

In sum, the vector is a good, general-purpose container that is especially useful for random access and when insertions and deletions only occur at the end.

A vector of `bools` has a special implementation that permits memory to be saved. However, it is actually not a standard container, so you shouldn't try to use it as such, for example in STL algorithms. Tip 26 explains why a vector of Booleans is convenient for manipulating bits and when to use it.

Another standard sequence container is the list. The *list* is a doubly linked list data structure. To use a list, you must include the header `<list>`. The list is made up of *nodes*, each of which contains an element, a pointer to the next node, and a pointer to the previous node. The big advantage of a list is that insertions and deletions anywhere take a constant amount of time. Its disadvantage is that it has no random access—to get to a particular element, you have to start at the beginning of the list and step to each element until you reach the one you're interested in.

Figure 2.11 shows an arrangement of a list's nodes in memory. The nodes, marked A, B, and C in the figure, are not contiguous in memory. The central part of each node represents an element. The shaded bar on the left part of the node contains the forward link (the pointer to the next node), which the figure shows as a solid arrow. The shaded bar on the right side of a node contains the backward link, shown as a dashed arrow. From the diagram, you can deduce a number of things:

■ Lists take up more memory per element than vectors because they have to store two links with each element.

■ Random access is slow because the list can't compute the location of an element. The list has to begin at the source node and step through the nodes one at a time until it gets to the destination node.

■ Deleting an element anywhere is fast because all the list has to do is redirect two pointers and call a node's destructor. For example, to delete node B in Figure 2.11, the list makes the forward link from node A point to node C and the backward link from node C point to node A.

■ Inserting an element anywhere is fast for a similar reason.

■ When you delete an element, none of the other nodes change in memory. Thus, all iterators, pointers, and references to the other elements remain valid. This is also true if you insert an element.

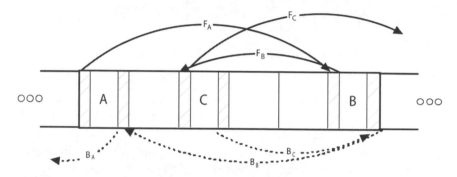

FIGURE 2.11   Arrangement of a list in memory.

Because a list's iterators are bidirectional, rather than random access, you can't use them with some STL algorithms, such as `sort` and `nth_element`. However, Table 9.2 shows that the list has member functions that are alternatives to some of these algorithms.

The third standard sequence container is the deque (which rhymes with "check"). A *deque* is a double-ended queue. To use a deque, you must include the header `<deque>`. In functionality, the deque is between a list and a vector. The deque has random access that is almost as efficient as a vector's. Inserting or deleting the first element is efficient, like it is for the list. However, insertions or deletions in the middle still perform poorly.

Figure 2.12 shows the logical structure of a deque. (This is not how it is stored in memory, though.) The deque is a dynamic array like the vector except that it is open at both ends. The practical effect of this is that it is easy to add or delete elements from either end of a deque. (The index of the first element in a deque is always zero.) Like the vector, the deque also has random access iterators and the subscript operator (`[]`). A deque does not have the vector's ability to reserve memory and check capacity (see Tip 17), but it does provide member functions (`push_front` and `pop_front`) to insert and delete elements from the front of the container.

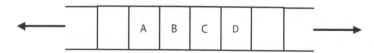

FIGURE 2.12   Logical structure of a deque.

Associative Containers

Vectors, deques, and lists make up the standard sequence containers. The other category of standard container is the associative container. An *associative container* is one that holds its elements in sorted order. The position of the element depends on its value, rather than on the time and place of insertion. Figure 2.13 illustrates this by showing values in a set (one type of associative container) entering out of order but being organized internally in numerical order. (Usually the elements are stored in memory using a balanced binary tree or red-black tree data structure.)

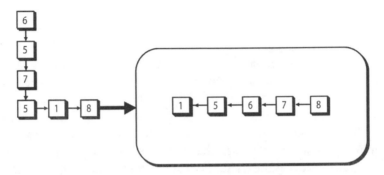

FIGURE 2.13   Associative containers order by value, not position.

By default, associative containers sort their elements into ascending order. If you iterate through the container, the first element is the smallest, the second is the second smallest, and so forth. Actually, when you insert an element and specify its position, the associative containers only take that position as a hint. They use it as a starting point to search for the right place to put the element.

Associative containers are designed for fast searching. They have very efficient member functions that perform searches and related actions such as counting the number of particular elements in the container and finding the first specified element. The four standard associative containers—set, multiset, map, and multimap—do have different interfaces and capabilities, though. The set searches for elements by their value and the elements must be unique. The multiset does the same but can store duplicate values. Maps and multimaps have elements that are pairs. The first member of the pair is the key, and the second is the value. Examples of key-value pairs are a country name and its national statistics, a person's national identification number and his address, and an engine's model number and its technical specifications. Maps can have any data type as a key, search by keys quickly, do not allow duplicate keys, and have a subscript operator ([ ]) that can take any data type that matches the key's type, not just an integer. Multimaps also search by key but do not have a subscript operator, nor do they prohibit duplicate keys.

A *set* is an associative container that stores its elements in order by value. Figure 2.13 is a good illustration of this property. Other properties of the set are as follows:

- It does not allow duplicate values.
- It automatically sorts the elements when the set is constructed or elements are inserted or deleted.
- You can use the default sorting criterion (less-than) or provide a criterion at compile time or at run time.
- A set's iterators are const, that is, you can read their values, but you can't change them.

You can find out how many of a particular element there are in a set by calling its member function count. The set can't have duplicates, so it will return either zero or one. You can also find that element by calling the member function find, which returns an iterator that marks the position of the found element. If the set can't find the element, the returned iterator is equal to the set's end iterator.

Multisets have the same characteristics except that they can have duplicate elements, as Figure 2.14 shows. They have the same count member function as the set, but multisets are more useful because they can have duplicate items. The member function find works the same way as for a set, returning the position of the first found element.

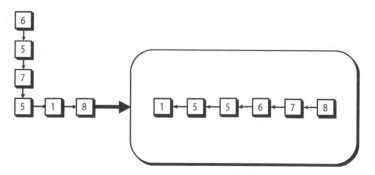

FIGURE 2.14   Inserting elements into a multiset.

Multisets also have three member functions that let you find the range of elements equal to a specified one. The first, lower_bound, returns the position of the first element that is greater than or equal to the given value. The second, upper_bound, produces the location of the first element that is greater than that specified. The third, equal_range, returns the first two in a pair data structure. The set also has these member functions. Although the first two can be useful, equal_range isn't because the set can't have duplicate elements.

A *map* is an associative container that stores its elements in order by *key*. Each key has a *value* associated with it. Figure 2.15 shows some key-value pairs. The map is excellent for fast searches by key, though searches by value are slow. Other properties of the map are as follows:

■ It does not allow duplicate keys.

■ It automatically sorts the elements by key when the map is constructed or elements are inserted or deleted.

■ You can use the default sorting criterion (less-than) or provide one at compile time or at run time.

■ A map's iterator points to a `pair` data structure, which the next section of this chapter describes. You can change the second member of the pair (the value) but not the first, that is, the key is `const`.

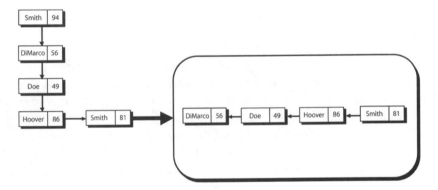

FIGURE 2.15   Inserting elements into a map.

Multimaps have the same characteristics except that they can have duplicate keys, as Figure 2.16 shows. Both types of containers have the five member functions `find`, `count`, `lower_bound`, `upper_bound`, and `equal_range` as sets and multisets do, but they work on keys, rather than values. For example, `count` gives you the number of elements that have the specified key. `equal_range` and `count` are not very useful for maps because they can't have duplicate keys.

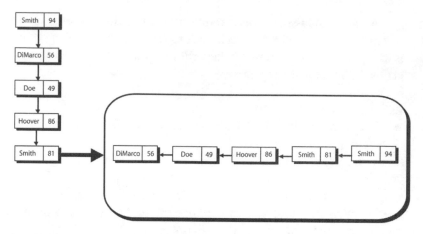

FIGURE 2.16   Inserting elements into a multimap.

Container Adaptors

(Multi)sets and (multi)maps make up the standard associative containers. The vector, list, and deque make up the standard sequence containers. They can't be built from each other (in the sense of one container being a wrapper for the other) without a substantial loss of efficiency. Some other classical data structures can, however, be feasibly constructed from the standard sequence containers. The STL gives you three of these structures—the stack, queue, and priority queue. They are not standard containers because they don't meet the requirements for those structures. Especially important is their lack of iterators. The three containers are actually *container adaptors*—wrappers around a standard container that provide a specialized interface.

The *stack*, which Figure 2.17 illustrates, is a data structure in which the last item added is the first one removed. That is, the stack keeps its elements in last-in, first-out (LIFO) order. A good example is a stack of cafeteria trays. Trays that have just been washed are placed on top of those already there and push them down. Only one tray is available for the taking—the one on top. Once it's removed, the next tray, and only that tray, can be taken.

To use a stack, you must include the header <stack>. By default, the stack is made out of the deque standard container, but you can use any sequence container that has the member functions back, push_back, and pop_back. The stack contains the deque as a class member and is not inherited from it. The stack hides almost all its container's members and gives the few it exposes names commonly associated with the stack. Thus, back becomes top, push_back becomes push, and pop_back becomes pop.

Another container adaptor is the queue. The *queue* is a first-in, first-out data structure, as Figure 2.18 shows. You insert elements only at the back of the queue and remove them only from the front. Usually, the elements come in faster than they are removed, so the queue functions as a *buffer*, that is, it temporarily stores elements until they are removed.

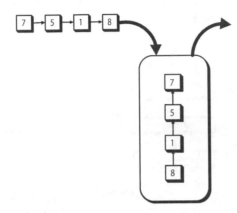

FIGURE 2.17   Stack.

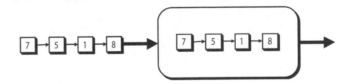

FIGURE 2.18   Queue.

To use a queue, you must include the header `<queue>`. By default, the queue is made out of the deque standard container, but you can use any sequence container that has the member functions `back`, `front`, `push_back`, and `pop_front`. The queue contains the deque as a class member and is not inherited from it. The queue hides almost all its container's members and renames some of the others with more common terms. The member functions `back` and `front` keep their names but `push_back` becomes `push` and `pop_front` becomes `pop`.

The third container adaptor is the *priority queue*, shown in Figure 2.19. It's almost the same as a queue except that elements come off the priority queue in order of importance. In other words, the priority queue holds ranked elements and the highest ranked ones are removed first. A good use of priority queues is in a situation where data or messages must be buffered and then processed in order of importance.

To use a priority queue, you must include the header <queue>. By default, the priority queue is made from the vector, but you can use any sequence container that has the member functions front, push_back, and pop_back and random access. You can also specify a comparison function that determines the priority of the elements. If you don't, the priority queue uses the element's less-than operator, which the element must define. The priority queue hides almost all its container's members and renames front to top.

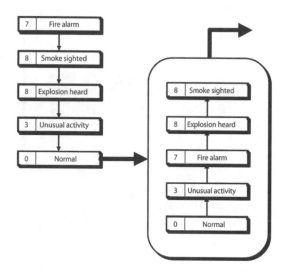

FIGURE 2.19   Priority queue.

Miscellaneous Containers

The stack, queue, and priority queue are the STL's container adaptors. Two other containers come with the STL. The first, *bitset*, allows you to easily manipulate a collection of bits and is available by including the header <bitset>. The bitset is neither a container adaptor nor a standard container. As Figure 2.20 illustrates, it can't hold different data types, only bits. Some properties of a bitset are the following:

- It can hold any number of bits, but you must specify the number at compile time and you can't change it after that.
- The bits are indexed, and you can access them with the subscript operator ([ ]).
- There are common bit operations for combining two bitsets—& (AND), | (OR), and ^ (XOR).
- Its bits can be shifted left or right by any amount.
- It can read and write itself from and to a stream.

- It has a limited (but useful) ability to provide a text string version of the bits.
- You can set, reset (clear), or flip (toggle) any or all bits.
- You can find out how many bits are set, if a particular bit is set, if any bits are set, or if no bits are set.

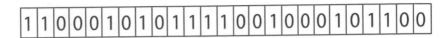

FIGURE 2.20   A bitset.

The other container, pair, is technically not even a container. The Standard Library includes it in the utilities section because several of the STL algorithms and standard containers use it. However, pair does hold two elements (as Figure 2.21 shows), so it is listed here as a miscellaneous container. The elements have public access and are called first and second. Some of the pair's properties are as follows:

- The two members can have different data types. (The pair is the only container that is like this, that is *heterogeneous*.)
- An element of a pair can also be a pair, which in turn can contain a pair, and so on. This rapidly becomes clumsy, though, and it's good to avoid too much of this nesting. Use a struct instead. (In the future, C++ may have a generalization of a pair called a *tuple* that will hold more than two elements [Jarvi02].)
- You can test two pairs for equality. They are equal if the two first members are equal and the two second members are also equal.
- One pair can be less than another. A pair x is less than a pair y if

```
x.first<y.first || ( !( y.first<x.first ) && x.second<y.second )
```

There's also a convenient utility function that creates a pair by deducing the argument data types, thus saving you a little typing. The function, make_pair, has the declaration

```
template< class T1, class T2 >
pair<T1,T2> make_pair( const T1& x, const T2& y );
```

make_pair and pair are available through the header <utility>.

To illustrate make_pair's use, consider the multimap standard container, which stores its elements as pairs. To insert an element in a multimap m that expects a pair made out of an integer and a floating-point number, you could use either the code

```
m.insert( pair<int,float>( 44, 2.178 ) )
```

or the code

```
m.insert( make_pair( 44, 2.178 ) ).
```

The latter is a tiny bit shorter but quite a bit clearer.

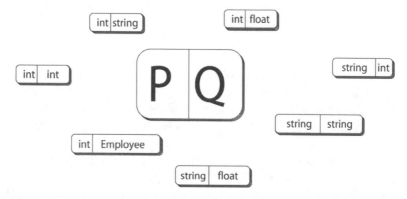

FIGURE 2.21   Members of a pair can have different data types.

FUNCTORS

The container adaptors and miscellaneous containers can't operate in STL algorithms. The standard containers, which are much more frequently used, work very nicely with the algorithms. However, before demonstrating how you can process containers with the algorithms, it is important to learn how to control their actions and specify the kind of processing they do.

C++ is an example of an *extensible* language, a language in which the user can add his versions of built-in operators. It's common to see arithmetic operators overloaded, either as class members or as global functions. For example, if you write a class that represents *rational numbers* (numbers that can be written as the ratio of two integers), you can define +, -, x, and / for the class. Actually, if you want to do arithmetic with rational numbers using those four symbols, you have to define those operators or your program won't even compile. You can always write functions such as add, subtract, multiply, and divide to do the operations, but your code will be much clearer and your classes easier to use if you overload the operators.

Interestingly enough, a pair of parentheses used to pass arguments is an operator. Its name is the *call operator*, and it is written as operator(). Unlike most other overloaded operators, it must be a member function, that is, it can't be a global function. You call it by writing the name of an instance of the class followed by the arguments within parentheses. You can have versions of operator() with different signatures. When the operator is used (called), the compiler chooses the overloaded version to use and follows the normal rules of function argument evaluation.

For example, suppose v and webster are instances of a class that has the call operator defined. Then int x = v(3) and if(!webster("frolic", "sangfroid")) are uses of the call operator. The first call operator would likely have the signature int operator()(int a) and the second would probably be declared as bool operator()(const string& s1, const string& s2).

To illustrate the call operator, suppose you have a class that counts how many integers of a sequence lie in a given range of values, as in Listing 2.6.

LISTING 2.6   A Class with a Call Operator

```
class Range
{
    public:
    Range( int a, int b ) : a_( a ), b_( b ), count_( 0 ) {}
    // a <= b

    void operator()( int n ) { if( n >= a_ && n <= b_ ) ++count_; }
    // increments the count if   a_ <= n <= b

    int count() const { return count_; }

    private:
    int a_, b_, count_;
};

int main( )
{
    vector<int> v( 100, 5 );
    Range r = for_each( v.begin(), v.end(), Range( 5, 10 ) );
    cout << "Count = " << r.count() << endl;
// ...
```

The constructor accepts the inclusive bounds, stores them, and sets the element count to zero. A member function returns the count. The call operator accepts a number, and if the number falls within the bounds, increments the counter. The main function demonstrates a use of operator(). The program declares a vector with 100 elements, each equal to five. Next, it passes the beginning and end of the vector's range to for_each, an STL algorithm. The algorithm goes through the sequence and makes each element be a parameter for its third argument, the function object. That results in the application of Range's call operator to each element.

The expression Range(5, 10) is an unnamed, temporary variable. "Stream Iterators" in Chapter 2 explains this construct in more detail. Call operators and unnamed, temporary variables become clearer when you see an implementation of for_each, as in Listing 2.7.

LISTING 2.7   An Implementation of for_each

```
template< class ForwardIterator, class Functor >
Functor for_each( ForwardIterator start, ForwardIterator stop,
    Functor f )
{
    for( ; start != stop; ++start )
      f( *start );
    return f;
}
```

The loop in Listing 2.7 shows how the code dereferences the iterator and passes that value to the call operator of the function argument f. for_each also returns a copy of f, its third argument. This is the only STL algorithm that returns such a copy. You can also see how general the algorithm is. It can move through a range of any data type that arises from any container and apply a call operator that does anything. There are some restraints on all this freedom, but the limitations are pretty minimal.

You can also pass a global function (template or not) to for_each. Listing 2.8 shows how to use both types of functions to square or cube all elements in a sequence.

LISTING 2.8   Using a Function in an Algorithm

```
inline
template< class T >
void square( T& n )
{ n *= n; }

inline
void cube( double& n )
{ n *= n * n; }


int main( )
{
    vector<int> v( 10, 5 );
```

```
list<double> d( 10, 5.0 );
for_each( v.begin(), v.end(), square<int> );
for_each( d.begin(), d.end(), cube );
  // ...
```

A *function-like object, function object,* or *functor* is an object that has a call operator, that is, `operator()`. A *function argument* is a functor or function that is passed to another function, for example, the third argument of `for_each`. Many of the STL algorithms use functors. It's certainly more work to write a class that has a call operator instead of just writing a function, so why bother with `operator()`? Well, a function object has three advantages over a function. The first is that a functor can have a state. It can have member functions and attributes, which makes it very powerful. You can also initialize a functor at runtime. In fact, a functor can have internal variables whose values are different for different instantiations of the functor. For example, in Listing 2.6 you could have `Range( 5, 10 )` and `Range( 50, 100 )` existing at the same time in the program. This isn't possible with functions.

The second advantage is that each functor has its own type. When you pass a functor to a template, it helps determine the signature. This lets you produce special behavior of the template for any or all functors. The last advantage is that function objects are usually faster than function pointers. This is because functors are passed by value and often have call operators written inline. On the other hand, functions are always passed by pointer, and on current computer architectures, jumps to function pointers are slow.

Predefined Function Objects

Although you certainly can write your own function objects, you often won't need to do that. The Standard Library contains a number of predefined function objects that make it easier to work with the STL algorithms. To use the functors, you must include the header `<functional>`. The predefined functors can be grouped according to similar functionality.

Table 2.6 lists the arithmetic functors. They cover all the arithmetic operations in the C++ language itself. To use the arithmetic functors, a custom data type must define any operator its objects are called on. For example, suppose you have a class called Color and want to call the functor `plus` on two color objects `c1` and `c2`, that is, `plus<Color>( c1, c2 )`. To do this, the Color class must define `operator+`, for example,

```
Color Color::operator+( const Color& rhs )
```

or a global function `operator+` must add two Color instances together, such as

```
Color operator+( const Color& left_color, const Color& right_color ).
```

As an illustration of using an arithmetic functor, consider the case of adding two vectors and storing them in a third, that is, the first element of the output vector is the sum of the first element of each input, the second element is the sum of the second element of each input vector, and so on. Assuming all vectors are the same size, a single statement with the STL algorithm transform does the job, as the final line in Listing 2.9 shows.

TABLE 2.6   Predefined Arithmetic Function Objects

Function Object	Operation
plus	parameter1 + parameter2
minus	parameter1 − parameter2
multiplies	parameter1 * parameter2
divides	parameter1 / parameter2
modulus	parameter1 % parameter2
negate	−parameter1

LISTING 2.9   Example of Adding Corresponding Elements of a Sequence

```
vector<float> a, b;
// fill a and b with numbers...

vector<float> c( a.size() );
transform( a.begin(), a.end(), b.begin(), c.begin(), plus<float>() );
```

transform starts at the beginning of vectors a and b, adds each pair of elements and puts the sum in the corresponding element of c.

Table 2.7 shows the built-in functors that compare two objects or numbers. Any class that has objects passed to a comparison function object must define the appropriate operation, for example, ==, <, >=, etc. The code in Listing 2.10 demonstrates the use of a comparison functor. The snippet examines two lists containing people's incomes. For each corresponding pair of elements, it calculates whether the first income is greater than the second by using transform, which starts at the beginning of the two lists, compares each pair of elements, and puts the resulting Boolean in the deque. It seems that the first choice of the container to store the results should be a vector of Booleans, but Tip 28 explains why this won't work.

TABLE 2.7 Predefined Comparison Function Objects

Function Object	Operation
equal_to	parameter1 == parameter2
not_equal_to	parameter1 != parameter2
greater	parameter1 > parameter2
less	parameter1 < parameter2
greater_equal	parameter1 >= parameter2
less_equal	parameter1 <= parameter2

LISTING 2.10 Example of Using a Comparison Function Object

```
list<int> income1, income2;
// enter numbers into income1 and income2...

deque<bool> income1_greater( income1.size() );

transform( income1.begin(), income1.end(), income2.begin(),
    income1_greater.begin(), greater<int>() );
```

The STL also has three functors (see Table 2.8) that perform logical operations. Classes passed to these functors must define the appropriate operation, that is, &&, ||, or !. To illustrate their use, assume called_by_Bob and called_by_Fred are deques of Booleans. Each element specifies whether that salesman has called a corresponding customer. If result is also a deque of Booleans, the statement

```
transform( called_by_Bob.begin(), called_by_Bob.end(),
    called_by_Fred.begin(), result.begin(), logical_and<bool>() );
```

computes all the customers whom both Bob and Fred have called. Likewise, the statement

```
transform( called_by_Bob.begin(), called_by_Bob.end(),
    called_by_Fred.begin(), result.begin(), logical_or<bool>() );
```

calculates all the customers that either Bob or Fred (or both) have called.

TABLE 2.8 Predefined Logical Function Objects

Function Object	Operation
`logical_and`	parameter1 && parameter2
`logical_or`	parameter1 || parameter2
`logical_not`	!parameter1

Binders (see Table 2.9) take a function object of two parameters and convert it to a functor that just accepts one argument. They do this by "freezing" one of the two arguments, that is, always passing the same value to that argument. `bind1st` binds the first argument and `bind2nd` the second one. Binders are particularly useful with arithmetic and comparison functors. The signature of both binders is `const Operation& op, const T& x`. The first argument is a function object that specifies the operation, and the second argument is the constant value to be fed to the operation. For example,

```
find_if( v.begin(), v.end(), bind2nd( greater<int>(), 5 ) )
```

finds the first element in the sequence that is greater than five. The call operator of `greater<int>()` takes two arguments and determines if the first is greater than the second. The second argument is bound to five, so the first argument comes from the sequence. In essence then, `find_if` computes `e > 5` for every element `e` in the sequence until it finds one that is greater than five or until it reaches the end of the sequence.

TABLE 2.9 Predefined Binder and Negator Function Objects

Function Object	Operation
`bind1st`	Hold first argument of a functor constant
`bind2nd`	Hold second argument of a functor constant
`not1`	Complement (logical negation) of unary predicate
`not2`	Complement (logical negation) of binary predicate

`bind1st` works the same way except that it freezes the first argument of a binary functor. One good use of this binder is in taking the inverse of a number.

```
transform( data.begin(), data.end(), inverted.begin(),
    bind1st( divides<double>(), 1.0 ) );
```

The statement takes every element from the container called data, divides one by the element, and puts the result in a container that holds these inverted numbers.

A *negator* is an adaptor that returns the complement (also called the logical inverse or NOT) of its argument. The STL has two negators—not1 and not2. The former operates on functors that take one argument and the latter on functors that take two.

The arguments to negators are predicates. A *predicate* is a function object that returns a Boolean, or a value that can be converted to a Boolean. In addition, a predicate must always return the same value for the same inputs. Thus,

```
bool check1( int a )
{ return a > 10; }
```

is a predicate but

```
bool check2( int b )
{
    static int count = 0;
    return ( b + count++ ) % 2 == 0; // even numbers
}
```

is not.

Suppose you have a predicate function valid1 and you want to replace all numbers in a sequence s that are not valid by 100. The statement

```
replace_if( s.begin(), s.end(), not1( ptr_fun( valid1 ) ), 100 );
```

does the trick. (Table 2.10 and Tip 47 provide more information on ptr_fun.) If you have a binary predicate valid2 and want to find what pairs of numbers are not valid, you can do it this way:

```
vector<int> v1;
vector<int> v2;
// put numbers in the vectors...

deque<bool> invalid( v1.size() );
transform( v1.begin(), v1.end(), v2.begin(), invalid.begin(),
    not2( ptr_fun( valid2 ) ) );
```

The STL comes with three functors that let you adapt functions for use with function objects. Table 2.10 lists these functors and describes their use. The first, ptr_fun, allows ordinary (also called global) functions to work in adaptors. For example, suppose you have an ordinary function `bool is_valid( int )` that returns `true` if its argument is valid and `false` otherwise. To find the first element in a list `l` of numbers that is valid, you can use the expression

```
find_if( l.begin(), l.end(), is_valid )
```

TABLE 2.10   Predefined Function Objects for Adapting Functions

Function Object	Operation
ptr_fun	Allows a pointer to an ordinary function to be used as a functor
mem_fun	Allows a member function of a pointer to a class object to be used as a functor
mem_fun_ref	Allows a member function of a class object to be used as a functor

However, if you want to find the first element that is *not* valid and try to use the code

```
find_if( l.begin(), l.end(), not1( is_valid ) )
```

you'll get a compiler error because `not1` expects a function object and `is_valid` is just a plain function. To fix this, wrap `is_valid` in a call to `ptr_fun`:

```
find_if( l.begin(), l.end(), not1( ptr_fun( is_valid ) ) )
```

Remember that when you pass the name of a function as an argument, you're actually passing a pointer to the function. This is how `ptr_fun` gets its name.

   `ptr_fun` also works with functions that take two arguments. Suppose you write a function with signature

```
double distance2d( pair<int,int> p1, pair<int,int> p2 )
```

that calculates the distance between two two-dimensional points. To compute the distance between corresponding points in two vectors, you can use the code

```
vector< pair<int,int> > points1;
vector< pair<int,int> > points2;
// load values into points1 and points2...

vector<double> d( points1.size() );
```

```
transform( points1.begin(), points1.end(), points2.begin(),
    d.begin(), distance2d );
```

To compute the distance of each point from the origin, that is, from the point (0,0), you can use the code

```
transform( points1.begin(), points1.end(), d.begin(),
    bind2nd( ptr_fun(distance2d), make_pair(0,0) ) );
```

Another adaptor for functions is `mem_fun_ref`, which provides the same capability as `ptr_fun` but for class member functions. To use this adaptor, wrap it around text consisting of the address operator (`&`), followed by the class name, followed by the scope operator (`::`), and the member function name, for example, `mem_fun_ref( &X::draw )`. This adaptor allows you to call a member function of each class object in a range. For example, suppose you have a class called Cow with a member function `moo` that makes the appropriate noise. To make the entire herd sound off, you can use code like this:

```
vector<Cow> herd;
// load cows into the herd...

for_each( herd.begin(), herd.end(), mem_fun_ref( &Cow::moo ) );
```

`for_each`, an STL algorithm, traverses the vector from start to finish and invokes the passed functor on every element. In this case, `for_each` calls the member function `moo` of each element. If you omitted `mem_fun_ref`, the code wouldn't compile. You can also call a member function that takes just one argument. If the Cow class has a member function

```
void Cow::print( string owner ) const
```

you can call it with a bound argument this way to show that Farmer John owns the whole herd:

```
for_each( herd.begin(), herd.end(),
    bind2nd( mem_fun_ref( &Cow::print ), "Farmer John" ) );
```

There are two caveats to be aware of, though. The first is that when you apply a binder to a member function that is wrapped in `mem_fun_ref`, the member function must be declared `const`, for example,

```
class Cow
```

```
{
    public:
        void moo();
        void print( string owner ) const;
};
```

(If you're not using a binder, the member function doesn't have to be `const`, as `moo` demonstrates.) The second caveat is that the argument must be passed by value, not reference. The member function `print` shows that although the string would typically be passed by (constant) reference, it's passed in the example by value so that the function can be used in a binder.

A final note on function objects: if you're interested in writing your own function objects, the Standard Library provides two base objects, `unary_function` and `binary_function`, to make life easier for you. You can derive function objects from them that will work with adaptors.

ALGORITHMS

Function objects aren't useful in and of themselves. They exist to specify the behavior of STL algorithms. This is important because containers and algorithms are the heart of the STL. You can think of an *algorithm*, in the STL sense, as a template function that processes a range or ranges of elements. All algorithms are independent of the internal implementation of the containers they work on. They do this by having their inputs specified as iterator ranges. As long as the passed iterators are the type required by the algorithm, it doesn't matter what the iterators point to. For example, the `copy` algorithm copies elements from an input range to an output range. Both ranges commonly come from containers. However, the input range can also come from a file, a string, or even the standard input stream. Likewise, the output range can be part of a file, a memory stream, or the standard output stream.

Some algorithms have both *in-place* and *copying* versions. The former uses one range as both the input and output. In the latter, the algorithm has both input and output ranges. If an algorithm `zzz` has a copying version, that version is called `zzz_copy`. For example, the algorithm `unique` removes all consecutive duplicates of an element. `unique_copy` removes all consecutive duplicates as it's copying the input range to the output range. In other words, it only copies unique elements.

Another suffix on algorithm names is `_if`. If an algorithm has two forms that have the same number of parameters, one of which can be a value or a predicate, the algorithm has two names. The one without the suffix `_if` accepts a value and the one with the suffix accepts the function object. For example, the algorithm `find` locates the first element in a range that is equal to a specified value. By using `find_if`, you can specify a different test, for example, the first element less than ten. Algorithms that take predicates have defaults that can be used in many cases. Typically, the defaults are less-than (<) and equals (==).

Finally, if an algorithm `zzz` has a copying version with an argument that takes a predicate or a function object, the predicate version is called `zzz_copy_if`. The only two such algorithms are `remove_copy_if` and `replace_copy_if`.

The algorithms in the Standard Library can be divided into five main groups, as Table 2.11 shows. *Nonmodifying algorithms* change neither the value nor the order of elements in the range they work on. They only use input and forward iterators, so you can use them on all standard containers. *Modifying algorithms* change the value but not the order of elements. Some modifying algorithms are in-place and others aren't. *Mutating algorithms* change the order but not the value of elements in a sequence. Again, some algorithms in this group are in-place but others aren't. *Sorting algorithms* sort their inputs. Although they are mutating algorithms, they are in a separate group because they are more complicated and take more time to run than the other mutating algorithms. *Numeric algorithms* are principally used in numerical computations. In fact, they are listed in a separate chapter of the C++ Standard. Finally, the Standard C Library is actually part of the C++ Standard Library. Although the tips in this book use some C functions occasionally, there won't be any substantial discussion of them.

TABLE 2.11   Five Main Groups of Algorithms

Group	Header
Modifying and Nonmodifying Algorithms	`<algorithm>`
Mutating Algorithms	`<algorithm>`
Sorting Algorithms	`<algorithm>`
Numeric Algorithms	`<numeric>`
C Library	`<cstdlib>`

The remainder of this section provides brief descriptions of all the STL algorithms. Unless otherwise stated, all elements operate on ranges. Appendix A has a more detailed explanation of the algorithms that this book uses. However, for even more information consult the C++ Standard [ISO98] or an STL reference book such as [Austern00], [Josuttis99], or [Musser01].

Nonmodifying Algorithms

The first group of STL algorithms are the modifying and nonmodifying algorithms. Table 2.12 shows part of this group—the nonmodifying algorithms. Most of them are used to locate an element or elements in a range. Note that `search` finds the first matching subsequence, but unfortunately the algorithm that finds the last matching subsequence, `find_end`, does not have an analogous name.

TABLE 2.12   Nonmodifying Algorithms

Algorithm	Description
adjacent_find	Find the first pair of consecutive elements that are equal or that satisfy a predicate.
count count_if	Find the number of elements that are equal to a given one or that satisfy a predicate.
equal	Return `true` if all corresponding elements in two ranges are equal or satisfy a predicate.
find find_if	Find the first element equal to a passed one or that satisfies a predicate.
find_end	Find the last subrange that equals or satisfies a predicate with a specified subrange.
find_first_of	Find the first element that equals or satisfies a predicate with any element of a specified group.
for_each	Apply to each element a function argument that only reads.
lexicographical_compare	Determine if the first range is lexicographically less than the second. You can provide a predicate.
max_element	Find the largest element. You can provide a predicate.
min_element	Find the smallest element. You can provide a predicate.
mismatch	Find the first pair of corresponding elements in two ranges that are not equal or that do not satisfy a predicate.
search	Find the first subrange that equals a specified subrange or satisfies a predicate with it.
search_n	Find the first consecutive n elements that equal a given value or satisfy a predicate.

Modifying Algorithms

The counterparts to the nonmodifying STL algorithms are, naturally enough, the modifying algorithms. Table 2.13 provides brief descriptions of each. `for_each` and `transform` are both general and similar. `for_each` only accepts one range, returns a copy of its function object, and is slightly faster because it passes the elements by reference. `transform` can take one or two input ranges, has an output range, does not return its function argument, and assigns the results of the function object to the elements. The output range can be one of the input ranges so `transform` can in effect modify the input range, as `for_each` does.

TABLE 2.13   Modifying Algorithms

Algorithm	Description
copy	Copy the input elements to the output.
fill	Set elements to a specified value.
fill_n	Set *n* elements to a specified value.
for_each	Apply a function argument that can modify a passed value to each element.
generate	For each element call a function object and store its returned value.
generate_n	For *n* elements call a function object and store its returned value.
remove remove_if	Remove all elements equal to a passed one or that satisfy a predicate.
remove_copy remove_copy_if	Copy to an output range all elements except for those that equal the specified one or that satisfy a predicate.
replace replace_if	Replace all elements equal to a passed one or that satisfy a predicate.
replace_copy replace_copy_if	Copy elements to an output while replacing all that are equal to a specified one or that satisfy a predicate.
transform	General modification from one or two inputs to an output.

Mutating Algorithms

The modifying and nonmodifying algorithms make up the first group of STL algorithms. The second group, shown in Table 2.14, contains the mutating algorithms. They just change the order of the elements. Some are simple changes, such as rotating and reversing. Some are incremental re-orderings, such as the permutation algorithms. And some are quite complicated, such as random shuffling.

FIGURE 2.14   Mutating Algorithms

Algorithm	Description
next_permutation	Get the next permutation of the elements.
prev_permutation	Get the previous permutation of the elements.
random_shuffle	Shuffle the elements.
reverse	Reverse the order of the elements.
reverse_copy	Reverse the order of the elements being copied to an output.
rotate	Rotate the order of the elements.
rotate_copy	Rotate the order of the elements being copied to an output.

Partitioning and Sorting Algorithms

After the mutating algorithms comes another group—the partitioning and sorting algorithms shown in Table 2.15. To *partition* a range is to break it up into two sub-ranges such that one contains all the elements that are equal to a specified value (or satisfy a given predicate) and the other holds the rest of the elements. Partitioning is a simple case of sorting.

Some of the algorithms have a version with the prefix stable. These functions take longer to run but preserve the relative ordering of equal elements. For example, if elements A and B are equal and A comes before B in the input range, A will also come before B in the output.

TABLE 2.15   Partitioning and Sorting Algorithms

Algorithm	Description
nth_element	Get the first *n* sorted elements of a range, in ascending or specified order.
partial_sort	Sort part of the input range into ascending or specified order.
partial_sort_copy	Copy the input to the output, sorting the first part of it into ascending or specified order. →

partition	Split the input into two parts—one that satisfies a predicate and one that doesn't. Equal elements may not retain their original, relative order.
sort	Sort the input range in ascending or specified order.
stable_partion	Split the input into two parts—one that satisfies a predicate and one that doesn't. Equal elements retain their original, relative order.
stable_sort	Sort the input range in ascending or specified order. Equal elements retain their original, relative order.

Sorted Range Algorithms

Once you've sorted the elements in a container, you can do a lot with them by using another group of STL algorithms—the sorted range algorithms that Table 2.16 lists. They all assume that the input range is sorted. Moreover, it has to be sorted with the same criterion that you use in the algorithm. If the input isn't sorted, the algorithms will run but won't produce correct answers.

TABLE 2.16   Sorted Range Algorithms

Algorithm	Description
binary_search	Search for a particular element.
equal_range	Find the first and last positions at which a specified element can be inserted.
includes	Determine if the first range is a subset of the second.
inplace_merge	Merge two sorted parts of a range into one.
lower_bound	Find the first position at which a specified element can be inserted.
merge	Merge two sorted input ranges into one sorted output range.
set_difference	Find the elements that are in the first range but not in the second.
set_intersection	Find the intersection of two input ranges.
set_symmetric_difference	Find the exclusive-or of two input ranges, that is, those elements that are in one but not both input ranges. $\rightarrow$

set_union	Find the union of two input ranges.
unique	Retain only one element from each group of consecutive elements.
unique_copy	Copy only the first element from each group of consecutive elements that equal or satisfy a predicate.
unique_if	Remove all but one element from each group of consecutive elements that equal or satisfy a predicate.
upper_bound	Find the last position at which a specified element can be inserted.

Heap Algorithms

In addition to the sorted range algorithms in Table 2.16, a quartet of related algorithms lets you work with heaps. A *heap* is a special organization of elements in a range between two random access iterators. Its two principal properties are that the first element is the largest and that an element can be added or removed in time proportional to the logarithm of the number of elements in the heap. Heaps are useful for making priority queues. Table 2.17 lists the heap algorithms.

TABLE 2.17   Heap Algorithms

Algorithm	Description
make_heap	Convert a range to a heap.
pop_heap	Remove the first element of the heap.
push_heap	Add an element to the heap.
sort_heap	Convert a heap to a sorted range.

Numeric Algorithms

The sorting and sorted range algorithms are useful in a wide variety of applications. However, members of the fourth group of STL algorithms appear chiefly in numerical software. Table 2.18 describes these algorithms, but because of their specialized nature, they may not be familiar to you.

TABLE 2.18   Numeric Algorithms

Algorithm	Description
accumulate	Sum the elements or apply a binary operator to all of them in turn.
adjacent_difference	Make each output element be the difference of the corresponding input element and the previous input element. You can also apply a binary operator other than subtraction.
inner_product	Compute the inner product (the sum of the product of corresponding elements in two ranges) or a generalized inner product.
partial_sum	Make each output element be the sum of the corresponding input element and all previous input elements. You can also apply a binary operator other than addition.

Binary Algorithms

The numeric algorithms, and in fact almost all of the STL algorithms, operate on ranges. A few useful algorithms, however, just operate on pairs of elements. Table 2.19 briefly describes each. Some of the other STL algorithms use them, but you can call them from your own code, too.

TABLE 2.19   Binary Algorithms

Algorithm	Description
iter_swap	Exchange the values pointed to by two iterators.
max	Find the larger of two values. You can use a custom comparison.
min	Find the smaller of two values. You can use a custom comparison.
swap	Exchange two values.

ERROR HANDLING

The STL algorithms are very powerful, but they're still software, and software almost always has errors in it. To understand how the STL handles errors, you have to look at its design philosophy. The STL was built for speed, not safety. Checking for errors takes time, so the STL basically avoids these precautions. It does virtually no checking of parameters—that's all up to you. The people who adopted the STL into the Standard Library chose this path for two reasons. The first was, as mentioned before, to avoid slowing down the STL. The second was that if a user prefers safety over speed, he can either make wrappers for the STL that provide error checking or can get a more protected version, for example, "safe STL" by Cay Horstmann [Horstmann04] or STLport at [STLport04]. However, it wouldn't be possible to go from a slow, safe library to a fast, unchecked one.

Program errors can be broken into two general categories. *Logic errors* are errors caused by incorrect programming, such as indexes that are out of range. They are in theory preventable. The only time the STL checks for a logical error is in the vector or deque's member function at. It's the same as the subscript operator ([]) except that it throws an error if the index is out of bounds. *Runtime errors* are caused by the program's environment and are typically beyond the scope of the program, for example, a low-memory condition. They are often hard to predict.

The C++ Standard Library (not just the STL) gives this *basic guarantee for exception safety*: the library will not leak resources or violate container *invariants* (prescribed states) if an exception occurs. There is also a stronger guarantee that an operation has no effect if an exception is thrown. In database programming, this is known as a *commit-or-rollback* or *transaction safe* action. In particular,

- Any failure to construct a node in the node-based containers (list, set multiset, map, multimap) leaves the container as it was. This applies to the initial construction and to the insert member function.
- Removing a node cannot fail.
- A single-element insertion in an associative container is transaction safe.
- All erase operations of both either one element or multiple elements always succeed.

All of these guarantees assume that the element's destructor doesn't throw an error. This is good programming practice anyway, but it's even more important to observe it in order to make the Standard Library function well in the face of errors.

In general, for safety in the presence of exceptions, associative containers are better than deques or vectors, and lists are the safest of all. Many of the container member functions have specific exception guarantees. See the Standard or a Standard Library reference book, for example, Table 6.35 of [Josuttis99].

Here are some tips that can help you avoid STL errors:

■ Make sure the output container has enough room to hold the results of an algorithm or use an inserter.

■ Don't use an iterator from one container in a different container, for example,

```
vector<float> x, y;
vector<float>::iterator x_iterator = x.begin();
y.erase( x_iterator );    // BAD — iterator for x used in y
```

■ Don't mix regular beginning and end iterators with their reverse iterator counterparts, such as begin and rend.

■ Don't let the iterators in a range come from different containers, for example,

```
count( a.begin(), b.end(), 100 )    // BAD — mixing iterators from
                                    // a and b
```

■ Don't forget, especially in search algorithms, to check that the returned iterator is not the end iterator before attempting to reference it, for example,

```
list<int>::iterator i = find_if( a.begin(), a.end(),
    bind2nd( greater<int>(), 500 ) );
if( i != a.end() )  // GOOD — check if equal to end iterator
    cout << "First number greater than 500 is " << *i << endl;
else
    cout << "Couldn't find a number greater than 500\n";
```

■ Don't dereference unitialized iterators, for example,

```
deque<Animal>::iterator pet;
cout << *pet;    // BAD — pet is not initialized
```

■ Don't use iterators that point to deallocated elements (see Tip 21).

■ Watch out for iterators that point to erased elements, for example,

```
list<Car>::iterator best = a.begin();
a.pop_front();
best->print();    // BAD — element "best" pointed to doesn't exist
```

■ Make sure all ranges are valid, that is, both iterators refer to the same container and the first iterator does not come after the second.

■ If you use an algorithm that has two input ranges, make sure the second one has at least as many elements as the first.

ENDNOTES

1. Actually, the requirement for the elements to be contiguous is not in the C++ Standard. It was mistakenly omitted and a correction has been submitted to the standards committee. However, everyone assumes that the elements are contiguous, and a vector is always implemented that way.

3 Tips on Containers in General

This chapter starts the heart of the book—a collection of practical tips to help you use the C++ Standard Library. Although the remaining chapters each focus on a specific type of container (list, vector, etc.) or a particular application of the Standard Library (text processing, numeric processing), this chapter gives you tips that apply to a variety of containers. Some tips are for all standard containers, and some are for just the standard sequence containers (vector, list and deque). You'll find that you'll use many of these tips quite often in your own work. In addition, the tips in the remaining chapters refer to them frequently, too.

ON THE CD

Feel free to test the source code on your compiler. All the tip programs are on the CD-ROM in the TIPS folder. The first line of each program in the book tells the file's name.

Here's what you'll get from this chapter:

- How to pick the right container to use
- What kind of elements can be in a container
- How to initialize a container with data or with the contents of another container
- How to store, append, or exchange the contents of one container with another
- How to tell if a container is empty
- How to get a container's current size or maximum size
- How to tell if containers are equal or if one is less than the other
- How to access a container from back to front
- How to fill a container with values from the standard input
- How to display a container's contents on the standard output

All tips in the book have the same format. First, the title describes the tip and gives the tip number. Next, a line tells what part of the Standard Library the tip applies to. This is usually an STL container or algorithm. After that, an optional line lists the tips that are related to the one you're reading.

Each tip presents its material in two ways. The first way, labeled "Quick Solution," is a very concise answer to the problem posed in the tip. It's useful if you already know what the solution is but don't quite remember the code. If you're an advanced programmer and just want a terse answer, this solution is for you. Be aware, though, that the code is meant to be short and because of this does not necessarily show good coding techniques. For example, these snippets don't parameterize constants and seldom check for runtime errors.

Because many of the tips involve containers, the programs use a custom-written template function to display the contents of a container. The function is called `tips::print` and is always qualified by the namespace `tips` so that you can easily tell that it is an auxiliary piece of code and not part of the Standard Library. The sample tip that follows (Tip 0) simultaneously explains this function and illustrates the format of the tips.

TIP 0   ## SAMPLE TIP—DISPLAY THE ELEMENTS OF A CONTAINER

Applies to: Standard containers
See also: Tip 5, Tip 16, Tip 21

Quick Solution

```
template <class T>
    void tips::print( const T& container, const char* text=0,
      const char* element_separator = " " );
// ... <-- indicates intervening, irrelevant code

deque<double> d;
// ... <-- indicates that the container is filled and perhaps processed

tips::print( d );
```

Detailed Solution

Many tips in this book involve containers. It's useful to be able to display the contents of a container, both to understand intermediate processing and to view the result. The custom written function `tips::print` does just that by sending each element in a container to the standard output stream. It displays all elements on one line. They are separated by a space, although you can change this to a different character or characters. The function can also display some text to the left of the container elements if you want. Because `tips::print` is a template function, it is in a header file and must be inserted in the code with #include. The file is called tips.hpp and looks like this:

```
// tips.hpp

#ifndef TIPS_HPP
#define TIPS_HPP

#include <iostream>

namespace tips
{

// Display on one line of cout each element of a container
// text - optional text to display before the elements
//    (if there is text it will be followed by a colon and a space)
// element_separator - character(s) to put between the elements
//    (default is a space)

template <class T>
void print( const T& container, const char* text=0,
   const char* element_separator = " " )
{
   const char* text_separator = ": ";

   // if there's text, display it and some separator characters
   if( text != 0 )
      std::cout << text << text_separator;

   // store the end iterator, which doesn't change
   typename T::const_iterator container_end = container.end();

   // display each element followed by the element separator
   for( typename T::const_iterator i = container.begin();
      i != container_end; ++i )
      std::cout << *i << element_separator;

   std::cout << std::endl;
}

}  // end namespace
#endif
```

The beginning of the file has the typical `#define` statement sentinels to avoid duplicate inclusion of the header file. The `#include` statement brings in the `iostream` header file that the code uses to get the standard output stream and end-of-line marker. The namespace `tips` enables you to distinguish the function `print` from a program function or one in the standard library.

The first argument to `tips::print` is a container. It can be any standard container and can have any element that can be inserted into an output stream. The second argument is a pointer to some optional text. By default, the pointer is set to zero, which signifies that there is no text to print. The third argument is again a pointer, but this time to text containing separator character(s). The function will display these characters between each element that it prints. The default element separator is a single space. Sometimes multiple spaces look better, especially if the container has words in it. You can change the element separator by explicitly passing the third argument.

The function starts by defining a text separator, which is a group of characters that it displays after the initial text string, if the string exists. The first two executable lines of code show how the function does this. Next, the software declares a constant iterator to store the end iterator returned by the container. This is a good optimization to do when using the end iterator of a container in a hand-coded loop because the loop calls the member function `end` at each iteration. You have to be sure that the end iterator won't change during the loop's execution. In this case, the container is passed by constant reference so there's no problem. However, Tip 21 explains how iterators can sometimes subtly become invalid.

The function then declares an iterator that it uses to cycle through the container's elements with a standard for-loop. It inserts each container element and the element separator into the standard output stream. The code finishes by writing an end-of-line character.

As an example, if the container were a vector called `original` that held the numbers 1, 1, 2, 3, and 5, the line

```
tips::print( original, "Original data" );
```

would produce the output

```
Original data: 1 1 2 3 5
```

Although many of the tips use `tips::print`, Tip 5 is a particularly good demonstration because it makes `tips::print` display a list container of double precision floating-point numbers and a vector of strings. Tip 16 shows an alternate way of displaying a container. That technique is a clever use of the STL algorithm copy that prints with only one line of code.

And now, here are the real tips for using the C++ Standard Library in your own code.

| TIP 1 | ## USE THE RIGHT CONTAINER |

Applies to: Standard containers

Quick Solution

Vector: Fast access to elements and rapid insertion/deletion at back

Deque: Fast access to elements and rapid insertion/deletion at front and back

List: Fast, safe insertion/deletion anywhere

Set: Fast search by value

Multiset: Fast search by value, duplicates allowed

Map: Fast search by key

Multimap: Fast search by key, duplicates allowed

Detailed Solution

The STL has seven different standard containers to choose from. Vectors and deques, sets and multisets, and maps and multimaps are pairs of containers whose purposes are related. However, these pairs and the list container are not similar to each other. Actually, their interfaces are different enough that it's hard to write substantial amounts of code using only member functions that are common to all containers. Because of this, it's best to decide ahead of time which container to use, and that leads to the question that this tip answers—"How do I pick a container?"

To help you decide, here are some questions to think about:

- Do you need random access to the container's elements? That is, will you be reading and writing elements nonsequentially?
- Will you be inserting or deleting in the middle of the container? At the front? At the back?
- Do you need the elements to stay in the order that they were inserted into the container?
- Will you be using iterators, pointers, or references to container elements? If so, Table 3.1 shows which containers are least likely to invalidate these objects.

- Would you like to use indexes for the locations of elements, instead of iterators?
- Does the container need to be compatible with a C-style array?
- Should the container free the memory it uses when it deletes an element?
- Must container operations be transaction-safe? This characteristic, also called *commit-or-rollback behavior,* means that if an element throws an exception during an operation (such as insert or delete), the operation doesn't succeed and the container stays in the state it was before the operation started.
- Do you need fast searching based on an element's value? Will there be multiple elements of the same value?
- Similarly, do you need fast searching based on a key? Will there be more than one element with the same key?

Table 3.1 will help you decide which container to use based on the preceding questions. Find the properties that are most important in your application, or the ones that you will use most frequently, and then see what container the table recommends.

TABLE 3.1 General Considerations for Choosing a Container

	Vector	Deque	List	Set	Multiset	Map	Multimap
Fast access to any element location	X	X					
Fast insertion/deletion at front		X	X				
Fast insertion/deletion in middle			X				
Fast insertion/deletion at end		X	X				
Keep in order of insertion	X	X	X				
Maintain iterators, pointers, or references to elements			X	X	X	X	X
Use indexes for element locations	X	X					
Compatible with C-style array	X						
Memory of deleted elements freed		X[a]	X	X	X	X	X

$\rightarrow$

	Vector	Deque	List	Set	Multiset	Map	Multimap
Operations are transaction safe			X[b]	X[b]	X[b]	X[b]	X[b]
Quick search based on value (without duplicates)				X			
Quick search based on value (with duplicates)					X		
Quick search based on key (without duplicates)						X	
Quick search based on key (with duplicates)							X

[a] Deques are not required to free memory when their elements are deleted, but often do.
[b] Lists are safe except for sorting and assignment. The associative containers are safe except for multiple-element insertion. There are also different degrees of safety in the member functions, for example, succeeding or having no effect; guaranteeing not to throw an error, and so forth. For details, see an STL reference book such as [Josuttis99].

TIP 2   REQUIREMENTS ON CONTAINER ELEMENTS

Applies to: Standard containers

Quick Solution

All elements must be copyable, assignable, and destroyable.

Detailed Solution

Even though standard containers are templates, there are some requirements regarding the types of data they can hold. Fortunately, these are mild restrictions. The requirements are the following:

1. All elements must be *copyable*. This means that an element must have a copy constructor and the copy that is made must be equivalent to the original. (This does not happen, for example, with auto-pointers.) Containers make copies of their elements very frequently, so it's good to make sure that the copy constructor is efficient.
2. All elements must be *assignable* by the assignment operator (=). Containers and algorithms use assignment to overwrite elements, sometimes in unexpected situations.

3. All elements must be *destroyable* by a destructor. Containers delete their elements by calling the elements' destructors.

All built-in data types are copyable, assignable, and destroyable. In addition, C++ provides default copy constructors, destructors, and assignment operators for classes, making them automatically suitable for use in containers. Your class might have its own versions of these functions, especially if the class needs to allocate and deallocate resources such as memory. Actually, if a class has a custom version of any of these three member functions (copy constructor, destructor, and assignment operator), it should have custom versions of all of them. The C++ FAQ calls this "The Law of the Big Three" [Cline99].

Elements used in sequence containers might also have to meet other requirements, namely:

1. Elements might need default constructors (constructors that take no arguments). For example, all sequence containers have a constructor with one argument—the size to make the container being constructed. The elements in the container are created by calling their default constructors. Another example is the sequence container member function `resize`, which might also call the elements' default constructors.
2. Elements might need the equality operator (==). It is used when searching for elements or testing to see if containers are equal.
3. Elements might need the less-than operator (<), for example, in the list member function `sort`, or when checking if one container is less than another.

Finally, elements in associative containers must have a sorting criterion, which by default is `operator<`.

Listing 3.1 has a program that clearly shows elements in a container being created, assigned, and destroyed.

LISTING 3.1   Elements Being Created, Assigned, and Destroyed

```
// general_requirements.cpp

#include <iostream>
#include <vector>

using namespace std;

class Element
{
```

```
   public:
   Element();
   Element( const Element& );
   ~Element();
   Element& operator=( const Element& );
};

inline
Element::Element()
{ cout << "\nIn default constructor"; }

inline
Element::Element( const Element& )
{ cout << "\nIn copy constructor"; }

inline
Element::~Element()
{ cout << "\nIn destructor"; }

inline
Element& Element::operator=( const Element& )
{
   cout << "\nIn assignment operator";
   return *this;
}

int main( )
{
   cout << "CONSTRUCTING VECTOR WITH THREE ELEMENTS";
   vector<Element> d( 3 );

   cout << "\n\nDELETING FIRST ELEMENT";
   d.erase( d.begin() );

   cout << "\n\nDELETING ALL ELEMENTS";
   d.clear();
}
```

The output is

```
CONSTRUCTING VECTOR WITH THREE ELEMENTS
In default constructor
In copy constructor
In copy constructor
In copy constructor
In destructor

DELETING FIRST ELEMENT
In assignment operator
In assignment operator
In destructor

DELETING ALL ELEMENTS
In destructor
In destructor
```

The program starts with a simple class called Element that has a custom default constructor, copy constructor, destructor, and assignment operator. All that these member functions do is print out what function they are. When the code makes a container with Elements in it, these functions produce a trace of the activity going on inside the container.

The program starts by creating a vector with three Elements. To construct them, the vector makes a temporary copy using Element's default constructor, creates the three copies to be stored in the vector by using Element's copy constructor, and then destroys the temporary copy by calling its destructor. The output shows this sequence of events.

Next, the program deletes the first element in the vector by calling the member function erase. Interestingly enough, erase does not call the destructor of the first element. Instead, it overwrites the first element with the second one, the second one with the third one, and then calls the destructor of the third element. (Your version of erase might operate differently.)

Finally, the program deletes all elements in the container by calling the member function clear. The output shows the two remaining destructors being called.

TIP 3   C-STYLE ARRAYS HAVE BEGINNING AND END ITERATORS

Applies to: Standard containers, many algorithms
See also: Tip 5, Tip 8, Tip 16, Listing 13.13

Quick Solution

```
const float cost[4] = { 4.78, 6.97, 8.81, 9.02 };
copy( cost, cost + 4, v.begin() );
```

Detailed Solution

The STL was designed so that pointers can act as iterators and C-style arrays can be used in many algorithms. In particular, many STL algorithms take an iterator range, as do a number of the member functions of STL containers. This tip shows how to get a beginning and end iterator for C-style arrays.

In C++, the name of an array is a constant pointer to the start of the memory holding that array's elements. You can access each element by adding the element index to the array name. Because the elements are numbered starting at zero, adding the number of elements in the array to the array name produces a pointer that is one element immediately past the end of the array. That may sound familiar because the end iterator of a range is also one element past the last member of the sequence. So to specify the beginning iterator of a C-style array, use the array name. To specify the end iterator, use the array name plus the number of elements.

There are different ways of stating the number of elements. The code in Listing 3.2 illustrates three of them. They are all correct, so you can use any of them. The text that accompanies the code explains the pros and cons of the different styles.

LISTING 3.2   Beginning and Ending Iterators of C-Style Arrays

```cpp
// general_array_iterators.cpp

#include <algorithm>
#include <iostream>
#include <iterator>

using namespace std;

int main( )
{
   // one way of declaring an array size
   const int num_costs = 4;
   const float cost[num_costs] = { 4.78, 6.97, 8.81, 9.02 };
   cout << "Costs: ";
   copy( cost, cost + num_costs,
         ostream_iterator<float>( cout, "   " ) );

   // another way of declaring an array size
   const char* fruit[] = { "Strawberry", "Apple", "Peach" };
```

```
    cout << "\nFruits: ";
    copy( fruit, fruit + sizeof( fruit ) / sizeof( fruit[0] ),
       ostream_iterator<const char*>( cout, "   " ) );

    // a third way of declaring an array size
    int year[] = { 1959, 1958, 1993, 1991, 1989 };
    const int num_years = sizeof( year ) / sizeof( year[0] );
    cout << "\nOriginal years: ";
    copy( year, year + num_years,
       ostream_iterator<int>( cout, "   " ) );

    // sort and display the years
    sort( year, year + num_years );
    cout << "\nSorted years: ";
    copy( year, year + num_years,
       ostream_iterator<int>( cout, "   " ) );

    // reverse the sorted years and display them
    reverse( year, year + num_years );
    cout << "\nSorted and reversed years: ";
    copy( year, year + num_years,
       ostream_iterator<int>( cout, "   " ) );
}
```

The output is

```
Costs: 4.78   6.97   8.81   9.02
Fruits: Strawberry   Apple   Peach
Original years: 1959   1958   1993   1991   1989
Sorted years: 1958   1959   1989   1991   1993
Sorted and reversed years: 1993   1991   1989   1959   1958
```

The first section of code shows one method of declaring and initializing a C-style array. In this style, you explicitly state the number of elements in the array declaration. The advantage of doing this is that it provides some safety from putting in the wrong number of values in the initializer list. If you put in too many values, the compiler produces an error. If you don't put in enough, the compiler sets the missing elements to zero. Although this isn't as useful as a compiler error, it may make it easier to track down the error during debugging because zero might be an illegitimate or unusual number in your data set. The disadvantage of this method is that if the number of array elements changes, you have to change both the initializer list and the constant that specifies the array size.

After declaring and initializing the array, the program uses the copy algorithm to print the values in the array (see Tip 16). The first two arguments are the iterator range, which for the C-array are the array name and the name plus the number of elements, as described earlier.

The next group of lines demonstrates a second method of specifying the array size. The array declaration does not explicitly state the number of elements in the array. Rather, the compiler infers it from the number of values in the initializer list. You can compute the number of elements by using the sizeof operator. If the argument to sizeof is an array name, the result is the number of bytes in the entire array. If the argument is an array element, the result is the number of bytes in that element. The quotient of these two gives the number of elements in the array. This value is used to compute the end iterator passed to copy.

The advantage of this method of specifying the array size is that if the number of elements in the array changes you only need to change one thing—the initializer list. The disadvantage is that if the number of values in the initializer list is incorrect, there's no indication of a problem. In addition, if you have to use the expression for the number of array elements more than once (perhaps in calls to multiple algorithms), it is inconvenient to retype the quotient. The next technique solves this minor problem.

The third method of specifying the array size creates a constant integer whose value is the quotient described previously. Using this constant produces clearer code and requires less typing. It has the same advantage and disadvantage as the second method.

For some important examples of using iterator ranges of a C-style array, see Tip 5 and Tip 8.

TIP 4   CONSTRUCT A CONTAINER FILLED WITH THE SAME VALUE

Applies to: Sequence containers, string
See also: Tip 5, Listing 13.14

Quick Solution

```
vector<float> v( 5, 3.14f ); // five elements of 3.14
```

Detailed Solution

Sometimes it may be useful to construct a container with a certain number of elements that are all the same and all equal to a specified value. For example, if you're going to be adding numbers to the elements, you probably want them all initialized to zero. If you're going to be multiplying numbers into the elements, they should be set to 1. Listing 3.3 shows how to initialize a standard sequence container with any number of copies of a specified value.

LISTING 3.3 Constructing a Container That Has Identical Elements

```
// general_initialize_single.cpp

#include <vector>

#include "tips.hpp"

using namespace std;

int main( )
{
   const int num_elements = 5;
   const float value = 3.14f;

   // construct a vector filled with copies of one value
   vector<float> v( num_elements, value );
   tips::print( v, "Initialized vector" );
}
```

The output is

```
Initialized vector: 3.14 3.14 3.14 3.14 3.14
```

The line in which the vector is declared shows that the constructor takes two arguments. The first is the number of elements to be constructed, and the second is the value that each element is set to. (The second element is passed by constant reference for the sequence containers and by value for the string.) Either argument can be a constant (as shown) or a variable.

The output shows that the vector does indeed have five elements, each of which is 3.14. If you're interested in creating a container with different values in it, see Tip 5.

CONSTRUCT A CONTAINER FILLED WITH SPECIFIED VALUES

TIP 5

TIP

Applies to: Sequence containers, string
See also: Tip 3, Tip 4, Tip 8, Tip 34

Quick Solution

```cpp
const double data[4] = { 4.78, 6.97, 8.81, 9.02 };
list<double> l( data, data + 4 );
```

Detailed Solution

It's often important to create a container with different specific values in it. Unfortunately, there aren't constructors that let you do this directly. However, it is easy to do by declaring a C-style array with an initializer list and then constructing the container from the array. You can always do this because all standard containers and the standard string have a constructor that takes the beginning and end iterators of a range as its arguments.

Tip 3 shows that for a C-style array you can use the name of the array as the beginning iterator and the name plus the number of elements as the end iterator. (The tip also explains different ways of declaring a C-style array.) The program in Listing 3.4 shows two examples of initializing sequence containers with specified data. See Tip 34 if you want to do the same with associative containers.

LISTING 3.4   Constructing a Container That Has Specified Values

```cpp
// general_initialize_many.cpp

#include <list>
#include <vector>

#include "tips.hpp"

using namespace std;

int main( )
{
   const int num_elements = 4;
   const double data[num_elements] = { 4.78, 6.97, 8.81, 9.02 };
   list<double> l( data, data + num_elements );

   const char* flavors[] = { "Strawberry", "Vanilla", "Chocolate" };
   vector<string> v( flavors,
      flavors + sizeof( flavors ) / sizeof( flavors[0] ) );

   // display containers
   tips::print( l, "List" );
   tips::print( v, "Vector", "   " );
}
```

The output is

```
List: 4.78 6.97 8.81 9.02
Vector: Strawberry  Vanilla  Chocolate
```

The container, in this case a list, is initialized by a constructor that takes the beginning and end of the C-style array as its arguments. (See Tip 3 for more information about the range of a C-style array.) The input data type can be any that is convertible to the data type of the container, though here both the array and the list have doubles.

The next group of lines demonstrates the initialization of a vector of strings. It also illustrates a different method of stating the number of elements in the array. Again, Tip 3 explains this method. The output shows that the two containers have been properly initialized.

If the container you want to fill already exists, Tip 8 explains how to put values of your choosing in it. If you want your new container to contain copies of a single value, see Tip 4.

TIP 6   **CONSTRUCT ONE CONTAINER FROM ANOTHER**

Applies to: Standard containers
See also: Tip 1, Tip 5

Quick Solution

```
list<int> original;
// ...

// make a vector from a list
vector<int> vector_copy( original.begin(), original.end() );

// make a list from a list
list<int> list_copy( original );
```

Detailed Solution

You can create a container that has the same contents as another container. Actually, you can do this regardless of whether the two are the same kind of container or not. Moreover, although the data types in the two containers are usually the same, this technique will work with different data types as long as the source type is convertible to the destination type.

One good reason to change container types is if you are going to be accessing the data in the containers differently. For example, suppose you initially gather a large amount of data, perhaps stored in the container elements as instances of a class. You know that you will be examining and discarding most of the raw data and keeping only the best pieces of information. Because you will be deleting many container elements, Tip 1 suggests that you use a list, which is optimized for deletions. After you have culled the data, you know that you will seldom delete container elements, but will often access them nonsequentially. For this, Tip 1 recommends that you use a vector, so you should transfer the contents of the list to a vector.

The code in Listing 3.5 shows how to construct one container from another.

LISTING 3.5   Constructing One Container from Another

```cpp
// general_construct.cpp

#include <iomanip>
#include <iostream>
#include <list>
#include <vector>

#include "tips.hpp"

using namespace std;

int main( )
{
   const int data[] = { 1, 1, 2, 3, 5 };
   list<int> original( data,
      data + sizeof( data ) / sizeof( data[0] ) );

   // make a vector from a list
   vector<int> vector_copy( original.begin(), original.end() );

   // make a list from a list
   list<int> list_copy( original );

   // make a list of floats from a list of ints
   list<float> list_float( original.begin(), original.end() );

   // show results
   tips::print( original, "Original list" );
   tips::print( vector_copy, "Vector copy" );
   tips::print( list_copy, "List copy" );
```

```
        cout << fixed << setprecision( 1 );
        tips::print( list_float, "List copy as floats" );
}
```

The output is

```
Original list: 1 1 2 3 5
Vector copy: 1 1 2 3 5
List copy: 1 1 2 3 5
List copy as floats: 1.0 1.0 2.0 3.0 5.0
```

The code starts by declaring a list and storing five integers in it to simulate the raw data described in the preceding text. (Tip 5 describes the technique for creating a container from an array.) Next, the code makes a vector with the same contents as the list by using the constructor that takes an iterator range. All standard containers have a constructor of this form, so you can always make any container from any other one, as long as the input data type is convertible to the data type in the container being created.

If both containers are the same kind and have exactly the same data type, you can make a new one from the old one by using a copy constructor, as the next line of code demonstrates. This is always possible because all standard containers have a copy constructor. Although you could also use the constructor that has an iterator range, the copy constructor is more convenient. The output shows that all three containers have the same contents.

If the container types are the same but the data types aren't—they're different but convertible—you have to use the iterator range form of the constructor. The program constructs a list of floating-point numbers from a list of integers to illustrate this. The last line of output demonstrates that the contents are indeed copies but are stored in different data types.

TIP 7   CONSTRUCT A CONTAINER FROM STANDARD INPUT

Applies to: Sequence containers, string
See also: Tip 5, Tip 6, Tip 78, Tip 97

Quick Solution

```
deque<float> data( (istream_iterator<float>( cin )),
    istream_iterator<float>() );
```

Detailed Solution

You can construct and initialize a container with values taken directly from the standard input stream. This is useful in quick-and-dirty programs. Moreover, Tip 78 and Tip 97 show that you can use the same technique with streams other than the standard input. The program in Listing 3.6 demonstrates how to create a container and fill it with values from the input stream.

LISTING 3.6   Constructing a Container with Values from the Standard Input

```cpp
// general_initialize_cin.cpp

#include <deque>
#include <iostream>
#include <iterator>

#include "tips.hpp"

using namespace std;

int main( )
{
    // load values from standard input stream
    deque<float> data( (istream_iterator<float>( cin )),
        istream_iterator<float>() );

    /***** If your compiler won't work on the above, try this

    istream_iterator<float> data_start( cin );
    istream_iterator<float> data_end;
    deque<float> data( data_start, data_end );

    *****/

    tips::print( data, "Values from cin" );
}
```

The program illustrates the technique by initializing a deque as an example. The container constructor has two iterators as arguments that specify an iterator range. (See Tip 5 and Tip 6 for other examples of this constructor.) The first iterator is a stream iterator made from the standard input cin. The second iterator is made by the default constructor for stream iterators. This serves as an end-of-stream marker, as "Stream Iterators" in Chapter 2 explains. You must have the extra set of parentheses around the first argument of the expression involving data or the compiler will interpret the expression very differently than what you intend. (It turns out to be a declaration of a function that returns a deque and has some strange arguments. See Item 6 of Scott Meyers' excellent book for details [Meyers01].)

When the program starts running, it immediately waits for user input. Type some numbers and press the Enter or Return key after each. When you've finished, press the end-of-file key. This is Ctrl-D on Unix and many other systems and Ctrl-Z on Windows. (Ctrl-X means to simultaneously press down both the Control key and the X key.)

If your input is the three numbers 3.14, 2.78 and 5.55, the output is

```
Values from cin: 3.14 2.78 5.55
```

Not all compilers can handle the code shown in the program. If yours won't compile, try the equivalent technique shown in the code comments. It's clearer but longer. The only runtime difference is that you'll have to enter the first number when the program constructs the beginning iterator `data_start`.

TIP 8   STORE SPECIFIED VALUES IN AN EXISTING CONTAINER

TIP

Applies to: Sequence containers, strings
See also: Tip 5

Quick Solution

```cpp
const int data[3] = { 14, 17, 220 };
vector<int> v;
// ...
v.assign( data, data + 3 );
```

Detailed Solution

Just as you can construct a container with specific values, you can store specific values in an existing container. The number of elements that you put in the container can be different than what it already has. The data type that you store does not have to be the same as the container's data type, but it does have to be convertible to that type. The program in Listing 3.7 demonstrates storing specified values in an existing container.

LISTING 3.7 Storing Specific Values in an Existing Container

```cpp
// general_assign_specific.cpp

#include <string>
#include <vector>

#include "tips.hpp"

using namespace std;

int main( )
{
   const char* student_answers[] =
      { "Berlin", "London", "Paris", "Madrid", "Don't know" };

   // create a vector and initialize it with the above strings
   vector<string> answers( student_answers, student_answers
      + sizeof( student_answers ) / sizeof( student_answers[0] ) );
   tips::print( answers, "Student answers", "  " );

   // reuse the vector by storing the correct answers in it
   const char* correct_answers[] = { "Berlin", "Paris", "London",
      "Madrid", "Vienna", "Oslo" };
   answers.assign( correct_answers, correct_answers
      + sizeof( correct_answers ) / sizeof( correct_answers[0] ) );
   tips::print( answers, "Correct answers", "  " );
}
```

The output is

```
Student answers: Berlin  London  Paris  Madrid  Don't know
Correct answers: Berlin  Paris  London  Madrid  Vienna  Oslo
```

The program simulates a geography quiz by first creating a vector of strings containing the student's answers and printing them. (Tip 5 explains how to construct a container with specific data.) Then it stores the correct answers in the same vector by using that container's `assign` member function.

The `assign` member function takes an iterator range as input. It replaces the entire contents of the container with the new sequence. The number of elements to be stored can be different than what the container originally had. The data type can be different too, as long as the type in the input sequence can be converted to the data type of the container. The output shows that the contents of the vector were indeed changed.

TIP 9 STORE CONTENTS OF ONE CONTAINER IN ANOTHER

Applies to: Sequence containers
See also: Tip 4, Tip 5, Tip 6

Quick Solution

```
list<int> l;
vector<int> v1, v2;
// ...
v1 = v2; // same container and data type
l.assign( v1.begin(), v1.end() ); // different container, same data
                                  // type
```

Detailed Solution

If you already have a container, you can replace its contents with that of another container. (Tip 6 gives a realistic situation for which you might want to do this.) The two container types can be the same or different, and the data types can even differ as long as the source type is convertible to the destination type. The code in Listing 3.8 demonstrates assigning one container to another.

LISTING 3.8 Storing Contents of One Container in Another

```
// general_assign.cpp

#include <list>
#include <vector>

#include "tips.hpp"

using namespace std;

int main( )
{
   const double data[] = { 3.14, 2.78, 1.51, 7.66, 9.65 };
   list<double> original( data,
      data + sizeof( data ) / sizeof( data[0] ) );

   // make a vector and list with data different from above
   vector<double> vector_data( 3, 3.33 );
```

```
list<double> list_data( 4, 4.44 );

// show results
tips::print( original, "Original data" );
tips::print( vector_data, "Original vector" );
tips::print( list_data, "Original list" );

// assign a list to a list
list_data = original;

// assign a list to a vector
vector_data.assign( original.begin(), original.end() );

// create an empty vector of int's and assign
// a list of doubles to it
vector<int> v;
v.assign( original.begin(), original.end() );

// show results
tips::print( list_data, "\nList   after assignment" );
tips::print( vector_data, "Vector after assignment" );
tips::print( v, "Vector of int from list of double" );
}
```

The output is

```
Original data: 3.14 2.78 1.51 7.66 9.65
Original vector: 3.33 3.33 3.33
Original list: 4.44 4.44 4.44 4.44

List   after assignment: 3.14 2.78 1.51 7.66 9.65
Vector after assignment: 3.14 2.78 1.51 7.66 9.65
Vector of int from list of double: 3 2 1 7 9
```

The code starts by declaring a list of doubles and storing five floating-point numbers in it. (Tip 5 describes the technique for creating a container from an array.) Then it creates a list and vector with different sets of floating-point numbers (see Tip 4) and displays all three containers. Next, the program makes one list become the same as another by using the assignment operator. This operator is available to all the standard containers, but the two containers it uses have to be the same kind and have the same data type.

The program continues by showing how to make one container have the contents of a different container. It does this by using the version of the `assign` member function that takes an iterator range. All standard sequence containers have this function. The data types of the source and destination can be different as long as the former can be converted to the latter. The end of the program demonstrates this by assigning a list of double precision values to a vector of integers.

The first part of the output shows that initially the three containers have different contents and sizes. After assigning the first container to the other two, they contain the same numbers. Finally, the last line illustrates the conversion of data types described previously.

TIP 10   APPEND ONE CONTAINER TO ANOTHER

Applies to: Sequence containers, string
See also: Tip 5, Tip 61

Quick Solution

```
list<int> l;
vector<int> v;
// ...
l.insert( l.end(), v.begin(), v.end() ); // append v to l
```

Detailed Solution

It's common to want to append one container to another. For example, data may be stored in various containers because it arises at different times or different places. These containers may then need to be "pasted together" so that all the data can be processed as a single collection. Another example is when the same data is copied into different containers for different processing and these containers are then reunited. Finally, appending can occur when different containers are to be processed in order. If the computations are the same for all containers, it may be convenient to put them into one container in the desired order (by appending them to each other) and then process the big container.

The way to append one container to another is to use the member function `insert`, which all standard sequence containers and the string have. (Actually, the associative containers have this member function too, but because they don't order by location, this tip doesn't apply to them.) The signature of insert is

```
insert( iterator position, InputIterator start, InputIterator stop )
```

The first argument is the position at which the following range should be inserted. For appending, this is the end iterator of the container into which elements are being inserted. The last two arguments are the beginning and end iterators of the container being inserted. The code in Listing 3.9 illustrates the call to `insert`.

By the way, although you may often see appending done by using the `copy` algorithm with a back inserter, `insert` can be more efficient. If you want to put elements into a container and are not appending them, definitely use `insert` instead of `copy`. It is likely to be much more efficient.

You can use the technique with `insert` to append characters to a string. However, for strings it is much more natural to use the "+=" operator, as Tip 61 shows. The program in Listing 3.9 demonstrates the method on a sequence container.

LISTING 3.9   Appending Containers

```cpp
// general_append.cpp

#include <algorithm>
#include <vector>

#include "tips.hpp"

using namespace std;

int main( )
{
    const char* names1[] = { "Smith", "Jones", "Bradbury" };
    const char* names2[] = { "Kelvin", "Ostrowski", "Lane", "Lord" };

    // create and initialize vectors with the above names
    vector<string> squad1( names1,
        names1 + sizeof( names1 ) / sizeof( names1[0] ) );
    vector<string> squad2( names2,
        names2 + sizeof( names2 ) / sizeof( names2[0] ) );

    // sort and print the separate squads
    sort( squad1.begin(), squad1.end() );
    tips::print( squad1, "Squad 1" );
    sort( squad2.begin(), squad2.end() );
    tips::print( squad2, "Squad 2" );

    // append the second squad to the first and print
    squad1.insert( squad1.end(), squad2.begin(), squad2.end() );
    tips::print( squad1, "Both squads" );
```

```
    // sort and print the merged squads
    sort( squad1.begin(), squad1.end() );
    tips::print( squad1, "Both squads sorted" );
}
```

The output is

```
Squad 1: Bradbury Jones Smith
Squad 2: Kelvin Lane Lord Ostrowski
Both squads: Bradbury Jones Smith Kelvin Lane Lord Ostrowski
Both squads sorted: Bradbury Jones Kelvin Lane Lord Ostrowski Smith
```

The program starts by creating two vectors of strings initialized with names of squad members (see Tip 5). It processes each vector by sorting it. The first two lines of the output show the result. Next, the code appends the second vector to the first and prints the large vector. Then it sorts the vector to get an alphabetical listing of all squad members.

TIP 11   **EXCHANGE CONTAINERS**

TIP

Applies to: Standard containers, string, swap, swap_ranges
See also: Tip 1, Tip 6, Tip 9, Tip 79, Tip 81

Quick Solution

```
list<float> l;
vector<float> v1, v2;
// ...
v1.swap( v2 ); // swap contents — same container and data type

// swap contents — different container, same data type
swap_ranges( l.begin(), l.end(), v1.begin() );
```

Detailed Solution

Tip 9 shows you how to put the contents of one container into another. However, there's a much faster way of doing this as long as (1) the two containers are the same kind, (2) their data types are the same, and (3) you don't mind the source container being changed. If this is your situation, you can swap (exchange) the containers' contents. Swapping is more efficient than using the assignment operator or the `assign` member function because swapping just resets some pointers inside the container and doesn't move or copy elements.

To swap containers that are the same kind and have the same data type, use the `swap` member function. Alternatively, you can pass both containers to the `swap` global function. Both ways are equivalent and both ways are very safe. The only time they can throw an exception is if associative containers are involved and copying or assigning the comparison criterion throws an exception.

Because swapping the same kind of container is so safe, a good use of `swap` is to work on a temporary copy of a container and if the processing completes successfully, swap the temporary and original containers. If the processing fails, the original container is untouched. This avoids the often-arduous task of trying to recreate the elements in a container that only made it partway through a computation.

To swap elements that have the same data type but reside in different containers, use the STL algorithm `swap_ranges`. This might occur if data has to undergo different kinds of processing and is stored in different containers to optimize the computations. For example, half the data might be in a list and half in a vector. The list processing might have numerous insertions and deletions and the vector processing might need nonsequential data access. After each half is processed, the data could be swapped and the remaining processing performed. `swap_ranges` is not fast like `swap`, but it does let you exchange the contents of different types of containers.

The program in Listing 3.10 demonstrates swapping between the same or different type of container.

LISTING 3.10   Swapping Containers

```cpp
// general_swap.cpp

#include <algorithm>
#include <functional>
#include <iomanip>
#include <list>
#include <numeric>
#include <vector>

#include "tips.hpp"

using namespace std;

int main( )
{
    // make a vector with the sequence 1.5, 3.0, 4.5 ...
    vector<float> v( 7, 1.5 );
```

```
partial_sum( v.begin(), v.end(), v.begin() );
cout << fixed << setprecision( 2 );
tips::print( v, "Original   data" );

list<float> l( v.begin(), v.end() );

try
{
   // find the inverses
   vector<float> temp( v );
   transform( temp.begin(), temp.end(), temp.begin(),
      bind1st( divides<float>(), 1.0 ) );
   v.swap( temp );
   tips::print( v, "Inverse of data" );
}
catch( ... )
{
   cout << "Failed to compute inverses\n";
   return 1;
}

// swap vector and list
swap_ranges( v.begin(), v.end(), l.begin() );

// delete two smallest numbers
l.sort();
l.pop_front();
l.pop_front();
tips::print( l, "\nList data" );
}
```

The output is

```
Original   data: 1.50 3.00 4.50 6.00 7.50 9.00 10.50
Inverse of data: 0.67 0.33 0.22 0.17 0.13 0.11 0.10

List data: 0.13 0.17 0.22 0.33 0.67
```

The program starts by creating a vector with a sequence of numbers (see Tip 79). The first line of the output shows the numbers. The code then stores the data in a list for later use. Next, it creates a temporary vector with the same contents as the original vector by using the technique that Tip 6 explains. The program processes the data by using the STL algorithm `transform` to calculate the inverse. (Tip 81 has more on computations with `transform`.) Because the vector construction and `transform` are both in a `try` block, if either fails (and so throws an exception) execution immediately passes to the `catch` block. There, the program simply prints an error and exits. If the construction and computation both succeed, the code swaps the original and temporary vectors to put the altered data set into the original vector. After the code prints the data, it leaves the `try` block and the temporary vector vanishes because it goes out of scope. The second line of the output shows the result of computing the inverse of the numbers.

Next, the program exchanges the contents of the vector and the list. It must do this with the STL algorithm `swap_ranges` instead of `swap` because the containers are different. The program then concludes by performing work better suited for a list than a vector—in this case, deleting two elements from the front of the container (see Tip 1). The last line of the output shows the sorted and shortened set of numbers.

TIP 12   GET A CONTAINER'S SIZE AND MAXIMUM SIZE

Applies to: Standard containers, strings
See also: Tip 4, Tip 17, Tip 64

Quick Solution

```
vector<double> v;
// ...

cout << "Vector empty? " << boolalpha << v.empty()
    << "\nElements in vector: " << v.size()
    << "\nMaximum elements vector can hold: " << v.max_size();
```

Detailed Solution

All standard containers and the string have member functions that provide three pieces of information about the container's size (the number of elements it has). The first, `empty`, returns `true` if the container has no elements and `false` if it does have some. The second, `size`, tells the number of elements currently in the container. (The string's member function `length` does the same thing as `size`, as Tip 64 demonstrates.) The third, `max_size`, provides the maximum number of elements that the container can ever hold. This number depends on the size of the element and on the size of data types used in a particular operating system.

The maximum size may be smaller for vectors than other containers. This is because vectors store their values in one contiguous stretch of memory whose length may be limited by the operating system. If you're interested in vectors, Tip 17 shows that they have some additional capabilities related to their size and number of elements.

You might wonder why there's a member function that checks if a container is empty and a member function that can tell you if the container has 0 elements. The reason empty is available is that it may run faster. This is especially true for lists. So if you only want to know whether or not there are any elements and not how many there are, it's best to use empty.

The code in Listing 3.11 demonstrates getting all three pieces of size information.

LISTING 3.11   Finding Size Information of a Container

```cpp
// general_size.cpp

#include <iostream>
#include <list>
#include <vector>

using namespace std;

int main( )
{
   vector<double> v( 3, 10.0 );
   list<double> l( 3, 10.0 );

   cout << "Vector empty? " << boolalpha << v.empty()
      << "\nElements in vector: " << v.size()
      << "\nMaximum elements vector can hold: " << v.max_size()

      << "\n\nList empty? " << l.empty()
      << "\nElements in list: " << l.size()
      << "\nMaximum elements list can hold: " << l.max_size();
}
```

The output is

```
Vector empty? false
Elements in vector: 3
Maximum elements vector can hold: 536870911

List empty? false
Elements in list: 3
Maximum elements list can hold: 4294967295
```

Using the technique in Tip 4, the program makes a vector and list, each with the same data type and number of elements. Then it prints whether the container is empty or not and displays each container's size and maximum size. The manipulator `boolalpha` causes the Boolean returned by `empty` to be displayed as a word ("true" or "false") rather than as a numeral (0 or 1).

The output shows the results. The numbers you get for the maximum number of elements may differ.

TIP 13   IS ONE CONTAINER GREATER THAN ANOTHER?

Applies to: Standard containers, lexicographical_compare
See also: Tip 5

Quick Solution

```
vector<double> v1, v2;
list<double> l;
// ...
if( v1 > v2 )
   cout << "v1 is greater than v2";

if( lexicographical_compare( v1.begin(), v1.end(), l.begin(), l.end() )
)
   cout << "v1 is greater than l";
```

Detailed Solution

Let's say you have two groups of people who owe you money, and you can only collect debts from one group at a time. Which group should you work on first? One answer is to find which person has the highest debt and start with that group. If the person with the most debt in each group owes the same amount of money, compare the second highest debts in the two groups. If they're the same, keep going until you find a pair that isn't the same. If all the values in the smaller group match the corresponding ones in the larger group, then just work on the larger one.

This procedure is called lexicographical comparison, and it's easy to do with the Standard Library. Specifically, in *lexicographical comparison*, the library starts at the beginning of the two sequences and compares corresponding elements until it finds one of the following results:

- The elements are not equal. The result of comparing the sequences is the result of comparing the unequal elements.
- One sequence runs out of elements. This sequence is less than the other.

■ Both sequences run out of elements. The two sequences are equal.

All standard containers define the operators less-than (<), less-than-or-equal-to (<=), greater-than (>), and greater-than-or-equal-to (>=). They carry out lexicographical comparisons on containers of the same kind and same data type. To compare different kinds of containers (but still with the same data type), use the lexicographical_compare STL algorithm. The program in Listing 3.12 illustrates both these techniques.

LISTING 3.12   Checking if One Container Is Less Than or Greater Than Another

```cpp
// general_greater_than.cpp

#include <algorithm>
#include <deque>
#include <vector>

#include "tips.hpp"

using namespace std;

int main( )
{
   const int data1[] = { 200, 250, 250, 100, 500, 500, 400 };
   const int data2[] = { 200, 200, 300, 500, 400, 400 };

   // create and initialize vectors to hold the debts
   vector<int> debts1( data1,
      data1 + sizeof( data1 ) / sizeof( data1[0] ) );
   vector<int> debts2( data2,
      data2 + sizeof( data2 ) / sizeof( data2[0] ) );

   // sort into descending order
   sort( debts1.begin(), debts1.end(), greater<int>() );
   sort( debts2.begin(), debts2.end(), greater<int>() );

   // display debts
   tips::print( debts1, "Group 1 debts" );
   tips::print( debts2, "Group 2 debts" );

   // compare debts
   if( debts1 > debts2 )
      cout << "\nCollect from Group 1 first";
   else
```

```
        cout << "\nCollect from Group 2 first";

    // store one group of debts in a different container
    deque<int> debts2_deque( debts2.begin(), debts2.end() );

    // compare the vector to the deque
    if( lexicographical_compare( debts2_deque.begin(),
        debts2_deque.end(), debts1.begin(), debts1.end() ) )
        cout << "\nCollect from Group 1 in vector first";
    else
        cout << "\nCollect from Group 2 in deque first";
}
```

The output is

```
Group 1 debts: 500 500 400 250 250 200 100
Group 2 debts: 500 400 400 300 200 200

Collect from Group 1 first
Collect from Group 1 in vector first
```

The code starts by constructing and initializing two vectors to hold the debts of the two groups. (Tip 5 provides the details on initializing a container with specific data.) The code then sorts the two containers into descending order so that the comparisons that follow will start with the highest debts. The first two arguments to sort are the iterator range. The optional third argument provides a comparison function. By default, this function is the less-than operator, so the code explicitly passes the Standard Library's greater-than functor to make the algorithm sort in descending order.

The program prints the two containers and then compares them in one line by using the greater-than operator. The output shows that although the first elements of the two vectors are the same, the second element (500) of the first vector is greater than the corresponding element (400) of the other vector. That makes the first vector greater, and those debts should be collected first, as the third line of the output reports.

Finally, to illustrate comparing different containers, the code stores the contents of the second vector in a deque. It calls lexicographical_compare with the first range from the deque and the second from the vector. The algorithm returns true if the first range is less than the second, which in this case is the same as the first group of debts being greater than the second. The output shows the corresponding message from the program.

ARE TWO CONTAINERS EQUAL?

Applies to: Standard containers, equal
See also: Tip 5, Tip 6

Quick Solution

```
vector<int> v1, v2;
list<int> l;
// ...
if( v1 == v2 )
   cout << "v1 is equal to v2";

if( v1.size() == l.size() && equal( v1.begin(), v1.end(), l.begin() ) )
      cout << "\nThe vector and list are equal";
```

Detailed Solution

Suppose you have a class with lots of attributes. You've chosen to store them in a class member that's a container and they're always stored in the same order. How can you tell if two instances of the class are equal? A reasonable definition is that they're equal if all their attributes are equal. This boils down to testing whether or not the containers with the attributes are equal. Fortunately, this is easy to do.

By definition, two containers are equal if they have the same data type, they have the same number of elements, and all the corresponding elements are equal. This implies that the values in the two containers must be the same, and they must be in the same order. As the code in Listing 3.13 shows, there are two ways to test equality, depending on whether the containers are the same kind.

LISTING 3.13 Checking If Two Containers Are Equal

```
// general_equal.cpp

#include <algorithm>
#include <iostream>
#include <list>
#include <vector>

using namespace std;

int main( )
{
   const short attributes[] = { 3, 7, -4, 6, 6, 98 };
```

```
// create and initialize vector with above data
vector<short> v1( attributes,
    attributes + sizeof( attributes ) / sizeof( attributes[0] ) );

// make a copy of the vector
vector<short> v2( v1 );

// see if the vectors are equal
if( v1 == v2 )
    cout << "The vectors are equal";
else
    cout << "The vectors are not equal";

// see if the vector and a reversed copy are equal
reverse( v2.begin(), v2.end() );
if( v1 == v2 )
    cout << "\nThe vector and reversed vector are equal";
else
    cout << "\nThe vector and reversed vector are not equal";

// make a list from a vector and see if they're equal
list<short> l( v1.begin(), v1.end() );
if( v1.size() == l.size()
    && equal( v1.begin(), v1.end(), l.begin() ) )
    cout << "\nThe vector and list are equal";
else
    cout << "\nThe vector and list are not equal";
}
```

The output is

```
The vectors are equal
The vector and reversed vector are not equal
The vector and list are equal
```

The code begins by creating a vector and initializing it with some numbers using the technique described in Tip 5. It then makes a copy of the vector (using that container's copy constructor) and tests whether the two vectors are equal by using the overloaded equals operator (==). This operator is defined for all containers, but the two containers must be the same kind and hold the same type of data. The first line of the output shows that the vectors are indeed equal.

Next, the code reverses the elements in one of the vectors and tests them for equality again. The second line of the output shows that the vectors are not equal, thus confirming that even if two containers are the same size and have the same elements, the elements must be in the same order.

Finally, the code creates a list with the same contents as the vector by using the technique described in Tip 6. The containers are different, so you can't use the == operator. What you can use is the STL `equal` algorithm.

`equal` verifies that two ranges are the same, that is, all the corresponding elements are equal. The first two arguments provide the first range, and the third argument is the start of the second range. As usual, the second range must be at least as long as the first. Because it could be longer, the code first verifies that the two containers have the same number of elements (are the same size) before it calls `equal` to actually compare the elements. In addition, failing to test the size can have serious effects if the second range is shorter than the first.

You can also test if two containers are not equal. If the containers are the same kind, use the inequality operator `!=`, which all containers have. If the containers are different, check that their sizes are different or that the output of `equal` is `false`.

TIP 15   ACCESS A CONTAINER IN REVERSE

Applies to: Standard containers, string
See also: Tip 30, Tip 49, Tip 59, Tip 72

Quick Solution

```
vector<int> v1, v2;
// ...

// copy v1 in reverse order to v2
copy( v1.rbegin(), v1.rend(), v2.begin() );
```

Detailed Solution

Sometimes it's handy to access a container in reverse. The first thought about how to do this is to simply reverse the elements in the container and then access them in the normal order. Actually, you can reverse a container's elements in a number of ways. There's the STL algorithm `reverse`. Another option is to use `reverse_copy` to reverse the order while copying to another container. And if your sequence is sorted, you can resort it in the reverse order. These methods all take time, though. A faster way works in many situations—using reverse iterators. They let you access the container's elements in reverse order without having to actually change the order by moving them around.

All standard containers have member functions that return reverse iterators, namely rbegin and rend. The former gives the start of the elements when accessed in reverse order, and the latter is one past their end. You can use the pair rbegin and rend in algorithms just as you use forward iterators. However, if you want to use either by itself, see "Reverse Iterators" in Chapter 2 first.

The program in Listing 3.14 is a simple example that displays a hand of cards. It demonstrates what to do if some players want their cards shown from lowest to highest and other players prefer them in the opposite order.

LISTING 3.14   Accessing a Container's Elements in Reverse

```cpp
// general_reverse.cpp

#include <algorithm>
#include <fstream>
#include <functional>
#include <iostream>
#include <iterator>
#include <list>

using namespace std;

class Card
{
   public:
   enum Suit { spades, clubs, hearts, diamonds };

   Card( int value = 1, Suit suit = spades );
   // value - 1 = Ace, 2-10, 11 = Jack, 12 = Queen, 13 = King

   bool operator<( const Card& rhs ) const;
   // return true if value on left less than value on right, else false

   void print() const;
   // display info on card

   int suit() const;
   int value() const;

   private:
   int value_;
   Suit suit_;
};
```

```cpp
inline
Card::Card( int value, Suit suit )
   : value_( value ), suit_( suit )
{} // empty

inline
bool Card::operator<( const Card& rhs ) const
{ return value() < rhs.value(); }

void Card::print() const
{
   if( value() >= 2 && value() <= 10 )
      cout << value();
   else
      switch( value() )
      {
         case  1: cout << "Ace"; break;
         case 11: cout << "Jack"; break;
         case 12: cout << "Queen"; break;
         case 13: cout << "King"; break;
      };

   cout << " of ";
   switch( suit() )
   {
     case spades: cout << "spades"; break;
     case clubs: cout << "clubs"; break;
     case diamonds: cout << "diamonds"; break;
     case hearts: cout << "hearts"; break;
   default: cout << "unknown suit"; break;
    }
   cout << endl;
}

inline
int Card::suit() const
{ return suit_; }

inline
int Card::value() const
{ return value_; }

int main( )
{
```

```
list<Card> hand;  // empty hand

// simulate dealing a poker hand
hand.push_back( Card( 12, Card::hearts ) );
hand.push_back( Card( 6, Card::clubs ) );
hand.push_back( Card( 12, Card::diamonds ) );
hand.push_back( Card( 1, Card::spades ) );
hand.push_back( Card( 11, Card::clubs ) );

// sort the hand in ascending order and display it
cout << "HAND IN ASCENDING ORDER\n";
hand.sort();
for_each( hand.begin(), hand.end(), mem_fun_ref( &Card::print ) );

// display in descending order
cout << "\nHAND IN DESCENDING ORDER\n";
for_each( hand.rbegin(), hand.rend(), mem_fun_ref( &Card::print ) );
}
```

The output is

```
HAND IN ASCENDING ORDER
Ace of spades
6 of clubs
Jack of clubs
Queen of hearts
Queen of diamonds

HAND IN DESCENDING ORDER
Queen of diamonds
Queen of hearts
Jack of clubs
6 of clubs
Ace of spades
```

The program starts by declaring a simple class to represent a playing card. The constructor accepts the card value and suit. (In a standard American card deck, the values are 1 (Ace), 2–10, 11 (Jack), 12 (Queen), and 13 (King). The four suits are spades, clubs, hearts, and diamonds.) The class has two accessors, a print member function, and the less-than operator. It compares two cards by comparing their values.

The function main starts by creating an empty hand from a list. (A list would be a good choice if the programmer expects to delete each played card.) It adds five cards to the hand, simulating the dealing of a poker hand. Next, it calls the list's sort member function (see Tip 30), which uses the card's less-than operator to sort into the default order of lowest to highest. It then displays the sorted hand by using for_each to call the print member function of each element (see Tip 49 and Tip 59). The first set of lines in the output shows the result.

To show the cards from highest to lowest, the code uses the same call to for_each but with the beginning reverse iterator rbegin instead of begin and the ending reverse iterator rend instead of end. It's very easy, fast, and clean. The second set of lines in the output shows what the program printed when using the reverse iterators. For another example of using them, see Tip 72.

TIP 16   DISPLAY A CONTAINER ON STANDARD OUTPUT

Applies to: Standard container, string, copy, ostream_iterator
See also: Tip 4, Tip 97, Listing 13.5

Quick Solution

```
vector<int> v;
// ...
copy( v.begin(), v.end(), ostream_iterator<int>( cout, " " ) );
```

Detailed Solution

It's very handy to print the contents of a container or, more specifically, to send them to the standard output stream cout. You can use the output for debugging or for the actual data display. The program in Listing 3.15 shows how to do it.

LISTING 3.15   Displaying a Container's Elements on the Standard Output

```cpp
// general_output.cpp

#include <algorithm>
#include <iostream>
#include <iterator>
#include <string>
#include <vector>

using namespace std;

int main( )
{
    // create and display a vector in one row
```

```
vector<int> v( 5, 9 );
cout << "Output in a row: ";
copy( v.begin(), v.end(), ostream_iterator<int>( cout, " " ) );

// display the vector in one column
cout << "\n\nOutput in a column\n";
copy( v.begin(), v.end(), ostream_iterator<int>( cout, "\n" ) );

// create and display a string
string s( "phlegm" );
cout << "\n\"" << s << "\" is spelled ";
copy( s.begin(), s.end(), ostream_iterator<char>( cout, " " ) );
}
```

The output is

```
Output in a row: 9 9 9 9 9

Output in a column
9
9
9
9
9

"phlegm" is spelled p h l e g m
```

The first line of the program uses the technique of Tip 4 to create a vector with five identical elements. The code then displays the container's contents on one row by using the copy algorithm. The first two arguments to copy are the beginning and end of the container. The third argument is an iterator made from cout. You get this iterator by creating an output stream iterator ostream_iterator as shown. Its template argument must be the same as the container's data type or be a data type that can be converted to the container's data type. The first argument of its constructor is an output stream, which in this case is cout. (If you had an output stream open to a file, you could use that stream with this code to write the containers to the file—this is what Tip 97 is about.) The second argument is a character string to write after each container element. The program makes the output appear on one line by simply writing a space after each element. The first line of the output shows the result.

To display the container elements in a column, use the newline character as the second argument in the `ostream_iterator` constructor. The output shows that the values are indeed printed in one column. The last sections of the code and output demonstrate that the technique works on strings too. If you're interested in stream iterators, "Stream Iterators" in Chapter 2 provides a lot more detail.

4 Tips on Vectors

The vector is the workhorse of the STL containers. It performs well in many cases and really excels in others. It's an excellent replacement for the C-style array and has the big advantage of being able to resize itself. This means that when you insert an element into a vector, if there's not enough memory to hold it, the vector allocates additional space for the element. This happens automatically and invisibly and is quite a leap up from a C-style array.

Vectors are great if you want fast access to any element. You can also get to the elements via subscripts, which make vectors compatible with older code that uses arrays. Tip 25 shows you how to work with a vector's data as if it were a C-style array.

The news isn't all rosy, however. The vector's Achilles heel is insertions and deletions—more specifically, those occurring anywhere but at the end. If you plan on inserting and deleting frequently, try a list.

This chapter on vectors will tell you the following:

- How to make the vector more efficient by setting aside the correct amount of internal memory
- How to use indexes and iterators with a vector
- How to work with the last element of the vector
- How to make the vector check if an index is valid
- How to use a vector as a C-style array
- How to use a vector to manipulate bits

TIP 17   RESERVE SPACE FOR ELEMENTS

Applies to: Vector
See also: Tip 21

Quick Solution

```
vector<int> v; // has zero elements
v.reserve( 100000 ); // still has zero elements but can accept
                     // 100000 without reallocating
```

Detailed Solution

The vector is a vast improvement over the standard C-style array. One of its chief advantages is that it automatically increases its size if it needs to. (Another major benefit is that it automatically calls the destructors of its elements.) When you add one or more elements, if the vector doesn't have enough space to hold the new element, it creates some. To do this, the vector first allocates enough memory to contain the old data and new data. Then it copies both the old elements and the new ones to the new memory, calls the destructors of the old elements, and deletes the old memory. This copying can take quite a bit of time, especially if the elements of the vector have nontrivial copy constructors. Moreover, if you add data one element at a time (perhaps in a loop with the push_back member function), the vector may have to do its memory allocation and copying procedure more than once. Thus, one disadvantage of automatic resizing is that it can waste time. In addition, Tip 21 explains that another drawback of reallocation is that it invalidates all references, pointers, and iterators to the vector's elements.

You can mitigate these problems if you know ahead of time how many elements your vector will have to hold. The fix is to use the vector's reserve member function to allocate the necessary amount of space. The C++ Standard guarantees that the vector will not reallocate memory as long as the number of elements you put into the vector doesn't exceed what you reserved. Note that reserve doesn't change the number of elements that vector is holding—it just sets aside enough space so that it can hold the specified number of elements without having to reallocate and copy. The program in Listing 4.1 provides an example.

LISTING 4.1 Reserving Space in a Vector

```
// vector_reserve.cpp

#include <vector>

using namespace std;

int main( )
{
   // fill a vector with one million numbers the slow way
   vector<int> v1;
   for( int i = 0; i < 1000000; ++i )
```

```
      v1.push_back( i );

   // fill a vector with one million numbers the fast way
   vector<int> v2;        // has zero elements
   v2.reserve( 1000000 ); // still has zero elements
   for( int i = 0; i < 1000000; ++i )
      v2.push_back( i );
}
```

The program starts by creating a vector with no elements in it. The code then inserts numerous elements into the vector. This will probably cause a substantial number of reallocations and, thus, will be a slow process. The second section of code shows a better way of doing the same thing. The code uses reserve to set aside enough memory for the numbers that will be stored in it. This is the first and only allocation of memory (other than any that may be allocated by the constructor). When the program then puts the numbers into the vector, this happens quickly because there is never any need to reallocate memory.

Because reserve allocates memory and such an allocation can fail, reserve could throw a bad_alloc exception. For this reason, if you're setting aside a lot of space, it's a good idea to put the reserve call in a try-catch block.

Note that because the vector allocates its memory exponentially—that is, doubling the amount of memory with each allocation—multiple allocations happen less frequently and deteriorate performance less than might be expected. If you happen to know the maximum size that your vector will have to be, go ahead and call reserve. However, because multiple allocations probably won't happen much, it's not worth jumping through several hoops to compute or predict the amount of memory to set aside.

TIP 18   REMOVE EXCESS MEMORY

Applies to: Vector

Quick Solution

```
vector<double> v;
// ...
vector<double>().swap( v );
```

Detailed Solution

Suppose you've stored a number of elements in a vector. After using it for a while you find that you've reduced the number of elements a lot or that you don't need the vector at all anymore. Unfortunately, deleting elements from a vector, resizing it to a smaller length, or even removing all elements doesn't free up memory. So how can you minimize the amount of memory your vector has allocated? You have to do it indirectly, as the next paragraph explains.

When you create a vector, it allocates at least enough memory to store the elements specified in the constructor. Some implementations allocate exactly that amount, but some allocate more. In any case, this is the smallest amount of memory that a vector of that size can have. The trick, then, is to create a vector with the same elements as yours and swap your vector with the temporary one. Swapping exchanges the elements and the memory allocated. After the swap, you must make sure that the vector you constructed is deleted, or you'll be wasting more memory than before. You can delete the vector by having it go out of scope or by making it be a temporary variable. The code in Listing 4.2 demonstrates both of these methods.

LISTING 4.2   Removing Memory from a Vector

```cpp
// vector_shrink.cpp

#include <algorithm>
#include <iostream>
#include <vector>

using namespace std;

int main( )
{
   // make a big vector and then deallocate all its memory
   const int big_size = 10000;
   vector<double> v( big_size );
   cout << "Before clearing, the capacity of the vector is "
      << v.capacity() << " and its size is " << v.size();
   v.clear();
   cout << "\nAfter clearing, the capacity of the vector is "
      << v.capacity() << " and its size is " << v.size();
   vector<double>().swap( v );

   /* if the above line doesn't compile use this code
   {
      vector<double> temporary;
      temporary.swap( v );
   } */

   cout << "\nAfter swapping, the capacity of the vector is "
```

```
    << v.capacity() << " and its size is " << v.size();

// make a big vector and then minimize its memory
v.assign( big_size, 3.33 );
cout << "\n\nBefore resizing, the capacity of the vector is "
    << v.capacity() << " and its size is " << v.size();
v.resize( 1 );
cout << "\nAfter resizing, the capacity of the vector is "
    << v.capacity() << " and its size is " << v.size();
vector<double>( v ).swap( v );

/* if the above line doesn't compile use this code
{
    vector<double> temporary( v );
    temporary.swap( v );
} */

cout << "\nAfter swapping, the capacity of the vector is "
    << v.capacity() << " and its size is " << v.size();
}
```

The output is

```
Before clearing, the capacity of the vector is 10000 and its size is
10000
After clearing, the capacity of the vector is 10000 and its size is 0
After swapping, the capacity of the vector is 0 and its size is 0

Before resizing, the capacity of the vector is 10000 and its size is
10000
After resizing, the capacity of the vector is 10000 and its size is 1
After swapping, the capacity of the vector is 1 and its size is 1
```

The program starts by demonstrating how to remove as much memory from a vector as possible. It begins by creating a large vector and displaying its capacity and size. (If you run this program, the capacities you get may be different than those shown. However, they will always be at least as great as the size.) The code then clears the vector to remove all the elements. The output shows that the size is now 0, but the capacity hasn't changed. In other words, the memory is still allocated. The program then swaps vectors, and the output shows that the capacity has been reduced, in this case to 0.

One line of code does the swapping:

```
vector<double>().swap( v );
```

`vector<double>()` creates an unnamed, temporary variable using the default constructor. (See "Predefined Function Objects" in Chapter 2 for more information on temporary, unnamed variables.) This makes an empty vector, which has the minimum possible capacity. (It may not be 0, though—that depends on the implementation.) `swap(v)` is a call of the swap member function of the temporary variable. It exchanges the empty contents and any allocated memory of the temporary variable with the contents and memory of v. After that, the expression ends, the temporary variable disappears (that's what temporary variables do) and v is left as an empty vector with the minimum amount of memory.

Be careful not to try to use the code

```
v.swap( vector<double>() );
```

which is similar to the line that does work. This does not work and shouldn't even compile because swap is accepting a nonconstant reference to a temporary variable and this is not allowed.

Although the code

```
vector<double>().swap( v );
```

is legal, some compilers may not accept it. If this happens, use the code that is commented out in the example. It does the same thing and is clearer. The braces around the two lines are necessary—they force the temporary vector to go out of scope and, thus, have its memory deleted.

The last half of the program is similar but shows how to minimize memory of a vector while keeping some of its elements. The code fills the empty vector used in the first half with many numbers and resizes the vector to contain only one element. The output shows that resizing doesn't change the capacity. Finally, the program constructs an unnamed, temporary variable but with the copy constructor instead of the default constructor. This makes the temporary variable have the same contents but with the minimum amount of memory. As before, the workaround is in comments in the code.

TIP 19   ## USE AN INDEX

Applies to: Vector, deque
See Also: Tip 4, Tip 5, Tip 20, Tip 21, Tip 83

Quick Solution

```
vector<double> v( 100 );
for( vector<double>::size_type i = 0; i < 100; ++i )
   v[i] = 2 * i + 1;
```

Detailed Solution

The vector is the Standard Library's replacement of the C-style array. Like the array, you can access its elements by an index. However, because the STL algorithms always use a vector's iterators and never an index, it's possible to forget about a vector's indexing capabilities. Here are some situations in which indexing may be helpful:

- Reallocation invalidates all iterators, references, and pointers to vector elements (see Tip 21), but it doesn't affect indexes.
- Mathematical algorithms might be coded more naturally as indexes than as iterators.
- An index can denote an element in one array that corresponds to an element in another array that is specified by an iterator.
- Code written for C-style arrays might be more easily converted to vectors if indexes are used.

The program in Listing 4.3 demonstrates several uses of indexes.

LISTING 4.3   Using an Index in a Vector

```
// vector_index.cpp

#include <algorithm>
#include <iostream>
#include <vector>

using namespace std;

int main( )
{
   vector<int> v( 10, 66 );
   v[1] = 100;

   // get an iterator that points to the maximum
   vector<int>::iterator before_itr =
      max_element( v.begin(), v.end() );
```

```
    cout << "The maximum before resizing is " << *before_itr;

    // make the index of the maximum
    vector<int>::difference_type max_index = before_itr - v.begin();

    // force the vector to reallocate
    v.resize( v.capacity() + 1 );

    // get a new iterator that points to the maximum
    vector<int>::iterator after_itr = max_element( v.begin(), v.end() );

    // the old iterator should no longer be valid
    if( before_itr == after_itr )
        cout << "\nThe first iterator is still valid";
    else
        cout << "\nThe first iterator is no longer valid";

    // the index is still valid
    cout << "\nThe maximum after resizing is " << v[max_index];

    const char* breed_array[] =
        { "Bulldogs", "Terriers", "Poodles", "St. Bernards" };
    const int weight_array[] = { 65, 34, 8, 175 };
    const int dogs
        = sizeof( weight_array ) / sizeof( weight_array[0] );

    // make vectors with breeds and weights
    vector<string> breeds( breed_array, breed_array+dogs );
    vector<int> weights( weight_array, weight_array+dogs );

    // find the heaviest breed weight
    vector<int>::iterator weight_itr =
        max_element( weights.begin(), weights.end() );

    // use an index to get the corresponding name
    cout << endl << endl << breeds[weight_itr-weights.begin()]
        << " are the heaviest breed";
}
```

The output is

```
The maximum before resizing is 100
The first iterator is no longer valid
The maximum after resizing is 100

St. Bernards are the heaviest breed
```

The program creates a vector of integers (see Tip 4) and finds the largest number with `max_element` (see Tip 83). This algorithm returns an iterator that points to the maximum. If there is more than one maximum, the iterator points to the first one.

The next line of code gets the equivalent index for the iterator by using the technique of Tip 20. The code stores the difference between the two iterators in the data type specified by vector's `difference_type`. The code then resizes the vector to one larger than the current capacity, which, depending on the implementation of the vector, can force a reallocation. This doesn't change the values of the elements, so the subsequent call to `max_element` finds the same value as before. However, because of the reallocation, the iterator pointing to the value is different than the iterator before the resizing. This is reflected in the output. Actually, the old iterator is invalid (as Tip 21 explains) and shouldn't even be compared with the new one. (On some systems, this may cause a crash.) However, the index computed before reallocation is still good, as the output shows.

The second half of the program illustrates another use of indexes. It starts by making two vectors with predefined values (see Tip 5). The names of dog breeds are in one vector, and the average weights are in the corresponding elements of the other vector. Again, `max_element` finds the largest value in the vector of weights, but the iterator it returns is not usable in the other vector. However, a simple computation of the index, as before, enables the program to find the breed name corresponding to the biggest weight.

TIP 20 CONVERT BETWEEN ITERATORS AND INDEXES

Applies to: Vector, deque, string
See also: Tip 5, Tip 83, Listing 13.1

Quick Solution

```
vector<int> v1, v2;
// ...
vector<int>::iterator v1_min = min_element( v1.begin(), v1.end() );
```

```
// convert iterator to index
vector<int>::size_type index = v1_min — v1.begin();
cout << "Minimum of v1 is " << *v1_min
    << "  Corresponding value of v2 is " << v2[index];

// convert index to iterator
vector<int>::iterator v2_iterator = v2.begin() + index;
```

Detailed Solution

A vector has random access iterators. One of the benefits of these iterators is that you can add and subtract integers and other random iterators from them. This is particularly useful with the indexing (subscripting) capability of vectors because it lets you convert from iterators to indexes and vice versa. For example, some vector member functions such as insert and erase require iterators, so you must convert indexes to use them. On the other hand, if you have an iterator from one vector and want to find the corresponding element in another vector, you can do this most easily by finding the index in the second vector.

To convert a vector's iterator to an index, subtract the beginning iterator (from the begin member function) from the iterator. To go in the opposite direction, add the index to the beginning iterator. Deques and strings also have random access iterators, so this technique applies to them, too.

The code in Listing 4.4 illustrates conversions between iterators and indexes.

LISTING 4.4   Converting Between Iterators and Indexes in a Vector

```
// vector_iterator_index.cpp

#include <algorithm>
#include <string>
#include <vector>

#include "tips.hpp"

using namespace std;

int main( )
{
    const char* name_array[] = { "John", "Harry", "Mark", "Abe" };
    const int age_array[] = { 89, 34, 12, 20 };
    const int people = sizeof( age_array ) / sizeof( age_array[0] );

    // make vectors with names and ages
    vector<string> names( name_array, name_array+people );
```

```
      vector<int> ages( age_array, age_array+people );

      // find the youngest age
      vector<int>::iterator age_itr =
        min_element( ages.begin(), ages.end() );

      // convert from iterator to index
      cout << names[age_itr-ages.begin()]
        << ", the youngest person, is " << *age_itr << " years old\n";

      // convert from index to iterator
      tips::print( names, "Before erasing" );
      names.erase( names.begin()+1 );  // erase the second element
      tips::print( names, "After erasing" );
}
```

The output is

```
Mark, the youngest person, is 12 years old
Before erasing: John Harry Mark Abe
After erasing: John Mark Abe
```

The code starts by constructing a vector of strings and a vector of integers filled with predefined values. (See Tip 5 for the details of this technique.) It then finds the smallest number by using the STL algorithm `min_element`, which, as Tip 83 explains, returns an iterator pointing to the desired value. Next, the code prints the name and age of the youngest person, as the first line of the output shows. To get the name corresponding to the age, the code subtracts the beginning iterator of the age vector from the iterator for the youngest age and uses this difference as an index in the name vector.

Finally, the program demonstrates converting from an index to an iterator. To illustrate this it assumes that you want to delete the second name, which has index 1 in the vector of names. The `erase` member function deletes the element, but it only accepts iterators, not indexes. However, getting the iterator is simple—just add the index (one) to the iterator for the start of the vector, as the code shows. The last two lines of the output are the result.

TIP 21   BE CAREFUL OF INVALIDATED ITERATORS

Applies to: Vector
See also: Tip 4, Tip 6, Tip 11, Tip 17, Tip 19, Tip 23, Tip 83

Quick Solution

If a vector reallocates, all iterators pointing to its elements become invalid.

Detailed Solution

Iterators, pointers, and references to elements in vectors can easily become invalidated. This can occur under a number of circumstances:

- Inserting elements invalidates all iterators, pointers, and references to elements after those inserted. If the insertion causes reallocation, it invalidates all iterators, pointers, and references.
- Deleting elements invalidates all iterators, pointers, and references to the elements after those deleted, but does not invalidate iterators, pointers, and references to elements before.
- Destruction of the vector invalidates all iterators, pointers, and references to elements.
- Reallocation invalidates all iterators, pointers, and references to elements.

This last item can be particularly pernicious because reallocation happens automatically. It may be implicitly triggered by a number of different member functions—assign, resize, reserve, insert, and push_back. Tip 6, Tip 17, and Tip 23 provide more information on these functions.

It's a good idea to set iterators, pointers, and references to vector elements after you have finished using the previously mentioned member functions. A safer alternative is to use an index, as Tip 19 demonstrates. Another possibility is a deque, which is a little bit less susceptible to invalidation. If you're really going to refer to elements frequently, you should probably switch to a list because insertions and deletions never invalidate iterators, pointers, or references to its elements.

Finally, note that when swapping two vectors (via the swap member function or the equivalent global function swap, as Tip 11 explains), iterators, pointers, and references to elements remain valid, but they now refer to elements in a different container.

The program in Listing 4.5 demonstrates how push_back can invalidate an iterator.

LISTING 4.5   Being Aware of Invalidated Iterators in Vectors

```cpp
// vector_invalidate.cpp

#include <algorithm>
#include <iostream>
#include <vector>

using namespace std;

int main( )
{
   vector<double> v( 5, 2.78 );
   v[2] = 0.0;

   // make the vector as large as possible without reallocating
   v.resize( v.capacity(), 2.78 );

   // find the smallest number
   vector<double>::iterator before_itr =
      min_element( v.begin(), v.end() );

   // append one more element. This causes reallocation
   v.push_back( 2.78 );

   // find the smallest number. (Its value is the same as before.)
   vector<double>::iterator after_itr =
      min_element( v.begin(), v.end() );

   // See if minimum is still in the same spot of memory
   if( before_itr == after_itr )
      cout << "The iterators are the same";
   else
      cout << "The iterators are not the same";
}
```

The output is

```
The iterators are not the same
```

The program starts by creating a vector with five identical values (see Tip 4) and sets the middle element to a smaller number. Next, it resizes the vector (see Tip 17), using the member function `capacity` to make the vector as large as possible without causing reallocation. The code then uses the STL algorithm `min_element` to get an iterator that points to the smallest number in the vector, as explained in Tip 83.

After calling the algorithm, the code uses `push_back` to add one more element and so force reallocation. (The value added is the same as those in the original vector, so the minimum value in the vector doesn't change.) Then the program gets another iterator with the location of the minimum and compares the new and the old iterators. Note that even though the minimum hasn't changed, the iterators are not pointing to the same location in memory. This is because the reallocation invalidated the first iterator. If you were to use it, your program might not work properly.

CLASSES SHOULD HAVE CONSTRUCTORS, DESTRUCTORS, AND AN ASSIGNMENT OPERATOR

TIP 22

TIP

Applies to: Vector
See also: Tip 2

Quick Solution

Vectors almost always use the default constructors, destructors, and assignment operators of their elements. Elements that are classes should have correct and efficient versions of these functions.

Detailed Solution

One of a vector's most useful capabilities is its ability to automatically resize itself when necessary. However, resizing and other uses of vector member functions implicitly and extensively copy, assign, and destroy the vector's elements. For this reason, it's important that classes used in vectors have a copy constructor, a destructor, and an assignment operator. The class may also need a default constructor because the vector may call that if the user has not specified an object to copy. These functions should work correctly. They should also be efficient because they are likely to be called frequently.

The program in Listing 4.6 demonstrates some simple manipulations of a vector. The vector's data element is a class that prints a message whenever its default constructor, copy constructor, destructor, or assignment operator is called. This allows you to see when and how often the vector uses these member functions of its data element. Because implementations of the vector may differ, your output may not be the same as the one shown. It should be close enough for you to get the idea, though.

LISTING 4.6   Requirements for Classes Used in Vectors

```cpp
// vector_default_constructor.cpp

#include <iostream>
#include <vector>

using namespace std;

class Element
{
   public:
   Element();
   ~Element();
   Element( const Element& );
   Element& operator=( const Element& );

   private:

   static int default_constructor_calls_;
   static int assignment_calls_;
   static int copy_constructor_calls_;
   static int destructor_calls_;
};

inline
Element::Element()
{  cout << "\nCall " << ++default_constructor_calls_
      << " of default constructor";
}

inline
Element::Element( const Element& )
{
   cout << "\nCall " << ++copy_constructor_calls_
      << " of copy constructor";
}

inline
Element::~Element()
{  cout << "\nCall " << ++destructor_calls_ << " of destructor"; }

inline
Element& Element::operator=( const Element& )
```

```
   {
      cout << "\nCall " << ++assignment_calls_
         << " of assignment operator";
      return *this;
   }

   int Element::default_constructor_calls_ = 0;
   int Element::assignment_calls_ = 0;
   int Element::copy_constructor_calls_ = 0;
   int Element::destructor_calls_ = 0;

   int main( )
   {
      cout << "CONSTRUCTING VECTOR WITH TWO ELEMENTS";
      vector<Element> d( 2 );

      cout << "\n\nRESIZING TO CAPACITY";
      d.resize( d.capacity() );

      cout << "\n\nADDING ONE MORE ELEMENT";
      d.push_back( Element() );

      cout << "\n\nDELETING FIRST ELEMENT";
      d.erase( d.begin() );
   }
```

The output is

```
CONSTRUCTING VECTOR WITH TWO ELEMENTS
Call 1 of default constructor
Call 1 of copy constructor
Call 2 of copy constructor
Call 1 of destructor

RESIZING TO CAPACITY
Call 2 of default constructor
Call 2 of destructor

ADDING ONE MORE ELEMENT
Call 3 of default constructor
Call 3 of copy constructor
Call 4 of copy constructor                          →
```

```
Call 5 of copy constructor
Call 3 of destructor
Call 4 of destructor
Call 5 of destructor

DELETING FIRST ELEMENT
Call 1 of assignment operator
Call 2 of assignment operator
Call 6 of destructor
Call 7 of destructor
Call 8 of destructor
```

The program starts by constructing a vector with two elements. The form of the vector constructor that the code uses accepts the number of elements to put in the vector as the first argument and an instance of the element as the optional second argument. If this argument exists, the vector will fill itself with copies of the instance. However, as in the code of Listing 4.6, if you omit that argument, the vector fills itself with copies made from the default constructor. Thus, the first section of the output starts with one call to the element's default constructor. This is the vector making a temporary instance of its data element. The vector then calls the copy constructor twice, making two copies of the temporary variable and storing them as the two elements. Finally, the first section of the output shows a call to the temporary instance's destructor.

In the next section of the program, the vector resizes itself to its capacity, which is the largest number of elements it can hold without reallocating memory. The `resize` member function takes the new size as its first argument and, optionally, an instance of the element as its second argument. If the latter is not passed, as in the sample program, `resize` creates a temporary instance. This produces the calls shown in the output to the default constructor and to the destructor. The vector is already at capacity in this implementation, so it takes no further action.

Next, the program forces reallocation by creating a temporary, unnamed variable and adding it to the end of the vector via the member function `push_back`. The creation of this variable produces the third call to the default constructor, as the output shows. The vector then copies the two old elements and the passed element into the newly allocated memory. The output shows the resulting three calls to the copy constructor. Finally, there are three calls to the element's destructor—two for the old elements and one for the temporary, unnamed variable.

The last thing the program does is to delete the first element in the vector. Surprisingly, there is no call to the first element's destructor. This is because the vector cleverly removes that element by overwriting it with the second element, producing an unexpected call to the assignment operator. Similarly, the vector overwrites the second element with the third, then calls the third element's destructor. The vector now has just two elements. It goes out of scope as the program ends, and this produces the last two calls to the destructor shown in the output.

This simple program illustrates the importance of having correct and efficient default and copy constructors, destructors, and assignment operators in classes that are to be stored in vectors. Again, although your STL implementation may not produce exactly the same output, the difference is just a matter of degree.

Tip 2 explains general restrictions on the elements in a standard container. These also apply to the vector.

TIP 23   FAST ACCESS AT THE BACK

Applies to: Vector, deque
See also: Tip 41

Quick Solution

```
vector<int> v;
// ...

if( !v.empty() ) // only access last element if it exists
{
   cout << v.back(); // access last element
   v.pop_back(); // remove last element
}
v.push_back( 13 ); // can append element even if vector is empty
```

Detailed Solution

It's common to think of accessing a vector by indexes or iterators. What is less well known is that the vector also provides efficient manipulation of its last element. This makes it ideal for some applications, for example, the LIFO (last-in, first-out) data structure known as a stack.

A vector has three member functions specifically designed to work with its last element. The first, back, returns a reference or constant reference to the last element. This makes it convenient to read or write the last element. Make sure not to use back on an empty vector because the result is undefined and probably pernicious.

The second relevant member function is pop_back, which removes the last element. However, because pop-back doesn't return the element, you'll often use back in tandem with pop_back to read the last element and then delete it. Again, calling pop_back on an empty vector results in an undefined action.

Finally, `push_back` appends an element to the vector and works even if the vector is empty. It is quick except on the occasional times when adding an element makes the vector reallocate memory. `push_back` and the other two functions described are also members of the deque.

The program in Listing 4.7 demonstrates how to work with the last element of a vector. It displays the last card played in a card game by examining the card on the top of the discard pile.

LISTING 4.7   Accessing the Back of a Vector

```cpp
// vector_back.cpp

#include <iostream>
#include <list>
#include <vector>

using namespace std;

class Card
{
    public:
    enum Suit { spades, clubs, hearts, diamonds };

    Card( int value = 1, Suit suit = spades );
    // value - 1 = Ace, 2-10, 11 = Jack, 12 = Queen, 13 = King

    int suit() const;
    int value() const;

    private:
    int value_;
    Suit suit_;
};

inline
Card::Card( int value, Suit suit )
    : value_( value ), suit_( suit )
{} // empty

inline
int Card::suit() const
{ return suit_; }

inline
```

```cpp
int Card::value() const
{ return value_; }

// global function
ostream& operator<<( ostream& out, const Card& card )
{
    if( card.value() >= 2 && card.value() <= 10 )
        out << card.value();
    else
        switch( card.value() )
        {
            case  1: out << "Ace"; break;
            case 11: out << "Jack"; break;
            case 12: out << "Queen"; break;
            case 13: out << "King"; break;
            default: out << "Unknown value"; break;
        };

    out << " of ";
    switch( card.suit() )
    {
        case Card::spades: out << "spades"; break;
        case Card::clubs: out << "clubs"; break;
        case Card::diamonds: out << "diamonds"; break;
        case Card::hearts: out << "hearts"; break;
        default: out << "unknown suit"; break;
    }
    return out;
}

int main( )
{
    const int num_players = 2;
    vector< list<Card> > hands( num_players );

    // deal first player a hand
    hands[0].push_front( Card( 12, Card::hearts ) );
    hands[0].push_front( Card( 1,  Card::spades ) );
    hands[0].push_front( Card( 4,  Card::spades ) );

    // deal second player a hand
    hands[1].push_front( Card( 13, Card::diamonds ) );
    hands[1].push_front( Card( 12, Card::clubs ) );
    hands[1].push_front( Card( 2,  Card::hearts ) );
```

```cpp
const int num_plays = 3;
bool discard[num_players][num_plays] = { { true, true, false },
                                          { true, false, false } };

vector<Card> discard_pile;

// simulate card play
for( int i = 0; i < num_plays; ++i )
   for( int j = 0; j < num_players; ++j )

      // if discard and hand not empty...
      if( discard[j][i] && !hands[j].empty() )
      {
         discard_pile.push_back( hands[j].front() );
         hands[j].pop_front();
         cout << "Player " << (j+1) << " discarded a "
            << discard_pile.back() << endl;
      }

      // if pick up and discard pile not empty...
      else if( !discard[j][i] && !discard_pile.empty() )
      {
         hands[j].push_back( discard_pile.back() );
         cout << "Player " << (j+1) << " picked up a "
            << discard_pile.back() << endl;
         discard_pile.pop_back();
      }
}
```

The output is

```
Player 1 discarded a 4 of spades
Player 2 discarded a 2 of hearts
Player 1 discarded a Ace of spades
Player 2 picked up a Ace of spades
Player 1 picked up a 2 of hearts
Player 2 picked up a 4 of spades
```

The program starts by declaring a simple class to represent a playing card. The constructor accepts the card value and suit. (In a standard American card deck, the values are 1 (Ace), 2–10, 11 (Jack), 12 (Queen), and 13 (King). The four suits are spades, clubs, hearts, and diamonds.) The class has two accessors, and a global stream insertion operator lets the class write information about itself to an output stream.

The function `main` simulates a game of cards between two players. It starts by creating a vector containing the two empty hands that are represented by lists. (A list is a good choice if you expect to delete cards at various positions in the hand.) The code simulates dealing by giving each player three cards and adding each card to the front of a list with the list's `push_front` member function (see Tip 29). The last preparatory step the program takes is to create a discard pile from a vector of `Cards`.

The heart of the program is a nested loop that simulates card play. The first part of the if-statement in the loop checks whether the current player is supposed to discard this round. If he is and if his hand is not empty, he discards one card, which comes from the front of the list for simplicity. The program puts the card onto the top of the discard pile by using the vector's `push_back` member function and removes the card from the front of the list.

If the player is not supposed to discard, he must pick up a card from the discard pile. After verifying that the pile is not empty, the program gets the top card from the pile by using the vector's `back` member function. After the code adds the card to the player's hand, it removes the card from the discard pile by calling the vector's `pop_back` member function. The output shows the result.

If you're just going to use the vector as a stack data structure and you don't need to use any STL algorithms on it, you'd be better off just using the STL stack container. It's a little bit easier to use, as Tip 41 demonstrates.

TIP 24   CHECKED AND UNCHECKED ACCESS

Applies to: Vector
See also: Tip 5

Quick Solution

```
vector<int> v;
// ...
cout << v[5] // doesn't check for valid index
    << "   " << v.at( 5 ); // checks for valid index
```

Detailed Solution

Valid indexes for a vector are zero up to the size of the vector minus one, inclusive. Calling the subscript operator [ ] with an invalid index produces undefined behavior—the *bête noire* of debugging. Although the STL rarely checks for logic errors, vector indexes are one situation where the STL does provide a modest safety net. This comes in the form of the `at` member function of vectors. The input to `at` has the same legal values as those for the subscript operator. The output is also the same. However, if the input is illegal, at throws an out_of_range exception (see "Exception Handling in the Standard Library" in Chapter 1). This is much better than doing something undefined, which may include accessing forbidden regions of memory and other disastrous actions. However, the downside of using at is that it is slower than access via subscripts.

One nice compromise is to use at during debugging and the subscript operator in the release version of the code. You can easily do this by conditional compilation. If the program is compiled *without* debugging code, the C++ compiler often defines the macro NDEBUG. If there is debugging code, the compiler does not define the macro. (There are also compilers that do the opposite, i.e., they define DEBUG when debugging and don't define it when not debugging.) Check your compiler's documentation to see if it will set one of these macros for you or if you have to do it yourself. You can easily set a macro, such as NDEBUG, manually by putting the line #define NDEBUG in your code as the program in Listing 4.8 shows. Comment the line out when you want to debug.

By using the #ifdef NDEBUG preprocessor directive, you can access vectors during debugging with at and in final versions with subscripts. The program in Listing 4.8 illustrates this technique.

LISTING 4.8   Checked and Unchecked Access of a Vector

```cpp
// vector_checked.cpp

#include <iostream>
#include <vector>

using namespace std;

// comment next line out when debugging
#define NDEBUG

class Ship
{
    public:
    Ship( const float cargo_weight[], int length );

    float operator[]( int index ) const;
    // REQUIRE: 0 <= index < cargo_loads()
    // RETURN: weight of load with specified index

    int cargo_loads() const;
```

```
    private:
    vector<float> weight_;
};

inline
Ship::Ship( const float weight[], int length )
    : weight_( weight, weight+length )
{} // empty

inline
float Ship::operator[]( int index ) const
{
#ifdef NDEBUG
    return weight_[index]; // don't check range when not debugging
#else
    return weight_.at( index ); // check range when debugging
#endif
}

inline
int Ship::cargo_loads() const
{ return static_cast<int>( weight_.size() ); }

int main( )
{
    const int num_loads = 3;
    const float weights[num_loads] = { 40.8f, 35.2f, 22.1f };

    // make a ship and load it with cargo
    Ship ship( weights, num_loads );

    // BAD LOOP - off-by-one error
    for( int i = 1; i <= ship.cargo_loads(); ++i )
      cout << "Cargo load " << i << " weighs "
        << ship[i] << " metric tons\n";
}
```

The output when NDEBUG is not defined is

```
Cargo load 1 weighs 35.2 metric tons
Cargo load 2 weighs 22.1 metric tons
```

Then the program throws the out_of_range exception.

The code starts by declaring a little class that represents a cargo ship. Its constructor accepts an array of cargo weights and stores them internally in a vector. The member function cargo_loads returns the number of loads of cargo, which is the size of the internal vector. The class defines the subscript operator to accept an index and return the weight of that load. Note that the comment in the class declaration beneath the operator documents the legal range of the index.

The code for the member functions comes next. Using the technique in Tip 5, the constructor initializes the vector of cargo weights with the passed array. cargo_loads returns the size of the vector of weights and operator[] shows the conditional vector access described previously.

The main program starts by constructing a ship with three loads of cargo. It then has a simple loop that attempts to print the index and weight of each load. However, this loop illustrates a common error by using 1, 2, and 3 as indexes instead of 0, 1, and 2. It produces the output shown earlier about the second and third cargo loads. (If your program doesn't produce output, it may be that cout is being buffered and not flushed at the exception. Try setting the unitbuf flag on cout. This forces output after each call to cout.)

What happens when the loop tries to use an index of three depends on whether NDEBUG is defined or not. If it isn't defined when the program runs, the vector will throw an out-of-range error and stop. If there is no debugging code (NDEBUG is defined), the outcome depends on the system. The program may crash, it may produce strange output, or it may do something else. The behavior at this point is, after all, undefined.

TIP 25   GET A C-STYLE ARRAY FROM A VECTOR

Applies to: Vector
See also: Tip 79, Listing 13.14

Quick Solution

```
void f( int a[], int length );

vector<int> v;
// ...

// pass vector as a C-array
if( !v.empty() )
    f( &v[0], static_cast<int>( v.size() ) );
```

Detailed Solution

Vectors are much better than C-style arrays. However, sometimes you may have to go back to the bad old ways, especially if you're working with legacy code. Fortunately, it's easy to get a C-style array, or, more specifically, a pointer to a C-style array, from a vector. All you have to do is use the address operator (&) on element 0 of the vector. For example, if the vector is v, the address of the C-style array containing the vector's data is &v[0].

There are a few caveats. First, if the vector is empty, the address of the first element might not even exist. So before using the address, have your code verify that the vector is not empty. Second, don't use the beginning iterator (from a vector's begin member function) as the address of the array. It might work because a vector's iterator is often just a plain pointer. However, it might also not work because there are cases when the iterator is not a pointer but, rather, a class, such as in a debugging implementation of vector. Finally, note that this technique applies to a vector but not to a deque.

The code in Listing 4.9 is an example of using a vector as a C-style array.

LISTING 4.9   Getting a C-Style Array from a Vector

```cpp
// vector_array.cpp

#include <numeric>
#include <vector>

#include "tips.hpp"

void doubler( int a[], int length );
// doubles each value in the array

using namespace std;

int main( )
{
    // make a vector of consecutive integers
    vector<int> data( 5, 1 );
    partial_sum( data.begin(), data.end(), data.begin() );
    tips::print( data, "Vector before use as array" );

    // pass vector as a C-array
    if( !data.empty() )
    {
        doubler( &data[0], static_cast<int>( data.size() ) );
        tips::print( data, "Vector after  use as array" );
```

```
        }
    }

    void doubler( int a[], int length )
    {
        for( int i = 0; i < length; ++i )
            a[i] *= 2;
    }
```

The output is

```
Vector before use as array: 1 2 3 4 5
Vector after  use as array: 2 4 6 8 10
```

The program creates a vector of consecutive integers by using the partial-sum STL algorithm as described in Tip 79. Then, after checking that the vector isn't empty, the program passes the values as a C-style array to the function `doubler`, which simulates legacy C code. Such code would need the length of the array, which you can easily get from the `size` member function of the vector. The earlier output, produced by printing the vector before and after the call to `doubler`, shows that operating on the C-style array does indeed change the values in the C++ vector.

TIP 26   USE A VECTOR OF BOOLEANS TO MANIPULATE BITS

Applies to: Vector of Booleans
See also: Tip 4, Tip 28, Tip 44

Quick Solution

```
vector<bool> v;
//...

v[1] = true; // set a particular bit
v[4].flip(); // toggle a particular bit
v.flip(); // toggle all bits
```

`vector<bool>` can't be used in STL algorithms

Detailed Solution

If you need to work with a collection of Boolean values such as bits or flags, `vector<bool>` may be what you're after. This template specialization of the vector class is designed to minimize the amount of space occupied by the flags, so it is especially useful for large collections of bit values. Actually, it often takes up only one-eighth of the memory that an unoptimized version would. (There are, however, implementations in which a `bool` and an `int` both take up four bytes.)

You can change the size of a vector of Booleans after you have created it. You can also access a single bit with the subscript operator (`[]`). Specifically, you can do the following:

■ Assign a Boolean value to a specific bit, such as `v[3] = true`. (If the right side is not `true` or `false`, it is converted to those values using the normal C++ rules.)
■ Assign the value of one bit to another, for example, `v[2] = v[0]`.
■ Complement (negate) a specific bit by using the `flip` member function on an indexed value, for example, `v[10].flip()`.
■ Complement all bits by using `flip` on the vector, for example, `v.flip()`.

`vector<bool>` does have its drawbacks. Access to the bits may be slower because they have to be packed and unpacked. More importantly, `vector<bool>` is not a true container and thus can't be used in the STL algorithms. If you do need to use algorithms on a collection of flags, Tip 28 explains how a deque of Booleans is an alternative. If you don't need to use algorithms and you don't need to change the size of the collection, use a bitset instead of a vector of Booleans. As Tip 44 shows, a bitset has much more bit-tweaking power. Table 8.1 summarizes the pros and cons of these three containers.

The program in Listing 4.10 is an example of using `vector<bool>`.

LISTING 4.10   Using a Vector of Booleans

```cpp
// vector_boolean.cpp

#include <vector>

#include "tips.hpp"

using namespace std;

int main( )
{
    vector<bool> shots( 5 ); // true if pet has shot
    tips::print( shots, "Initial pets with shots" );

    // give shots to two pets
    shots[1] = true;
```

```
    shots[4].flip();
    tips::print( shots, "Subsequent pets with shots" );

    // delete the first element because that pet was adopted
    shots.erase( shots.begin() );
    tips::print( shots, "After adoption, pets with shots" );

    // flip bits to show pets needing shots
    shots.flip();
    tips::print( shots, "Pets needing shots" );
}
```

The output is

```
Initial pets with shots: 0 0 0 0 0
Subsequent pets with shots: 0 1 0 0 1
After adoption, pets with shots: 1 0 0 1
Pets needing shots: 0 1 1 0
```

The program starts by declaring a vector of Booleans that represents whether or not an animal at a pound has had its shots. The vector has five elements that are initialized to their default value (see Tip 4). For `bool`, this is `false`, as the first line of output shows.

Next, two pets are given shots, so the corresponding bits in the vector must be set to `true`. The code demonstrates two ways of doing this. The first is to assign `true` to a specific bit by using an index and the subscript operator to denote that bit. The second method is to complement that particular bit by using the `flip` member function. (You have to know that the bit is `false` before you can set it to `true` by flipping.) The second line of output shows that two bits have been turned on.

The program simulates the adoption of a pet by deleting that pet's record of whether or not it has had a shot. The third line of output shows that after deleting the first pet, there are only four pets, thus demonstrating that `vector<bool>` can change size after it is created. Finally, to print the pets that still need shots instead of the pets that already have them, the program uses the `flip` member function on the entire container. The last line of the output shows the result.

5 | Tips on Deques

The double-ended queue, or deque, is a container that's partway between a vector and a list. Like a vector, it allows indexing of its elements and has random access iterators. In general, though, accessing elements is a little slower than in a vector. Like a list, the deque has efficient access to elements at the front and back. Inserting or removing from the front or back does not move elements unless there is a reallocation. Unlike a list, inserting elements to or deleting them from the middle is not fast. Thus, the ideal application of a deque is one that requires fast access, insertion to and deletion from the front or back, and quick access to any of the elements. This chapter demonstrates how to

■ Work with the front of a deque
■ Use the deque as an alternative to a vector of Booleans

| TIP 27 | **OPERATIONS AT FRONT** |

Applies to: Deque
See also: Tip 23, Tip 42

Quick Solution

```
deque<float> d;
// ...
cout << d.front(); // first element
d.pop_front(); // remove first element
d.push_front( 3.14 ); // prepend element
```

Detailed Solution

In many ways, a deque is similar to a vector. One handy difference is that it gives you quick access to the front of the container. You can get a reference to the first element with the deque member function `front`, you can insert an element in the front with `push_front`, and remove the first element with `pop_front`. And, like a vector (see Tip 23), a deque has the analogous member functions `back`, `push_back`, and `pop_back` to manipulate the last element.

The efficient access to both ends of the container makes the deque well-suited for use as a queue, though not surprisingly, the STL queue container (Tip 42) is even better. You can also use the deque to good advantage if your container elements can be split into two parts. For example, suppose you have a group of items to be sold at an auction. To maintain interest, you'd like to alternate selling cheap ones with those that are expensive. A nice way to do this is to load all the inexpensive items at the front of a deque, load all the costly ones at the back, and then sell the goods by alternately popping items off the front and the back. Listing 5.1 has code to do this.

LISTING 5.1   Using the Front of a Deque

```cpp
// deque_front.cpp

#include <deque>
#include <iostream>
#include <string>
#include <vector>

using namespace std;

class Auction_item
{
   public:
   Auction_item( const string& name = "nothing",
      int minimum_bid = 0 );
   int minimum_bid() const;
   string name() const;

   private:
   int minimum_bid_;
   string name_;
};

inline
Auction_item::Auction_item( const string& name, int minimum_bid )
   : name_( name ), minimum_bid_( minimum_bid )
{} // empty
```

```
inline
int Auction_item::minimum_bid() const
{   return minimum_bid_; }

inline
string Auction_item::name() const
{   return name_; }

int main( )
{
    vector<Auction_item> v( 5 );
    v[0] = Auction_item( "dinner for two", 150 );
    v[1] = Auction_item( "1000 piece jigsaw puzzle", 10 );
    v[2] = Auction_item( "25-year old bottle of wine", 75 );
    v[3] = Auction_item( "night of babysitting", 20 );
    v[4] = Auction_item( "limousine ride", 100 );

    deque<Auction_item> items;

    // load auction items with cheap ones in front, expensive at back
    const int min_expensive_item = 50;
    for( vector<Auction_item>::iterator i = v.begin();
       i != v.end(); ++i )
       if( i->minimum_bid() >= min_expensive_item )
          items.push_back( *i );
       else
          items.push_front( *i );

    // sell the items
    bool sell_cheap = true;
    while( !items.empty() )
    {
       if( sell_cheap )
       {
          cout << "Now selling: a " << items.front().name()
             << " for a minimum bid of "
             << items.front().minimum_bid() << endl;
          items.pop_front();
       }
       else
       {
          cout << "Now selling: a " << items.back().name()
             << " for a minimum bid of "
             << items.back().minimum_bid() << endl;
```

```
            items.pop_back();
        }

        // Alternate selling cheap and expensive
        sell_cheap = !sell_cheap;
    }
}
```

The output is

```
Now selling: a night of babysitting for a minimum bid of 20
Now selling: a limousine ride for a minimum bid of 100
Now selling: a 1000 piece jigsaw puzzle for a minimum bid of 10
Now selling: a 25-year old bottle of wine for a minimum bid of 75
Now selling: a dinner for two for a minimum bid of 150
```

The top of the code shows a simple class that stores the name and minimum bid of an auction item. The program starts by storing some items in a vector, simulating an auction database. Next, the code declares a deque and loads the expensive items at the back of the deque and the cheap ones up front. It does this by comparing the item's minimum bid to a threshold and then using push_back or push_front. Note that this doesn't sort the items by cost—rather, it separates them into two groups, with all the cheap items together at the front of the deque and all the expensive goodies at the back. Finally, the code carries out the auction by alternately selling the front and back elements in the deck. The deque's front and back member functions return references, so you can chain them to easily access those elements' members, for example, items.front().minimum_bid().

The threshold for expensive items is 50, and the output shows the offerings alternating between inexpensive and costly. The last two are expensive because there are more of those items than of the cheap ones.

TIP 28   ALTERNATIVE TO A VECTOR OF BOOLEANS

Applies to: Deque
See also: Tip 5, Tip 26, Tip 44

Quick Solution

```
deque<bool> d1, d2;
// ...
```

```
deque<bool> d3( d1.size() );
transform( d1.begin(), d1.end(), d2.begin(), d3.begin(),
    logical_and<bool>() );
```

Use `deque<bool>` for bit manipulation if you also want to use STL algorithms.

Detailed Solution

The Standard Library has two containers optimized for working with bits, namely, `bitset` (Tip 44) and `vector<bool>` (Tip 26). Both of these may use less memory to store a bit or a Boolean than a typical `bool` variable does. Unfortunately, neither of these are standard containers, which means that you can't use them with the STL algorithms.

An alternative is to use a deque of Booleans, which is a standard container. You don't get any special memory savings, but you do get to use the power of the STL algorithms. Table 8.1 summarizes the pros and cons of these three containers.

Listing 5.2 provides an example of using a deque of Booleans.

LISTING 5.2 Using a Deque Instead of a Vector of Booleans

```cpp
// deque_bool.cpp

#include <algorithm>
#include <deque>
#include <iostream>

using namespace std;

bool logical_xor( bool a, bool b );
// return true only if exactly one argument is true

void print_result( const char* names[], const deque<bool>& print,
    const char* text );
// display the elements in names for which the corresponding elements
// in print are true

int main( )
{
    const char* contacts[] ={ "Alex Pendrod", "Joseph deSilva",
        "Sally Weh", "Donald O'Brien", "Julia Rosenstein" };
    const bool salesman1_data[] = { true, true, false, false, true };
    const bool salesman2_data[] = { false, false, true, true, true };
```

```
        const int num_customers = sizeof( salesman1_data )
           / sizeof( salesman1_data[0] );

        // create deques and initialize with above data
        deque<bool> salesman1( salesman1_data,
           salesman1_data+num_customers );
        deque<bool> salesman2( salesman2_data,
           salesman2_data+num_customers );
        deque<bool> result( num_customers );

        print_result( contacts, salesman1,
           "has been called by Salesman 1" );
        print_result( contacts, salesman2,
           "has been called by Salesman 2" );

        // customers called by both salesmen
        transform( salesman1.begin(), salesman1.end(), salesman2.begin(),
           result.begin(), logical_and<bool>() );
        print_result( contacts, result,
           "has been called by both salesmen" );

        // customers called by at least one salesman
        transform( salesman1.begin(), salesman1.end(), salesman2.begin(),
           result.begin(), logical_or<bool>() );
        print_result( contacts, result,
           "has been called by at least one salesman" );

        // customers called by only one salesman
        transform( salesman1.begin(), salesman1.end(), salesman2.begin(),
           result.begin(), logical_xor );
        print_result( contacts, result,
           "has been called by only one salesman" );

        // customers not called by Salesman 1
        transform( salesman1.begin(), salesman1.end(),
           result.begin(), logical_not<bool>() );
        print_result( contacts, result,
           "has not been called by Salesman 1" );
     }

inline
bool logical_xor( bool a, bool b )
{  return a ? !b : b;  }
```

```
void print_result( const char* names[], const deque<bool>& which,
    const char* text )
{
    for( deque<bool>::size_type i = 0; i < which.size(); ++i )
        if( which[i] )
            cout << names[i] << " " << text << endl;
    cout << endl;
}
```

The output is

```
Alex Pendrod has been called by Salesman 1
Joseph deSilva has been called by Salesman 1
Julia Rosenstein has been called by Salesman 1

Sally Weh has been called by Salesman 2
Donald O'Brien has been called by Salesman 2
Julia Rosenstein has been called by Salesman 2

Julia Rosenstein has been called by both salesmen

Alex Pendrod has been called by at least one salesman
Joseph deSilva has been called by at least one salesman
Sally Weh has been called by at least one salesman
Donald O'Brien has been called by at least one salesman
Julia Rosenstein has been called by at least one salesman

Alex Pendrod has been called by only one salesman
Joseph deSilva has been called by only one salesman
Sally Weh has been called by only one salesman
Donald O'Brien has been called by only one salesman

Sally Weh has not been called by Salesman 1
Donald O'Brien has not been called by Salesman 1
```

The program has some names of customers and records of whether each of two salesmen has called those customers. The program starts by loading the data from the arrays into the deques by using the technique of Tip 5. Each element of the deques salesman1 and salesman2 tells whether that salesman has called the person in the corresponding element of the names array. The custom function print_result produces the output. It receives the names and a deque of Booleans but only displays the names corresponding to elements in the deque that are true. The first two sections of the output show which customer each salesman has called.

The first calculation is to find which customers have been called by both salesmen. This is simply the logical AND of the elements in the two deques. The STL algorithm transform accomplishes this easily with the use of the functor logical_ and that is part of the Standard Library. transform stores the result in a third deque. The third section of the output shows the result.

Next, the program decides which customers have been called by at least one salesman. It uses transform as before, but this time with the predefined functor logical_or. The fourth part of the output shows the result. Similarly, the code also computes which customers have only been called by one salesman. The exclusive-or logical operation provides this information, but the STL doesn't have a functor for this. However, it's easy to write one, as the one-line function at the end of the program shows.

The last section of the program shows transform operating on only one input deque. It uses the built-in functor logical_not to store the opposite of each input element in the output deque. This produces a list of the customers who have *not* been called by the first salesmen. The last part of the output displays these people's names.

6 | Tips on Lists

The STL list container is a doubly linked list. It's the antithesis, or perhaps the complement, of a vector. Whereas the vector has very fast random access, the list has slow access to an element in general. On the other hand, inserting or deleting an element in a vector anywhere but at its end takes a lot of time. The list can do this very quickly, so if you're going to be inserting and deleting at various spots in a container, use a list. It really does make a difference.

The list has a number of member functions that allow you to do a special kind of inserting called *splicing*. It also has member functions that do the same thing as some of the STL algorithms. The list has its own versions, either because the algorithm won't work at all on a list or because the list can provide a more efficient version. This chapter has tips about all these things and more. You'll find out the following:

- How to easily work with the front and back of the list
- How to splice and merge lists
- How to sort lists
- How to remove duplicate values from a list

TIP 29 **USE THE FRONT AND BACK**

Applies to: List
See also: Tip 27, Tip 45

Quick Solution

```
list<float> l;
// ...
cout << l.front(); // first element
l.pop_front(); // remove first element
l.push_front( 3.14 ); // prepend element
```

161

```
cout << l.back(); // last element
l.pop_back(); // remove last element
l.push_back( 2.718 ); // append element
```

Detailed Solution

If you're planning on inserting or deleting in the middle of a container, you've probably decided to use a list because that's what it's really good at. However, don't forget that it also provides efficient access to its front and back. It has six member functions that make it convenient to work at these positions. `front` and `back` return references to the elements at those sites, `pop_front` and `pop_back` erase those elements, and `push_front` and `push_back` add an element to the appropriate end of the list. Here are a few tips on using these handy member functions:

- The behavior of `front`, `back`, `pop_front`, and `pop_back` is undefined if the list has no elements. You should check that the list is not empty before calling these member functions. `push_front` and `push_back` have no such restriction.
- `pop_front` and `pop_back` remove an element but do not return it. If you need to do something with an element, access it before you pop it off the list.
- `front` and `back` return references (or constant references) to an element. This lets you chain calls to it with calls to a function or data member. The program in this tip gives an example of chaining.

Because of this easy manipulation of elements at the front and back of a list, you may find that container useful if your data is divided into two parts. When creating a list, you can put elements from one part at the front and the other elements at the back. They won't be sorted, but that's an easy way to partition them during creation. The program in Listing 6.1 is an example.

LISTING 6.1   Accessing the Front and Back of a List

```
// list_front_back.cpp

#include <algorithm>
#include <iostream>
#include <list>

using namespace std;

int main( )
{
    const char* name_data[] = { "Cindy Winkelman", "Ann Smith",
```

```
      "Joe Johnston", "Edward Koppelman", "Janice Weitz",
      "Gail Hickford", "Candy Kauffman" };
  const bool girl_data[] = { true, true, false, false, true,
      true, true };
  const int num_graduates = sizeof( girl_data )
      / sizeof( girl_data[0] );

  list< pair< string, bool > > graduate;
  // first - person's name     second - true if girl, false if boy

  // list of graduates - girls in front, boys in back
  for( int i = 0; i < num_graduates; ++i )
      if( girl_data[i] )
        graduate.push_front(
            make_pair( name_data[i], girl_data[i] ) );
      else
        graduate.push_back(
            make_pair( name_data[i], girl_data[i] ) );

  // march in the graduates in boy-girl pairs
  cout << "LADIES AND GENTLEMEN, THE GRADUATES ARE\n";
  while( !graduate.empty() )
  {
    cout << graduate.front().first;
    graduate.pop_front();
    if( !graduate.empty() )
    {
      cout << " and " << graduate.back().first;
      graduate.pop_back();
    }
    cout << endl;
  }
}
```

The output is

```
LADIES AND GENTLEMEN, THE GRADUATES ARE
Candy Kauffman and Edward Koppelman
Gail Hickford and Joe Johnston
Janice Weitz and Cindy Winkelman
Ann Smith
```

The program simulates a printout or announcement of graduating students. It's traditional for the students to march into the ceremony in boy-girl pairs. The start of the program has some kids' names and their sexes. The code creates a list containing the STL utility data structure pair (see Tip 45). The first element is a string with the kid's name and the second is a Boolean that's true if the child is a girl and false if it's a boy.

As the program creates the list, it puts the girls on the front and the boys at the back. Later, when the program shows the graduating pairs, it can simply pull one person from the front and one from the back, which will automatically produce boy-girl pairs. To put the data in the list, the code loops through the stored names and sexes and uses the predefined auxiliary function make_pair, also described in Tip 45. The function returns a pair that the program pushes on the front or back of the list, depending on whether the child is a male or a female.

The second half of the code displays the names of the graduating children. The program keeps working on the list as long as it's not empty. The loop prints the name of the first child in a graduating couple. You can see that it gets the name by calling the front member function of the list and then appending a call to the first data member in the pair, appropriately called first. This technique is known as chaining. After printing the name, the loop gets rid of that element by calling pop_front. It then checks if the list is empty, which could happen if there were an odd number of students. If the list is empty, there's nothing to do. If it's not empty, the code prints the name of the last student in the list and removes that element. Pretty simple and clean.

The output shows the boy-girl pairs. The last two lines illustrate that the code automatically handles situations in which there are more girls than boys (or vice versa) or in which there are an odd number of students. In this case, all the students march in pairs except for the one loner at the end.

If you need this kind of quick access to the front and end of a container, but you don't have to insert or delete from the middle a lot, check out the deque. This container has the same six member functions, is efficient at those operations, and gives you random access to boot. Tip 27 has the details.

TIP 30   SORT

Applies to: List
See also: Tip 49, Tip 59

Quick Solution

```
list<float> l;
// ...
```

```
l.sort(); // default sort is ascending
l.sort( greater<float>() ); // descending sort
```

Detailed Solution

Sorting is a fundamental procedure in programming. However, if you call the STL algorithm sort on a list, you'll get a nasty surprise—your program won't even compile. This is because sort requires random-access iterators, and a list doesn't have any. Not to worry, though—list has a member function to do sorting. It's called sort (appropriately) and comes in two versions. The first takes no parameters and sorts by the less-than operator. The second accepts a comparison function that defines the sort order. The code in Listing 6.2 is an example that demonstrates both of these member functions.

LISTING 6.2   Sorting Lists

```cpp
// list_sort.cpp

#include <algorithm>
#include <functional>
#include <iomanip>
#include <iostream>
#include <list>

using namespace std;

class Player
{
   public:
   Player( const string& first_name = "John",
      const string& last_name = "Doe", int height = 60,
      float field_goal_percentage = 10 ); // height in inches
   bool operator<( const Player& rhs ) const;

   float field_goal_percentage() const;
   string first_name() const;
   int height() const;   // in inches
   void height( int& feet, int& inches ) const;
   string last_name() const;
   void print() const;

   private:
   float field_goal_percentage_;
```

```cpp
    string first_name_;
    int height_;    // in inches
    string last_name_;
};

inline
Player::Player( const string& first_name, const string& last_name,
   int height, float field_goal_percentage )
   : field_goal_percentage_( field_goal_percentage ),
     first_name_( first_name ), height_( height ),
     last_name_( last_name )
{} // empty

inline
float Player::field_goal_percentage() const
{  return field_goal_percentage_; }

inline
string Player::first_name() const
{  return first_name_; }

inline
int Player::height() const   // in inches
{  return height_; }

inline
void Player::height( int& feet, int& inches ) const
{
   feet = height() / 12;
   inches = height() % 12;
}

inline
string Player::last_name() const
{  return last_name_; }

void Player::print() const
{
   int feet, inches;
   height( feet, inches );
   string name( first_name() );
   name += " ";
   name += last_name();
   cout << setw( 20 ) << left << name << feet << " feet " << inches
```

```
               << " inches   Field goal percentage: "
               << field_goal_percentage() << endl;
}

inline
bool Player::operator<( const Player& rhs ) const
{ return last_name() < rhs.last_name(); }

inline
bool greater_height( const Player& lhs, const Player& rhs )
{ return lhs.height() > rhs.height(); }

inline
bool greater_field_goal_percentage( const Player& lhs,
   const Player& rhs )
{ return lhs.field_goal_percentage()
   > rhs.field_goal_percentage(); }

int main( )
{
   list<Player> players;

   // statistics for 2003-2004 season
   players.push_back( Player( "Kobe", "Bryant", 78, 0.422 ) );
   players.push_back( Player( "Allen", "Iverson", 72, 0.392 ) );
   players.push_back( Player( "Shaquille", "O'Neal", 85, 0.555 ) );
   players.push_back( Player( "Yao", "Ming", 90, 0.531 ) );
   players.push_back( Player( "Tim", "Duncan", 84, 0.502) );

   // sort by name
   cout << "PLAYERS BY LAST NAME\n";
   players.sort();
   for_each( players.begin(), players.end(),
      mem_fun_ref( &Player::print ) );

   // descending sort by height
   cout << "\nPLAYERS BY HEIGHT\n";
   players.sort( greater_height );
   for_each( players.begin(), players.end(),
      mem_fun_ref( &Player::print ) );

   // descending sort by field goal percentage
   cout << "\nPLAYERS BY FIELD GOAL PERCENTAGE\n";
   players.sort( greater_field_goal_percentage );
```

```
      for_each( players.begin(), players.end(),
         mem_fun_ref( &Player::print ) );
   }
```

The output of the program is

```
PLAYERS BY LAST NAME
Kobe Bryant          6 feet 6 inches    Field goal percentage: 0.422
Tim Duncan           7 feet 0 inches    Field goal percentage: 0.502
Allen Iverson        6 feet 0 inches    Field goal percentage: 0.392
Yao Ming             7 feet 6 inches    Field goal percentage: 0.531
Shaquille O'Neal     7 feet 1 inches    Field goal percentage: 0.555

PLAYERS BY HEIGHT
Yao Ming             7 feet 6 inches    Field goal percentage: 0.531
Shaquille O'Neal     7 feet 1 inches    Field goal percentage: 0.555
Tim Duncan           7 feet 0 inches    Field goal percentage: 0.502
Kobe Bryant          6 feet 6 inches    Field goal percentage: 0.422
Allen Iverson        6 feet 0 inches    Field goal percentage: 0.392

PLAYERS BY FIELD GOAL PERCENTAGE
Shaquille O'Neal     7 feet 1 inches    Field goal percentage: 0.555
Yao Ming             7 feet 6 inches    Field goal percentage: 0.531
Tim Duncan           7 feet 0 inches    Field goal percentage: 0.502
Kobe Bryant          6 feet 6 inches    Field goal percentage: 0.422
Allen Iverson        6 feet 0 inches    Field goal percentage: 0.392
```

The top of the source code contains the definition of a simple class that represents a basketball player. The class holds the player's first and last names, his height, and the percentage of field goals (shots other than free throws) that he made. After the class, two nonmember functions compare aspects of one player with those of another. For example, greater_height returns true if the first player passed to it is taller than the second and false otherwise. These functions will be the arguments to the list's sort function.

The program starts by making a list containing five players from the National Basketball Association (NBA), the professional basketball league in the United States [Basketball04]. It puts them into alphabetical order by calling the list's sort member function with no arguments. This makes the list sort itself with the less-than operator, which is defined in the Player class and which in turn sorts by last name. The program then prints the list members by using the STL algorithm for_each to call each element's print member function (see Tip 49 and Tip 59). The first section of the output shows that the players are indeed in alphabetical order.

Next, the code resorts the players, this time into descending order of height. Because the sort member function without arguments arranges the elements into ascending order by last name, you need to customize the sorting. Do this by passing a comparison function, in this case greater_height. The output now shows the same five players sorted by height. Finally, the program sorts in descending order of field goal percentage. The last section of the output shows the result.

TIP 31   SPLICE

Applies to: List
See also: Tip 29, Tip 30, Tip 48

Quick Solution

There are three different variations of the splice member function.

```
list<float> list1, list2, list3, list4;
list<float>::iterator i;
// ... fill lists and make iterator point to element in list1

// splice all list2 elements into list1 at i. list2 is empty after
// splice
list1.splice( i, list2 );

list<float>::iterator i3;
// ... make iterator point to element in list3

// splice element at i3 into list1 at i. Element is not in list3 after
// splice
list1.splice( i, list3, i3 );

list<float>::iterator i4a, i4b;
// ... make iterators point to elements in list4

// splice elements in range [i4a, i4b) into list1 at position i
// elements in range are not in list4 anymore after splice
list1.splice( i, list4, i4a, i4b );
```

Detailed Solution

"To splice" originally meant "to unite two ropes by intertwining their strands." It now is more general, applying to other materials (such as magnetic tape) or referring to the removal of material from one source and its insertion in another location. For example, in molecular biology a section of DNA can be removed from one strand of DNA and spliced (inserted) into another.

In lists, splicing is the moving of elements from one list to another. After the move, the elements are no longer in the source. The big difference between splicing and other kinds of element movement, such as insertion, assignment, and copying, is that in the former, the elements are never duplicated, but in the latter, they are. Lists accomplish splicing by adjusting internal pointers to the list nodes. This doesn't involve creating, copying, assigning, or destroying elements, so it can be much faster than insertion, especially if the elements are classes. It's also very safe—splicing never throws errors.

Splicing is helpful and efficient when you need to process sections of a list separately but still keep the original list. You can splice a part of one list into another, do your computations on that list and then splice the results back into the original list. (The sample program in Listing 6.3 demonstrates this.)

There are three overloaded list member functions called splice that let you splice. The first is

```
void splice(iterator position, list<T,Allocator>& x)
```

This member function removes all the elements from the list x and puts them into the calling list in front of the element specified by position. The source and destination lists must be different. If you want to splice an element within a list, use

```
void splice(iterator position, list<T,Allocator>& x, iterator i)
```

This version of splice moves the element in x at i in front of the element in the calling list specified by position. (If position is the same as i or the element after i (++i), nothing happens.) Here, the source list can (but need not) be the same as the destination list. The third version of splice is

```
void splice(iterator position, list<T,Allocator>& x, iterator first,
iterator last)
```

It moves a range from list x and puts it in front of position in the calling list. x and the calling list can be the same but position can't be in the range.

The program in Listing 6.3 uses all three versions of splice and demonstrates how to process parts of a list separately.

LISTING 6.3   Splicing Lists

```cpp
// list_splice.cpp

#include <algorithm>
#include <functional>
#include <iostream>
#include <list>

using namespace std;

class Judge
{
   public:
   Judge( int id = 1, int panel = 1, int score = 1,
      bool award = false );
   // id >= 1, ID number of judge
   // 1 <= panel <= 3
   // 1 <= score <= 10
   // award - if true, judge gives a special award

   bool operator>( const Judge& rhs ) const;
   // compare scores

   bool is_award() const;
   int panel() const;

   void print() const;
   // display info about judge

   private:

   bool award_;
   int id_;
   int panel_;
   int score_;
};

inline
Judge::Judge( int id, int panel, int score, bool award )
   : award_( award ), id_( id ), panel_( panel ), score_( score )
{} // empty

inline
```

```
bool Judge::operator>( const Judge& rhs ) const
{ return score_ > rhs.score_; }

inline
bool Judge::is_award() const
{ return award_; }

inline
int Judge::panel() const
{ return panel_; }

inline
void Judge::print() const
{
   cout << "Judge " << id_ << " of Panel " << panel()
      << " gives a score of " << score_;
   if( is_award() )
      cout << " and a SPECIAL AWARD";
   cout << endl;
}

bool is_panel( const Judge judge, int panel_number );
// returns true if panel number of judge is equal to passed number,
// false otherwise

bool less_panel( const Judge& lhs, const Judge& rhs );
// returns true if panel number of first judge is less than
// panel number of second judge, false otherwise

int main( )
{
   const int id[]     = { 1, 5, 2, 4, 2, 3, 6, 2, 1, 4, 3, 3 };
   const int panel[]  = { 1, 1, 3, 1, 2, 1, 2, 1, 3, 2, 2, 3 };
   const int score[]  = { 7, 7, 1, 6, 6, 4, 6, 5, 4, 3, 4, 5 };
   const bool award[] = { false, false, false, false, false,
      false, true, true, true, false, false, false,  };

   list<Judge> judge;
   for( int i = 0; i < sizeof( id ) / sizeof( id[0] ); ++i )
      judge.push_back( Judge( id[i], panel[i], score[i], award[i] ) );

   cout << "ORIGINAL LIST\n";
   for_each( judge.begin(), judge.end(),
      mem_fun_ref( &Judge::print ) );
```

```cpp
// sort by panel number and display
judge.sort( less_panel );
cout << "\nLIST SORTED BY PANEL\n";
for_each( judge.begin(), judge.end(),
   mem_fun_ref( &Judge::print ) );

const int num_panels = 3;
for( int i = 1; i <= num_panels; ++i )
{
   // find the first judge from the current panel
   list<Judge>::iterator start =
      find_if( judge.begin(), judge.end(),
         bind2nd( ptr_fun( is_panel ), i ) );

   // find the first judge from the next panel
   list<Judge>::iterator stop =
      find_if( judge.begin(), judge.end(),
         bind2nd( ptr_fun( is_panel ), i+1 ) );

   // splice all the current panel judges into a temporary list
   list<Judge> work;
   work.splice( work.begin(), judge, start, stop );

   // sort judges by score in descending order
   work.sort( greater<Judge>() );

   // remove the highest and lowest
   work.pop_front();
   work.pop_back();

   // move any special award to the front of the original list
   list<Judge>::iterator j = find_if( work.begin(), work.end(),
         mem_fun_ref( &Judge::is_award ) );
   if( j != work.end() )
      judge.splice( judge.begin(), work, j );

   // put the sorted, remaining judges back into original list
   judge.splice( stop, work );
}

cout <<
   "\nLIST SORTED BY PANEL AND SCORE, SPECIAL AWARDS FIRST\n";
for_each( judge.begin(), judge.end(),
   mem_fun_ref( &Judge::print ) );
```

```
}

inline
bool less_panel( const Judge& lhs, const Judge& rhs )
{ return lhs.panel() < rhs.panel(); }

inline
bool is_panel( const Judge judge, int panel_number )
{ return judge.panel() == panel_number; }
```

The output is

```
ORIGINAL LIST
Judge 1 of Panel 1 gives a score of 7
Judge 5 of Panel 1 gives a score of 7
Judge 2 of Panel 3 gives a score of 1
Judge 4 of Panel 1 gives a score of 6
Judge 2 of Panel 2 gives a score of 6
Judge 3 of Panel 1 gives a score of 4

Judge 6 of Panel 2 gives a score of 6 and a SPECIAL AWARD
Judge 2 of Panel 1 gives a score of 5 and a SPECIAL AWARD
Judge 1 of Panel 3 gives a score of 4 and a SPECIAL AWARD
Judge 4 of Panel 2 gives a score of 3
Judge 3 of Panel 2 gives a score of 4
Judge 3 of Panel 3 gives a score of 5

LIST SORTED BY PANEL
Judge 1 of Panel 1 gives a score of 7
Judge 5 of Panel 1 gives a score of 7
Judge 4 of Panel 1 gives a score of 6
Judge 3 of Panel 1 gives a score of 4
Judge 2 of Panel 1 gives a score of 5 and a SPECIAL AWARD
Judge 2 of Panel 2 gives a score of 6
Judge 6 of Panel 2 gives a score of 6 and a SPECIAL AWARD
Judge 4 of Panel 2 gives a score of 3
Judge 3 of Panel 2 gives a score of 4
Judge 2 of Panel 3 gives a score of 1
Judge 1 of Panel 3 gives a score of 4 and a SPECIAL AWARD
Judge 3 of Panel 3 gives a score of 5
```

$\rightarrow$

```
LIST SORTED BY PANEL AND SCORE, SPECIAL AWARDS FIRST
Judge 1 of Panel 3 gives a score of 4 and a SPECIAL AWARD
Judge 6 of Panel 2 gives a score of 6 and a SPECIAL AWARD
Judge 2 of Panel 1 gives a score of 5 and a SPECIAL AWARD
Judge 5 of Panel 1 gives a score of 7
Judge 4 of Panel 1 gives a score of 6
Judge 3 of Panel 2 gives a score of 4
```

Suppose there's a contest with three panels of judges. After each contestant performs, the judges are given a certain amount of time to record their scores. You receive the scores in a list container, and you know the following:

- The scores can be in any order because the judges can make their decisions in any order.
- There are exactly three panels.
- Because the scores aren't sent to you until three judges per panel have voted, there will always be scores from at least three judges from each panel.
- A judge can only vote once per contestant.
- Only one judge per panel can grant a special award, though a panel need not give the award.

Your job is to write software to rearrange the list so that (1) the judges' decisions are sorted in ascending order of panel number, (2) within a panel, the decisions are in descending order of score, (3) the highest and lowest scores from each panel have been eliminated (as in Olympic ice skating judging), and (4) any judges who have given a special award and who have not been eliminated are placed at the front of the list.

The code starts by declaring a class to hold information about the judge. It contains his identification number, panel number, score, and whether or not he has granted a special award. There are member functions to display the information in the class, to tell if the judge has made an award, and to rank the judges in descending order of score (the greater-than operator). There are also two global functions. One decides whether a passed judge is a member of a particular panel, and the other tells whether one judge's panel number is less than another's.

The main part of the program starts by loading a bunch of judges' votes onto a list by pushing them onto the back of the list (see Tip 29). It then displays the votes by calling the print member function of each element in the list, using the technique of Tip 48. The first section of the output shows the votes in their original order. You can see that the panel numbers are mixed up.

The code then sorts the list by panel number. The code uses the `sort` member function (see Tip 30) with the custom global function `less_panel` as an argument. (The class could define a less-than operator instead to compare votes by score. However, this would be confusing because the greater-than operator compares votes by panel number.) The second section of the output shows the judges' decisions sorted by panel number.

The next part of the program is a loop that does the bulk of the work. It processes the three panels but is parameterized so that it will work with other numbers of panels. The loop starts by using the STL algorithm `find_if` to look for the first judge who's a member of the current panel. (The loop counter is, in fact, the panel number.) Similarly, the loop also finds the first judge from the next panel. These two iterators define the range of judges in the current panel. (Remember that as with all STL ranges, the last iterator, which in this case points to the next panel's first judge, is one past the last element of interest. Note also that if `find_if` doesn't find a member of the next panel (and this happens on the final loop iteration because there is no next panel), it returns the ending iterator of the container. That iterator works just fine in the code that follows the call to `find_if`.

Once the loop has the range of the judges in the current panel, it declares a temporary list and splices those elements into it. Then the loop sorts those judges into descending order of score using the greater-than predefined functor. Removing the judges with the highest and lowest scores is easy with the use of `pop_front` and `pop_back` (see Tip 29). Finally, the code uses `find_if` again to search for a judge who has given out the special award. There can be at most one such judge in the panel, so the program only calls `find_if` once. However, there might not be any judges who gave awards, so the code verifies that the algorithm didn't return the ending iterator before it splices the element onto the front of the original list.

The last thing the loop does is to splice any remaining elements in the working list back into the original, at the same spot from which they were taken. The last section of the output shows the result. All special awards are at the head of the list, the highest and lowest score from each panel has been eliminated, and the remaining judges are sorted by panel and within panel by score.

TIP 32   MERGE

Applies to: List
See also: Tip 30, Tip 48

Quick Solution

```
list<int> list1, list2;
// ...
```

```
list1.sort();
list2.sort();

// after call, list2 is empty, list1 has both lists sorted
list1.merge( list2 );
```

Detailed Solution

Sometimes you need to merge two sorted lists together, that is, combine them into one sorted list. For example, suppose at the start of the day, you have just one list of items available. You sort the list and then work with it. As the day progresses, you get more lists that you process the same way. At the end of the day, you need to put all the lists together, sort the composite list, and do your computations on it. Instead of re-sorting the master list, you can merge all the lists together. This produces a sorted list, and more quickly, too.

Although the STL has the algorithm merge, lists have a member function with the same name. It is more efficient because it just splices nodes rather than create new ones. merge has two signatures. The first takes no arguments and sorts using the less-than operator. The second takes one argument—a binary predicate that determines the sorting order. Here are some other things to keep in mind:

- Sort all lists that you merge the same way, that is, with the sorting criterion.
- merge will run on unsorted lists, but the result is not very useful.
- The list member function merge removes all elements from the source list and puts them into the destination list. The algorithm version doesn't modify either source list.

The program in Listing 6.4 has some examples of sorting and merging lists.

LISTING 6.4   Merging Lists

```
// list_merge.cpp

#include <algorithm>
#include <functional>
#include <iostream>
#include <iterator>
#include <list>

using namespace std;

class Salesperson
{
```

```cpp
  public:
  Salesperson( const string& name = "", int sales = 0,
     int district = 0 );
  // name - salesperson's last name
  // sales - >= 0, last year's sales in dollars
  // district - district number

  bool operator>( const Salesperson& rhs ) const;
  // true is sales of *this is > than rhs.sales(), else false

  void print() const;
  // print info on salesperson

  private:
  int district_;
  string name_;
  int sales_;
};

inline
Salesperson::Salesperson( const string& name, int sales,
   int district )
   : district_( district ), name_( name ), sales_( sales )
{} // empty

inline
bool Salesperson::operator>( const Salesperson& rhs ) const
{ return sales_ > rhs.sales_; }

inline
void Salesperson::print() const
{ cout << name_ << " from District " << district_
   << " has sales of $" << sales_ << endl;
}

int main( )
{
  list<Salesperson> list1;
  list1.push_back( Salesperson( "Gutierrez", 37000, 1 ) );
  list1.push_back( Salesperson( "Gonzalez", 49000, 1 ) );
  list1.push_back( Salesperson( "Ochoa", 48500, 1 ) );

  // sort District 1 salespeople in descending order and display
  list1.sort( greater<Salesperson>() );
```

```
cout << "Top three salespeople for District 1\n";
for_each( list1.begin(), list1.end(),
   mem_fun_ref( &Salesperson::print ) );

list<Salesperson> list2;
list2.push_back( Salesperson( "Yashimoto", 65000, 2 ) );
list2.push_back( Salesperson( "de la Cruz", 33000, 2 ) );
list2.push_back( Salesperson( "Duke", 47000, 2 ) );

// sort District 2 salespeople in descending order and display
list2.sort( greater<Salesperson>() );
cout << "\nTop three salespeople for District 2\n";
for_each( list2.begin(), list2.end(),
   mem_fun_ref( &Salesperson::print ) );

list<Salesperson> list3;
list3.push_back( Salesperson( "White", 30000, 3 ) );
list3.push_back( Salesperson( "Kline", 44000, 3 ) );
list3.push_back( Salesperson( "Bradley", 42500, 3 ) );

// sort District 3 salespeople in descending order and display
list3.sort( greater<Salesperson>() );
cout << "\nTop three salespeople for District 3\n";
for_each( list3.begin(), list3.end(),
   mem_fun_ref( &Salesperson::print ) );

list<Salesperson> list4;
list4.push_back( Salesperson( "Smith", 51000, 4 ) );
list4.push_back( Salesperson( "Kleinenberg", 33000, 4 ) );
list4.push_back( Salesperson( "Schwartz", 44000, 4 ) );

// sort District 4 salespeople in descending order and display
list4.sort( greater<Salesperson>() );
cout << "\nTop three salespeople for District 4\n";
for_each( list4.begin(), list4.end(),
   mem_fun_ref( &Salesperson::print ) );

// merge Districts 1 and 2 into Western Region
list1.merge( list2, greater<Salesperson>() );

// keep only the top 3 salespeople
const int top_positions = 3;
list<Salesperson>::iterator position = list1.begin();
advance( position, top_positions );
```

```
list1.erase( position, list1.end() );

cout << "\nTop three salespeople for Western Region "
   << "(Districts 1 and 2 )\n";
for_each( list1.begin(), list1.end(),
   mem_fun_ref( &Salesperson::print ) );

// merge Districts 3 and 4 into Eastern Region
list3.merge( list4, greater<Salesperson>() );

// keep only the top 3 salespeople
position = list3.begin();
advance( position, top_positions );
list3.erase( position, list3.end() );

cout << "\nTop three salespeople for Eastern Region "
   << "(Districts 3 and 4)\n";
for_each( list3.begin(), list3.end(),
   mem_fun_ref( &Salesperson::print ) );

// merge two regions into whole country
list1.merge( list3, greater<Salesperson>() );

// keep only the top 3 salespeople
position = list1.begin();
advance( position, top_positions );
list1.erase( position, list1.end() );

cout << "\nTop three salespeople in the country\n";
for_each( list1.begin(), list1.end(),
   mem_fun_ref( &Salesperson::print ) );
}
```

The output is

```
Top three salespeople for District 1
Gonzalez from District 1 has sales of $49000
Ochoa from District 1 has sales of $48500
Gutierrez from District 1 has sales of $37000

Top three salespeople for District 2
Yashimoto from District 2 has sales of $65000
Duke from District 2 has sales of $47000
de la Cruz from District 2 has sales of $33000                    →
```

```
Top three salespeople for District 3
Kline from District 3 has sales of $44000
Bradley from District 3 has sales of $42500
White from District 3 has sales of $30000

Top three salespeople for District 4
Smith from District 4 has sales of $51000
Schwartz from District 4 has sales of $44000
Kleinenberg from District 4 has sales of $33000

Top three salespeople for Western Region (Districts 1 and 2 )
Yashimoto from District 2 has sales of $65000
Gonzalez from District 1 has sales of $49000
Ochoa from District 1 has sales of $48500

Top three salespeople for Eastern Region (Districts 3 and 4)
Smith from District 4 has sales of $51000
Kline from District 3 has sales of $44000
Schwartz from District 4 has sales of $44000

Top three salespeople in the country
Yashimoto from District 2 has sales of $65000
Smith from District 4 has sales of $51000
Gonzalez from District 1 has sales of $49000
```

The sample program illustrates the use of merge to make a hierarchy of comparisons. First, the program sorts salespeople within one district. Next, it does the same thing for regions, with each region being made up of several districts. Finally, the program combines the top sellers for the regions into a list for the whole country and finds the champions in that list.

The program starts by declaring a little class to hold the name, yearly sales total, and district number of a salesperson. It also has the greater-than operator, which ranks the class by sales. The main part of the code declares a list for District 1 and puts three salespeople in it. It puts them into descending order of sales by calling the list's sort member function (see Tip 30) with the greater-than predefined functor as the sorting criterion. Then it displays the sorted salespeople by using the STL algorithm for_each to call every element's print member function, as Tip 48 explains. The first section of the output shows the three salespeople in descending order of amount sold. The code creates, sorts, and displays lists for the other three districts. The output shows these sorted salespeople.

After seeing the top three sellers for each of the four districts, the company's management says it wants to see the top sellers for each region. Districts 1 and 2 make up the western region, and the other two districts constitute the eastern region. Because all the lists are sorted, it's more efficient to merge two lists than to combine them and re-sort. The program merges the second list into the first. It passes the greater-than functor because that's how the original lists were sorted. (If it didn't pass, a sorting criterion sort would use less-than. This would cause problems when used on lists sorted with greater-than.)

The program could just print the top three from the longer list, but because it's going to merge that list later on, it deletes all but the top three now. To do this, the program first creates a list iterator and sets it to the start of the list. Then it calls the utility function advance (available in the <iterator> header) to advance the iterator by three. (You can't just add three to the iterator because that only works with random access iterators. A list iterator is bidirectional, not random access.) Finally, the program calls the list member function erase to remove all elements from the fourth to the end. The output shows the result. Notice that salespeople from both districts are in the output.

The code does the same thing for the other two districts to get the top three sellers for the eastern region. In its final use of merge, it combines the two regions into a list for the whole country and gets the best three salespeople all around. The output shows the winning salespeople for the regions and the country.

TIP 33   REMOVE DUPLICATES

Applies to: List
See also: Tip 29, Tip 30, Tip 45, Tip 59

Quick Solution

```
list<int> l;
// ...

l.sort();
l.unique(); // remove all duplicates
```

Detailed Solution

There are times when you need to remove all but one copy of items stored in a list. In other words, you need to get rid of all duplicates. For example, your list might contain the hits from a Web search, which is likely to have duplicates. You might have a list with all the scores on a test, but you're just interested in the different numbers that occurred, regardless of how many students got a particular score.

Finally, you might have a list of all the cars at an auto dealer. The customers might want to look at the different cars available. If the dealer has several cars that are the same, the customers wouldn't want to look at the duplicates.

The STL algorithm `unique` removes consecutive duplicates in a range. Lists have a member function with the same name that is optimized for the list, so use it instead of the algorithm. The function has two versions—one that compares by equality and one that accepts a binary predicate. In the former case, `unique` eliminates the current element if it is equal to the previous element. (This means that classes in the list must define an equality operator.) The latter case operates the same way except that `unique` deletes the current element if the predicate returns `true`.

It's important to remember that `unique` only eliminates consecutive duplicates. Sorting will make all duplicates of an item fall consecutively in the list, so it's often done before calling `unique`. However, there may be times when you only want to eliminate consecutive duplicates from the original list ordering. The program in Listing 6.5 illustrates both situations.

LISTING 6.5   Removing Duplicates from Lists

```cpp
// list_unique.cpp

#include <algorithm>
#include <iostream>
#include <list>
#include <string>
#include <utility>

using namespace std;

void print_message( const pair<int,string>& message );

int main( )
{
    list< pair< int, string > > message;
    message.push_back( make_pair( 40449, "Shift key down" ) );
    message.push_back( make_pair( 40443, "Mouse key down" ) );
    message.push_back( make_pair( 40443, "Mouse key down" ) );
    message.push_back( make_pair( 40444, "Mouse key up" ) );
    message.push_back( make_pair( 40448, "Mouse move" ) );
    message.push_back( make_pair( 40443, "Mouse key down" ) );

    cout << "ORIGINAL MESSAGES" << endl;
    for_each( message.begin(), message.end(), print_message );
```

```
    message.unique();
    cout << "\nSEQUENTIAL DUPLICATES REMOVED" << endl;
    for_each( message.begin(), message.end(), print_message );

    message.sort();
    message.unique();
    cout << "\nALL DUPLICATES REMOVED" << endl;
    for_each( message.begin(), message.end(), print_message );
}

void print_message( const pair<int,string>& message )
{
    cout << message.first << " - " << message.second << endl;
}
```

The output is

```
ORIGINAL MESSAGES
40449 - Shift key down
40443 - Mouse key down
40443 - Mouse key down
40444 - Mouse key up
40448 - Mouse move
40443 - Mouse key down

SEQUENTIAL DUPLICATES REMOVED
40449 - Shift key down
40443 - Mouse key down
40444 - Mouse key up
40448 - Mouse move
40443 - Mouse key down

ALL DUPLICATES REMOVED
40443 - Mouse key down
40444 - Mouse key up
40448 - Mouse move
40449 - Shift key down
```

Most modern graphical user interfaces (GUIs) are message based. This means that each interface action has information about it stored in a data packet (a message), and this message is passed to the appropriate piece of software to be handled.

Messages usually have the time the action occurred and an identification number. Keystrokes will also have the key that was hit. Mouse actions may have the button that was pushed and the mouse location. Occasionally, because of quirks or bugs in the GUI, some messages are duplicated. If you're working with the messages, you need to eliminate those duplicates.

The sample program simulates a message by an STL `pair` data structure containing an identification number and explanatory text. The program makes a list to hold the messages, creates a number of messages with the STL utility `make_pair` (see Tip 45), and adds them to the list by using the member function `push_back` (see Tip 29). The program then prints the message by using the STL algorithm `for_each` (see Tip 59) to call a custom function. This function, at the bottom of the source code, just has one statement that sends the identification number and text to the standard output stream. The first section of the output shows the result.

To eliminate any consecutive duplicates, the code calls the list member function `unique`. The second part of the output shows the messages that are left. Note that there are still two duplicate messages—number 40443. This is because there were three originally, but only two occurred consecutively. `unique` only eliminated the duplicate of the consecutive pair.

Suppose it's also of interest (for example, for debugging) to show only the unique messages, that is, to eliminate all duplicates regardless of where in the list they occur. The program shows that the code is the same as before except that it sorts the list first (see Tip 30). The last section of the output shows that this time the messages are unique throughout the whole list. Sorting and calling `unique` got rid of one of the duo of duplicates. If there had been three or more duplications, `unique` would have still done its job. However, instead of just eliminating one of the duplicated elements, `unique` would have eliminated as many as necessary so that only one remained.

7 Tips on Associative Containers

A sequence container holds its elements in linear order. The location of an element depends on when and where it was inserted, but is independent of the value of the element. Associative containers are quite different. They hold *sorted* collections of objects. The position in the container depends on the object's value rather than on whether it was inserted before or after another object.

When you insert elements into an associative container, it automatically sorts them. This doesn't mean that associative containers are designed for sorting per se because you can also sort sequence containers. The big advantage of associative containers comes in searching for a value. The search is always logarithmic, which for large sequences is much faster than a search on an unsorted sequence container. Nevertheless, there are some situations in which alternative containers or search methods may be better:

- Hash maps, under the name "unordered associative containers" are available from Boost (see Tip 99) and perform substantially better in some applications.
- If the collection of elements is fixed, sorting a vector and using a binary search, such as the STL algorithm `lower_bound`, performs better and takes up significantly less memory.
- Storing small collections in a sequence container and using the STL algorithms `find` or `find_if` normally gives superior performance.

The STL has two general types of associative containers—sets/multisets and maps/multimaps. Sets order their elements by value and don't permit duplicates. Multisets order the same way but do permit duplicates. Maps store elements in pairs. One member of the pair is the key and the other is the value. Maps order their elements by key and the keys must be unique. Multimaps do the same but permit duplicate keys.

Maps have indexing, that is, access to an element's value by passing the key to the subscript operator (`[]`). The interesting and powerful feature of this capability is that the index can be any data type, not just an integer. For example, the index can be a text string. The clear application of that is a dictionary in which the key is a word and the value is the word's definition. Because of this use, maps are sometimes called *dictionaries*. A container that permits indexing by any data type is known as *associative memory*, and that is where the name for the four containers in this chapter comes from.

The obvious use of a set is as a model of a mathematical set. A map can be used as a dictionary. Here are some other applications of associative containers:

- Sometimes, especially with large objects, inserting them into a multiset so that they are automatically sorted is faster than putting them into a sequence container and sorting them with the STL `sort` algorithm or the container's `sort` member function.
- If an application uses only a few of a large number of possible integer indexes, a map can take up much less memory than a vector. This is because the map only needs room for the elements that are present but a vector must allocate space for all possible indexes.
- Maps are useful in scientific calculations involving sparse matrices. (A *matrix* is a rectangular array of numbers, and a *sparse matrix* is a matrix that has only a few nonzero values.) The map stores the location and value only of the nonzero elements.

Associative containers store their elements in order. By default, the containers compare two elements with the less-than operator, though you can specify something else. If you want to see whether one element is the same as another, for example, when using a container's `find` member function to search for an element, a subtle issue arises—what does "same" mean? The most obvious answer is that two elements are the same if they make the equals operator (`==`) return `true`. However, the STL does not use this definition.

To understand what the STL does, first consider ordering two numbers, x and y. There are only three possibilities—x is less than y, y is less than x, or x is equal to y. Intuition says that x and y are the same if they are equal. The simplest way to test this is just to see if x equals y. A more complicated way to see if the two are equal is to verify that x is not less than y and that y is not less than x. The only possibility that remains is that x must be equal to y. For example, $2 + 3$ is equal to 5 because $2 + 3$ is not less than 5 and 5 is not less than $2 + 3$.

In the STL, two objects x and y are *equal* if they satisfy the equals operator, that is, if `operator==( x, y )` returns `true`. Two objects are *equivalent* if the first is not less than the second and the second is not less than the first, that is, if `!( x < y ) && !( y < x )` is true. Another way of defining equivalence, which is logically the same as the first definition, is that two objects are *equivalent* if it's not true that the first is less than the second or the second is less than the first, that is, `!( x < y || y`

< x) is true. This expression is a little better because there is only one "not" (!) to evaluate. By analogy, if you provide a custom comparison function (say *compare*) to put objects in order, the two objects are equivalent if !(compare(x, y) || compare(y, x)) is true.

Associative containers always use equivalence to see if elements are the same. Using equivalence instead of equality in associative containers has some advantages. First, since the container must have the less-than operator anyway to order the elements, classes in the container don't need to also define an equality operator. Second, the containers' constructors accept an optional argument that specifies the sorting criterion. If the containers used equality, you would have to specify two arguments, one for comparison and one for equality. Finally, by using equivalence, you can make a class that defines an equality operator (==) that is independent of its less-than operator. Be careful with this, though, because you want results to be consistent. For example, suppose you put the elements into a multiset and search for a particular one with the container's find member function. You probably want the one found to be the same as if you put the elements into a vector and searched with the STL algorithm find, which uses equality to compare two elements.

A word of caution—be careful when reading about associative containers. Authors often say that two elements are equal even though they mean equivalent. In this book, comparisons of elements in associative containers are always done by equivalence, so phrases such as "the same" and "equal" mean "equivalent" in this context.

Here's what this chapter has in store for you:

- How to initialize associative containers with specified values
- How to use a map or multimap as a dictionary
- How to search, modify or remove elements
- How to use sorted range algorithms with sets and multisets

TIP 34   INITIALIZE WITH SPECIFIED VALUES

Applies to: Associative containers
See also: Tip 3, Tip 5, Tip 45, Tip 47, Tip 54, Tip 81

Quick Solution

```
const int n[3] = { 4, 2, 6 };
const char* text[3] = { "Four", "Two", "Six" };
```

```
set<int> s( n, n + 3 );

multiset<int> ms( n, n + 3 );

map<int,string> m;
transform( n, n+n_size, text, inserter( m, m.end() ),
    make_pair<int,string> );

multimap<int,string> mm;
transform( n, n+n_size, text, inserter( mm, mm.end() ),
    make_pair<int,string> );
```

Detailed Solution

You may want to construct an associative container with given data in it. Unlike C-style arrays, which let you do exactly this with initializer lists, associative containers don't have constructors that can do the job. However, you can combine arrays and associative container constructors to easily create sets and multisets with specified values. Doing the same for maps and multimaps takes just one line more. The technique is very similar to that for initializing standard sequence containers (see Tip 5), but there are a couple of twists.

To initialize sets or multisets, make a C-style array with the data specified in an initializer list and pass the beginning and end iterators of the array to the set/multisets constructor. (Tip 3 shows that for a C-style array, you use the name of the array as the beginning iterator and the name plus the number of elements as the end iterator.) For multisets, you'll have all your numbers sorted by key. A set will sort the numbers, too, but will also eliminate any duplicates, because no elements in a set can be the same. Notice that by constructing a set from an array as described, in just one line of code you're sorting a group of numbers and getting rid of all duplicates.

Initializing maps and multimaps takes a little bit more code. The problem is that those containers accept and store values in the `pair` data structure (see Tip 45), so you first have to move the data from the C-style arrays into pairs and then pass the pairs to the containers. After that, multimaps will contain all the data in sorted order. Maps will also be that way, but without duplicate keys. Listing 7.1 demonstrates the initialization of all four kinds of associative containers.

LISTING 7.1   Initializing Associative Containers

```
// associative_initialize.cpp

#include <algorithm>
#include <functional>
```

```cpp
#include <iostream>
#include <map>
#include <set>
#include <utility>

#include "tips.hpp"

using namespace std;

int main( )
{
   const int num_cars = 6;
   const int year[num_cars] = { 1998, 1970, 1966, 2004, 1998, 1930 };
   const char* name[num_cars] = { "Toyota Sienna", "Dodge Dart",
      "Chevrolet Corvette", "BMW 645Ci", "Toyota Sienna",
      "Ford Model A" };

   // initialize set and multiset with given data
   set<int> unique_years( year, year + num_cars );
   multiset<int> all_years( year, year + num_cars );
   tips::print( unique_years, "Unique model years" );
   tips::print( all_years,    "All    model years" );

   // initialize map with given data
   typedef map<string,int> Car_map;
   Car_map unique_cars;
   transform( name, name+num_cars, year,
      inserter( unique_cars, unique_cars.end() ),
      make_pair<string,int> );

   cout << "\nUNIQUE CARS\n";
   Car_map::const_iterator unique_cars_end = unique_cars.end();
   for( Car_map::const_iterator i = unique_cars.begin();
      i != unique_cars_end; ++i )
      cout << i->second << " " << i->first << endl;

   // initialize multimap with given data
   typedef multimap<string,int> Car_multimap;
   Car_multimap all_cars;
   transform( name, name+num_cars, year,
      inserter( all_cars, all_cars.end() ),
      make_pair<string,int> );

   cout << "\nALL CARS\n";
```

```
Car_multimap::const_iterator all_cars_end = all_cars.end();
for( Car_multimap::const_iterator i = all_cars.begin();
    i != all_cars_end; ++i )
    cout << i->second << " " << i->first << endl;
}
```

The output is

```
Unique model years: 1930 1966 1970 1998 2004
All    model years: 1930 1966 1970 1998 1998 2004

UNIQUE CARS
2004 BMW 645Ci
1966 Chevrolet Corvette
1970 Dodge Dart
1930 Ford Model A
1998 Toyota Sienna

ALL CARS
2004 BMW 645Ci
1966 Chevrolet Corvette
1970 Dodge Dart
1930 Ford Model A
1998 Toyota Sienna
1998 Toyota Sienna
```

The program starts by storing the names and model years of some cars in C-style arrays. Then it creates and initializes a set and multiset by passing the array of dates to the constructors using the method of Tip 5. The first two lines of output show what's in the two containers. You can see that the numbers are now sorted. The set has one less item because it did not accept the duplicate value of 1998.

Before creating a map, the program uses a typedef statement to make a synonym for the map. (This is common shorthand when working with maps and multimaps because the container and iterator specifications tend to get pretty long.) The code constructs an empty map that uses strings as keys and integers as values. It can't pass them to the constructor because they are stored in two separate arrays. Instead, the code uses the STL algorithm transform to make key/value pairs out of the text and numbers and pass them to the map. Tip 47 and Tip 81 describe the use of this algorithm. Here, the first two arguments to transform specify the range of the first input array. (Tip 3 explains how to get the range of a C-style array.) The third argument is the start of the second input range and the fourth argument is the start of the output range, that is, the map. Typically, this argument would be a back inserter (see, for example, Tip 47 and Tip 54.) Unfortunately, you can't use back inserters with associative containers. However, you can get the same effect by calling a general inserter and specifying the position as the end of the container. The fifth and last argument is the binary function that accepts a value from each input range and makes a value that goes into the output range. The function, make_pair, is a predefined template function available in the <utility> header (see Tip 45). make_pair makes a pair out of its two arguments and returns it. The template parameter specification (<string,int>) in the code ensures that the first element in the pair is a string, rather than a pointer to a char. The second section of the output shows the result. The map has sorted its entries in alphabetical order, but it stored only five of the six cars. The map eliminated the sixth vehicle (the Toyota Sienna) because it's a duplicate and map keys must be unique.

Finally, the program creates and initializes a multimap using the same technique as for the map. Note that in both cases the program stored a local copy of the map or multimap's end iterator. This speeds up the execution of the subsequent loop because refers-to-loop doesn't have to call the container's end member function at each loop iteration.

The last section of the output shows the result. This time the container has all six cars because multimaps can contain duplicate keys.

TIP 35   USE A MAP OR MULTIMAP AS A DICTIONARY

Applies to: Map, multimap
See also: Tip 6, Tip 34, Tip 45

Quick Solution

```
const char* key[3] = { "one", "two", "three" };
const char* value[3] = { "uno", "dos", "tres" };

map<string,string> dictionary;
transform( key, key+3, value,
    inserter( dictionary, dictionary.end() ),
    make_pair<string,string> );

cout << "English: two   Spanish: " << dictionary["two"] << endl;
dictionary["four"] = "cuatro";
```

Detailed Solution

Maps and multimaps store data in pairs. One member of the pair is the key and the other is the value associated with that key. The containers sort their elements by key and are able to quickly look for and retrieve elements with a specified key. Another neat thing is that the key can be any data type (subject to some very mild restrictions), not just an integer. Actually, it's common for the key to be a text string. For example, you can retrieve information about a person by entering his name, or statistics on a sports team by using its name, and so on. In addition, the map provides an elegant interface for retrieving values by key—you pass the key via the subscript operator. This is just like using an array or vector except the argument is not necessarily an integer. A container with non-integer subscripting is often called associative memory. If both the key and value are text strings, the container may be called a dictionary.

Multimaps don't have this subscript capability because they can have multiple elements with the same key, so which element a key refers to would be ambiguous. However, they can have more than one value per key, and so, because most words have several definitions, they are more practical for dictionaries. Listing 7.2 shows how to use either a map or multimap as a dictionary.

LISTING 7.2   Using Maps and Multimaps as Dictionaries

```cpp
// associative_dictionary.cpp

#include <algorithm>
#include <iostream>
#include <map>
#include <utility>

using namespace std;

int main( )
{
   const char* word[] = { "POPS", "TAT", "ESPOO", "HABITFORMING",
      "ADAM" };
   const char* clue[] = { "Sodas", "Not solace, sew-lace?",
      "Second largest Finnish city", "Making nuns' clothes?",
      "Alpha male?" };

   // make a dictionary out of a map
   map<string,string> dictionary1;
   transform( word, word+sizeof(word)/sizeof(word[0]), clue,
      inserter( dictionary1, dictionary1.end() ),
      make_pair<string,string> );
```

```cpp
cout << "There are " << dictionary1.size()
   << " words in the dictionary\n\n";

// use subscript operator to read value
cout << "The clue for POPS is \"" << dictionary1["POPS"] << "\"\n"
   << "The clue for TAT is \"" << dictionary1["TAT"] << "\"\n"
   << "The clue for ESPOO is \"" << dictionary1["ESPOO"] << "\"\n";

cout << "\nThere are " << dictionary1.size()
   << " words in the dictionary\n\n";

// use subscript operator to write value
dictionary1["ESPOO"] = "Typo in name";
cout << "The clue for ESPOO is \"" << dictionary1["ESPOO"] << "\"";

// get rid of mis-spelling
dictionary1.erase( "ESPOO" );

// make a dictionary out of a multimap
typedef multimap<string,string> Dictionary;
Dictionary dictionary2( dictionary1.begin(),
   dictionary1.end() );
dictionary2.insert( make_pair( "POPS", "Bursts" ) );
dictionary2.insert( make_pair( "POPS", "Fathers" ) );
dictionary2.insert( make_pair( "ADAM", "Madam I'm ____" ) );

// display all clues for one word
cout << "\n\nALL CLUES FOR \"POPS\"";
pair<Dictionary::iterator,Dictionary::iterator> range =
   dictionary2.equal_range( "POPS" );
for( Dictionary::iterator i = range.first; i != range.second; ++i )
   cout << "\nPOPS - " << i->second;

cout << "\n\nALL WORDS IN THE DICTIONARY\n";
for( Dictionary::iterator i = dictionary2.begin();
   i != dictionary2.end(); ++i )
   cout << i->first << " - " << i->second << endl;
}
```

The output is

```
There are 5 words in the dictionary

The clue for POPS is "Sodas"
The clue for TAT is "Not solace, sew-lace?"
The clue for ESPOO is ""

There are 6 words in the dictionary

The clue for ESPOO is "Typo in name"

ALL CLUES FOR "POPS"
POPS - Sodas
POPS - Bursts
POPS - Fathers

ALL WORDS IN THE DICTIONARY
ADAM - Alpha male?
ADAM - Madam I'm ____
ESPOO - Second largest Finnish city
HABITFORMING - Making nuns' clothes?
POPS - Sodas
POPS - Bursts
POPS - Fathers
TAT - Not solace, sew-lace?
```

The program in Listing 7.2 is an example of making a crossword puzzle dictionary. The key is a single puzzle word, though it may actually contain more than one word. The value is a clue that the player uses to guess the word. The code starts by initializing a map with some values using the technique of Tip 34. The map key is a text string and the value is also text. The first line of the output shows that there are five words in the dictionary.

The next statement in the code demonstrates the use of the subscript operator ([]) to get the value associated with a key. An important difference between map subscripting and that of a vector or C-style array is that a map index can't be wrong. If the indexed key doesn't exist, the map adds a new element with that key. The map makes the value associated with the key by calling the value's default constructor, so if you're using a class as a key, make sure it has this kind of constructor. (For numbers, this is 0.)

There are several implications of this automatic addition of keys. One is that the subscript operator is not available for constant maps because you can't write to them. Another implication is that although having indexing that always works lets you write some code more cleanly, it also can lead to accidental insertions into the map, especially when there are misspellings. For example, the program gets the values associated with three keys by using the keys as indexes, but the third key has a common error—the numeral 0 instead of the letter "O." The output shows that the clue for that word is the blank string (there's nothing between the quotation marks). That value arises because when the map can't find the misspelled key, it turns the key into a new key with a value given by a string's default constructor, namely, the empty string. The next line of the output confirms that the map has one more element than it had before.

Because the subscript operator returns a reference to the key's value, you can use this operator on the left side of an assignment to change the value. The code demonstrates this by replacing the empty string with some text, as the output shows. Then the program deletes that key before using the map in the next step.

Words in crossword puzzles have many different clues. Part of the fun of making puzzles is thinking of funny or clever clues. A map can't accept multiple clues for a single word because the word is a key and keys must be unique. However, a multimap doesn't have to have distinct keys, so it's perfect for storing words with multiple clues.

The program makes a multimap by using the form of its constructor that accepts an input range, as Tip 6 explains. The program then inserts some entries with duplicate keys into the multimap. There are various ways of putting a key and value together into a pair data structure, but using the STL utility function `make_pair` as shown is the easiest. (Tip 45 provides details on `pair` and `make_pair`.)

To confirm that a multimap can hold duplicate keys, the program displays all the clues for one of the words. A multimap holds all keys in one contiguous stretch of its iterator range. To get this range, use the member function `equal_range`, which returns the position of the first element with the given key and one past the position of the last element with that key. If `equal_range` can't find any elements with the key, both returned values are the same and equal to the end iterator of the multimap. This prevents the subsequent loop in the code from executing. In this application, the loop does run and the output shows all of the clues for one word. Finally, to display the whole dictionary, the program loops over the entire range of the container. Again, the output demonstrates that multimaps can hold elements with the same key.

TIP 36   SEARCH IN SETS AND MULTISETS

Applies to: Set, multiset, find, find_if
See also: Tip 34, Tip 45, Tip 47, Tip 48, Tip 50, Tip 59

Quick Solution

```
set<int> s;
// ...

set<int>::iterator site = s.find( 45 );
if( site != s.end() )
    cout << value << " in set";
else
    cout << value << " not in set";
```

See detailed solution for finding entries by variables other than value and searching in multisets.

Detailed Solution

The *raison d'être* of sets and multisets is quick searching and retrieval. You can search for a particular value in these associative containers tremendously faster than in the standard sequential containers, but to get this great performance, you need to use the find member function of the set and multiset. If you use the find or find_if STL algorithm, they'll work, but you'll be reduced to sluggish searching and miss the chief benefit of sets and multisets.

Sometimes, however, you need to search in a set or multiset for something other than the container's data type. For example, if the container holds a class, you might be looking for instances with a data member that has a particular value. You can do that kind of searching, but you won't be able to use the power of the associative container's find member function.

The program in Listing 7.3 shows how to find the first and last matching elements in a set and multiset and how to find all such elements. The searches can be by value (data type) or not by value.

LISTING 7.3 Searching in Sets and Multisets

```
// associative_search_set.cpp

#include <algorithm>
#include <functional>
#include <iostream>
#include <set>
#include <string>
#include <utility>
#include <vector>

using namespace std;
```

```cpp
class Dog
{
    public:
    Dog( string name = "Unknown", string breed = "Poodle",
        int year = 2000 );
    bool operator<( const Dog& rhs ) const;
    // return true if name is less than passed name, false otherwise

    string breed() const;
    string name() const;

    void print() const;
    // display info on the dog

    int year() const;

    private:
    string breed_;
    string name_;
    int year_;
};

inline
Dog::Dog( string name, string breed, int year )
    : breed_( breed ), name_( name ), year_( year )
{} // empty

inline
bool Dog::operator<( const Dog& rhs ) const
{ return name() < rhs.name(); }

inline
string Dog::breed() const
{ return breed_; }

inline
string Dog::name() const
{ return name_; }

inline
void Dog::print() const
{
    cout << name() << ", a " << breed() << ", won in " << year()
        << endl;
```

```cpp
}

inline
int Dog::year() const
{ return year_; }

bool equal_breed( const Dog winner, string breed );
// return true if Dog is the passed breed, false otherwise

int main( )
{
   // winners of the Westminster Kennel Club championship for 1971-1975
   const char* breed[] = { "Spaniel (English Springer)",
      "Spaniel (English Springer)", "Poodle (Standard)",
      "Pointer (German Shorthaired)", "Old English Sheepdog" };
   const char* name[] = { "Chinoe's Adamant James",
      "Chinoe's Adamant James", "Acadia Command Performance",
      "Gretchenhof  Columbia River", "Sir Lancelot of Barvan" };
   const int year[] = { 1971, 1972, 1973, 1974, 1975 };
   const int num_dogs = sizeof( breed ) / sizeof( breed[0] );

   // create and store breeds for use below
   vector<Dog> v;
   for( int i = 0; i < num_dogs; ++i )
      v.push_back( Dog( name[i], breed[i], year[i] ) );

   // dog to inquire about
   const Dog query( "Chinoe's Adamant James" );
   cout << "*** SET ***\nDID " << query.name()
      << " EVER WIN BEST-IN-SHOW?\n";

   // make a set. The values are instances of the Dog class
   set<Dog> winner_set( v.begin(), v.end() );
   set<Dog>::const_iterator winner_set_end = winner_set.end();

   // search in the set by value
   set<Dog>::const_iterator spot = winner_set.find( query );
   if( spot != winner_set_end )
      spot->print();
   else
      cout << query.name() << " never won best-in-show\n";

   const string query_breed( "Spaniel (English Springer)" );
```

```cpp
// first occurrence in set, not by value
cout << "\nFIRST ENTRY FOR A " << query_breed << endl;
for( spot = winner_set.begin(); spot != winner_set_end; ++spot )
   if( spot->breed() == query_breed )
      break;

if( spot != winner_set_end )
   spot->print();
else
   cout << "A " << query_breed << " didn't win in 1971-1975\n";

// last occurrence in set, not by value
cout << "\nLAST ENTRY FOR A " << query_breed << endl;
set<Dog>::const_reverse_iterator last1;
set<Dog>::const_reverse_iterator winner_set_rend
   = winner_set.rend();
for( last1 = winner_set.rbegin(); last1 != winner_set_rend;
   ++last1 )
   if( last1->breed() == query_breed )
      break;

if( last1 != winner_set_rend )
   last1->print();
else
   cout << "A " << query_breed << " didn't win in 1971-1975\n";

// all occurrences in a set, not by value
cout << "\nALL ENTRIES FOR A " << query_breed << endl;
bool found = false;
for( spot = winner_set.begin(); spot != winner_set_end; ++spot )
   if( spot->breed() == query_breed )
   {
      found = true;
      spot->print();
   }
if( !found )
   cout << "A " << query_breed << " didn't win in 1971-1975\n";

// now work with a multiset
multiset<Dog> winner_multiset( v.begin(), v.end() );

// find first occurrence in multiset, by value
cout << "\n*** MULTISET ***\nFIRST ENTRY FOR " << query.name()
   << endl;
```

```cpp
multiset<Dog>::const_iterator site = winner_multiset.find( query );
if( site != winner_multiset.end() )
   site->print();
else
   cout << query.name() << " never won in 1971-1975\n";

// search for all occurrences by value
pair<multiset<Dog>::iterator,multiset<Dog>::iterator>
   range = winner_multiset.equal_range( query );

// find last occurrence in multiset, by value
cout << "\nLAST ENTRY FOR " << query.name() << endl;
if( range.first != range.second )
{
   site = range.second;
   (--site)->print();
}
else
   cout << query.name() << " never won in 1971-1975\n";

// find all occurrences in multiset, by value
cout << "\nEVERY WIN BY " << query.name() << endl;
if( range.first != range.second )
   for_each( range.first, range.second,
      mem_fun_ref( &Dog::print ) );
else
   cout << query.name() << " never won in 1971-1975\n";

// first occurrence in multiset, not by value
cout << "\nFIRST ENTRY FOR A " << query_breed << endl;
site = find_if( winner_multiset.begin(), winner_multiset.end(),
   bind2nd( ptr_fun( equal_breed ), query_breed ) );
if( site != winner_multiset.end() )
   site->print();
else
   cout << "A " << query_breed << " didn't win in 1971-1975\n";

// last occurrence in multiset, not by value
cout << "\nLAST ENTRY FOR A " << query_breed << endl;
multiset<Dog>::reverse_iterator last2 =
   find_if( winner_multiset.rbegin(), winner_multiset.rend(),
   bind2nd( ptr_fun( equal_breed ), query_breed ) );
if( last2 != winner_multiset.rend() )
   last2->print();
```

```
      else
         cout << "A " << query_breed << " didn't win in 1971-1975\n";

      // all occurrences in a multiset, not by value
      cout << "\nALL ENTRIES FOR A " << query_breed << endl;
      multiset<Dog>::const_iterator winner_multiset_end
         = winner_multiset.end();
      found = false;
      for( site = winner_multiset.begin(); site != winner_multiset_end;
         ++site )
         if( equal_breed( *site, query_breed ) )
         {  found = true;
            site->print();
         }
      if( !found )
         cout << "A " << query_breed << " didn't win in 1971-1975\n";
}

inline
bool equal_breed( const Dog winner, string breed )
{ return winner.breed() == breed; }
```

The output is

```
*** SET ***
DID Chinoe's Adamant James EVER WIN BEST-IN-SHOW?
Chinoe's Adamant James, a Spaniel (English Springer), won in 1971

FIRST ENTRY FOR A Spaniel (English Springer)
Chinoe's Adamant James, a Spaniel (English Springer), won in 1971

LAST ENTRY FOR A Spaniel (English Springer)
Chinoe's Adamant James, a Spaniel (English Springer), won in 1971

ALL ENTRIES FOR A Spaniel (English Springer)
Chinoe's Adamant James, a Spaniel (English Springer), won in 1971

*** MULTISET ***
FIRST ENTRY FOR Chinoe's Adamant James
Chinoe's Adamant James, a Spaniel (English Springer), won in 1971

LAST ENTRY FOR Chinoe's Adamant James
Chinoe's Adamant James, a Spaniel (English Springer), won in 1972  →
```

```
EVERY WIN BY Chinoe's Adamant James
Chinoe's Adamant James, a Spaniel (English Springer), won in 1971
Chinoe's Adamant James, a Spaniel (English Springer), won in 1972

FIRST ENTRY FOR A Spaniel (English Springer)
Chinoe's Adamant James, a Spaniel (English Springer), won in 1971

LAST ENTRY FOR A Spaniel (English Springer)
Chinoe's Adamant James, a Spaniel (English Springer), won in 1972

ALL ENTRIES FOR A Spaniel (English Springer)
Chinoe's Adamant James, a Spaniel (English Springer), won in 1971
Chinoe's Adamant James, a Spaniel (English Springer), won in 1972
```

The program illustrates searching in sets and multisets by using them to hold information about winners of a dog show. The code starts by declaring a class that holds the dog's name, breed, and the year the dog won the show. The code declares the less-than operator, which is necessary because it's used as the default sorting criterion in the associative containers. In this code, the operator sorts by the dog's name. The class also has accessors to retrieve the information and a member function to display its data.

The main part of the program starts by creating and storing instances of the class in a vector. In fact, the code uses the best-in-show winners from 1971 to 1975 at the Westminster Kennel Club competition. This is the oldest and most prestigious dog show in the United States [Dog04].

To search the values in a set, you need to pass its `find` member function the same data type that the set has. `find` uses the element's less-than operator to find an equivalent to the value passed, but the dog class's less-than operator only uses one of the three data members—the dog's name. Thus, the program creates an instance of the dog class with the name of the dog to be looked for as a parameter to the constructor. Because the other two parameters are irrelevant to the search, the code uses the constructor's default values.

Next, the program creates a set from the vector by passing the begin and end vector iterators to the set's constructor. This technique is similar to the one in Tip 34. The program then searches the set for the particular dog by using the set's `find` member function, which returns an iterator that marks the desired element. If one isn't found, the code sets the iterator equal to the set's end iterator. The output shows that there is a winner with the given name. In fact, that dog won twice, but the set's constructor ignored the second win because a set can't hold duplicate elements. Only having unique elements also means that there is no need for special techniques to find the last matching element or all matching elements because those are the same as the first matching element.

You might want to find out if a particular breed has won the show. The less-than operator doesn't use the dog's breed, so the program can't use the `find` member function to look at the winner's breeds. There are a couple of solutions to this problem, though. One is to write a loop that marches through the set's elements until it finds a dog of the right breed. Another is to use the STL algorithm `find_if`. Each method has its pros and cons, but both ways are much slower than searching with the set's `find` member function.

The code first illustrates using a loop by looking for the first dog of a specified breed. As soon as it finds one, the program makes the element display its internal information and breaks out of the loop. If there isn't a match, the loop iterator is equal to the set's end iterator. The code tests for this after the loop and displays a message saying that it couldn't find that particular breed. Note that the program stores a local copy of the set's (and later the multiset's) end iterator. This speeds up the execution of the subsequent loop because it doesn't have to call the container's `end` member function at each loop iteration.

To find the last winner with the specified breed, the software uses an identical loop, but with reverse iterators instead of the normal, forward iterators. The advantage of using loops to find the first and last matching elements is that you don't have to write a functor or a global function as you do to use `find_if`. The disadvantage is that you have more code to write in the main body.

To find all dogs of the particular breed, the code uses a loop that is similar to the previous ones. In this case, though, the loop must examine every element, so the last value of the loop iterator is always equal to the set's end iterator. Because the code can't determine from the loop iterator if the search was successful or not, the loop sets a Boolean variable to `true` whenever the loop finds a match. The code then tests this variable after the loop finishes. The output shows the results of searching for the first, last, and all dogs of the indicated breed.

The second half of the program does the same searches, but on a multiset. To find the first matching value, the program uses the multiset's `find` member function as before. To find the last and all matching values, the program uses another member function, `equal_range`. This function returns two iterators in a `pair` data structure (see Tip 45). The first member of the pair, `first`, points to the first element in the multiset that is not less than the value passed to `find`. The second member of the pair, `second`, points to the first element that is greater than the passed value. In other words, this is the range (in the standard STL sense) of the matching values. If the two iterators in the pair are the same, there were no matches.

If `find` did locate something, the code makes a copy of the second iterator and decrements it to get the last matching element. The program can decrement the iterator because a multiset's iterators are bidirectional. The program needs to decrement the iterator because it is the last one in the range and, thus, is actually one past the last matching element.

The principal use of the two iterators is to define the range of all matching values, not just the last one. Once you have the range, you can do many things with the elements. The code gives an example by having each of the elements in the range display its information. (Tip 48 and Tip 59 explain this technique.) The output shows the results of searching for the first, last, and all matching values. A multiset can contain duplicate entries, so both wins of the dog now appear. Note, too, that all these searches are fast because the code performs them with the multiset's find member function.

As with a set, sometimes it may be necessary to search a multiset containing a class, not for matching values (elements), but for matching data members. The first half of the program shows how to do that using loops. The code for the multiset illustrates an alternative. To look for the first dog of a specified breed the program uses the STL algorithm find_if. The first two arguments are the range of the multiset and the last argument is the match criterion. find_if applies the criterion to each element in turn and stops when the criterion is true or when it reaches the end of the range. The criterion is a custom global function that accepts two arguments—an instance of the dog class and a string with the desired dog breed. The function returns true if the dog's breed is the desired one and false otherwise. The predefined functor bind2nd makes the second argument to the function be constant during the execution of find_if (see Tip 50). To use the binder on the global function, Tip 47 explains that you must wrap the function in a call to ptr_fun, another predefined functor. find_if returns an iterator that marks the first element that makes the criterion be true. If the iterator is equal to the end of the range, the algorithm can't find a suitable element. To find the last value with the specified breed, the code uses the same technique, but with reverse iterators. The output shows the results of both searches.

Even though the program uses an STL algorithm, the searches are much slower than those performed by the multiset's find member function. The advantage of using the algorithm over a loop (as the search of the set demonstrates) is that there is less code to write. The disadvantage is that you have to create a functor or a global function to pass to find_if. If you can use the function at least a few times, it's better to go the STL route than to code the loops.

The last thing the program does is to find all dogs of the specified breed. Although you can do this with find_if, it's cleaner to just write a loop as shown. The loop is the same as that used to search the set except that it calls the global function to test the breed instead of doing the comparison explicitly. Using a function instead of an explicit test is better style because it reuses software (the function) and increases modularity by encapsulating the test for the breed inside that function. The output shows that two of the wins were by dogs of the specified breed.

The real power of sets and multisets is their extremely fast searches for matching values. If you find yourself searching a lot for things other than the values, such as data members in classes, you're missing the benefit of these containers. You may want to change your sorting criterion or perhaps switch to a different container.

TIP 37   SEARCH IN MAPS AND MULTIMAPS

Applies to: Map, multimap, find, find_if
See also: Tip 34, Tip 45, Tip 47, Tip 50

Quick Solution

```
map<string,Employee> m;
// ...

map<string,Employee>::iterator site = m.find( "492-87-7844" );
if( site != m.end() )
   cout << key << "in map";
else
   cout << key << " not in map";
```

See detailed solution for finding entries by value and searching in multimaps.

Detailed Solution

Maps and multimaps store indexed data. Each element of these containers has a key and a value. A map or multimap gives you extremely fast searching of and access to elements by key. To get this benefit, though, you must use the containers' `find` member function. The `find` or `find_if` STL algorithms will work, but they'll be much slower. Occasionally, however, you might need to search in a map or multimap for a value, not a key. In this case, the two STL algorithms can be quite helpful.

The program in Listing 7.4 demonstrates finding the first and last matching elements in a map and multimap, shows how to find all such elements, and shows how to search for them by key or value.

LISTING 7.4   Searching in Maps and Multimaps

```
// associative_search_map.cpp

#include <algorithm>
#include <functional>
```

```
#include <iomanip>
#include <iostream>
#include <map>
#include <string>
#include <utility>
#include <vector>

using namespace std;

class Appliance
{
   public:
   enum Appliance_type { washer, dryer, refrigerator, freezer };

   Appliance( Appliance_type appliance = washer, int model = 220,
      int serial = 0 );

   bool operator<( const Appliance& rhs ) const;
   // order by ascending appliance number and within appliance number
   // by ascending model number

   Appliance_type appliance() const;
   int model() const;
   string name() const;

   void print() const;
   // display information about the appliance

   int serial() const;

   private:
   Appliance_type appliance_;
   int model_;
   int serial_;

};

inline
Appliance::Appliance( Appliance::Appliance_type appliance, int model,
   int serial )
   : appliance_( appliance ), model_( model ), serial_( serial )
{} // empty

inline
```

```
bool Appliance::operator<( const Appliance& rhs ) const
{ return appliance() < rhs.appliance() ||
   ( appliance() == rhs.appliance() && model() < rhs.model() );
}

inline
Appliance::Appliance_type Appliance::appliance() const
{ return appliance_; }

inline
int Appliance::model() const
{ return model_; }

string Appliance::name() const
{
   string what;
   switch( appliance() )
   {
      case washer:         what = "Washer";              break;
      case dryer:          what = "Dryer";               break;
      case refrigerator:   what = "Refrigerator";        break;
      case freezer:        what = "Freezer";             break;
      default:             what = "Unknown appliance";   break;
   }
   return what;
}

inline
void Appliance::print() const
{
   char oldfill = cout.fill();
   cout << setw( 12 ) << setfill( ' ' ) << name() << " - Model "
      << setw( 3 ) << model() << ", Serial number " << setw( 8 )
      << setfill( '0' ) << serial() << setfill( oldfill ) << endl;
}

inline
int Appliance::serial() const
{ return serial_; }

bool greater_model( const pair<Appliance::Appliance_type,Appliance> p,
   int min_model );
// return true if the model in p.second is >= min_model,
// otherwise returns false
```

```cpp
int main( )
{
   const Appliance::Appliance_type kind[] = { Appliance::refrigerator,
      Appliance::refrigerator, Appliance::washer, Appliance::dryer,
      Appliance::dryer, Appliance::dryer };
   const int model[] = { 220, 221, 19, 250, 350, 350 };
   const int serial[] = { 457792, 549970, 33447, 2298764, 2302971,
      2298765 };
   const int num_appliances = sizeof( kind ) / sizeof( kind[0] );

   // create and store appliances for use below
   vector<Appliance> v;
   for( int i = 0; i < num_appliances; ++i )
      v.push_back( Appliance( kind[i], model[i], serial[i] ) );

   // map key is serial number, value is Appliance
   map<int,Appliance> sold;

   // load the appliances into the map and display them
   transform( serial, serial+num_appliances, v.begin(),
      inserter( sold, sold.end() ),
      make_pair<int,Appliance> );
   map<int,Appliance>::const_iterator sold_end = sold.end();

   // first work with a map
   cout << "*** MAP ***\nAPPLIANCES BY SERIAL NUMBER\n";
   map<int,Appliance>::const_iterator site;
   for( site = sold.begin(); site != sold_end; ++site )
      site->second.print();

   // search by key
   const int desired_serial = 33447;
   cout << "\nINFORMATION AVAILABLE FOR SERIAL NUMBER "
      << desired_serial << "?\n";
   site = sold.find( desired_serial );
   if( site != sold_end )
      site->second.print();
   else
      cout << "There is no appliance with serial number "
         << desired_serial << endl;

   const Appliance::Appliance_type desired_type
      = Appliance::refrigerator;
   cout << "\nANY REFRIGERATORS SOLD?\n";
```

```cpp
// find the first element by value
cout << "\nFIRST REFRIGERATOR SOLD\n";
for( site = sold.begin(); site != sold_end; ++site )
   if( site->second.appliance() == desired_type )
      break;

if( site != sold_end )
   site->second.print();
else
   cout << "No refrigerators sold\n";

// find the last element by value
cout << "\nLAST REFRIGERATOR SOLD\n";
map<int,Appliance>::const_reverse_iterator reverse_site;
map<int,Appliance>::const_reverse_iterator sold_rend
   = sold.rend();
for( reverse_site = sold.rbegin(); reverse_site != sold_rend;
   ++reverse_site )
   if( reverse_site->second.appliance() == desired_type )
      break;

if( reverse_site != sold_rend )
   reverse_site->second.print();
else
   cout << "No refrigerators sold\n";

// find all elements by value
cout << "\nALL REFRIGERATORS SOLD\n";
bool found = false;
for( site = sold.begin(); site != sold_end; ++site )
   if( site->second.appliance() == desired_type )
   {
      found = true;
      site->second.print();
   }
if( !found )
   cout << "No refrigerators sold\n";

// work with a multimap. key is appliance type, value is Appliance
typedef multimap<Appliance::Appliance_type,Appliance>
   Appliance_multimap_type;

Appliance_multimap_type stock;
```

```cpp
// appliance that customer desires
const Appliance desired( Appliance::dryer );
cout << "\n\nCUSTOMER WOULD LIKE A " << desired.name()
   << endl << endl;

// load the appliances into the multimap
transform( kind, kind+num_appliances, v.begin(),
   inserter( stock, stock.end() ),
   make_pair<Appliance::Appliance_type,Appliance> );
Appliance_multimap_type::const_iterator stock_end = stock.end();

// search for first occurrence of key
Appliance_multimap_type::const_iterator spot
   = stock.find( desired.appliance() );
cout << "FIRST " << desired.name() << " IN STOCK\n";
if( spot != stock_end )
   spot->second.print();
else
   cout << "Don't have a " << desired.name() << " in stock\n";

// search for all occurrences of key
pair<Appliance_multimap_type::iterator,
   Appliance_multimap_type::iterator>
   range = stock.equal_range( desired.appliance() );

// last occurrence of key
cout << "\nLAST " << desired.name() << " IN STOCK\n";
if( range.first != range.second )
{
   spot = range.second;
   --spot;
   spot->second.print();
}
else
   cout << "Don't have a " << desired.name() << " in stock\n";

// all occurrences of key
cout << "\nEVERY " << desired.name() << " IN STOCK\n";
if( range.first != range.second )
   for( spot = range.first; spot != range.second; ++spot )
      spot->second.print();
else
   cout << "Don't have a " << desired.name() << " in stock\n";
```

```
// search for first occurrence of value
const int min_model = 221;
spot = find_if( stock.begin(), stock.end(),
  bind2nd( ptr_fun( greater_model ), min_model ) );

cout << "\nFIRST APPLIANCE WITH MODEL AT LEAST " << min_model
  << endl;
if( spot != stock_end )
  spot->second.print();
else
  cout << "No appliance with model at least than " << min_model
    << endl;

// search for last occurrence of value
multimap<Appliance::Appliance_type,Appliance>::reverse_iterator j =
  find_if( stock.rbegin(), stock.rend(),
    bind2nd( ptr_fun( greater_model ), min_model ) );

cout << "\nLAST APPLIANCE WITH MODEL AT LEAST " << min_model
  << endl;
if( j != stock.rend() )
  j->second.print();
else
  cout << "No appliance with model number at least "
    << min_model << endl;

// search for all occurrences of value
cout << "\nALL APPLIANCES WITH MODEL AT LEAST " << min_model
  << endl;
found = false;
for( spot = stock.begin(); spot != stock_end; ++spot )
  if( greater_model( *spot, min_model ) )
  {
    found = true;
    spot->second.print();
  }
if( !found )
  cout << "No appliance with model number at least "
    << min_model << endl;
}

inline
bool greater_model( const pair<Appliance::Appliance_type,Appliance> p,
  int min_model )
```

```
{ return p.second.model() >= min_model; }
```

The output is

```
*** MAP ***
APPLIANCES BY SERIAL NUMBER
      Washer - Model  19, Serial number 00033447
Refrigerator - Model 220, Serial number 00457792
Refrigerator - Model 221, Serial number 00549970
       Dryer - Model 250, Serial number 02298764
       Dryer - Model 350, Serial number 02298765
       Dryer - Model 350, Serial number 02302971

INFORMATION AVAILABLE FOR SERIAL NUMBER 33447?
      Washer - Model  19, Serial number 00033447

ANY REFRIGERATORS SOLD?

FIRST REFRIGERATOR SOLD
Refrigerator - Model 220, Serial number 00457792

LAST REFRIGERATOR SOLD
Refrigerator - Model 221, Serial number 00549970

ALL REFRIGERATORS SOLD
Refrigerator - Model 220, Serial number 00457792
Refrigerator - Model 221, Serial number 00549970

CUSTOMER WOULD LIKE A Dryer

FIRST Dryer IN STOCK
       Dryer - Model 250, Serial number 02298764

LAST Dryer IN STOCK
       Dryer - Model 350, Serial number 02298765

EVERY Dryer IN STOCK
       Dryer - Model 250, Serial number 02298764
       Dryer - Model 350, Serial number 02302971
       Dryer - Model 350, Serial number 02298765

FIRST APPLIANCE WITH MODEL AT LEAST 221
       Dryer - Model 250, Serial number 02298764            →
```

```
LAST APPLIANCE WITH MODEL AT LEAST 221
Refrigerator - Model 221, Serial number 00549970

ALL APPLIANCES WITH MODEL AT LEAST 221
        Dryer - Model 250, Serial number 02298764
        Dryer - Model 350, Serial number 02302971
        Dryer - Model 350, Serial number 02298765
  Refrigerator - Model 221, Serial number 00549970
```

The program illustrates searching in maps and multimaps by using them to hold information about appliances. This might be used, for example, at an appliance store or warehouse to monitor the stock or to look up information about a particular machine that was sold. The code starts by declaring a class that holds the kind of appliance and the model and serial numbers. The code declares the less-than operator, which is necessary because it's used as the default sorting criterion in associative containers. In the class in the program, the operator returns `true` if the appliance type on the left is less than that on the right (the types are numbered in the class by an `enum` statement) or if the types are the same and the model number on the left is less than that on the right. In all other cases, the operator returns `false`. In effect, this sorts the appliances by type and within type by model. The class also has accessors to retrieve the information and a member function to display its data.

The main part of the program starts by creating and storing instances of the class in a vector, then uses the technique of Tip 34 to initialize the map. The map key is the serial number, and the map values are instances of the appliance class. The program then displays all the elements in the map, as the output shows. Although a map can't have duplicate keys, all the machines that have been sold are present because they (presumably) have unique serial numbers.

The first search is by key, which is the typical way to look for something in a map. In this case, the code looks for a machine with a particular serial number, perhaps because a customer has reported a problem with it. The map's `find` member function does the work and passes back an iterator that marks the desired element. If `find` can't locate the key, it sets the iterator equal to the map's end iterator. The element that the iterator actually points to is a `pair` data structure (see Tip 45) whose second member (`second`) is the value associated with the specified key. Thus, to get to the element's value from the iterator, you first have to go to the pair's second member and then access the display member function from there. These operations can be chained, as the code illustrates. The output shows that a washer has the given serial number. Note that because all keys in a map are unique, you don't need any special techniques to find the last matching key or all matching keys—they're the same as the first matching key.

You might want to find out if the store has sold a particular kind of appliance, and if so, to see the information about that machine. The appliance type is not the key, so you can't use the map's `find` member function. There are a couple of alternatives, though. One is to write a loop that goes through the map's elements until it finds an element value that has the right kind of appliance. Another alternative is to use the STL algorithm `find_if`. Each method has its pros and cons, but both ways are much slower than is searching by key.

The code first illustrates using a loop by looking for the first appliance sold that is a refrigerator. As soon as the loop finds an element with such an appliance, the program makes the element display information about the appliance and breaks out of the loop. If there isn't a match, the loop iterator is equal to the map's end iterator. The code tests for this after the loop and displays a message saying that it couldn't find a refrigerator. Throughout the program, the code stores a local copy of the map or multimap's end iterator. This speeds up the execution of the subsequent loop because it doesn't have to call the container's `end` member function at each loop iteration.

To find the last refrigerator, the software uses an identical loop but with reverse iterators instead of the forward iterators. The advantage of using loops to find the first and last matching elements is that you don't have to write a functor or a global function as you do to use `find_if`. The disadvantage is that you have more code to write in the main body.

To find all refrigerators sold, the code uses a loop that is similar to the previous ones. In this case, though, the program must examine every element, so the last value of the loop iterator is always equal to the map's end iterator. Because the code can't determine from the loop iterator if the search was successful or not, the loop sets a Boolean variable to true whenever it finds a match. The code then tests this variable after the loop finishes. The output shows the results of searching for the first, last, and all refrigerators that the store has sold.

The second half of the program illustrates a situation in which the software should keep track of the appliances in stock. A customer is likely to be looking for one particular kind of appliance, so the key to use is the appliance type. Many machines of this kind could be in stock, so the data structure must be able to hold duplicate keys, that is, it must be a multimap, not a map.

To find the first matching key, the code uses the multimap's `find` member function. To find the last or all matching keys, the code uses another member function, `equal_range`. This function returns two iterators in a `pair` data structure (see Tip 45). The first member of the pair, `first`, points to the first element in the multimap whose key is not less than that passed to `find`. The second member of the pair, `second`, points to the first element whose key is greater than the passed key. In other words, this is the range of the matching keys. If the two iterators in the pair are the same, there were no matches.

If `find` does locate something, the code makes a copy of the second iterator and decrements it to get the last matching element. The program can decrement the iterator because a multimap's iterators are bidirectional. The program has to decrement the iterator because it is the last one in the range, that is, it's actually one past the last matching element.

The main use of the two iterators is to define the range of all matching values, not just the last one. Once you have the range, you can do several things with the elements, for example, have each display its information. The output shows the results of searching for the first, last, and all matching dryers. All these searches are fast because the code performs them with the multimap's `find` member function.

Sometimes it may be necessary to search a multimap for matching values rather than for matching keys. The first half of the program shows how to do that using loops. The code for the multimap illustrates an alternative. To look for the first appliance whose model number has a specified minimum value, the program uses the STL algorithm `find_if`. (This search might occur if higher model numbers imply newer models and the customer requests an appliance made within the last so many years.) The first two arguments of `find_if` are the range of the multimap and the last argument is the match criterion. `find_if` applies the criterion to each element in turn and stops when the criterion is true or when it reaches the end of the range. The criterion is a custom global function that accepts two arguments—a pair data structure with a key and value and an integer with the minimum model number. The function returns `true` if the model number of the appliance in the value is at least as great as the minimum one and `false` otherwise. The predefined functor `bind2nd` makes the second argument to the function be constant during the execution of `find_if` (see Tip 50). To use the binder on the global function, Tip 47 explains that you must wrap the function in a call to `ptr_fun`, another predefined functor. `find_if` returns an iterator that marks the first element that makes the criterion be true. If the iterator is equal to the end of the range, the algorithm can't find a suitable element. To find the last value with the specified breed, the code uses the same technique, but with reverse iterators. The output shows the results of both searches.

Even though the program uses an STL algorithm, the searches are much slower than those performed by the multimap's `find` member function. The advantage of using the algorithm over a loop is that there is less to write, as the code for searching the map demonstrates. The disadvantage is that you have to create a global function to pass to `find_if`. However, if you can reuse the function, do so and avoid writing loops by hand.

The last thing the program does is to find all appliances whose model number is at least some minimum value. Although you can do this with `find_if`, it's cleaner to just write a loop as shown. The loop is very similar to that used for searching the map except that it calls the global function to test the model number instead of doing the comparison explicitly. This is better style because it reuses software (the function) and increases modularity by encapsulating the test for the model number inside that function. The output shows that there are four appliances in stock whose model number is at least 221.

The real power of maps and multimaps is their extremely fast searches for keys. If you find yourself searching frequently for values, you're missing the benefit of these containers. You may want to change your key or perhaps switch to a different container.

TIP 38   MODIFY OR REMOVE ELEMENTS IN A SET OR MULTISET

Applies to: Set, multiset
See also: Tip 4, Tip 36, Tip 45

Quick Solution

```
set<int> s;
// ...

s.erase( 45 ); // remove value

// modify by replacing old with new
if( s.erase( 77 ) == 1 ) // did remove one entry

    if( s.insert( 80 ).second )
        cout << "Inserted new value";
    else
        cout << "New value already exists";
```

See detailed solution for removing and modifying in multisets.

Detailed Solution

Once you've created your set or multiset and filled it with data, you're ready to start using its speedy search and retrieval capabilities. It's perfectly reasonable to occasionally want to change or delete some values. This tip shows you how to modify or remove a value in a set and how to do the same for a single value or all values in a multiset. As the program in Listing 7.5 shows, to modify a value you have to erase it and insert a new one. Be aware that each time you do either of these actions, the container takes the time to re-sort itself. This isn't very lengthy, though—it's approximately the time to search the container.

Although the program in Listing 7.5 is a little longer than usual, it shows you quite a bit, namely, how to insert, delete, or modify elements in either a set or multiset.

LISTING 7.5   Modify or Remove a Value in a Set or Multiset

```cpp
// associative_modify_set.cpp

#include <iostream>
#include <set>
#include <vector>

#include "tips.hpp"

using namespace std;

int main( )
{
   const int num_grades = 11;
   const int grade[num_grades] = { 2, 5, 3, 8, 9, 9, 6, 3, 5, 9, 10 };

   set<int> unique( grade, grade+num_grades );
   multiset<int> all( grade, grade+num_grades );
   tips::print( unique, "Unique grades" );
   tips::print( all,    "All    grades" );

   const int wrong_grade = 9;
   const int right_grade = 10;
   cout << "\nGRADING ERROR - CHANGE ALL " << wrong_grade << "'S TO "
      << right_grade << "'S\n";

   // modify wrong grade in a set by removing it and inserting the
   // right one in its place
   if( unique.erase( wrong_grade ) == 1 )
   {
      if( unique.insert( right_grade ).second )
         cout << "Added new, unique grade of " << right_grade << endl;
      else
         cout << "Already have unique grade of " << right_grade
            << endl;
   }
   else
      cout << "No unique grade of " << wrong_grade << endl;
```

```cpp
    // modify wrong grades by removing them and inserting the right ones
    // in their place
    multiset<int>::size_type num_wrong = all.erase( wrong_grade );
    if( num_wrong > 0 )
    {
        vector<int> right( num_wrong, right_grade );
        all.insert( right.begin(), right.end() );
        unique.erase( wrong_grade );
        unique.insert( right_grade );
        cout << "Changed " << num_wrong << " grades of "
            << wrong_grade << " to " << right_grade << endl;
    }
    else
        cout << "No wrong grades of " << wrong_grade << endl;

    // one student drops class. Remove just his grade
    const int drop_grade = 5;
    cout << "\nDROP ONE GRADE OF " << drop_grade << endl;
    multiset<int>::iterator spot = all.find( drop_grade );
    if( spot != all.end() )
    {
        all.erase( spot );

        // if no more of that grade left, drop it from the unique grades
        if( all.count( drop_grade ) == 0 )
            unique.erase( drop_grade );
    }
    else
        cout << "Couldn't find a grade of " << drop_grade << endl;

    tips::print( unique, "Final unique grades" );
    tips::print( all,    "All    final grades" );
}
```

The output is

```
Unique grades: 2 3 5 6 8 9 10
All    grades: 2 3 3 5 5 6 8 9 9 9 10

GRADING ERROR - CHANGE ALL 9'S TO 10'S
Already have unique grade of 10
Changed 3 grades of 9 to 10                                    →
```

```
DROP ONE GRADE OF 5
Final unique grades: 2 3 5 6 8 10
All final grades:  2 3 3 5 6 8 10 10 10 10
```

The program starts by storing some quiz grades in a set and multiset and displaying them. Although the original grades are unordered and contain duplicates, the output shows that the grades stored in the set are unique and in ascending order. Thus, the set is good for showing the different grades made in the class, but not the grade for each student. The multiset, which can contain duplicates, keeps all the grades and orders them.

Suppose the teacher discovers he's made a grading error on all students who received a 9 and needs to change all those grades to a 10. For the set, the code would need to change the single value 9 (if it exists) to 10. Unfortunately, the set doesn't have a modify command. You have to change a value indirectly by first deleting it and then adding the new one. To delete a particular value in a set, use the member function erase. It returns the number of values erased, which for a set can only be 0 or 1. To add a value to a set, use its overloaded insert member function. The signature of this version of insert is

```
pair<iterator,bool> insert( value )
```

which inserts a value into the set if the value is not already there. insert returns a pair data structure (see Tip 45). The first member points to the value in the set, either the one that was already there or the newly inserted one. The second member is a Boolean that indicates whether the function inserted the new value. The code checks the second member, appropriately called second, using chained access and displays a message telling whether or not the program inserted a new value into the set. Doing this check isn't necessary because if the value to be inserted already exists, insert doesn't do anything.

Multisets operate very much as sets do. To modify all copies of a value in a multiset, remove all of the old copies and insert the same number of new values. The program does this by first calling the member function erase with the old value. The function returns the number of elements actually removed. If it did erase some, the code creates a vector with the same number of copies of the new value (see Tip 4) and puts them into the multiset using its insert member function. The code also erases the old grade and inserts the new one into the set in order to keep it synchronized with the multiset.

Now suppose one student drops the class. You can't pass his grade to the multiset's erase member function because that will get rid of all such values in the container. To remove just one copy of the value, you can get an iterator that points to the first copy and then delete only that. Tip 36 explains that you can locate the first occurrence of an element by using the `find` member function of the multiset, as the program does. If the function can't find the value, it returns an iterator equal to the container's end iterator. The program verifies that this isn't true and passes the iterator to the multiset's `erase` member function, which deletes only the value marked by that iterator. Again, to make the set reflect what is in the multiset, the code erases the grade from the former if there are no more copies of the grade left in the latter. The code learns this by calling the `count` member function, which returns the number of copies of the passed value that are in the multiset.

TIP 39	

MODIFY OR REMOVE ELEMENTS IN A MAP OR MULTIMAP

Applies to: Map, multimaps
See also: Tip 34, Tip 35, Tip 37, Tip 79

Quick Solution

```
map<string,int> m;
// ...

m["Waikiki"] = 2; // modify value, assuming key is present

// modify key by adding new key, storing old value, and deleting old
// key
m["St. John's"] = m["Waikiki"];
m.erase( "Waikiki" );
```

See detailed solution for modifying and removing in multimaps.

Detailed Solution

Maps and multimaps are handy containers that let you quickly access data based on a key. A map permits only unique keys but has an elegant interface to them—indexing via the subscript operator. A multimap allows duplicate keys, but doesn't have indexing. Both allow you to conveniently change the value associated with a key. However, you may want to do other things, such as changing the key itself, removing a key, and so on. This tip demonstrates many of these operations, including the following:

- Change a map key's associated value
- Change or remove a map key

- Change the first, last, or all copies of a multimap key's associated values
- Change the first, last, or all copies of a value in a multimap
- Remove the first, last, or all copies of a multimap key
- Remove the first, last, or all copies of a multimap value

Keep in mind that the power of the map and multimap comes from accessing their elements by key, not by value. Despite this, sometimes you do have to search through the container by value, as Listing 7.6 shows.

LISTING 7.6   Modify or Remove a Value in a Map or Multimap

```cpp
// associative_modify_map.cpp

#include <algorithm>
#include <iomanip>
#include <iostream>
#include <numeric>
#include <map>
#include <utility>
#include <vector>

using namespace std;

typedef multimap< string, pair<int,int> > city_multimap;
// key = city name, value = <rank,decade>

void print_city( const city_multimap& city );
// display names and ranks of all cities

int main( )
{
    const char* country1950[] = { "China", "India", "United States",
        "Russia", "Japan", "Indonesia" };
    const int num_countries = sizeof( country1950 )
        / sizeof( country1950[0] );

    // make rank contain 1, 2, 3, ... , num_countries
    vector<int> rank( num_countries, 1 );
    partial_sum( rank.begin(), rank.end(), rank.begin() );

    // put country and population rank together and store in map
    map<string,int> country;
    transform( country1950, country1950+num_countries, rank.begin(),
```

```
        inserter( country, country.end() ), make_pair<string,int> );

    cout << "MOST POPULOUS " << country.size()
        << " COUNTRIES IN 1950\n";
    for( map<string,int>::iterator i = country.begin();
        i != country.end(); ++i )
        cout << i->first << " ranks " << i->second << endl;

    // 50 years later, in the year 2000, things have changed

    // modify value of specified key
    country["Indonesia"] = 4;
    country["Russia"] = 6;

    // modify key
    country["Brazil"] = country["Japan"]; // Brazil now has Japan's rank
    country.erase( "Japan" ); // Japan no longer in top 6


    cout << "\nMOST POPULOUS " << country.size()
        << " COUNTRIES IN 2000\n";
    for( map<string,int>::iterator i = country.begin();
        i != country.end(); ++i )
        cout << i->first << " ranks " << i->second << endl;

    // most populous 5 cities (agglomerations) at start of each decade
    const int num_top_cities = 5;
    const char* top_city[] =
        { "Tokyo", "New York", "Shanghai", "Osaka", // 1970
            "Mexico City",
            "Tokyo", "New York", "Mexico City", "Sao Paulo", // 1980
            "Shanghai",
            "Tokyo", "New York", "Mexico City", "Sao Paulo", // 1990
            "Shanghai",
            "Tokyo", "Mexico City", "Sao Paulo", "New York", // 2000
            "Bombay" };
    const int num_cities = sizeof( top_city ) / sizeof( top_city[0] );

    city_multimap city;

    int decade = 1970;
    vector< pair<int,int> > city_info( num_cities );
    for( int i = 0; i < num_cities; ++i )
    {
```

```
      city_info[i] = make_pair( i%num_top_cities + 1, decade );
      if( ( i + 1 ) % num_top_cities == 0 )
         decade += 10;
}

// put city and rank together and store in multimap
transform( top_city, top_city + num_cities, city_info.begin(),
   inserter( city, city.end() ),
   make_pair< string, pair<int,int> > );

cout << "\n\nMOST POPULOUS " << num_top_cities
   << " CITIES IN EACH DECADE OF 1970-2000";
print_city( city );

// modify value of first element that has given key
const char modify_city[] = "New York";
const int modify_rank1 = 8;
city_multimap::iterator site = city.find( modify_city );
if( site != city.end() )
   site->second.first = modify_rank1;
else
   cout << "\nNo elements with key \"" << modify_city << "\"";

// find range of elements with given key
pair<city_multimap::iterator,city_multimap::iterator> range =
   city.equal_range( modify_city );

// modify value of last element with passed key
if( range.first != range.second )
{
   site = range.second;
   --site;
   site->second.first = modify_rank1;
}
else
   cout << "\nNo elements with key \"" << modify_city << "\"";

// modify values of all elements with passed key
if( range.first != range.second )
   for( site = range.first; site != range.second; ++site )
      site->second.first = modify_rank1;
else
   cout << "\nNo elements with key \"" << modify_city << "\"";
```

```cpp
         cout << "\n\nPREVIOUS CITIES WITH RANK OF " << modify_city
            << " CHANGED";
         print_city( city );

         // modify value of first element with specified value
         const int modify_rank2 = modify_rank1 + 1;
         for( site = city.begin(); site != city.end(); ++site )
            if( site->second.first == modify_rank1 )
               break;

         if( site != city.end() )
            site->second.first = modify_rank2;
         else
            cout << "\nNo elements with value " << modify_rank1;

         // modify value of last element with specified value
         city_multimap::reverse_iterator reverse_site = city.rbegin();
         for( ; reverse_site != city.rend(); ++reverse_site )
            if( reverse_site->second.first == modify_rank1 )
               break;

         if( reverse_site != city.rend() )
            reverse_site->second.first = modify_rank2;
         else
            cout << "\nNo elements with value " << modify_rank1;

         // modify value of all elements with specified value
         bool found = false;
         for( site = city.begin(); site != city.end(); ++site )
            if( site->second.first == modify_rank1 )
            {
               site->second.first = modify_rank2;
               found = true;
            }
         if( !found )
            cout << "\nNo elements with value " << modify_rank1;

         cout << "\n\nPREVIOUS CITIES WITH RANK OF " << modify_city
            << " CHANGED AGAIN";
         print_city( city );

         // remove first element with specified key
         site = city.find( modify_city );
         if( site != city.end() )
```

```cpp
      city.erase( site );
else
   cout << "\nNo elements with key \"" << modify_city << "\"";

// remove last element with specified key
range = city.equal_range( modify_city );
if( range.first != range.second )
   city.erase( --range.second );
else
   cout << "\nNo elements with key \"" << modify_city << "\"";

// remove all elements with specified key
city.erase( modify_city );

cout << "\n\nPREVIOUS CITIES WITHOUT " << modify_city;
print_city( city );

// remove first element with value higher than that given
const int max_rank = 3;
for( site = city.begin(); site != city.end(); ++site )
   if( site->second.first > max_rank )
      break;

if( site != city.end() )
   city.erase( site );
else
   cout << "\nNo elements with rank greater than " << max_rank;

// remove last element with value higher than that given
for( reverse_site = city.rbegin(); reverse_site != city.rend();
   ++reverse_site )
   if( reverse_site->second.first > max_rank )
      break;

if( reverse_site != city.rend() )
   city.erase( --reverse_site.base() );
else
   cout << "\nNo elements with rank greater than " << max_rank;

// remove all elements with value higher than that given
found = false;
for( site = city.begin(); site != city.end(); )
   if( site->second.first > max_rank )
   {
```

```
                     city.erase( site++ );
                     found = true;
                }
                else
                   ++site;
           if( !found )
              cout << "\nNo elements with rank greater than " << max_rank;

           cout << "\n\nPREVIOUS CITIES THAT RANK IN TOP " << max_rank;
           print_city( city );

     }


     void print_city( const city_multimap& city )
     {
        if( city.empty() )
           return;

        string city_name;
        for( city_multimap::const_iterator i = city.begin();
           i != city.end(); ++i )
        {
           // if city name not printed, do so
           if( i->first != city_name )
           {
              cout << endl << setw( 11 ) << right << i->first << " ranked: "
                 << left;
              city_name = i->first;
           }

           // print rank and decade
           cout << i->second.first << " in " << setw( 7 )
              << i->second.second;
        }
     }
```

The output is

```
MOST POPULOUS 6 COUNTRIES IN 1950
China ranks 1
India ranks 2
Indonesia ranks 6
Japan ranks 5
Russia ranks 4
United States ranks 3

MOST POPULOUS 6 COUNTRIES IN 2000
Brazil ranks 5
China ranks 1
India ranks 2
Indonesia ranks 4
Russia ranks 6
United States ranks 3

MOST POPULOUS 5 CITIES IN EACH DECADE OF 1970-2000
      Bombay ranked: 5 in 2000
Mexico City ranked: 5 in 1970    3 in 1980    3 in 1990    2 in 2000
   New York ranked: 2 in 1970    2 in 1980    2 in 1990    4 in 2000
       Osaka ranked: 4 in 1970
  Sao Paulo ranked: 4 in 1980    4 in 1990    3 in 2000
   Shanghai ranked: 5 in 1990    5 in 1980    3 in 1970
      Tokyo ranked: 1 in 1990    1 in 1970    1 in 1980    1 in 2000

PREVIOUS CITIES WITH RANK OF New York CHANGED
      Bombay ranked: 5 in 2000
Mexico City ranked: 5 in 1970    3 in 1980    3 in 1990    2 in 2000
   New York ranked: 8 in 1970    8 in 1980    8 in 1990    8 in 2000
       Osaka ranked: 4 in 1970
  Sao Paulo ranked: 4 in 1980    4 in 1990    3 in 2000
   Shanghai ranked: 5 in 1990    5 in 1980    3 in 1970
      Tokyo ranked: 1 in 1990    1 in 1970    1 in 1980    1 in 2000

PREVIOUS CITIES WITH RANK OF New York CHANGED AGAIN
      Bombay ranked: 5 in 2000
Mexico City ranked: 5 in 1970    3 in 1980    3 in 1990    2 in 2000
   New York ranked: 9 in 1970    9 in 1980    9 in 1990    9 in 2000
       Osaka ranked: 4 in 1970
  Sao Paulo ranked: 4 in 1980    4 in 1990    3 in 2000
   Shanghai ranked: 5 in 1990    5 in 1980    3 in 1970
      Tokyo ranked: 1 in 1990    1 in 1970    1 in 1980    1 in 2000
```

$\rightarrow$

```
PREVIOUS CITIES WITHOUT New York
      Bombay ranked: 5 in 2000
Mexico City ranked: 5 in 1970   3 in 1980   3 in 1990   2 in 2000
       Osaka ranked: 4 in 1970
   Sao Paulo ranked: 4 in 1980   4 in 1990   3 in 2000
    Shanghai ranked: 5 in 1990   5 in 1980   3 in 1970
       Tokyo ranked: 1 in 1990   1 in 1970   1 in 1980   1 in 2000

PREVIOUS CITIES THAT RANK IN TOP 3
Mexico City ranked: 3 in 1980   3 in 1990   2 in 2000
   Sao Paulo ranked: 3 in 2000
    Shanghai ranked: 3 in 1970
       Tokyo ranked: 1 in 1990   1 in 1970   1 in 1980   1 in 2000
```

The program demonstrates modifying and removing elements in maps and multimaps by working with population data. The program starts with a C-style array containing the names of the six most populous countries in 1950 [Countries04]. The code also makes a vector with the numbers one through six, using the technique of Tip 79. Then the software declares a map that uses the country name as a key and its population rank as a value and loads the data into the map using the STL algorithm `transform`, a method that Tip 34 explains. The output shows the result. The countries are listed alphabetically because the key is a text string and the map sorts by key.

A half century later, in the year 2000, Brazil has replaced Japan as the fifth most populous country, and Indonesia and Russia have traded places in the listing. The first thing the program demonstrates is how to change the value associated with a map key. Just assign the new value to the indexed map name, as the code shows. The indexing occurs through the subscript operator, which returns a reference to the key's value. You can use this reference on the left side of an assignment, as the program does.

To replace Japan with Brazil as the fifth most populous country, the program needs to change a key, the country name. You can't do this directly. You can't even do it through an iterator by changing the value of the first member of the pair that the iterator points to, which is the key. The reason is that iterators that point at elements in maps, and multimaps, even if the containers are not declared const, behave as if they were pointing to a pair whose first element *is* const. This prevents you from accidentally changing the key, which would disturb the internal organization of the container's elements.

Instead, to modify a key, you have to insert a new key that has the old key's associated value and then remove the old key. The program does this in the two lines

```
country["Brazil"] = country["Japan"]; // Brazil now has Japan's rank
country.erase( "Japan" ); // Japan no longer in top 6
```

On the right side of the first line, the code country["Japan"] returns the value of that element, that is, Japan's rank. On the left side, country["Brazil"] returns a reference to the value associated with the key "Brazil," which the assignment operator (=) sets equal to Japan's rank. What's interesting is that this works even though the map doesn't have the key "Brazil" in it. That's because, as Tip 35 explains, if you access an element that doesn't exist with the map's subscript operator ([ ]), it creates the element. In this case, the operator creates an element with the key "Brazil" and initial value of 0, and then the rest of the line sets the value to 5, Japan's rank. Once the program has inserted an element with the new key and old value, the code deletes the original element by passing its key to the member function erase, as shown. The net effect of these actions is to change an element's key while keeping its value the same. The output shows the six countries with the highest populations in 2000.

The advantage of using a multimap rather than a map is that a multimap can have duplicate indexes. To demonstrate working with the multimap, the program uses data for the five most populated cities in 1970, 1980, 1990, and 2000 [Cities04]. (These are actually figures for agglomerations, that is, cities with their surrounding urban areas.) The key in the multimap is a string with the city's name. The value is a pair data structure with two integers. The first integer is the city's population rank, and the second integer is the decade.

To create the multimap, the program first makes a vector with the rank-decade pairs. Then the code puts the city names and rank-decade pairs together and inserts them into the multimap by using transform, as before. Finally, the software displays the data using print_city, a custom function that prints each city's rank and the decade when it achieved that rank.

The first example of working with a multimap is to modify the value of the first element that has a given key. Tip 37 explains that you can locate this element by using the container's find member function. If the iterator that find returned is not equal to the multimap's end iterator, the returned iterator points to the first element with the desired key. The element is a pair data structure with another pair structure as the second member. The first member of this second pair is the rank, so the code simply sets that value to the new number.

Tip 37 also explains how to find the last element and all elements with a given key. The program next calls the member function equal_range, which returns a pair of iterators that denote the range of elements with the specified key. If the iterators are equal, the function didn't find any matching elements. Otherwise, the code makes a copy of the second iterator (the end of the range) and decrements it. (The program has to decrement the iterator once because it is the end of an STL range, and, thus, actually points to one past the elements of interest.) After that, the code simply sets the rank in that element to the new rank.

Modifying all members with the given key is almost easier—just loop over the range and set the first member of each element's pair to the new value. The program illustrates all three of these value-modification techniques by supposing that there was an error in New York's ranking and changing all of those numbers to eight. The output shows the result.

Sometimes it may be necessary to modify the first element that has a given value, not a given key. Tip 37 provides two ways of finding this element. The program in Listing 7.6 uses one of those methods. The code simply loops through the entire range and checks each element for the desired value. As soon as the program finds a desired value, it changes the value as before and breaks out of the loop. If the code never finds such a value, the loop variable is equal to the multimap's end iterator. The program checks this and reports that it didn't find a desired element.

Modifying the last element with a given value works the same way but with reverse iterators. Finally, to change the values of all elements that have the specified value, the program loops through the entire range, checks each element's value and changes it if necessary. (If you need more details on searching for the last matching element and for all elements of a given value, see Tip 37.) The output shows the result. All of New York's rankings have been changed from 8 to 9.

The last part of the program demonstrates removing elements from a multimap. To get rid of the first element with a particular key, the code searches with the `find` member function for an element with that key. If the code finds one, the software passes the iterator that points to the element to the multimap's `erase` member function, which deletes the element. To remove the last element with a specified key, the code finds that element with the `equal_range` member function as before, decrements the second member of the range, and passes that iterator to the `erase` member function. To remove all elements with a particular key, just pass the key to the `erase` member function. The output shows the list of cities without New York.

Instead of removing elements with a certain key, you can get rid of elements whose values meet a criterion. For example, suppose you only want to consider the three most populous cities. To delete the first element whose value (rank) is more than three, the code marches through the multimap's range with a loop. If the program finds an element with the correct value, the code deletes the element as before and exits the loop.

To remove the last element that meets the criterion, the code searches backward using reverse iterators. If the program finds such an element, the code deletes the element with the member function `erase` and exits the loop. There's a little twist in the code, though, because `erase` doesn't accept reverse iterators. To convert one to a regular iterator, the program uses the reverse iterator's `base` member function and decrements by one. See "Reverse Iterators" in Chapter 2 for an explanation.

The last thing the program does is to delete all elements whose values match the criterion. The code uses a for-loop to do this. However, the code increments the counter within the body of the loop instead of in the normal place, that is, in the for-statement itself. That's because the standard loop form leads to a subtle error. For example, suppose the code were written in the usual way:

```
found = false;
for( site = city.begin(); site != city.end(); ++site )
   if( site->second > max_rank )
   {
      city.erase( site );
      found = true;
   }
```

The problem is that as soon as `erase` deletes the element that `site` points to, the value in `site` becomes invalid. Attempting to increment that value (`++site` in the for-statement) produces a runtime error. Another possible solution might be to store the value returned by the `erase` member function, which presumably would be the location after the element just deleted. Unfortunately, `erase` doesn't return anything at all, so this won't work either.

The code in Listing 7.6 has the statement `city.erase( site++ )`. The way the statement executes is as follows: (1) the increment operator saves the current value of `site`, (2) the operator then increments the value in `site`, and (3) the operator returns the saved value, which is passed to `erase`. It doesn't matter, then, that `erase` invalidates the value of `site` that `erase` receives because the code has stored the correct, incremented value before the iterator becomes bad.

As a final note, remember that although many of the modify and remove operations illustrated in this tip can be done without using the `find` member function, such searches are not efficient. Maps and multimaps are optimized for searching by key, and searches by value or searches that don't use the member function `find` are comparatively slow.

USE THE SORTED RANGE ALGORITHMS WITH SETS AND MULTISETS

TIP 40

Applies to: Set, multiset, merge, set_difference, set_intersection, set_
                    symmetric_difference, set_union, unique
See also: Tip 34, Tip 53

Quick Solution

```
set<int> s1, s2;
// ...

vector<int> v( s1.size() + s2.size() );
vector<int>::iterator logical_end;

// elements in s1 and not in s2
logical_end =
set_difference( s1.begin(), s1.end(), s2.begin(), s2.end(),
   v.begin() );

// elements in s1 or s2 but not in both
logical_end =
set_symmetric_difference( s1.begin(), s1.end(), s2.begin(), s2.end(),
   v.begin() );

// elements in s1 and s2
logical_end =
set_intersection( s1.begin(), s1.end(), s2.begin(), s2.end(),
   v.begin() );

// elements in s1 or s2 or both
logical_end =
set_union( s1.begin(), s1.end(), s2.begin(), s2.end(), v.begin() );

// elements in both sets put in order
logical_end =
merge( s1.begin(), s1.end(), s2.begin(), s2.end(), v.begin() );
```

Detailed Solution

The handy thing about sets and multisets is that they automatically keep their elements sorted. When working with these containers, you fill them with values or search them for particular elements. You might also insert or delete some values from time to time. However, you can do a lot more with them. The STL comes with some powerful algorithms that let you combine sorted ranges, and because sets and multisets are always sorted, they make perfect inputs to these algorithms.

The names of the algorithms are often taken from analogous operations on mathematical sets, for example, set_union, set_intersection. Table 9.3 in Chapter 9 lists the algorithms and their functionality. The text by that table gives some suggestions on using the algorithms. The program in Listing 7.7 demonstrates the use of multisets with the sorted range algorithms.

LISTING 7.7   Using Multisets with the Sorted Range Algorithms

```cpp
// associative_set_algorithms.cpp

#include <algorithm>
#include <iostream>
#include <set>
#include <string>
#include <vector>

using namespace std;

#include "tips.hpp"

int main( )
{
    // 1991-95 Belmont, Preakness, and Kentucky Derby winners
    const int num_years = 5;
    const char* belmont_winner[num_years] = { "Hansel", "A. P. Indy",
        "Colonial Affair", "Tabasco Cat", "Thunder Gulch" };
    const char* preakness_winner[num_years] = { "Hansel", "Pine Bluff",
        "Prairie Bayou", "Tabasco Cat", "Timber Country" };
    const char* kentucky_winner[num_years] = { "Strike the Gold",
        "Lil. E. Tee", "Sea Hero",  "Go for Gin", "Thunder Gulch" };

    multiset<string> belmont( belmont_winner,
        belmont_winner+num_years );
    multiset<string> preakness( preakness_winner,
        preakness_winner+num_years );
    multiset<string> kentucky( kentucky_winner,
        kentucky_winner+num_years );

    cout << "BELMONT WINNERS\n";
    tips::print( belmont, 0, "  " );
    cout << "\nPREAKNESS WINNERS\n";
    tips::print( preakness, 0, "  " );
    cout << "\nKENTUCKY WINNERS\n";
    tips::print( kentucky, 0, "  " );

    // find winners of Belmont but not Preakness
    vector<string> winner;
    set_difference( belmont.begin(), belmont.end(), preakness.begin(),
        preakness.end(), back_inserter( winner ) );
    cout << "\nWINNERS OF BELMONT BUT NOT PREAKNESS\n";
```

```
if( !winner.empty() )
{
    tips::print( winner, 0, "   " );
}
else
    cout << "No horse won Belmont but not Preakness\n";

// find winners of Belmont or Preakness but not both
winner.clear();
set_symmetric_difference( belmont.begin(), belmont.end(),
    preakness.begin(), preakness.end(), back_inserter( winner ) );
cout << "\nWINNERS OF BELMONT OR PREAKNESS BUT NOT BOTH\n";
if( !winner.empty() )
{
    tips::print( winner, 0, "   " );
}
else
    cout << "No horse won Belmont or Preakness but not both\n";


// find winners of both Belmont and Preakness
winner.clear();
set_intersection( belmont.begin(), belmont.end(),
    preakness.begin(), preakness.end(), back_inserter( winner ) );
cout << "\nWINNERS OF BOTH BELMONT AND PREAKNESS\n";
if( !winner.empty() )
{
    tips::print( winner, 0, "   " );
}
else
    cout << "No horse won both Belmont and Preakness\n";

// find winners of all three
vector<string> triple_winner;
set_intersection( winner.begin(), winner.end(), kentucky.begin(),
    kentucky.end(), back_inserter( triple_winner ) );
cout << "\nTRIPLE WINNERS\n";
if( !triple_winner.empty() )
{
    tips::print( triple_winner, 0, "   " );
}
else
    cout << "No horse won all three races in 1991-1995\n";
```

```
// display all winners in alphabetical order
winner.clear();
merge( belmont.begin(), belmont.end(),
   preakness.begin(), preakness.end(), back_inserter( winner ) );
vector<string> all_winner;
merge( winner.begin(), winner.end(),
   kentucky.begin(), kentucky.end(), back_inserter( all_winner ) );

cout << "\nALL 15 WINNERS\n";
for( vector<string>::size_type i = 0; i < all_winner.size(); ++i )
{
   cout << all_winner[i] << "  ";
   if( (i+1) % 5 == 0 )
      cout << endl;
}

// find different horses that have won
all_winner.erase( unique( all_winner.begin(), all_winner.end() ),
   all_winner.end() );
cout << endl << all_winner.size() << " UNIQUE WINNERS\n";
for( vector<string>::size_type i = 0; i < all_winner.size(); ++i )
{
   cout << all_winner[i] << "  ";
   if( (i+1) % 5 == 0 )
      cout << endl;
}
}
```

The output is

```
BELMONT WINNERS
A. P. Indy  Colonial Affair  Hansel  Tabasco Cat  Thunder Gulch

PREAKNESS WINNERS
Hansel  Pine Bluff  Prairie Bayou  Tabasco Cat  Timber Country

KENTUCKY WINNERS
Go for Gin  Lil. E. Tee  Sea Hero  Strike the Gold  Thunder Gulch

WINNERS OF BELMONT BUT NOT PREAKNESS
A. P. Indy  Colonial Affair  Thunder Gulch

WINNERS OF BELMONT OR PREAKNESS BUT NOT BOTH
A. P. Indy  Colonial Affair  Pine Bluff  Prairie Bayou
Thunder Gulch  Timber Country                              →
```

```
WINNERS OF BOTH BELMONT AND PREAKNESS
Hansel  Tabasco Cat

TRIPLE WINNERS
No horse won all three races in 1991-1995

ALL 15 WINNERS
A. P. Indy  Colonial Affair  Go for Gin  Hansel  Hansel
Lil. E. Tee  Pine Bluff  Prairie Bayou  Sea Hero  Strike the Gold
Tabasco Cat  Tabasco Cat  Thunder Gulch  Thunder Gulch  Timber Coun-
try

12 UNIQUE WINNERS
A. P. Indy  Colonial Affair  Go for Gin  Hansel  Lil. E. Tee
Pine Bluff  Prairie Bayou  Sea Hero  Strike the Gold  Tabasco Cat
Thunder Gulch  Timber Country
```

The program in Listing 7.7 uses multisets and the winners of some American horse races to demonstrate the sorted range algorithms. In the United States, the three most important horse races are the Belmont Stakes, the Preakness Stakes, and the Kentucky Derby. Any horse that triumphs in all three in one year is called a Triple Crown winner.

The program starts by loading the winners of the three races during 1991 to 1995 [Horse04] into multisets by using the technique of Tip 34. Multisets can hold duplicate entries and should be used instead of sets because it's possible for a horse to win the same race more than once. The first three sections of the output show the Belmont, Preakness, and Kentucky Derby winners.

To find values that are in one container but not another, use `set_difference`. The code illustrates this by finding the horses that won Belmont but not Preakness. Because the number of output elements is unknown, the program puts the output into a vector with a back inserter. The output shows the result and demonstrates that the elements in the output range are sorted. This is true for all of the sorted range algorithms.

Another operation on sorted ranges is determining what values are in exactly one of two ranges, that is, in one or the other range but not in both. The algorithm that computes this is `set_symmetric_difference`. Call this algorithm the same way that you call `set_difference`. The output shows the result of using `set_symmetric_difference` to find the winners of the Belmont or Preakness Stakes but not both. If you do want to find values that are in both ranges, use `set_intersection`. The output shows that during 1991 to 1995, two horses won both the Belmont and Preakness.

You can also use the sorted range algorithms on more than two ranges, but not directly. You have to first call an algorithm on two ranges, store the result, and then repeatedly call the function on the result and a new range. As a small example, the program uses `set_intersection` to determine which horses won all three races in 1991 to 1995. (Note that these are not necessarily Triple Crown winners because they might not have won the races in the same year.) The program takes the vector that has the winners of both the Belmont and Preakness Stakes and finds the intersection of that with the horses that won the Kentucky Derby. The result goes into a new vector, rather than one of the source vectors, because source and destination ranges shouldn't overlap. The output shows that no horse won all three races during the period in question.

To combine sorted ranges into a sorted result, use `merge`. The number of destination elements is the sum of the number of source elements. The output shows the 15 horses (three race winners per year for five years) in alphabetical order.

Finally, the program computes a list of the different horses that have won, that is, a list with no duplicate names. The program does this by calling the STL algorithm `unique`, which eliminates any consecutive, duplicate elements so that only one copy on any element remains. The program doesn't actually delete the elements from the container. Instead, the program returns an iterator that points to the logical end of the container's range, that is, to one past the last element that is in the range of unique elements. This iterator is the first argument to the vector's `erase` member function. The last argument is the end of the vector's range, so overall the call to `erase` deletes all elements that are not unique in the vector. The technique of putting `unique` in the call to erase is the same as the remove-erase idiom that Tip 53 describes.

8 Tips on Other Containers

This chapter describes the other containers that come in the STL, the ones that aren't standard containers. Three of them are *container adaptors*, which are containers made from other containers. The container adaptor provides a much smaller and more specialized interface than its constituent container. This makes it very convenient to use the adaptor in the restricted setting for which it is intended. Note that container adaptors aren't standard containers because they don't meet the requirements for that type of container. Their principal missing feature is iterators. This precludes using them in STL algorithms. The three container adaptors described in this chapter are the following:

> **Stack:** The last element entered is the first one that can be taken out.
>
> **Queue:** The elements can only be extracted in the order they were entered.
>
> **Priority queue:** The elements are taken out by priority.

The fourth container in this chapter is the bitset, which holds and manipulates a collection of bits whose number is fixed on compile time. The fifth container, the pair, is more like a data structure than a container. The pair holds two elements, which can be of different types. The pair is used in a number of places in the STL but is also handy in its own right. For more information on all five of these containers, see "Container Adaptors" and "Miscellaneous Containers" in Chapter 2.

TIP 41 USING A STACK DATA STRUCTURE

Applies to: Stack
See also: Tip 45

Quick Solution

```
stack<int> s;
s.push( 1 );
```

```
s.push( 2 );
s.push( 3 );
cout << s.top() << endl; // 3
s.pop();
cout << s.top() << endl; // 2
s.pop();
cout << s.top() << endl; // 1
s.pop();
```

Detailed Solution

The stack is a handy data structure in which the last item added is the first one removed. That is, the stack keeps its elements in last-in, first-out (LIFO) order. A good example of a stack is, naturally, a stack of cafeteria trays. Trays that have just been washed are placed on top of the ones already there and push them down in the stack. Only one tray is available for the taking—the one that is on top. Once that tray is removed, the next tray—and only that tray—can be taken.

Stacks are common in computer science. Most computer programs have a run-time stack. Whenever a function is called, information such as its parameters, local variables, and the caller are placed (pushed) onto the stack. When a function finishes executing, it is removed from (popped off) the stack and the function underneath executes.

The stack is a good model for some real-world situations. One of the author's summer jobs was loading palettes of records onto a semi-trailer truck for shipping throughout the country. The only way to get cargo in and out of a semi is at the back, so the palettes to be delivered last must be loaded first so they don't block the door. Those that are to be dropped off first must be loaded last so that they can be reached right away.

The program in Listing 8.1 simulates loading and unloading a semi-trailer. The truck is loaded in California, which is on the West Coast of the United States, and travels east. The records for the easternmost city (Houston) are loaded first and those for the westernmost (Los Angeles) are loaded last.

LISTING 8.1   Using a Stack

```cpp
// adaptor_stack.cpp

#include <iostream>
#include <stack>
#include <string>
#include <utility>

using namespace std;
```

```cpp
int main( )
{
   const int num_loads = 5;
   const int palettes[num_loads] = { 7, 6, 2, 5, 10 };
   const char* destinations[num_loads] = { "Houston", "Dallas",
      "Albuquerque", "Phoenix", "Los Angeles" };

   // load up the truck
   stack< pair<int,string> > truck;
   cout << "LOADING TRUCK";
   for( int i = 0; i < num_loads; ++i )
   {
      truck.push( make_pair( palettes[i], destinations[i] ) );
      cout << "\nLoaded " << truck.top().first << " palettes for "
         << truck.top().second;
   }

   // make the trip
   cout << "\n\nTRUCK EN ROUTE";
   while( !truck.empty() )
   {
      cout << "\nDelivered " << truck.top().first << " palettes to "
         << truck.top().second;
      truck.pop();
   }

}
```

The output is

```
LOADING TRUCK
Loaded 7 palettes for Houston
Loaded 6 palettes for Dallas
Loaded 2 palettes for Albuquerque
Loaded 5 palettes for Phoenix
Loaded 10 palettes for Los Angeles

TRUCK EN ROUTE
Delivered 10 palettes to Los Angeles
Delivered 5 palettes to Phoenix
Delivered 2 palettes to Albuquerque
Delivered 6 palettes to Dallas
Delivered 7 palettes to Houston
```

The program has a primitive representation of a load of cargo, namely, the number of palettes and the destination city. These two items can be stored in a `pair` data structure, which Tip 45 and "Miscellaneous Containers" in Chapter 2 describe. The pair contains an integer (the number of palettes) and a string (the destination city). You must put a space between the two closing angle brackets in the declaration of the stack. Otherwise, the compiler will interpret two consecutive right angle brackets as the right shift operator.

The program starts by creating an empty stack to represent the truck. The first loop in the code loads the cargo onto the truck. `make_pair`, also described in "Miscellaneous Containers" (Chapter 2), is a nice way of creating a `pair`. In the loop, the code uses the stack's member function `push` to add each load to the truck. This function is the only way to add elements to the stack. The cargo is put onto the truck with the easternmost cities first and the westernmost last. The first part of the output shows the loading order.

When the truck makes its deliveries, it is unloaded in reverse order. The only way to remove an item from a stack is to use the `pop` member function. `pop` does not return the item but just removes it. Thus, the code first calls the member function `top`, which returns a reference to the only item that can be accessed in a stack, namely, the one on top. A reference can be chained to access the two public data members of the pair, called `first` and `second`. The code prints these values and then pops the item off the stack.

Although the program could have unloaded the truck with a for-loop, it's cleaner to use a while-loop and the member function `empty` as shown. The second half of the output shows that the cargo is unloaded in reverse order.

TIP 42 — A FIRST-IN, FIRST-OUT DATA STRUCTURE AND BUFFERING

Applies to: Queue
See also: Tip 43

Quick Solution

```
queue<int> q;
q.push( 1 );
q.push( 2 );
cout << q.front() << endl; // 1
q.pop();
q.push( 3 );
cout << q.front() << endl; // 2
q.pop();
```

```
cout << q.front() << endl; // 3
q.pop();
```

Detailed Solution

The STL comes with a queue container. This is a first-in, first-out (FIFO) queue that lets you insert any number of elements and remove them in the order you inserted them. You can remove the elements after you've inserted them all, but it's much more common to remove them at various times during the insertions. The classic application of this is a data buffer. For example, two pieces of hardware may run at different speeds. If the faster one processes data and passes it to the slower one, that data must be stored, or buffered, until the slowpoke is ready for the data.

The need for buffering occurs in the real world, too, especially in commerce. Customers often arrive at checkout counters faster than the clerks can ring up their orders and have to wait in line or, as they say in Britain, queue up. The program in Listing 8.2 provides an example of queuing by keeping track of vehicles coming to a car wash. Because the customers can arrive more quickly than cars can be cleaned, the software stores the objects representing the cars in a queue. This ensures that the cars will be cleaned in the order they arrived.

LISTING 8.2 Using a Queue

```cpp
// adaptor_queue.cpp

#include <iostream>
#include <queue>
#include <string>

using namespace std;

class Vehicle
{
   public:
   Vehicle( string description = "Unknown car",
      string license = "Unknown license", bool wax = false );
   string description() const;
   string license() const;
   bool wax() const;

   private:
   string description_, license_;
   bool wax_;
};
```

```cpp
inline
Vehicle::Vehicle( string description, string license, bool wax )
   : description_( description ), license_( license ), wax_( wax )
{} // empty

string Vehicle::description() const
{  return description_; }

string Vehicle::license() const
{  return license_; }

bool Vehicle::wax() const
{  return wax_; }

int main( )
{
   const char* description[] = { "blue Toyota Camry", "red VW",
      "green Toyota Sienna", "black Ford Mustang",
      "white Pontiac" };
   const char* license[] = { "ZD43UY", "CRO611", "AUW9046",
      "KW45JK", "ZQU342" };
   const bool wax[] = { false, true, false, true, false };
   const int num_cars = sizeof( wax ) / sizeof( wax[0] );

   queue<Vehicle> line;

   int count = 0;
   while( count < num_cars || !line.empty() )
   {
      for( int i = 0; i < 2; ++i )
         if( count < num_cars )
         {
            cout << "A " << description[count] << ", license "
               << license[count] << ", is here for a wash";
            if( wax[count] )
               cout << " and a wax";
            cout << endl << endl;

            // put the car in the queue
            line.push( Vehicle( description[count], license[count],
               wax[count] ) );
            ++count;
         }
         else
```

```
        break;

    // wash one car and call for it to be picked up
    cout << "ATTENTION PLEASE: a " << line.front().description()
        << ", license " << line.front().license()
        << ",\n\has been carefully washed ";
    if( line.front().wax() )
        cout << "and waxed ";
    cout << "and is available for pick-up\n\n";
    line.pop();
    }
}
```

The output is

```
A blue Toyota Camry, license ZD43UY, is here for a wash

A red VW, license CRO611, is here for a wash and a wax

ATTENTION PLEASE: a blue Toyota Camry, license ZD43UY, has been
carefully washed and is available for pick-up

A green Toyota Sienna, license AUW9046, is here for a wash

A black Ford Mustang, license KW45JK, is here for a wash and a wax

ATTENTION PLEASE: a red VW, license CRO611, has been carefully
washed and waxed and is available for pick-up

A white Pontiac, license ZQU342, is here for a wash

ATTENTION PLEASE: a green Toyota Sienna, license AUW9046, has been
carefully washed and is available for pick-up

ATTENTION PLEASE: a black Ford Mustang, license KW45JK, has been
carefully washed and waxed and is available for pick-up

ATTENTION PLEASE: a white Pontiac, license ZQU342, has been
carefully washed and is available for pick-up
```

The program starts by declaring a little class that holds a description of a car coming to the carwash, along with its license plate number and whether the car needs to be waxed. The remainder of the program is a loop that loads arriving cars into a queue and removes them when they have been cleaned. In each iteration of the loop, two cars can enter the carwash but only one can be washed and leave.

The code displays information about each customer's vehicle as it arrives and puts it on the queue by using the member function push. The cars should be processed from the head (front) of the queue to maintain the first-in, first-out order. The code demonstrates this by getting the characteristics of a finished car with the front queue member function. This deletes the car from the front of the queue with the member function pop. This function removes the next element but does not return it as front does, which is why you'll often see these two used in conjunction.

If you need something a little more powerful than a queue, try a priority queue. As Tip 43 explains, elements come off the queue in order of importance.

TIP 43   BUFFERING WITH PRIORITY REMOVAL

Applies to: Priority queue
See also: Tip 42

Quick Solution

```
priority_queue<int> p;
p.push( 1 );
p.push( 7 );
p.push( 5 );
cout << p.top() << endl; // 7
p.pop();
cout << p.top() << endl; // 5
p.pop();
cout << p.top() << endl; // 1
p.pop();
```

Detailed Solution

Tip 42 explains that a queue is a data structure in which elements are removed in the order they are inserted. The queue is commonly used as a buffer to manage situations in which data arrives more quickly than it can be processed. A priority queue can also serve as a buffer, but the data is removed according to how important it is, rather than on a first-come, first-served basis. The priority queue holds ranked elements, and the higher an element's ranking, the sooner the element can be removed.

A good use of a priority queue is to process incoming pieces of information that have an importance attached to them. The program in Listing 8.3 illustrates messages from a security system that is monitoring a group of buildings. The guards should respond to the events according to the danger they represent; for example, it's more important to handle a smoke alarm going off than to help an employee jump-start his car.

LISTING 8.3   Using a Priority Queue

```
// adaptor_priority_queue.cpp

#include <iostream>
#include <queue>
#include <string>

using namespace std;

class Message
{
   public:
   Message( string message = "Software problem",
      string source = "Message constructor", int security_level = 0 );
   // message - description of problem
   // source - site of problem
   // security_level - 0-10, 10 is most important

   bool operator<( const Message& rhs ) const;
   // compare security levels

   string message() const;
   int security_level() const;
   string source() const;

   private:
   string message_, source_;
   int security_level_;
};

inline
Message::Message( string message, string source, int security_level )
   : message_( message ), source_( source ),
     security_level_( security_level )
{} // empty
```

```cpp
bool Message::operator<( const Message& rhs ) const
{  return security_level() < rhs.security_level(); }

string Message::message() const
{  return message_; }

string Message::source() const
{  return source_; }

int Message::security_level() const
{  return security_level_; }

int main( )
{
   const char* message[] = { "situation normal",
      "visitor needs a pass", "lights on in Building 7",
      "visitor still needs a pass",
      "smoke from corner of Building 7",
      "call from Lab 46, Building 7 - they smell smoke",
      "fire alarm, Building 7, Lab 46" };
   const char* source[] = { "South gate", "West gate", "South gate",
      "West gate", "South gate", "South gate", "South gate" };
   const int security_level[] = { 0, 1, 3, 2, 6, 7, 8 };
   const int num_messages
      = sizeof( security_level ) / sizeof( security_level[0] );

   priority_queue<Message> messages;

   cout << "MESSAGES IN CHRONOLOGICAL ORDER\n";
   for( int i = 0; i < num_messages; ++i )
   {
      cout << "Event " << (i+1) << ": Security level - "
         << security_level[i] << "\n\t" << source[i] << " reports "
         << message[i] << endl;

      messages.push( Message( message[i], source[i],
         security_level[i] ) );
   }

   cout << "\n\nMESSAGES IN PRIORITY ORDER\n";
   while( !messages.empty() )
   {
      cout << "Security level - "
         << messages.top().security_level() << "\n\t"
         << messages.top().source() << " reports "
```

```
                    << messages.top().message() << endl;
            messages.pop();
    }
}
```

The output is

```
MESSAGES IN CHRONOLOGICAL ORDER
Event 1: Security level - 0
        South gate reports situation normal
Event 2: Security level - 1
        West gate reports visitor needs a pass
Event 3: Security level - 3
        South gate reports lights on in Building 7
Event 4: Security level - 2
        West gate reports visitor still needs a pass
Event 5: Security level - 6
        South gate reports smoke from corner of Building 7
Event 6: Security level - 7
        South gate reports call from Lab 46, Building 7 - they smell
        smoke
Event 7: Security level - 8
        South gate reports fire alarm, Building 7, Lab 46

MESSAGES IN PRIORITY ORDER
Security level - 8
        South gate reports fire alarm, Building 7, Lab 46
Security level - 7
        South gate reports call from Lab 46, Building 7 - they smell
        smoke
Security level - 6
        South gate reports smoke from corner of Building 7
Security level - 3
        South gate reports lights on in Building 7
Security level - 2
        West gate reports visitor still needs a pass
Security level - 1
        West gate reports visitor needs a pass
Security level - 0
        South gate reports situation normal
```

The program starts by declaring a class to represent a message from the security system. Each message consists of a text string that describes the problem, another text string with the origin of the message, and a security level. The higher this number is, the more important the message is. Because the program doesn't expect to ever call the class' default constructor, the program sets strange default values in the constructor so that an accidental call becomes apparent. The class also declares the less-than operator, which compares the security levels of two class instances. By default, the priority queue uses the less-than operator to determine the priority of each of its elements. Note also that the priority queue does not have its own header—it's in <queue>.

The first loop simulates messages coming into the security center. Each message is loaded into the priority queue as the message comes in by using the push member function. This is the only way to add elements to the data structure. The first part of the output shows the messages in the order they were inserted into the priority queue.

The second loop simulates the guards handling the security messages. The loop keeps executing as long as the member function empty returns false. The loop removes the message with the highest priority by using the pop member function. Unfortunately, this function removes the element but does not return it, so before calling pop, the code displays the message by using top. This member function returns a reference to the top element in the priority queue, that is, the one with the highest ranking. The reference can be chained as shown to access members of the element in the container, in this case the Message class. The second half of the output illustrates that the messages are indeed removed in descending order of security level.

If the priority queue is more than you need, try a regular queue. Tip 42 demonstrates that elements come out of the queue in the order they came in, regardless of importance.

TIP 44   USING A FIXED-SIZE COLLECTION OF BITS

Applies to: Bitset
See also: Tip 26, Tip 28, Tip 91

Quick Solution

```
bitset<50> a( 0xff0 );
const bitset<50> b( 0xf );

a |= b; // bitwise OR
a &= b; // bitwise AND
a.flip(); // toggle all bits
a.reset( 4 ); // clear bit 4
```

```
a.set(); // set all bits
```

See the detailed solution and a Standard Library reference book for the many more capabilities of the bitset.

Detailed Solution

In C programs and old C++ code, you'll often see the `unsigned long` data type used to hold a group of bits. The bits can be manipulated with the operators &, |, and ~. The C++ Standard Library has a big improvement of this process—the bitset. Its advantages are that it can be any size, that the bits can be accessed by a subscript (index), and that bitset has more bitwise operators than the three mentioned earlier. Although the bitset is also useful for performing binary (base two) I/O (see Tip 91), its primary function is bit-tweaking. To have access to the bitset you must include the header `<bitset>`.

A vector or deque of Booleans can serve as an alternative to a bitset (see Tip 26 and Tip 28). Their chief benefit is that they can be resized. Table 8.1 summarizes the pros and cons of these three containers.

TABLE 8.1 Comparison of `bitset`, `vector<bool>`, and `deque<bool>`

Property	bitset	vector<bool>	deque<bool>
Designed for compressed storage	X	X	
Works in STL algorithms			X
Resizing		X	X
Indexing	X	X	X
Quick access to front and back		X	X
Binary (base two) I/O	X		
Construction from string	X		
Count number of set bits	X		
Report if any or no bits set	X		
Containerwise equality, inequality	X	X	X
Convenient set, clear of all bits	X		
Flip (complement) any or all bits	X	X	
OR, EXCLUSIVE OR, AND (returning itself or new bitset)	X		
Left and right shifts	X		
Convert to unsigned int or string	X		

The program in Listing 8.4 is an example of its use.

LISTING 8.4   Using a Bitset

```cpp
// adaptor_bitset.cpp

#include <bitset>
#include <iostream>

using namespace std;

int main( )
{
   const int num_lights = 15;
   const bitset<num_lights> outside( 0xf );
   const bitset<num_lights> inside( 0xff0 );
   const bitset<num_lights> driveway( 0x7000 );

   // on creation all bits are off
   bitset<num_lights> lights;
   cout << "Lights are off during the day: " << lights;
   lights |= outside;
   cout << "\nAt dusk, turn on outside lights: " << lights;
   lights |= driveway;
   cout << "\nAdd driveway lights: " << lights;
   lights |= inside;
   cout << "\nAdd inside lights: " << lights;

   // to save electricity turn off half the lights
   for( int i = 0; i < num_lights; i +=2 )
     lights.reset( i );
   cout << "\nTo save electricity turn on only every other light:"
     << lights;

   // turn off inside lights at night
   lights &= bitset<num_lights>( inside ).flip();
   cout << "\nAt bedtime turn off inside lights: " << lights;

   // turn off all lights at sunrise
   lights.reset();
   cout << "\nTurn off all lights at sunrise: " << lights << endl;
}
```

The output is

```
Lights are off during the day: 000000000000000
At dusk, turn on outside lights: 000000000001111
Add driveway lights: 111000000001111
Add inside lights: 111111111111111
To save electricity turn on only every other light:010101010101010
At bedtime turn off inside lights: 010000000001010
Turn off all lights at sunrise: 000000000000000
```

The program demonstrates bitsets by simulating the control of lights around a house. The code declares a constant integer that specifies the number of lights and then uses that as the template parameter to 3 bitsets. These bitsets define groups of lights for the inside, outside, and driveway of the house. The code declares the bitsets to be constants because they define the sets of lights and so shouldn't be changed. Even though the groups are smaller than the total number of lights (3, 4, and 8 versus 15), they are declared to each contain 15 bits because only bitsets of the same size can be combined with the bitset operators. Besides the default constructor, the bitset has constructors that accept an unsigned long value or a C++ text string as the initial specification of the bit states. There are only 15 bits in this example, so it's easy to specify the bits by using an unsigned long and a hexadecimal value.

Next, the program models a panel of light switches with a bitset. On creation, a bitset made with the default constructor has all bits set to 0. You can display the bits as a group of 1s and 0s by simply inserting the bitset into an output stream. The first line of the output shows that all of the bits are initially off (0). The code then turns on sets of lights by ORing the panel bitset with each group bitset. The second, third, and fourth lines of output show the result.

With the high cost of electricity nowadays, it's a good idea to save money by turning off some of the lights around the house. The program shows how to turn off every other light by using a loop and the bitset member function `reset`, which sets the specified bit to 0. The output statement displays the bits.

When everyone goes to sleep, all the lights inside the house should be turned off. The bit-tweaking for this is to AND the bits in the panel with a bitset that has all inside-light bits set to 0 and all other bits set to 1. The code accomplishes this with the expression

```
lights &= bitset<num_lights>( inside ).flip()
```

This is the common STL use of an unnamed, temporary variable (see "Predefined Function Objects" in Chapter 2) and is equivalent to

```
bitset<num_lights> temp( inside );
temp.flip();
lights &= temp;
```

The member function `flip` toggles (reverses the value of) all bits in the bitset. Finally, the program turns off all lights with the member function `reset`. Use its complement `set` to turn on all bits in the bitset.

USING A PAIR OF THE SAME OR DIFFERENT
TIP 45   **DATA TYPES**

Applies to: Pair
See also: Tip 17, Tip 55

Quick Solution

```
pair<int,double> p( 1, 32.56 );
cout << p.first << "   " << p.second; // 1    32.56
```

Detailed Solution

The `pair` is not a container adaptor but is a very handy little data structure that holds two items, which can have the same or different data types. Pairs have a variety of uses:

■ In the map and multimaps containers (see "Associative Containers" in Chapter 2)
■ In the STL algorithms `equal_range` and `mismatch`
■ To return two values from a function
■ To manipulate two items at once, for example, Tip 55
■ As a mini-`struct` to hold two items that are logically related

You can make the pair hold three items by making one of the pair's members hold another pair. You could continue this nesting, but that quickly becomes a mess. It's better to use a `struct` instead. (Future versions of C++ may have a data structure similar to a pair called a tuple. It holds more than two elements [Jarvi02]).

The pair has two data members, `first` and `second`, that are both public. It has all six relational operators. There are two equality operators, `==` and `!=`. Two pairs are equal if the `first` members are equal and the `second` members are equal. They are not equal if the `first` members are not equal and/or the `second` members are.

The four relational operators are <, >, <=, and >=. When testing for inequality, if the `first` data members are not equal, they decide the result. If they are equal, the comparison of the `second` data members determines the answer.

Listing 8.5 has a program that shows the pair in action.

LISTING 8.5   Using a Pair

```cpp
// adaptor_pair.cpp

#include <algorithm>
#include <iostream>
#include <iterator>
#include <string>
#include <vector>
#include <utility>

using namespace std;

typedef pair<int,string> Billionaire;

bool less_than_second( const Billionaire& b1, const Billionaire& b2 );
// return true if the first billionaire name comes before the second

int main( )
{
   const char* names[] = { "Alsaud, Alwaleed Bin Talal",
      "Allen, Paul", "Albrecht, Karl and Theo", "Buffett, Warren",
      "Gates, Bill" };
   const int billion[] = { 18, 20, 26, 30, 41 };
   const int num_billionaires = sizeof( names ) / sizeof( names[0] );

   // create vector and initialize with above info
   vector<Billionaire> billionaire( num_billionaires );
   transform( billion, billion+num_billionaires, names,
      billionaire.begin(), make_pair<int,string> );

   // compare two billionaires
   if( billionaire[1].first > billionaire[3].first )
      cout << billionaire[1].second << " has more money than "
         << billionaire[3].second << endl;
   else if( billionaire[1].first == billionaire[3].first )
      cout << billionaire[1].second << " and "
         << billionaire[3].second
         << " have the same amount of money\n";
```

```
        else
          cout << billionaire[1].second << " has less money than "
            << billionaire[3].second << endl;

        // default sort is in ascending order by money.
        sort( billionaire.begin(), billionaire.end() );

        // Display in reverse to see richest first
        cout << "\nFIVE RICHEST PEOPLE BY WEALTH";
        vector<Billionaire>::const_reverse_iterator billionaire_rend
          = billionaire.rend();
        for( vector<Billionaire>::const_reverse_iterator i
          = billionaire.rbegin(); i != billionaire_rend; ++i )
          cout << "\n$" << i->first << " billion - " << i->second;

        // sort into ascending order by last name and display
        sort( billionaire.begin(), billionaire.end(), less_than_second );
        cout << "\n\nFIVE RICHEST PEOPLE BY NAME\n";
        vector<Billionaire>::const_iterator billionaire_end
          = billionaire.end();
        for( vector<Billionaire>::const_iterator i = billionaire.begin();
          i != billionaire_end; ++i )
          cout << i->second << " - $" << i->first << " billion\n";
}

inline
bool less_than_second( const Billionaire& b1, const Billionaire& b2 )
{
    return b1.second < b2.second;
}
```

The output is

```
Allen, Paul has less money than Buffett, Warren

FIVE RICHEST PEOPLE BY WEALTH
$41 billion - Gates, Bill
$30 billion - Buffett, Warren
$26 billion - Albrecht, Karl and Theo
$20 billion - Allen, Paul

                                                            →
```

```
$18 billion - Alsaud, Alwaleed Bin Talal

FIVE RICHEST PEOPLE BY NAME
Albrecht, Karl and Theo - $26 billion
Allen, Paul - $20 billion
Alsaud, Alwaleed Bin Talal - $18 billion
Buffett, Warren - $30 billion
Gates, Bill - $41 billion
```

The program stores a billionaire's name and how much money he has [Billionaire04] together in a pair. The `<utility>` header allows access to the pair and the utility function `make_pair` described later in this tip. The code starts by making a `typedef` called `Billionaire` for the pair. This is common when working with pairs and cuts down on the amount of typing. Next, the program declares a vector with enough elements to hold the pairs that will be put into it.

The code constructs the pairs with the function `make_pair`. This utility function lets you construct a pair without explicitly declaring the data types. In general, it saves a little typing, though, in function templates, it can save a lot. The alternative to using it in the program would be to construct a temporary, unnamed variable like this:

```
billionaires.push_back( pair<int,string>( billions[i], names[i] ) );
```

After filling the vector, the program demonstrates access to the two public data members by comparing the wealth of a couple of the billionaires. Notice that the code compares the `first` data members and doesn't use the pair's comparison operators because they could give an incorrect result. For example, if the first line of the comparison were

```
if( billionaires[1] > billionaires[3] )
```

and the two billionaires had the same amount of money, the result of the inequality would be decided by their last names, which is not what you want.

The next section of code shows a situation where it is fine to use the pair's less-than operator. In this case, the program calls the STL algorithm `sort`, which does what its name says it does. By default, it uses the less-than operator to sort. If two billionaires had equal amounts of money, it would just sort them alphabetically, which is not only acceptable here but desirable. The loop that follows the sorting prints the vector in reverse order to list the people with the biggest hoard first.

Finally, the program ends by sorting the vector of billionaires by name. The person's name is in the second data member of the pair and, because the pair's less-than operator (which sort uses by default) compares the first data members, the program has a custom comparison function. This function, shown at the end of the program, returns `true` if the second data member of the pair on the left of the less-than sign (<) is less than the second data member of the pair on the right. Otherwise, it returns `false`. The code passes the function to the sorting routine and the bottom half of the output shows that the billionaires are indeed sorted by name and not by money.

9 Tips on Algorithms

lgorithms are one of the two major parts of the Standard Template Library. (The other big part is the containers.) Most of the algorithms are conceptually simple to understand—count counts the number of elements equal to a specified one, fill fills a range with a value, find finds a particular value. STL reference books can fill in the details for you. This chapter will provide you with other things, such as how to know what algorithms to use and when to use them, and how to use ordinary functions and class member functions in algorithms. This chapter will also give you some good advice on sorting. Here's what you will see:

- How to choose among similar algorithms
- How to use ordinary functions, pointers to ordinary functions and class member functions in algorithms
- How to use a two-argument function in an algorithm that expects a one-argument function
- How to find or erase the first or last matching element
- How to remove all matching elements, logically or permanently
- What to do before using the set algorithms
- How to sort on one of many fields
- How to sort without copying
- How to copy elements that meet a criterion
- How to operate on each element of a container

TIP 46   USE THE MOST SPECIFIC ALGORITHM

Applies to: All algorithms

Quick Solution

If an algorithm is available that does what you want, use it instead of for_each; for example, use count or count_if to count specific elements. If available, use a con-

261

tainer's member function instead of the equivalent STL algorithm; for example, the find member function of a set instead of the find STL algorithm.

Detailed Solution

for_each is a very useful algorithm that takes a function or function object that you've written and marches it through a range of elements, doing your bidding on each. You can just examine the elements or you can modify them. There's room for a lot of creativity and a lot of power with for_each, but don't use it. Okay, that's a little strong, so how about this—look for another algorithm that does what you want before using for_each.

The advice in this tip is to use the most specific STL algorithm you can. There are two different ways you can do this. The first is to see if there's an algorithm other than for_each with the functionality you need. For example, suppose you wanted to count how many numbers in a vector are greater than 100. You could easily write a class that could be passed to for_each, and each time it received an element, it would increment a counter if the number were more than 100. for_each returns a copy of the class with the gathered information and voilà—you have your answer. The problem with this is that there's already an algorithm (count_if) that is designed for counting. When used in conjunction with the built-in functors, this algorithm lets you count the specified numbers much more easily.

There are a number of advantages to using a more specific algorithm than for_each:

- There is often less code to write.
- The code that you do write is often simpler.
- The specific algorithm may be more efficient.
- The intent of the code is clearer. It's easier to tell that you're counting if the algorithm is called "count" than if it's called "for_each."

You don't have to memorize all the algorithms to know what's available. Just flip through a list of them occasionally so they'll be in the back of your mind. Table 9.1 may help you recall what's in the STL algorithmic toolkit. It lists (by functionality) specific algorithms that serve as alternatives to for_each.

There's a second meaning to using the most specific algorithm that you can—be aware of container member functions that do the same thing as STL algorithms. (Fortunately, they have the same names.) Sometimes the containers provide the functionality because they can't be used with the algorithm; for example, the sort algorithm requires random iterators, which a list doesn't have. In other cases, the container provides an algorithm because that version is more efficient; for example, the find member function of sets.

TABLE 9.1   Alternatives to `for_each`

Purpose	Algorithms
Counting	`count`, `count_if`
Minimum/maximum	`min_element`, `max_element`
Searching	`find`, `find_if`, `search`, `search_n`, `find_first_of`, `find_end`, `adjacent_find`
Changing values	`fill`, `fill_n`, `generate`, `generate_n`, `replace`, `replace_if`
Computing	`accumulate`, `adjacent_difference`, `partial_sum`

Lists tend to have member function alternatives that are related to modifying or moving elements. Associative containers provide alternatives for finding elements. Table 9.2 shows the algorithms for which you should substitute member functions.

TABLE 9.2   Member Function Alternatives to Algorithms

Algorithm	List	Set/multisets	Map/multimap
`count`		X	X
`equal_range`		X	X
`find`		X	X
`lower_bound`		X	X
`merge`	X		
`remove`, `remove_if`	X		
`reverse`	X		
`sort`	X		
`unique`	X		
`upper_bound`		X	X

The algorithms are in alphabetical order and an X indicates that the container provides a member function (with the same name).

TIP 47   USE A FUNCTION IN ALGORITHMS

Applies to: Algorithms with functional arguments
See also: Tip 4, Tip 20, Tip 50, Tip 58, Tip 79, Listing 13.1, Listing 13.11

Quick Solution

```
int f1( int n );
int f2( int n1, int n2 );
// ...

vector<int> in;
// ...
vector<int> out( in.size() );
transform( in.begin(), in.end(), out.begin(), f1 ); // use function alone
transform( in.begin(), in.end(), out.begin(),
   bind2nd( ptr_fun( f2 ), 10 ) ); // use function with adaptor
```

Detailed Solution

Many of the STL algorithms take functional arguments that allow you to customize their behavior. For example, you can pass the sorting criterion to `sort`, the condition for equality to `count_if` or `find_if` and the operation to `for_each` or `transform`. A functional argument can be an ordinary function. A functional argument must have the correct number of arguments, which is either one or two, depending on the algorithm. The argument type should be the same as the type in the input range, and if the output is going into an output range, those types should match. A function that is a predicate must always produce the same output for the same input. "Predefined Function Objects" in Chapter 2 explains this in more detail.

To use an ordinary function as a functional argument, you simply pass the function's name. However, if you want to use the function with a function adaptor, you need to wrap the function name in a call to the predefined adaptor `ptr_fun`. The program in Listing 9.1 gives you some good examples of both ways of using an ordinary function.

LISTING 9.1   Using a Function in Algorithms

```
// algorithm_function.cpp

#include <algorithm>
#include <functional>
#include <iostream>
#include <iterator>
#include <numeric>
```

```cpp
#include <vector>

#include "tips.hpp"

using namespace std;

// ***** The phrase "the sum of the proper divisors" of a
//        number means the sum of all the divisors of the number
//        except for that number itself, e.g.
//        the sum of the proper divisors of 8 is 1 + 2 + 4 = 7

bool is_amicable_pair( int m, int n );
// returns true if the sum of the proper divisors of m is n and
// vice versa. Otherwise, returns false
// m > 1, n > 1

bool is_perfect( int n );
// returns true if the sum of the proper divisors of n is n itself
// otherwise, returns false
// n > 1

int proper_divisor_sum( int n );
// compute the sum of the proper divisors of n
// n > 1

int main( )
{
   // make the sequence 2, 3, ..., divisor_length+1
   const int divisor_length = 11;
   vector<int> sequence( divisor_length, 1 );
   sequence[0] = 2;
   partial_sum( sequence.begin(), sequence.end(), sequence.begin() );

   // for each number compute the sum of the proper divisors
   vector<int> result( divisor_length );
   transform( sequence.begin(), sequence.end(), result.begin(),
      proper_divisor_sum );
   tips::print( sequence, "                  Numbers" );
   tips::print( result,    "Sum of proper divisors" );

   // make the sequence 2, 3, ..., perfect_length+1
   const int perfect_length = 9999;
   sequence.assign( perfect_length, 1 );
   sequence[0] = 2;
```

```cpp
partial_sum( sequence.begin(), sequence.end(), sequence.begin() );

// find all the perfect numbers in the sequence
result.clear();
remove_copy_if( sequence.begin(), sequence.end(),
   back_inserter( result ), not1( ptr_fun( is_perfect ) ) );
cout << endl;
tips::print( result, "Perfect numbers" );

// make the sequence 0, 1, 2, 3, ..., amicable_last
const int amicable_last = 1500;
sequence.assign( amicable_last+1, 1 );
sequence[0] = 0;
partial_sum( sequence.begin(), sequence.end(), sequence.begin() );

// find all the amicable pairs in the sequence
cout << "\nAmicable pairs\n";
result.resize( 1 );
for( int i = 2; i <= amicable_last; ++i )
{
   vector<int>::iterator out =
      remove_copy_if( sequence.begin()+i, sequence.end(),
      result.begin(),
      not1( bind1st( ptr_fun( is_amicable_pair ), i ) ) );
   if( out != result.begin() )
      cout << i << " " << result[0] << endl;
}

// faster way to find all the amicable pairs in the sequence
cout << "\nFaster amicable pairs\n";
result.resize( sequence.size() );
transform( sequence.begin()+2, sequence.end(), result.begin()+2,
   proper_divisor_sum );

for( int i = 2; i <= amicable_last; ++i )
   if( result[i] > 1 // no prime numbers
      && result[i] != i // no perfect numbers
      && i < result[i] // no duplicate pairs
      && result[i] <= amicable_last // don't go past end
      && result[result[i]] == i // other number is amicable
      )
   {
      cout << i << " " << result[i] << endl;
   }
```

```
}

inline
bool is_amicable_pair( int m, int n )
{ return m != n &&
   proper_divisor_sum( m ) == n && proper_divisor_sum( n ) == m; }

inline
bool is_perfect( int n )
{ return proper_divisor_sum( n ) == n; }

int proper_divisor_sum( int n )
{
   int sum = 1;
   int stop = n;
   for( int i = 2; i < stop; ++i )
     if( n % i == 0 )
     {
        sum += i;
        stop = n / i;
        sum += stop;
     }
   return sum;
}
```

The output is

```
             Numbers: 2 3 4 5 6 7 8 9 10 11 12
Sum of proper divisors: 1 1 5 1 6 1 7 7 8 1 16

Perfect numbers: 6 28 496 8128

Amicable pairs
220 284
1184 1210

Faster amicable pairs
220 284
1184 1210
```

Some of the many things studied in number theory are perfect numbers and their close relatives, amicable pairs. A *perfect number* is an integer greater than one such that the sum of all its divisors other than itself is equal to that integer. This sum is called the *sum of the proper divisors*. Six is a perfect number because 1 + 2 + 3 is 6. Eight is not a perfect number because 1 + 2 + 4 is 7, not 8. An *amicable pair* of numbers is two different integers (each greater than one) such that the sum of the first integer's proper divisors is equal to the second integer and vice versa. The program in this tip calculates sums of proper divisors, perfect numbers, and amicable pairs.

The function that does the work is `proper_divisor_sum`. It expects an argument that's greater than one and then does what the name says—finds the sum of the proper divisors. In a show of good modularity, the other two functions are simple uses of the first. `is_amicable_pair` returns `true` if its two arguments are different and if the sum of the proper divisors of the first is equal to the second argument and vice versa. Otherwise, `is_amicable_pair` returns `false`. `is_perfect` performs the eponymous operation, returning `true` if the sum of the proper divisors of its argument is equal to the argument itself and `false` otherwise.

The main program starts by making a vector filled with ones, as described in Tip 4, then uses the STL algorithm `partial_sum` and Tip 79 to make a consecutive sequence of integers starting with two. To calculate the sum of the proper divisors of each of these numbers, the program uses another STL algorithm, `transform`. Its first two arguments are the input range, the third argument is the start of the output range, and the last argument is the operation to perform. This is just the ordinary function `proper_divisor_sum`. Note that the output vector doesn't need a back inserter because it was created with the same size as the input vector.

The first section of the output shows the integer sequence. Beneath it are the sums of each numbers, proper divisors. Most of the sums are smaller than the numbers they come from, some are larger, and one is the same, six. It's the first perfect number.

Next, the program illustrates how to find all perfect numbers in a sequence. The program changes the size and contents of the current vector by passing a new length and element value to the vector's `assign` member function. Then the program creates a sequence starting with two as before. The goal is to put copies of all the numbers in the input vector that are perfect into an output vector. The most logical way to do this would be to use a `copy_if` algorithm with `is_perfect` as the functional argument. Unfortunately, as Tip 58 explains, the STL doesn't have a `copy_if` algorithm. That tip provides a custom-written one and explains how to use the STL algorithm `remove_copy_if` instead.

`remove_copy_if` copies elements in an input range that *fail* a criterion to an output range. If you used `is_perfect` as the functional argument, it would copy all input elements that were *not* perfect numbers to the output, which is the opposite of what you want. To fix this, you can take the logical negation of the result of `is_perfect` by using the predefined function adaptor `not1`. You can't apply that directly to an ordinary function, though, or you'll get a compiler error. To make such a function usable with an adaptor, you need to wrap the function in a call to another adaptor, `ptr_fun`. The call to `remove_copy_if` demonstrates this and shows that the third argument is a back inserter to the output vector. You need a back inserter here because you don't know how large the output will be, that is, how many elements will be copied. The output shows that there are four, the first four perfect numbers.

The last part of the program shows two different ways of finding amicable pairs with values of 1500 or less. The first method starts by making the sequence of integers 0, 1, 2, . . . , 1500 in a vector. (The algorithm doesn't use the first two numbers in the sequence, but having them there makes the code cleaner.) The program also resizes the output vector to have one element because when the loop that follows uses the vector, the vector will never need to hold more than one element.

The way the program uses that loop is to look for an amicable pair with the number 2, an amicable pair with the number 3, and so forth. The loop contains a call to `remove_copy_if`. To avoid redundant comparisons, the loop only tests values in the sequence that are greater than the loop counter. This is why the start of the input range is the vector's begin iterator plus the loop counter. (Tip 20 explains how you can do some kinds of arithmetic with random iterators such as those of a vector.)

The third argument to `remove_copy_if` is the start of the output sequence. There's no need for a back inserter because any given number can be part of at most one amicable pair and the output vector is big enough to contain one element. For the last argument, the code again uses an ordinary function. This time the function takes two arguments—the two integers that may be an amicable pair. One of the integers stays the same while it is compared to all the other integers in the vector. To always pass this number as the first argument to `is_amicable_pair` whenever `remove_copy_if` calls it, use the predefined function adaptor `bind1st`. Tip 50 explains that this makes the first argument to `is_amicable_pair` always be the indicated number. The second argument is the element that `remove_copy_if` passes to it. (In this program, you could also use the function adaptor `bind2nd` to freeze the second argument and let the element be the first argument—the result would be the same.)

`remove_copy_if` returns an iterator that points to one past the last element inserted in the output range, so if the algorithm didn't insert anything, the iterator would be equal to the beginning iterator of the output vector. If it did insert something, there's an amicable pair, which the code prints. The output shows the two amicable pairs that the program found.

Although this first method uses only a loop with a call to one STL algorithm, it's very inefficient. There are three problems:

- `remove_copy_if` calls `is_amicable_pair`, which computes the sum of the proper divisors for each of the two numbers passed to it. The first number is fixed during every call to `remove_copy_if`. Its sum should only be computed once, not at every call.
- Similarly, each iteration recomputes the sum of the proper divisors, even though these numbers don't change during the execution of the loop.
- If `remove_copy_if` does find an amicable pair in the sequence, it doesn't need to look any further in that sequence for more pairs because there can't be any more.

The last problem isn't very important because amicable pairs are rare. However, the first two problems are serious.

The last part of the program shows another way of finding amicable pairs. It uses `transform` to compute the sum of the proper divisors of each number in the sequence 2, 3, ..., 1500. (The input and output vectors have two additional elements, but adding two to the start of the corresponding begin iterators causes `transform` to ignore those elements.) Once the code has computed and stored all of the necessary sums of proper divisors, a single loop with no STL algorithms in it finishes the work. For each number from 2 to 1500 inclusive, the code checks if

- The corresponding sum is greater than 1. If the sum is 1, the number is prime and a prime number can't be in an amicable pair. Also, by definition, 1 cannot be a member of an amicable pair, which is why the loop counter starts at 2.
- The sum is not equal to the loop counter. The two numbers in an amicable pair must be different and if this check weren't here, perfect numbers, such as 6 and 28, would produce amicable pairs.
- The loop counter is less than the sum. This avoids the same amicable pair being found twice, once for the two numbers and again when they are reversed.
- The sum is less than or equal to the last index in the vector of sums. This is necessary because the next condition uses the sum as an index.
- The sum at the index of the current sum is the current loop counter. This means the numbers are an amicable pair.

The output shows that both methods find the same amicable pairs. However, the second method is much faster. On one computer here, the first technique takes about 10 seconds and the second one runs instantaneously. There are two morals, then, to this story:

- Often, the algorithm you use rather than the code makes the big difference in speed.
- You don't have to do everything with STL algorithms. You can solve part of a problem with them and use regular C++ techniques to solve the rest.

TIP 48   USE A CLASS MEMBER FUNCTION IN AN ALGORITHM

Applies to: Mem_fun_ref, bind2nd, algorithms with function arguments
See also: Tip 49, Tip 59, Tip 81, Tip 86, Listing 13.4

Quick Solution

```
class Player
{
   public:
   // ...
   int bonus( int games_won ) const;
   void add_win();

   private:
};

// ...

vector<Player> team;
// ...

// member function need not be const if used only with mem_fun_ref
for_each( team.begin(), team.end(), mem_fun_ref( &Player::add_win ) );

vector<int> bonus( team.size() );

// member function must be const if used with mem_fun_ref and binder
transform( team.begin(), team.end(), bonus.begin(),
      bind2nd( mem_fun_ref( &Player::bonus ), 7 ) );
```

Detailed Solution

C++ is great for object-oriented programming, a powerful and enjoyable coding technique. It also meshes well with the Standard Template Library. STL containers can easily hold classes, and you can even use some of the class member functions with STL algorithms. One common thing to do is to iterate over a container of classes and call a member function at each element that prints out information in that class instantiation. Such a member function is often called `print` or `display`. You can also go through a container, calling a getter (accessor) member function and storing the results in another container. Then you can analyze the numbers, for example, by finding the average value.

Unfortunately, there are some strict limitations on using member functions:

- Member functions used with `mem_fun_ref` (explained later) and passed to `bind1st` or `bind2nd` must be constant, that is, declared with the `const` keyword after the function name.
- You can only work with member functions that take zero or one arguments.
- You can't use the member functions as arguments to the predefined function objects. For example, you can't have a member function that returns a number be an argument to the predefined function object `multiplies`, which computes the product of two numbers.

Nevertheless, being able to call a class member function is handy. The program in Listing 9.2 gives a couple of examples of this.

LISTING 9.2   Using a Class Member Function in an Algorithm

```cpp
// algorithm_member.cpp

#include <algorithm>
#include <functional>
#include <iomanip>
#include <iostream>
#include <numeric>
#include <string>
#include <vector>

using namespace std;

class Player
{
   public:
   Player( string name = "Unknown", int income = 0,
      int bonus_percentage = 0 );
   // name - player's last name
   // income - yearly income (salary+endorsements+ads) in euro
   // bonus_percentage - percent of salary bonus per game won

   int bonus( int games_won ) const;
   // bonus in euro = 30% of income * bonus_percentage * games_won

   void print() const;
   // display info about player

   string name() const;
```

```
      int income() const;

   private:

      int salary() const;   // in euro
      int bonus_percentage_;
      int income_;
      string name_;
};

inline
Player::Player( string name, int income, int bonus_percentage )
   : bonus_percentage_( bonus_percentage ), income_( income ),
     name_( name )
{} // empty

inline
int Player::bonus( int games_won ) const
{ return static_cast<int>(
   salary() * ( bonus_percentage_ / 100.0 ) * games_won ); }

inline
void Player::print() const
{
   cout << setw( 10 ) << left << name() << "Income: " << setw( 8 )
      << right << income() << " euro per year   Bonus: "
      << bonus_percentage_ << "% of salary per game won\n";
}

inline
int Player::income() const
{ return income_; }

inline
string Player::name() const
{ return name_; }

inline
int Player::salary() const
{ return static_cast<int>( 0.3 * income() ); }

int main( )
{
   // 5 highest paid players on Real Madrid in 2004
```

```
vector<Player> real_madrid;
real_madrid.push_back( Player( "Beckham", 22400000, 3 ) );
real_madrid.push_back( Player( "Ronaldo", 16500000, 3 ) );
real_madrid.push_back( Player( "Zidane",  14000000, 3 ) );
real_madrid.push_back( Player( "Raul",     9300000, 2 ) );
real_madrid.push_back( Player( "Figo",     8500000, 1 ) );

// print the info for each player
for_each( real_madrid.begin(), real_madrid.end(),
   mem_fun_ref( &Player::print ) );

// get all the incomes
vector<int> temporary( real_madrid.size() );
transform( real_madrid.begin(), real_madrid.end(),
   temporary.begin(), mem_fun_ref( &Player::income ) );

// compute and display the average income
int average_income = accumulate( temporary.begin(),
   temporary.end(), 0 ) / temporary.size();
cout << "\nAverage income for the " << real_madrid.size()
   << " highest paid players on Real Madrid: "
   << average_income << " euro\n\n";

// compute and display the bonuses to-date
const int games_won = 5;
transform( real_madrid.begin(), real_madrid.end(),
   temporary.begin(),
   bind2nd( mem_fun_ref( &Player::bonus ), games_won ) );
cout << "With " << games_won << " games won to-date"
   << " the average bonus is "
   << accumulate( temporary.begin(), temporary.end(), 0 )
      / temporary.size() << " euro\n";
}
```

The output is

```
Beckham    Income: 22400000 euro per year    Bonus: 3% of salary per
game won
Ronaldo    Income: 16500000 euro per year    Bonus: 3% of salary per
game won
Zidane     Income: 14000000 euro per year    Bonus: 3% of salary per
game won                                                           →
```

```
Raul        Income:  9300000 euro per year    Bonus: 2% of salary per
game won
Figo        Income:  8500000 euro per year    Bonus: 1% of salary per
game won

Average income for the 5 highest paid players on Real Madrid:
14140000 euro

With 5 games won to-date the average bonus is 557399 euro
```

The program starts by declaring a class to represent soccer players ("football" players, for European readers). The class has the player's last name, his yearly income (in euro), and a number that specifies the percentage of his salary that he gets as a bonus for each game his team wins. Member functions print information about the player and return his income, name, or salary. Actually, a player's salary is often just a small part of his income. The remainder comes from endorsements, advertising, and so forth. For example, David Beckham's salary in 2004 was a little less than 30% of his income for that year [Soccer04]. The code assumes other players have similar income breakdowns, and in computing the bonus, the code uses 30% of the total income as their salary.

The main part of the program declares a vector to hold the players. It then pushes on to it the five highest paid players in 2004 from the Real Madrid (Royal Madrid) soccer club. (They also happen to be among the top ten highest paid soccer players for any team, as shown in [Soccer04].) Each constructor has the person's last name, his yearly income in euro, and his bonus percentage. Although the salaries are correct, the percentages have been made up. Don't worry if it looks like your favorite player has been slighted, and don't send us any hate mail either.

Once the players have been loaded into the vector, the program prints them by calling each element's `print` member function. It does this by using the STL algorithm `for_each` (see Tip 59). Its first two arguments specify the container's range and the last argument is the operation that will be done on each element. The code illustrates how to call a member function of the element—put in the reference operator (`&`), class name, scope operator (`::`) and function name and surround the whole mess with the function adaptor `mem_fun_ref`, which is available through the header `<functional>`. You have to use the adaptor—if you don't, you'll get a compiler error. The output shows the information for the five players.

It's possible to also call constant member functions that return a value. To do this, the code first declares a vector with the same number of elements as there are players. Then the code cycles through all the players by calling `transform` (see Tip 81 for more details on this STL algorithm). The first two arguments are the input range, the third argument is the start of the output range, and the last argument is a function that takes an element from the input and returns a value that is placed in the output. In this case, the argument is the member function `income`, called the same way as before. Once the incomes are in a container, you can analyze them, for example, finding the highest and lowest, the median, and so forth. The program computes the average income by using the STL algorithm `accumulate` to add the incomes and dividing by the number of incomes (see Tip 86). The second section of the output shows the result.

Finally, the program computes the total bonuses paid out to the players so far. It uses `transform` as before, but this time calls the member function `bonus`, which takes one argument—the number of games won so far. That member function is again inside `mem_fun_ref`, and now that whole mess is in a call to the function adaptor `bind2nd`. `bind2nd` takes its second argument (the number of games) and passes it to `bonus` every time it's called by `transform`. (Remember that the member function must be constant if you use it with `bind1st` or `bind2nd`.) When `transform` is finished, the code computes the average as before and prints it without even storing it in an intermediate variable. The last line of the output is the result.

This tip gives you some ideas about how and when to call member functions of classes in containers. You can also do similar things if you have a container with pointers to classes. If you're in this situation, take a look at the next tip, Tip 49.

TIP 49 — USE A POINTER TO A CLASS MEMBER FUNCTION IN AN ALGORITHM

Applies to: Mem_fun, algorithms with function arguments
See also: Tip 48, Tip 59, Listing 13.4

Quick Solution

```
class Player
{
   public:
   // ...
   int bonus( int games_won ) const;
   void add_win();

   private:
};

// ...

vector<Player*> team;
```

```
// ...

// member function need not be const if used only with mem_fun
for_each( team.begin(), team.end(), mem_fun( &Player::add_win ) );

vector<int> bonus( team.size() );

// member function must be const if used with mem_fun and binder
transform( team.begin(), team.end(), bonus.begin(),
     bind2nd( mem_fun( &Player::bonus ), 7 ) );
```

Detailed Solution

Tip 48 shows you how to call the member function of a class that's stored in a container. You can also do this if you have pointers to the class in the container. And having pointers to classes just screams out for polymorphism. *Polymorphism* is the ability to call one function (signature) and have different functions respond. The functions have to belong to classes in the same inheritance tree, they have to be declared virtual, and you have to access them through pointers or references. If you have several classes that are derived from one base class and you call the member function through a pointer to that base class, the function of whatever class was actually assigned to that pointer responds.

The restrictions on the member functions you can use are the same as in Tip 48, namely the following:

- Member functions used with mem_fun (explained later) and passed to bind1st or bind2nd must be constant, that is, declared with the const keyword after the function name.
- You can only work with member functions that take zero or one arguments.
- You can't use the member functions as arguments to the predefined function objects. For example, you can't have a member function that returns a number be an argument to the predefined function object multiplies, which computes the product of two numbers.

The code in Listing 9.3 is a good example of using polymorphism with STL containers and algorithms.

LISTING 9.3   Using a Pointer to a Member Function in Algorithms

```
// algorithm_member_pointer.cpp

#include <algorithm>
#include <cmath>
```

```cpp
#include <functional>
#include <iostream>
#include <numeric>
#include <string>
#include <vector>

using namespace std;

class Shape
{
   public:
   Shape( const string& name = "Unknown" );

   virtual float area() const = 0;

   virtual void draw() const = 0;
   // REQUIRE: print shape on cout, no larger than 11x11 characters

   void draw_captioned( string caption ) const;
   // calls draw() and prints the caption and name on the next line

   string name() const;

   virtual float perimeter() const = 0;

   void print() const;
   // print name, area and perimeter

   private:
   string name_;
};

inline
Shape::Shape( const string& name )
   : name_( name )
{} // empty

inline
void Shape::draw_captioned( string caption ) const
{
   draw();
   cout << caption << name() << endl << endl;
}
```

```cpp
inline
string Shape::name() const
{ return name_; }

inline
void Shape::print() const
{  cout << name() << " with area " << area() << " and perimeter "
   << perimeter() << endl;
}

// **** First derived class

class Square : public Shape
{
   public:
   Square( int width = 5 );
   // 1 <= width <= 11

   virtual float area() const;
   virtual void draw() const;
   // REQUIRE: print shape on cout, no larger than 11x11 characters

   virtual float perimeter() const;

   private:
   int width_;
};

inline
Square::Square( int width )
   : Shape( "Square" ), width_( width )
{}    // empty

inline
float Square::area() const
{  return width_ * width_; }

void Square::draw() const
{
   for( int i = 0; i < width_; ++i )
   {
      for( int j = 0; j < width_; ++j )
         cout << '*';
      cout << endl;
```

```cpp
   }
}

inline
float Square::perimeter() const
{ return 4 * width_; }

// **** Second derived class

class Pyramid : public Shape
{
   public:
   Pyramid( int height = 4 );
   // makes an isosceles triangle with given height and base equal
   // to 2*height-1 . 2 <= height <= 6

   virtual float area() const;
   virtual void draw() const;
   virtual float perimeter() const;

   private:
   int base_;
   int height_;
};

inline
Pyramid::Pyramid( int height )
   : Shape( "Pyramid" ), base_( 2*height-1 ), height_( height )
{}    // empty

inline
float Pyramid::area() const
{   return 0.5 * height_ * base_; }

void Pyramid::draw() const
{
   for( int i = 1; i <= height_; ++i )
   {
      for( int j = -(height_-1); j <= (height_-1); ++j )
         cout << ( abs( j ) < i  ? '*' : ' ' );
      cout << endl;
   }
}

inline
```

```
float Pyramid::perimeter() const
{ return base_ + 2 * sqrt( height_*height_ + base_*base_/4.0 ); }

int main( )
{
   Square s1( 2 );
   Pyramid p( 6 );
   Square s2( 4 );

   vector<Shape*> shape( 3 );
   shape[0] = &s1;
   shape[1] = &p;
   shape[2] = &s2;

   // have each shape print its information
   for_each( shape.begin(), shape.end(), mem_fun( &Shape::print ) );
   cout << endl;

   // have each shape draw itself with a caption
   for_each( shape.begin(), shape.end(),
     bind2nd( mem_fun( &Shape::draw_captioned ), "Geometry I: " ) );

   // find the total area of the shapes
   vector<float> size( shape.size() );
   transform( shape.begin(), shape.end(), size.begin(),
     mem_fun( &Shape::area ) );
   cout << "\nTotal area: "
     << accumulate( size.begin(), size.end(), 0.0f ) << endl;
}
```

The output is

```
Square with area 4 and perimeter 8
Pyramid with area 33 and perimeter 27.2788
Square with area 16 and perimeter 16

**
**
Geometry I: Square                                         →
```

```
       *
      ***
     *****
    *******
   *********
  ***********
Geometry I: Pyramid

****
****
****
****
Geometry I: Square

Total area: 53
```

The program starts by declaring an abstract base class called Shape. You can tell it's abstract because it has a member function set equal to 0. This is called a *pure virtual function*. Abstract classes specify an interface (the member functions) but not an implementation. The derived classes provide the code for the pure virtual functions.

You can't instantiate an abstract class, but you can derive from it. You can, however, instantiate any derived class that provides code for all the pure virtual functions. Shape, an abstract class from which to derive classes representing shapes, has three abstract member functions. They provide the perimeter and area of the shape and make a simple drawing of it on the standard output stream. The class also has nonvirtual functions that return the name of the shape, draw it with a specified caption, and display the name, area, and perimeter.

The first derived class represents a square. Its constructor accepts the width of the square, the area member function returns the square of the width, and the perimeter member function returns four times the width. The code to draw the square makes a simple drawing with asterisks.

The second derived class represents a two-dimensional pyramid. This is a triangle whose two sides are the same length and whose base is twice the height minus one. The class provides implementations of its base class's three pure virtual functions.

The main program starts by constructing two squares and a pyramid. Then the program makes a vector with pointers to the abstract base class and points the first and third pointers to the squares and the second pointer to the pyramid. (Remember that a pointer to a base class can point to derived classes.) Next, the program uses the STL algorithm for_each (see Tip 59) and the adaptor mem_fun to call the print member function associated with each pointer. (If you tried to call the member function without using mem_fun, you'd get a compiler error.) The first section of the output shows the result. You can see that although the algorithm only called the member function print, the first and third calls ran that function from the square class and the second call ran the function from the pyramid class. This is polymorphism in action.

Next, to show that you can call a constant member function that accepts one argument, the program uses for_each to call the member function draw_captioned. The program passes the same figure caption to each call. The different figures in the second section of the output again show how the calls to the same member function produce different results, depending on what derived class the pointers are aimed at.

Finally, the program shows another way to use containers with pointers to classes by using the STL algorithm transform to get the area of each shape. The first two arguments are the input range, the third is the start of the output range (a container the code created to hold the areas), and the last is the name of the member function to be called, surrounded once again by mem_fun. To get the total area, the code calls accumulate, an STL algorithm that adds all the numbers in its input range. The last line of the output shows the result.

This tip showed how you can combine two of the neatest features of C++—the Standard Template Library and polymorphism. The containers had pointers to classes, which enabled polymorphism to work. If your containers have the classes themselves rather than pointers to them, you don't get polymorphism but Tip 48 demonstrates some cool things that you can still do.

TIP 50   **FREEZE AN ARGUMENT TO A FUNCTION OBJECT**

Applies to: Bind1st, bind2nd, binary function objects, binary predicates
See also: Tip 47, Tip 62, Tip 79, Tip 81, Listing 13.1, Listing 13.7, Listing 13.9, Listing 13.11

Quick Solution

```
vector<double> v1, v2;
// ...

transform( v1.begin(), v1.end(), v1.begin(), // compute inverse
    bind1st( divides<double>(), 1.0 ) ); // freeze first argument
transform( v2.begin(), v2.end(), v2.begin(), // compute percent
    bind2nd( multiplies<double>(), 100.0 ) ); // freeze second argument
```

Detailed Solution

All but two of the Standard Library's built-in function objects take two arguments. Sometimes both of these arguments can come from containers, for example, when using the STL algorithm `transform`. Often, however, you want one of the arguments to have a fixed value and the other to change, to be the different elements of a container. For example, you might want to subtract the smallest element in a container from all elements to make the minimum container value be 0. You might want to remove all elements in a container that are less than a certain value, or you might want to operate on a bunch of integers with the modulus of two to see which ones are even.

The Standard Library has two functors (function objects) that let you convert binary function objects to unary ones. They do this by binding or freezing either the first or the second argument to some constant value. The functor `bind1st` freezes the first (left) argument of a binary function object. `bind2nd` does the same for the second argument. Both of these are function adaptors, which are function objects that let you combine function objects with each other, combine them with special functions, or, as in this tip, combine them with specific values.

Each of the binding functors takes two arguments. The first is an adaptable binary function object (see "Functors" in Chapter 2), and the second is the fixed value that will be used for one of that object's two arguments. You can't use the binding functions on objects with more than two arguments. Also, there are no predefined binding functors for arguments other than the first and second ones. Nonetheless, the two binders available let you do some very practical things, as the program in Listing 9.4 shows.

LISTING 9.4   Freezing an Argument to a Function Object

```
// algorithm_freeze.cpp

#include <algorithm>
#include <functional>
#include <iomanip>
#include <numeric>
#include <string>
#include <vector>

#include "tips.hpp"

using namespace std;

bool in_string( char c, const string target );
// returns true if c is in target, false otherwise

int main( )
{
    // make the sequence 1 2 3 4 5
    vector<float> v( 5, 1 );
```

```
   partial_sum( v.begin(), v.end(), v.begin() );
   tips::print( v, "Original numbers" );

   // compute the inverses
   transform( v.begin(), v.end(), v.begin(),
      bind1st( divides<float>(), 1 ) );
   cout << fixed << setprecision( 2 );
   tips::print( v, "Inverses" );

   // convert to percentages
   transform( v.begin(), v.end(), v.begin(),
      bind1st( multiplies<float>(), 100 ) );
   tips::print( v, "Percentages" );

   // make a sequence starting at -10 and increasing by 100
   v.assign( v.size(), 100 );
   v[0] = -10;
   partial_sum( v.begin(), v.end(), v.begin() );
   tips::print( v, "\nOriginal numbers" );

   // truncate numbers to fall between 0 and 255 inclusive
   replace_if( v.begin(), v.end(),
      bind2nd( greater<float>(), 255 ), 255 );
   replace_if( v.begin(), v.end(), bind2nd( less<float>(), 0 ), 0 );
   tips::print( v, "Saturated numbers" );

   // count the vowels in a sentence
   const string vowels( "aeiouAEIOU" );
   string phrase( "The quick brown fox jumps over the lazy dog." );
   cout << "\nThere are " << count_if( phrase.begin(), phrase.end(),
      bind2nd( ptr_fun( in_string ), vowels ) )
      << " vowels in \n\"" << phrase << "\"\n";
}


inline
bool in_string( char c, const string target )
{  return target.find( c ) != string::npos; }
```

The output is

```
Original numbers: 1 2 3 4 5
Inverses: 1.00 0.50 0.33 0.25 0.20
Percentages: 100.00 50.00 33.33 25.00 20.00                    →
```

```
Original numbers: -10.00 90.00 190.00 290.00 390.00
Saturated numbers: 0.00 90.00 190.00 255.00 255.00

There are 11 vowels in
"The quick brown fox jumps over the lazy dog."
```

The program starts by making a vector with five consecutive numbers, using the `partial_sum` algorithm and the technique of Tip 79. The first line of the output shows the numbers. Next, the program uses `transform` (see Tip 81) to take the inverse of each number. The inverse is simply 1 divided by the number, so the code uses `bind1st` to freeze at 1 the first argument of the built-in adaptor `divides`. The program then converts the inverses to percentages by multiplying by 100. The code does this by freezing the first argument of a built-in functor (`multiplies`) to 100. The software could have frozen the second argument instead and the result would have been the same. The second and third lines of the output show the inverses and percentages.

To illustrate binding arguments for functors that compute things other than arithmetic, the program makes another sequence of numbers and runs some relational operators on them. It forces all integers in the container to lie between 0 and 255 inclusive. (This action is common in digital image processing and computer graphics.) First, the program calls the STL algorithm `replace_if` to replace all values that are greater than 255 by 255 itself. `bind2nd` freezes the second argument at 255. Another call to `replace_if` sets any values less than zero to zero. Again, the code uses `bind2nd` to always compare the container elements to a fixed value, in this case, zero. The middle section of the output confirms that all processed numbers are in the correct range.

The last part of the code demonstrates a method of counting the vowels in a string of text. The `count_if` STL algorithm passes every character in the text string to a predicate that returns `true` if the character is in a text string passed to it and `false` otherwise. In the code, the text string passed to the predicate is the lower and upper case vowels. The predicate is a custom one—the function `in_string`. It simply uses the string's `find` member function to see if the character is in the text. (See Tip 62 for details on searching in text strings.) However, before `in_string` or any regular function can be used in `bind2nd`, it must be wrapped in the function adaptor `ptr_fun` (see Tip 47). This is because `bind2nd` expects an adaptable function object as its first argument. A plain function is not adaptable (because it's missing certain type definitions that the binders expect), but it can be made so by putting it in `ptr_fun`. The last line of the output shows that the code did indeed count the number of vowels in the pangram.

FIND AND ERASE THE FIRST OR LAST MATCHING ELEMENT

TIP 51

Applies to: Sequence container
See also: Tip 1, Tip 30, Tip 42, Tip 47, Tip 49, Tip 50, Tip 52, Tip 53

Quick Solution

```
list<int> l;
// ...

list<int>::iterator itr = find( l.begin(), l.end(), 5 ); // find first 5
if( itr != l.end() ) // if found, erase
   l.erase( itr );

list<int>::reverse_iterator last = find_if( l.rbegin(), l.rend(),
   bind2nd( greater<int>(), 10 ) ); // find last greater than 10
if( last != l.rend() ) // if found, erase
   l.erase( --last.base() );
```

Detailed Solution

Sometimes you'd like to find the first occurrence of an object in your container and perhaps even remove it. For example, you might have a deque serving as a queue that contains rental cars. As the cars come in, they're placed on the end of the queue. Cars at the head of the queue are cleaned and made ready to rent again first, so to find the most prepared kind of car your customer wants, for example, a blue, subcompact car with manual transmission, you would search from the top of the queue. Once you've rented it, you would remove it from the list of available autos. (By the way, the STL has a queue container [see Tip 42], but unfortunately, you can neither search through it nor remove any element except the one at the head of the queue.)

Although `find` (the STL algorithm that finds the first occurrence of a particular item in a range) works on unsorted ranges, it's often useful to sort the range first. This effectively adds an extra condition to your search criteria because the element you find matches the search criteria while having the lowest possible sorting criterion. Similarly, by searching in reverse from the end of the sorted container, you get the element with the highest sorting value that also matches the search criteria.

As an example, suppose you have a list of military personnel, with each element having the soldier's name, rank, and type of job. It's your job to fill vacant positions with troops of the right rank and job skill. If you sorted the list in ascending order of rank and searched from the beginning by job, you would find the lowest ranked person who could do the work. If you searched in reverse from the end, you would find the highest ranked person of the appropriate capability.

The STL algorithm `find` finds the first element equal to a specified one, that is, the element closest to the start of the range. By using reverse iterators, `find` locates the last such element. Its close relative `find_if` works the same way, except that you give it the matching criterion instead of letting it use equality as the test.

Once you have the location of the element, you can use the container's `erase` member function to delete it. The program in Listing 9.5 illustrates these techniques by looking for certain publications in a list and removing those that it finds.

LISTING 9.5 Finding and Erasing the First or Last Matching Element

```cpp
// algorithm_find_first.cpp

#include <algorithm>
#include <functional>
#include <iostream>
#include <list>
#include <string>

using namespace std;

class Publication
{
   public:
   Publication( string first_name = "", string last_name = "",
      string title = "", string journal = "", int year = 0 );
   bool operator<( const Publication& rhs ) const;
   // order by date

   string last_name() const;
   void print() const;
   // display publication data

   int year() const;

   private:

   string first_name_;
   string journal_;
   string last_name_;
   string title_;
   int year_;
```

```
};

inline
Publication::Publication( string first_name, string last_name,
   string title, string journal, int year )
   : first_name_( first_name ), journal_( journal ),
     last_name_( last_name ), title_( title ), year_( year )
{} // empty

inline
bool Publication::operator<( const Publication& rhs ) const
{  return year() < rhs.year(); }

inline
string Publication::last_name() const
{  return last_name_; }

inline
void Publication::print() const
{
   cout << last_name() << ", " << first_name_ << endl
      << title_ << endl << journal_ << ", " << year()
      << endl << endl;
}

inline
int Publication::year() const
{  return year_; }

inline
bool equals_last_name( const Publication publication,
   string last_name )
{  return publication.last_name() == last_name; }


int main( )
{
   list<Publication> publication;

   publication.push_back( Publication( "Greg", "Reese",
      "Target detection against narrow band noise backgrounds",
      "Vision Research", 1999 ) );

   publication.push_back( Publication( "Greg", "Reese",
```

```
                      "Image Enhancement by Intensity Dependent Spread Functions",
                      "Computer Vision, Graphics and Image Processing", 1992 ) );

               publication.push_back( Publication( "Greg", "Reese",
                  "Theoretical Results for Intensity Dependent Spread Functions",
                  "Journal of the Optical Society of America A", 1992 ) );

               publication.push_back( Publication( "Tom", "Cornsweet",
                  "Intensity-dependent spatial summation",
                  "Journal of the Optical Society of America A", 1985 ) );

               publication.push_back( Publication( "Chris", "Woodward",
                  "Site Preferences and Formations Energies...",
                  "Physics Review B", 1998 ) );

               publication.push_back( Publication( "Chris", "Woodward",
                  "Equilibrium Mg Segregation at Al/Al3Sc Heterophase...",
                  "Physical Review Letters", 2003 ) );

               // sort in chronologically ascending order
               publication.sort();

               // display all publications
               cout << "THERE ARE " << publication.size() << " PUBLICATIONS\n";
               for_each( publication.begin(), publication.end(),
                  mem_fun_ref( &Publication::print ) );

               // find earliest publication by Reese
               string author( "Reese" );
               list<Publication>::iterator earliest =
                  find_if( publication.begin(), publication.end(),
                     bind2nd( ptr_fun( equals_last_name ), author ) );

               // if publication found, display and delete it
               if( earliest != publication.end() )
               {
                  cout << "\nEARLIEST PUBLICATION BY " << author << endl;
                  earliest->print();
                  publication.erase( earliest );
               }
               else
                  cout << "NO PUBLICATIONS BY " << author << endl;

               // find latest publication by Reese
```

```cpp
    list<Publication>::reverse_iterator latest =
       find_if( publication.rbegin(), publication.rend(),
          bind2nd( ptr_fun( equals_last_name ), author ) );

    // if publication found, display and delete it
    if( latest != publication.rend() )
    {
       cout << "\nLATEST PUBLICATION BY " << author << endl;
       latest->print();
       publication.erase( --latest.base() );
    }
    else
       cout << "NO PUBLICATIONS BY " << author << endl;

    // display all remaining publications
    cout << "THERE ARE " << publication.size()
       << " PUBLICATIONS REMAINING\n";
    for_each( publication.begin(), publication.end(),
       mem_fun_ref( &Publication::print ) );
}
```

The output is

```
THERE ARE 6 PUBLICATIONS
Cornsweet, Tom
Intensity-dependent spatial summation
Journal of the Optical Society of America A, 1985

Reese, Greg
Image Enhancement by Intensity Dependent Spread Functions
Computer Vision, Graphics and Image Processing, 1992

Reese, Greg
Theoretical Results for Intensity Dependent Spread Functions
Journal of the Optical Society of America A, 1992

Woodward, Chris
Site Preferences and Formations Energies...
Physics Review B, 1998

Reese, Greg
Target detection against narrow band noise backgrounds
Vision Research, 1999                                      →
```

```
Woodward, Chris
Equilibrium Mg Segregation at Al/Al3Sc Heterophase...
Physical Review Letters, 2003

EARLIEST PUBLICATION BY Reese
Reese, Greg
Image Enhancement by Intensity Dependent Spread Functions
Computer Vision, Graphics and Image Processing, 1992

LATEST PUBLICATION BY Reese
Reese, Greg
Target detection against narrow band noise backgrounds
Vision Research, 1999

THERE ARE 4 PUBLICATIONS REMAINING
Cornsweet, Tom
Intensity-dependent spatial summation
Journal of the Optical Society of America A, 1985

Reese, Greg
Theoretical Results for Intensity Dependent Spread Functions
Journal of the Optical Society of America A, 1992

Woodward, Chris
Site Preferences and Formations Energies...
Physics Review B, 1998

Woodward, Chris
Equilibrium Mg Segregation at Al/Al3Sc Heterophase...
Physical Review Letters, 2003
```

Suppose the user has a number of journal articles that he can cite in a paper he's writing. Once he cites one, he'd like to remove it so he doesn't include it in his list of references again. The program simulates these actions. It starts by declaring a class to hold information about a journal publication. The class contains the author's first and last names, the article's title, the name of the journal, and the year of publication. The class's member functions include the less-than operator, which sorts in ascending order of publication date, getters for the last name and year of publication, and a function that prints the internal information. There's also the global function equals_last_name, which returns true only if the passed publication's last name is equal to the passed last name. This is the predicate that find_if will use.

The aim of the program is to find the earliest and latest publications of an author, display them, and remove them from the collection of articles. To do this, the program starts by creating a list to hold the publications. (A list is a good container to use because the program will be deleting elements throughout the container and, as Tip 1 points out, lists are designed for this.) The program then adds some articles by the author or his colleagues to the list.

The goal is to find the earliest and latest publications, so the software sorts the elements into ascending chronological order by calling the list's sort member function (see Tip 30). The program uses for_each to call each element's print member function, as Tip 49 explains. The output shows that the six publications are indeed in chronological order. However, the code can't just take the first and last of the sorted publications as its result because they might not be by the right author.

To find the first publication by a particular author, the code uses find_if. The first two arguments are the container's range and the last is the match condition. Because the code sorts from the start of the container and the elements are in order of date, the first matching element will automatically be the earliest suitable publication. Thus, the match condition only needs to verify that the publication's author is the desired one.

The third argument to find_if does this. It calls the global function equals_last_name, which returns true only if the passed publication's last name is the same as the name that is the function's second argument. This argument is the same throughout the call to find_if, and its value is held constant through the use of the adaptor bind2nd (see Tip 50). Unfortunately, you can't just use an adaptor on a normal function like equals_last_name—it has to be adapted for the adaptor. Tip 47 and the program in Listing 9.5 show that you do this with the predefined function adaptor ptr_fun. The upshot is that the call to find_if returns an iterator that marks the earliest publication by the specified author, in this case, "Reese." If there are no works by him, the value returned is the container's end iterator.

If the program does find the publication, it prints the information about the article and deletes it by passing the iterator to the list's erase member function. All standard containers have this function, and all those functions require that the iterator lie strictly within the container's range; that is, the iterator can't be equal to the end iterator. This is why it's important to make sure that find_if did find an element before you try to erase it. The output shows that the result is the earliest of Reese's publications in the list.

The list is in chronological order, so if you search from the back to the front, you can find the latest publication by a particular author. Reverse iterators make it easy to do this. The first two arguments to the second call to find_if are the list's reverse begin iterator (rbegin) and reverse end iterator (rend). The third argument is the same as before, but the algorithm's return value is a reverse iterator. Again, the code verifies that find_if found something, but notice that this time, the code compares the returned iterator to the list's reverse end iterator, not to the normal end iterator. The program prints the element's information as before.

When it comes to deleting the elements, there's a problem—the `erase` member functions don't accept reverse iterators. To convert them to regular iterators, use the reverse iterator's `base` member function and decrement by one. "Reverse Iterators" in Chapter 2 explains this peculiar behavior.

The remainder of the output shows that the second call to `find_if` did find Reese's latest journal publication and that the list now only has four elements because the calls to `erase` permanently removed two.

Well, now you know how to find and remove the first or last specified element in a range. Sometimes, you might want to remove all elements that meet some criteria. If so, check Tip 52 and Tip 53.

TIP 52   REMOVE ALL MATCHING ELEMENTS

Applies to: Sequence container, remove, remove_if
See also: Tip 16, Tip 50, Tip 53, Tip 76, Tip 79

Quick Solution

```
deque<int> d;
// ...

deque<int>::iterator logical_end = // remove all odd elements
    remove_if( d.begin(), d.end(), bind2nd( modulus<int>(), 2 ) );
vector<int> v( d.begin(), logical_end ); // make vector of even numbers
```

When you remove elements from a container using `remove` or `remove_if`, the size of the container does not change.

Detailed Solution

It's not uncommon to want to get rid of some of the elements in a container. For example, suppose you're trying to determine which students qualify for a scholarship. Assume you have elements representing students and your container has the entire student body. First, you could remove all students whose grade-point average is not high enough to qualify for the scholarship. Then you could remove from the container all students who have too much money to receive the grant. After continuing this culling, you would be left with a container that has all the students that are eligible for the scholarship.

The STL algorithm `remove` gets rid of all elements in a range that are equal to a specified element. For example, you can use it to remove all values of 0 from a range of integers. remove's close relative remove_if does the same thing, except that you pass it the criterion that determines whether or not an element is removed. This lets you remove all values that are greater than a certain value, less than or equal to a certain value, and so on.

There's a twist to using these algorithms, and that is that neither of them permanently eliminate the elements in a container that they operate on. That's right, remove and remove_if don't really remove elements; that is, they don't change the size of the container. What they do is return an iterator to the logical end of the container, that is, to one element past all the elements that have not been removed. You then use the container's begin iterator and the logical end iterator to specify the range of all elements that should be considered in further processing because they have not been removed from the original range. You have to carry this end iterator around in the code and make sure to use it instead of the iterator given by the container's end member function. Don't try to use the values in the removed area. What is there is undefined, and those elements are often not even the ones that were removed.

The reason the removal algorithms don't change the size of the container when they remove elements is that they operate on an iterator range that might belong to a container whose elements can't be erased, that is, permanently removed. For example, if the range represents a C-style array, you can't change that array's size. If you do want to decrease a container's size when you get rid of elements, Tip 53 explains how to really remove elements from a container. The program in Listing 9.6 shows an elegant use of logically removing container elements.

LISTING 9.6   Removing All Matching Elements

```
// algorithm_remove_all.cpp

#include <algorithm>
#include <functional>
#include <iostream>
#include <iterator>
#include <numeric>
#include <vector>

using namespace std;

int main( )
{
    const int last_number = 50;
    vector<int> v( last_number - 1, 1 );
    v[0] = 2;
```

```
    // make the sequence 2, 3, ..., 49, 50
    partial_sum( v.begin(), v.end(), v.begin() );

    vector<int>::iterator stop = v.end();
    for( vector<int>::iterator start = v.begin(); start != stop;
       ++start )

       // remove all subsequent numbers that are not divisible by
       // the current one
       stop = remove_if( start+1, stop,
         not1( bind2nd( modulus<int>(), *start ) ) );

    cout << "Prime numbers: ";
    copy( v.begin(), stop, ostream_iterator<int>( cout, " " ) );
}
```

The output is

```
Prime numbers: 2 3 5 7 11 13 17 19 23 29 31 37 41 43 47
```

The program uses an ancient algorithm for finding prime numbers. (A *prime number* is a positive integer that is divisible by only two different positive integers, 1 and itself.) The Greek mathematician Eratosthenes (275–194 BC) created a procedure for finding all the primes up to a certain number. Here's a version of his algorithm:

- List all the integers from 2 up to some other integer of your choice.
- Remove all numbers after 2 that are divisible by 2.
- The next remaining number is 3. Remove all numbers after 3 that are divisible by 3.
- Start with the next remaining number and remove all numbers after it that are divisible by it.
- Repeat the preceding step until no numbers remain. The numbers left are all the primes from 2 (the first prime) through the integer you chose.

Because this algorithm strains out the numbers that are not prime from those that are, it's known as the Sieve of Eratosthenes.

The program starts by using the STL algorithm partial_sum to make the integers 2 through 50. (Tip 79 explains this technique.) The subsequent one-statement for-loop then carries out the entire sieve. The code first declares an iterator that stores the logical end of the sequence, that is, that marks the end of the numbers that have not been removed. Initially, this is simply the end iterator of the vector.

Next, in the initialization section of the loop, the program declares another iterator that points to the current number used to test divisibility and sets it to the start of the vector. The STL algorithm remove_if then does the work.

The first argument is the start of the sequence that remove_if should operate on. As the preceding algorithm explains, this is 1 after the current starting position in the vector, which is why the iterator in the argument has 1 added to it. The second argument marks the end of the sequence, and this is the logical end returned from the previous call to remove_if, or the actual end of the vector on the first call to remove_if.

The last argument is the condition for removing a number, namely, that it be divisible by the current starting number. To test this, you can divide the two numbers and examine the integer remainder. If it's 0, the two numbers are divisible, otherwise they are not. Fortunately, the Standard Library provides a functor for finding the remainder when dividing two integers—it's called modulus. Tip 76 explains how to use modulus and the other Standard Library functors for doing arithmetic.

The first argument that remove_if passes to modulus is an integer in the vector. The second argument (the divisor) is the current starting number. On any call to remove_if, the divisor is always the same because it is "frozen" by the built-in functor bind2nd, as Tip 50 explains. Finally, a third Standard Library functor, not1, returns the logical negation of the integer. This makes the condition for removal true if the remainder is 0 and false if it isn't. Thus, the entire statement removes all numbers after the current one that are exactly divisible by the current number, which is just what Eratosthenes wants us to do.

remove_if returns the end position of the numbers that it has not removed. This spot is used as the stopping point in the next call to remove_if. The output shows the result, which is all the prime numbers from 2 through 50. The code uses the STL algorithm copy and the technique of Tip 16 to display the numbers. Notice that stop, rather than the end iterator of the container, specifies the end of the range.

TIP 53	**REALLY REMOVE ALL MATCHING ELEMENTS**

Applies to: Sequence container, remove, remove_if
See also: Tip 5, Tip 50, Tip 51, Tip 52, Tip 76, Tip 84, Tip 86, Tip 90,
Listing 13.4, Listing 13.7, Listing 13.13

Quick Solution

```
deque<int> d;
// ...

d.erase( remove_if( d.begin(), d.end(), bind2nd( modulus<int>(), 2 ) ),
    d.end() ); // erase all odd elements from the deque
```

When you remove elements from a container as shown, the size of the container does change.

Detailed Solution

Tip 52 shows that you can logically remove elements from a container. This means that the elements that have not been removed are at the beginning of the container and a separate iterator marks the end of those elements. The container's size doesn't change, though. The advantages of this system are that you can avoid the expense of permanently deleting elements and that you can remove elements from ranges in which the elements can't be deleted, for example, a C-style array. The disadvantage is that you have to tote around an extra variable to mark the logical end of the container. This is a pain and takes us back to the bad old days of C-style arrays, which needed a separate variable to specify their length.

This tip shows you how to erase (permanently remove) elements from a standard sequence container. The size of the container decreases as elements are erased so that the container's length truly represents the number of elements that have not been removed. The program in Listing 9.7 demonstrates erasing elements by getting rid of fluke points in a set of experimental data.

LISTING 9.7   Really Removing All Matching Elements

```cpp
// algorithm_really_remove_all.cpp

#include <algorithm>
#include <cmath>
#include <functional>
#include <iostream>
#include <list>
#include <numeric>
#include <vector>

#include "tips.hpp"

using namespace std;

int main( )
{
    const float data_array[] = { 1, 1.3, 1.5, 0.9, 0.1, 0.2, -0.1,
        -0.9, -1.1, 0.1, 0.5, 55.4, 0.8, -7.2, -1.4 };

    // create and initialize vector with above data
    vector<float> data( data_array,
```

```cpp
        data_array + sizeof( data_array ) / sizeof( data_array[0] ) );

cout << "BEFORE ERASING OUTLIERS DATA VECTOR HAS "
    << data.size() << " ELEMENTS\n";
tips::print( data, "Data" );

// compute the mean
float mean = accumulate( data.begin(), data.end(), 0.0f )
    / data.size();

// subtract the mean from every data point
vector<float> zero_mean( data );
transform( zero_mean.begin(), zero_mean.end(), zero_mean.begin(),
    bind2nd( minus<float>(), mean ) );

// compute the sample standard deviation
float deviation = inner_product( zero_mean.begin(),
    zero_mean.end(), zero_mean.begin(), 0.0f );
deviation = sqrt( deviation / ( data.size() - 1 ) );

// erase all points more than three standard deviations
// greater than the mean
const int num_deviations = 3;
vector<float>::iterator end =
  remove_if( data.begin(), data.end(), bind2nd( greater<float>(),
      mean + num_deviations * deviation ) );
data.erase( end, data.end() );

// erase all points more than three standard deviations
// less than the mean
data.erase( remove_if( data.begin(), data.end(),
    bind2nd( less<float>(), mean - num_deviations * deviation ) ),
    data.end() );

cout << "\nAFTER ERASING OUTLIERS DATA VECTOR HAS "
    << data.size() << " ELEMENTS\n";
tips::print( data, "Data" );

// transfer to a list and remove all negative numbers
list<float> l( data.begin(), data.end() );
cout << "\nSize of list before calling remove_if: "
    << l.size() << endl;
l.remove_if( bind2nd( less<float>(), 0 ) );
cout << "Size of list after calling remove_if: "
```

```
        << l.size() << endl;
   tips::print( l, "List" );
}
```

The output is

```
BEFORE ERASING OUTLIERS DATA VECTOR HAS 15 ELEMENTS
Data: 1 1.3 1.5 0.9 0.1 0.2 -0.1 -0.9 -1.1 0.1 0.5 55.4 0.8 -7.2 -1.4

AFTER ERASING OUTLIERS DATA VECTOR HAS 14 ELEMENTS
Data: 1 1.3 1.5 0.9 0.1 0.2 -0.1 -0.9 -1.1 0.1 0.5 0.8 -7.2 -1.4

Size of list before calling remove_if: 14
Size of list after calling remove_if: 9
List: 1 1.3 1.5 0.9 0.1 0.2 0.1 0.5 0.8
```

In experimental data, there may occasionally be a few data points that are vastly different than the rest of the numbers. These anomalous values are called *outliers* and may come from equipment failures or gross human errors. A common way to get rid of outliers from a data set is to use these steps:

1. Compute the (sample) mean or average of the data.
2. Compute the (sample) standard deviation of the data by
     a. Subtracting the mean from each data point,
     b. Finding the sum of the squares of these differences,
     c. Dividing by the number of points minus one, and
     d. Taking the square root.
3. Eliminate all points that are greater than the mean plus three times the standard deviation or less than the mean minus three times the standard deviation. These points are the outliers.

The previous algorithm for computing the standard deviation makes three passes through the data—one to compute the mean, one to subtract it from the data, and one to add the sum of the squares of these differences. If you're interested, Tip 90 shows a different method of computing the variance, which is just the square of the standard deviation.

Before examining how the program removes outliers, look at the data array in the first line of the main function. Notice how all the values are between −2 and 2, except for 55.4 and −7.2. These two may be outliers, especially the first one.

The code starts by loading the numbers into a vector using the technique of Tip 5. The first section of the output shows the data set. Next, the program computes the mean by adding up all the values and dividing by the number of values. The STL algorithm accumulate does the sum nicely, as Tip 86 explains. The code then makes a copy of the vector with the data (using the vector's copy constructor) so that it can compute the standard deviation without changing the original data.

To subtract the mean from each data point, the program calls the STL algorithm transform. (Tip 76 explains how to do subtraction or any of the other three types of arithmetic on all elements of a container.) At this point, each element of the new vector of data is the corresponding original element minus the mean. As the code shows, you can easily get the sum of the squares of the elements by using yet another STL algorithm, inner_product. (Tip 84 provides the details for this technique.) Finally, the program divides the sum of the squares by one less than the number of data points and this gives the standard deviation.

The program removes outliers in two steps. The first call to remove_if gets rid of all points that are more than three standard deviations above the mean. The criterion passed to remove_if is easily made by combining the built-in STL function object greater with the mean plus three standard deviations. These constants are passed to the functors with another standard functor, bind2nd. Tip 50 provides more details on passing constants to functors.

remove_if returns an iterator that marks the end of the elements in the range that have not been removed. At this point, though, the vector still has its original size. To permanently remove the elements, call the erase member function, which all standard sequence containers have. This function accepts a range specified in the normal way—start of the range and one past the end of the range. The start is simply the iterator returned by remove_if and the end is the iterator provided by the container's end member function.

The second call to remove_if erases all points more than three standard deviations below the mean and combines the calls to remove_if and erase into one call. This way of coding is common and is called the remove-erase idiom. It works even when remove_if doesn't remove any elements. In that case, it returns an iterator to the end of the container. This makes the start and end of the range passed to erase be the same, so it does nothing. This is what happens in the sample program. By looking at the output, you can see that only the first call to erase removed any elements. You can also see that the actual size of the container has changed.

The last section of code is not part of removing outliers, but shows the special case of erasing from a list. Unfortunately, the terminology is confusing—a list has remove and remove_if member functions that actually do erase. A list also has erase member functions, but at least they erase, not remove. The difference is that remove and remove_if erase all elements in the list that equal a value or satisfy a predicate, whereas the erase functions erase an element at a given iterator or elements in a range of iterators.

The end of the output demonstrates that the list changes size when you call its remove_if member function. Because the two removal member functions are optimized for lists, you should use them instead of the corresponding STL algorithms.

This tip showed you how to erase all elements. If you just want to erase the first or last such element, check out Tip 51. If you want to remove all elements from a range that match a criterion without actually erasing them, see Tip 52.

TIP 54   SORT BEFORE PERFORMING SET OPERATIONS

Applies to: Sequence containers, merge, set_difference, set_intersection, set_symmetric_difference, set_union, unique

See also: Tip 17, Tip 30, Tip 49, Tip 59

Quick Solution

```
vector<int> v1, v2;
// ...

vector<int> v3( v1.size() + v2.size() );

sort( v1.begin(), v1.end() ); // must sort v1 and v2 first
sort( v2.begin(), v2.end() );

// elements in v1 and not in v2
set_difference( v1.begin(), v1.end(), v2.begin(), v2.end(), v3.begin()
);

// elements in v1 or v2 but not in both
set_symmetric_difference( v1.begin(), v1.end(), v2.begin(), v2.end(),
   v3.begin() );

// elements in v1 and v2
set_intersection( v1.begin(), v1.end(), v2.begin(), v2.end(),
   v3.begin() );

// elements in v1 or v2 or both
set_union( v1.begin(), v1.end(), v2.begin(), v2.end(), v3.begin() );

// elements in both vectors put in order in one vector
merge( v1.begin(), v1.end(), v2.begin(), v2.end(), v3.begin() );
```

```
// remove duplicate elements (size unchanged)
unique( v1.begin(), v1.end() );
```

Detailed Solution

The STL has a number of algorithms (see Table 9.3) for combining two ranges in different ways. Although the algorithms perform operations from mathematical set theory, they are quite useful for other purposes, as the code in Listing 9.8 illustrates.

TABLE 9.3   Sorted-Range Algorithms

Algorithm	Purpose
merge	Puts all elements from both input ranges into an output range. All elements in the input ranges end up in the output range
set_difference	Puts all elements that are in the first range but not in the second range in the output range
set_intersection	Puts all elements that are in both ranges in the sorted output range
set_symmetric_difference	Puts all elements that are in the first range or the second but not in both ranges into the output range
set_union	Puts all elements that are in either or both ranges into a sorted output range.
unique	Removes consecutive duplicates

All the algorithms have two versions. One version uses the default sorting criterion (less-than) and the other accepts a predicate that specifies the sorting. The signatures for each version are the same for all five algorithms. For example, for set_union the two signatures are

```
OutputIterator
set_union( InputIterator start1, InputIterator stop1,
    InputIterator start2, InputIterator stop2, OutputIterator startOut )

OutputIterator
set_union( InputIterator start1, InputIterator stop1,
    InputIterator start2, InputIterator stop2, OutputIterator startOut,
    BinaryPredicate predicate )
```

The second input range is a little unusual in that the end of that range needs to be specified. This is necessary because the two ranges could have different sizes. However, the output range, as usual, only has the start specified. You have to make sure the output range can contain the output or else use an inserter. If you make the output size be the sum of the two input sizes, you'll always be able to hold the results of these algorithms. This will probably waste a good amount of memory, though, so the best bet is to use an inserter.

The most important thing to remember when using these algorithms is that the input ranges must be sorted before you use the algorithms. They also have to be sorted according to the same criterion you use in the algorithm, either the default function or a specified one. If you use unsorted input ranges, neither the compiler nor the algorithms will report that, and the results will generally be incorrect. This bug can be hard to track down.

Here are a few other tips for using the sorted range algorithms:

- All algorithms return the end of the output range.
- The output is always sorted.
- For merge, all elements (including all copies) end up in the output range so that the number of elements is the sum of the number of elements in the two input ranges.
- For set_union, if one or both ranges have duplicates of some element, the number of times that element appears in the output is the maximum of the number of times it appears in the first or second range. For example, if one input range has five 2s and the other input range has three 2s, the output will contain five 2s. If those ranges were used in merge, the output would contain eight 2s.
- For set_intersection, duplicates occur in the output if both input ranges have the same element duplicated. The number of times that element appears in the output is the minimum of the number of times it appears in the two input ranges. For example, if one input range has five 2s and the other input range has three 2s, the output will contain three 2s.
- For set_difference, output duplicates are possible if the first input range has duplicates. The number of duplicates in the output is the number of times an element appears in the first input range minus the number of times the element appears in the second range. (If the element appears more times in the second range, it won't be in the output at all.) For example, if one input range has five 2s and the other input range has three 2s, the output will contain two 2s.
- For set_symmetric_difference, output duplicates can occur if elements are duplicated in an input range. The number of duplicates in the output is the larger number of duplicates in one input range minus the number of times it appears in the second range. For example, if one input range has five 2s and the other input range has three 2s, the output will contain two 2s.

The program in Listing 9.8 shows a good application of the sorted set algorithms.

LISTING 9.8   Using Sorted Set Algorithms

```cpp
// algorithm_sort_sets.cpp

#include <algorithm>
#include <functional>
#include <iomanip>
#include <iostream>
#include <list>
#include <string>
#include <vector>

using namespace std;

class Part
{
   public:
   enum part { engine, transmission, body };

   Part( part a_part = Part::engine, int id = 0 );
   bool operator<( const Part& rhs ) const;
   // sort by ID

   void print() const;
   // display information about part

   private:
   part part_;
   int id_;
};

inline
Part::Part( part a_part, int id )
   : part_( a_part ), id_( id )
{} // empty

inline
bool Part::operator<( const Part& rhs ) const
{   return id_ < rhs.id_;   }

void Part::print() const
{
```

```
      string component;
      if( part_ == engine )
         component = "engine";
      else if( part_ == transmission )
         component = "transmission";
      else
         component = "body";

      cout << "ID: " << setw( 8 ) << left << id_
         << " Part: " << component << endl;
}

int main( )
{
   // make the list of parts that Inspector A has examined
   list<Part> inspector_A;
   inspector_A.push_back( Part( Part::engine, 341002 ) );
   inspector_A.push_back( Part( Part::transmission, 1001 ) );
   inspector_A.push_back( Part( Part::body, 97344 ) );
   inspector_A.push_back( Part( Part::engine, 222145 ) );
   inspector_A.push_back( Part( Part::body, 8877 ) );

   // make the list of parts that Inspector B has examined
   list<Part> inspector_B( inspector_A );
   inspector_B.front() = Part( Part::transmission, 62804 );
   inspector_B.back() = Part( Part::body, 111359 );

   // must sort before using set algorithms
   inspector_A.sort();
   inspector_B.sort();

   cout << "ALL PARTS EXAMINED BY INSPECTOR A\n";
   for_each( inspector_A.begin(), inspector_A.end(),
      mem_fun_ref( &Part::print ) );

   cout << "\n\nALL PARTS EXAMINED BY INSPECTOR B\n";
   for_each( inspector_B.begin(), inspector_B.end(),
      mem_fun_ref( &Part::print ) );

   vector<Part> result;

   cout << "\n\nALL PARTS EXAMINED BY BOTH INSPECTORS\n";
   set_intersection( inspector_A.begin(), inspector_A.end(),
      inspector_B.begin(), inspector_B.end(),
```

```
      back_inserter( result ) );
for_each( result.begin(), result.end(),
   mem_fun_ref( &Part::print ) );

cout << "\n\nALL PARTS EXAMINED BY INSPECTOR A ONLY\n";
result.clear();
set_difference( inspector_A.begin(), inspector_A.end(),
   inspector_B.begin(), inspector_B.end(),
   back_inserter( result ) );
for_each( result.begin(), result.end(),
   mem_fun_ref( &Part::print ) );

// make vector large enough to hold all inspected parts
result.resize( inspector_A.size() + inspector_B.size() );

cout << "\n\nALL PARTS EXAMINED BY INSPECTOR B ONLY\n";
vector<Part>::iterator the_end =
   set_difference( inspector_B.begin(), inspector_B.end(),
   inspector_A.begin(), inspector_A.end(), result.begin() );
for_each( result.begin(), the_end, mem_fun_ref( &Part::print ) );

cout << "\n\nALL PARTS EXAMINED BY ONLY ONE INSPECTOR\n";
the_end = set_symmetric_difference( inspector_A.begin(),
   inspector_A.end(), inspector_B.begin(), inspector_B.end(),
   result.begin() );
for_each( result.begin(), the_end, mem_fun_ref( &Part::print ) );

cout << "\n\nALL PARTS EXAMINED BY AT LEAST ONE INSPECTOR\n";
the_end = set_union( inspector_A.begin(), inspector_A.end(),
   inspector_B.begin(), inspector_B.end(), result.begin() );
for_each( result.begin(), the_end, mem_fun_ref( &Part::print ) );

cout << "\n\nALL PARTS EXAMINED\n";
the_end = merge( inspector_A.begin(), inspector_A.end(),
   inspector_B.begin(), inspector_B.end(), result.begin() );
for_each( result.begin(), the_end, mem_fun_ref( &Part::print ) );
}
```

The output is

```
ALL PARTS EXAMINED BY INSPECTOR A
ID: 1001     Part: transmission
ID: 8877     Part: body
ID: 97344    Part: body
ID: 222145   Part: engine
ID: 341002   Part: engine


ALL PARTS EXAMINED BY INSPECTOR B
ID: 1001     Part: transmission
ID: 62804    Part: transmission
ID: 97344    Part: body
ID: 111359   Part: body
ID: 222145   Part: engine


ALL PARTS EXAMINED BY BOTH INSPECTORS
ID: 1001     Part: transmission
ID: 97344    Part: body
ID: 222145   Part: engine


ALL PARTS EXAMINED BY INSPECTOR A ONLY
ID: 8877     Part: body
ID: 341002   Part: engine


ALL PARTS EXAMINED BY INSPECTOR B ONLY
ID: 62804    Part: transmission
ID: 111359   Part: body


ALL PARTS EXAMINED BY ONLY ONE INSPECTOR
ID: 8877     Part: body
ID: 62804    Part: transmission
ID: 111359   Part: body
ID: 341002   Part: engine


ALL PARTS EXAMINED BY AT LEAST ONE INSPECTOR
ID: 1001     Part: transmission
ID: 8877     Part: body
ID: 62804    Part: transmission
ID: 97344    Part: body
ID: 111359   Part: body
ID: 222145   Part: engine
ID: 341002   Part: engine
```

$\rightarrow$

```
ALL PARTS EXAMINED
ID: 1001      Part: transmission
ID: 1001      Part: transmission
ID: 8877      Part: body
ID: 62804     Part: transmission
ID: 97344     Part: body
ID: 97344     Part: body
ID: 111359    Part: body
ID: 222145    Part: engine
ID: 222145    Part: engine
ID: 341002    Part: engine
```

Here's the situation: in a car manufacturing plant, two quality-control inspectors must examine each major part. The software has a list of the parts that each inspector has examined so far. By using the sorted set algorithms, you can get lots of information about the status of the inspections, such as which parts have been examined by only one inspector or already looked at by both inspectors.

The program starts by declaring a simple class to represent a car part. The class has the type of part (engine, transmission, or body) and the identification number (ID) of part. It has a less-than operator that sorts according to the ID. Finally, there's a little print function that shows the part type and identification number.

The main program starts by creating a list of parts that Inspector A has looked at and another list for Inspector B. It displays these two lists by having for_each (see Tip 59) call the print member function (see Tip 49) of each element in the lists. Next, the code sorts the lists by calling the list's sort member function (see Tip 30). The program must do this before using any of the sorted range functions. (If the parts were stored in vectors or deques, the program would use the STL sort algorithm instead.) The first two sections of the output show the result, which is simply what parts each inspector has examined. This output is also useful for verifying that subsequent calls to the sorted range algorithms work correctly.

After declaring a vector to hold the results of the algorithms, the code calls set_intersection, which finds the elements common to both lists. These are the parts that both inspectors have examined. If this meant that they were finished with this stage of quality control, more complicated code would send them along to the next phase of manufacturing. You can see that the output from this algorithm and the others described next is sorted, by default, into ascending value of the part ID.

The first call to set_difference shows the parts that only Inspector A has looked at. It also illustrates one of two techniques for working with the output of the sorted set algorithms. In this method, the code declares an empty output vector or clears the vector before using it in the algorithm to ensure that there are no elements present. When the code passes the vector to the algorithm, the software wraps the vector in a call to a back inserter, which simply pushes each output element onto the back of the vector. The advantage of this method is that the output vector only contains as many elements as the algorithm produces. This conserves memory and makes it convenient to use the vector because the size tells you the number of elements in the output. The disadvantages are that the back inserter may cause reallocation (see Tip 17) and that you have to remember to clear the vector each time before using it in one of the sorted set algorithms.

The next call to set_difference has the two input ranges switched, so the result is the parts that only Inspector B has examined. It also illustrates the second method of working with the output. First, the program resizes the vector to hold the maximum possible number of output elements that any call to the algorithms could produce. This is just the total number of input elements in all the input containers. Next, the program declares an iterator for the output vector. All the algorithms in Table 9.3 return an iterator that marks the end of the output range, that is, it's 1 past the last element written. The code then uses this value instead of the vector's end iterator when specifying the range of elements in the vector, for example, in the call to for_each. The advantages of this method are that the output vector will never reallocate and that you don't need to clear the vector each time before using it. The disadvantages are that you must know ahead of time the maximum possible number of elements, you might allocate more memory than necessary, and you have to tote around the end-of-range iterator instead of using the one in the vector. The remainder of the program uses this method.

Next, the code calls set_symmetric_difference, which produces the parts that only one inspector has looked at. This tells the Quality Control department how many parts are halfway done with inspection. The program also calls set_union to list all parts that have been examined by at least one inspector. Note that there are no duplicates in this list. That's the difference from the output to merge (called next), which does include duplicates and thus is not as useful in this application.

TIP 55   SORT ON ONE OF MANY FIELDS

Applies to: Vector, deque
See also: Tip 3, Tip 4, Tip 5, Tip 9, Tip 45, Tip 79

Quick Solution

See the detailed solution.

Detailed Solution

Sometimes the situation arises in which you have a number of containers with related data, and you need to sort them based only on the values in one container, the key. For example, one vector may contain the names of some cars, a second vector may have their horsepower, and a third vector may have the year in which they were made. The first elements in all the containers correspond to one car, the second elements correspond to another car, and so on. If you want to sort by horsepower, you'll need to move the other fields around too, so that after sorting all corresponding elements are still together.

You might ask, "If all elements at a given index are related to each other, why aren't they in a class? Then you would just have one container of objects which you could easily sort." The answer is that this *is* what you should do. Unfortunately, sometimes you have to deal with code written by people who haven't yet embraced object-oriented programming—they aren't using classes. The program might be legacy code, that is, old software, that doesn't even use standard containers, just C-style arrays. The program in Listing 9.9 shows you how to sort on one of many fields, even if those fields are stored in arrays.

LISTING 9.9   Sorting on One of Many Fields

```
// algorithm_sort_fields.cpp

#include <algorithm>
#include <iomanip>
#include <iostream>
#include <numeric>
#include <vector>

using namespace std;

void display( float price[], float height[], int weight[],
   int array_length );

void legacy_sorter( float price[], float height[], int weight[],
   int array_length );
// sort on price, other fields rearranged accordingly

int main( )
{
   float price[] = { 299.99, 174.95, 199.99, 198.99, 329.00 };
   float height[] = { 2.9, 2.2, 2.3, 2.4, 3.2 };
   int weight[] = { 84, 62, 70, 72, 94 };
```

```cpp
      const int n = sizeof( price ) / sizeof( price[0] );

      cout << "BEFORE SORTING BY PRICE\n";
      display( price, height, weight, n );

      legacy_sorter( price, height, weight, n );

      cout << "\nAFTER SORTING BY PRICE\n";
      display( price, height, weight, n );
   }

   void legacy_sorter( float price[], float height[], int weight[],
      int array_length )
   {
      // need space between > and >
      vector< pair<float,int> > index( array_length );

      // make the sequence 0, 1, 2, ..., array_length-1
      vector<int> temp_int( array_length, 1 );
      temp_int[0] = 0;
      partial_sum( temp_int.begin(), temp_int.end(), temp_int.begin() );

      // make a vector of pairs of prices and indexes
      transform( price, price+array_length, temp_int.begin(),
         index.begin(), make_pair<float,int> );

      // sort by price
      sort( index.begin(), index.end() );

      // rearrange the prices
      vector<float> temp_float( price, price+array_length );
      for( int i = 0; i < array_length; ++i )
         price[i] = temp_float[index[i].second];

      // rearrange the heights
      temp_float.assign( height, height+array_length );
      for( int i = 0; i < array_length; ++i )
         height[i] = temp_float[index[i].second];

      // rearrange the weights
      temp_int.assign( weight, weight+array_length );
      for( int i = 0; i < array_length; ++i )
         weight[i] = temp_int[index[i].second];
   }
```

```
void display( float price[], float height[], int weight[],
   int array_length )
{
   cout << fixed;
   for( int i = 0; i < array_length; ++i )
      cout << "Price: " << fixed << setprecision( 2 ) << setw( 6 )
         << price[i] << setprecision( 1 ) << setw( 5 ) << height[i]
         << setw( 4 ) << weight[i] << endl;
}
```

The output is

```
BEFORE SORTING BY PRICE
Price: 299.99  2.9  84
Price: 174.95  2.2  62
Price: 199.99  2.3  70
Price: 198.99  2.4  72
Price: 329.00  3.2  94

AFTER SORTING BY PRICE
Price: 174.95  2.2  62
Price: 198.99  2.4  72
Price: 199.99  2.3  70
Price: 299.99  2.9  84
Price: 329.00  3.2  94
```

The example program demonstrates sorting on one of many fields by having three C-style arrays with the price, height, and weight of some machines. The program declares two global functions to perform the work. The first, display, simply displays the information in the arrays. The second, legacy_sorter, sorts the data in the arrays based on price. It's best not to use arrays at all (vectors are much better), but because this type of sorting arises in structured programming, it's likely that arrays will be around too.

The code for sorting is in legacy_sorter. The idea is to store the original index of each price with the price, and as the prices are sorted, the indexes stay with them. When the sorting is finished, the other arrays are rearranged according to the shuffled indexes. That is, the first rearranged element originally had the first index, the second rearranged element originally had the second index, and so forth.

The function starts by making a vector with the same length as the arrays (see Tip 4) and containing pairs. A pair is a handy data structure (see Tip 45) that contains two elements that can have different data types. In this case, the first is a floating-point number (the price) and the second is an integer, the index. The two elements are in that order because one pair being less than another is first determined by comparing the first elements, rather than the second. Note also that there must be a space between the two closing angle brackets in the declaration of the vector. Otherwise, the compiler would interpret two consecutive right angle brackets as the right shift operator.

Next, the program uses the STL algorithm `partial_sum` and Tip 79 to make the integers from 0 up to the array length minus 1. These serve as the indexes of the original positions of the data. The code continues by putting the prices and corresponding indexes together into pairs and storing them in a vector. The STL algorithm `transform` does the work. Its first two arguments are the range of the C-style array. Tip 3 explains that the STL was fortunately designed to let arrays be used this way.

Once the vector is filled with the price-index pairs, it becomes trivial to sort it. The code does this in one line by calling the STL algorithm `sort`. By default, `sort` uses the less-than operator, which for pairs is the result of comparing the first elements with their less-than operator. The upshot is that the pairs are sorted by increasing price.

Finally, the function rearranges the arrays. It creates a vector of floating-point numbers and initializes them with the values in the price array (see Tip 5). Then the function uses a simple loop to copy those numbers back into the array in sorted order. Next, the function stores the array of heights in the same vector using the vector's `assign` member function (as Tip 9 describes) and uses a loop to put the heights back into the array in the correct order. Finally, the function rearranges the weights the same way. The output shows the data in the arrays before and after sorting and confirms that the information is in ascending order of price.

TIP 56   SORT WITH MULTIPLE CRITERIA

TIP

Applies to: Sequence containers
See also: Tip 48, Tip 59, Listing 13.7

Quick Solution

See the detailed solution.

Detailed Solution

The default sorting criterion in both the STL `sort` algorithm and the `sort` member function of lists is less-than. By using the predefined functors in the STL, you can easily change that to other simple criteria, such as greater-than, equal-to, and so on. However, you can't use those functors to do many things that are even slightly more complicated, such as the absolute value of the first argument being less than the absolute value of the second.

One way to make a complex sorting criterion is to code it as a function. This has several disadvantages. First off, the function can only take two arguments—the values that sort passes to it. If you need any other values, they have to be stored inside the function as constants or passed as global variables. That first alternative is not flexible because you can't change the values of the constants. The second alternative is bad programming practice.

Another drawback is that the number of functions you need can proliferate dramatically. For example, suppose you have a class that represents a car. It contains the model year, price, engine power, and gas mileage. You'd like to let the user sort on any of these items. When there are ties, you'd like to sort the tied values by another one of the items, for example, sort by price and, within price, sort by year. There are four fields for the first sorting and three for the second (assume the two sorting values can't be the same), so there are a total of 12 different ways to sort. This means you'd have the unenviable job of writing 12 different sorting functions.

The way to handle multiple or complex sorting criteria is to write a class that makes the sorting decision. It must define operator() as a binary predicate that decides if the first argument should come before the second. You pass an instance of the class to sort, and it calls the call operator. You can set in the class constructor any values you need or change them with mutators. You can also make the sorting decision as complicated as you want. If you have lots of combinations of things that go into making the decision, you can handle them by logic in one member function (the call operator) instead of writing many different global functions. Although this can make the member function pretty ugly, it's better than having to write a lot of global functions to do the work.

Here's an example of sorting with many different criteria. The code in Listing 9.10 demonstrates with the sort algorithm, but the list sort member function works the same way.

LISTING 9.10   Sorting with Multiple Criteria

```
// algorithm_sort_criteria.cpp

#include <algorithm>
#include <functional>
#include <iomanip>
#include <iostream>
#include <vector>

using namespace std;
```

```cpp
class Resistor_lot
{
  public:
  Resistor_lot( int lot = 0, int pieces = 0, int price = 1,
    int resistance = 1 );
  // lot >= 0 - lot number
  // pieces >= 0 - number of resistors in lot
  // price > 0 - price in dollars per hundred resistors
  // resistance > 0 - resistance in ohms

  int lot() const;
  int pieces() const;
  int price() const;

  void print() const;
  // display info on lot

  int resistance() const;

  private:
  int lot_, pieces_, price_, resistance_;
};

inline
Resistor_lot::Resistor_lot( int lot, int pieces, int price,
  int resistance) : lot_( lot ), pieces_( pieces ), price_( price ),
  resistance_( resistance )
{} // empty

inline
int Resistor_lot::lot() const
{ return lot_; }

inline
int Resistor_lot::pieces() const
{ return pieces_; }

inline
int Resistor_lot::price() const
{ return price_; }

inline
void Resistor_lot::print() const
{ cout << left << "Lot #: " << setw( 5 ) << lot()
```

```cpp
        << "Resistance (ohms): " << setw( 7 ) << resistance()
        << "Pieces: " << setw( 6 ) << pieces()
        << "Price/100: $" << setw( 5 ) << price() << endl;
}

inline
int Resistor_lot::resistance() const
{ return resistance_; }

class Resistor_lot_sorter
{
    public:
    enum sort_field { none, lot, pieces, price, resistance };

    Resistor_lot_sorter( bool ascending = true,
        sort_field field1 = lot,
        sort_field field2 = none );
    // ascending - if true sort in ascending order, else descending
    // field1 - first field to sort on. Can't be none
    // field2 - second field to sort on. Can be equal to none but
    //          must be different than field1

    bool operator()( const Resistor_lot& lhs,
        const Resistor_lot& rhs );
    // returns true if field1 of lhs is less than field1 of rhs
    // returns false if field1 of lhs is greater than field1 of rhs
    // returns false if field1 of both are equal and field2 is none
    // if field2 is not none returns true if field2 of lhs is less
    // than field2 of rhs, otherwise returns false

    void ascending( bool ascend );
    // ascend - if true sort in ascending order, else descending

    bool is_ascending() const;

    void field( sort_field field1 = lot, sort_field field2 = none );
    // field1 - first field to sort on. Can't be none
    // field2 - second field to sort on. Must be different than field1

    private:

    bool compare( const Resistor_lot& x, const Resistor_lot& y );
    // carries out comparison for operator()
```

```cpp
      bool ascending_;
      sort_field field1_;
      sort_field field2_;
};

inline
Resistor_lot_sorter::Resistor_lot_sorter( bool ascending,
   sort_field field1, sort_field field2 )
   : ascending_( ascending ), field1_( field1 ), field2_( field2 )
{} // empty

inline
bool Resistor_lot_sorter::operator()( const Resistor_lot& lhs,
   const Resistor_lot& rhs )
{
   if( is_ascending() )
      return compare( lhs, rhs );
   else
      return compare( rhs, lhs );
}

inline
void Resistor_lot_sorter::ascending( bool ascend )
{ ascending_ = ascend; }

bool Resistor_lot_sorter::compare( const Resistor_lot& x,
   const Resistor_lot& y )
{
   bool result = false;

   // store the values to compare
   int x_value, y_value;
   if( field1_ == lot )
   {
      x_value = x.lot();
      y_value = y.lot();
   }
   else if( field1_ == pieces )
   {
      x_value = x.pieces();
      y_value = y.pieces();
   }
   else if( field1_ == price )
   {
```

```
         x_value = x.price();
         y_value = y.price();
   }
   else
   {
         x_value = x.resistance();
         y_value = y.resistance();
   }

   // compare values and return if not equal
   if( x_value < y_value )
      return true;
   else if( x_value > y_value )
      return false;

   // at this point the two values are equal. If we're not sorting
   // on a second field, return false
   if( field2_ == none )
      return false;

   // now let the second field decide. If the two fields are equal
   // this code still works but having them be the same doesn't
   // make sense
   if( field2_ == lot )
      result = x.lot() < y.lot();
   else if( field2_ == pieces )
      result = x.pieces() < y.pieces();
   else if( field2_ == price )
      result = x.price() < y.price();
   else
      result = x.resistance() < y.resistance();

   return result;
}

inline
bool Resistor_lot_sorter::is_ascending() const
{ return ascending_; }

inline
void Resistor_lot_sorter::field( sort_field field1,
   sort_field field2 )
{
   field1_ = field1;
```

```
      field2_ = field2;
}

int main( )
{
   vector<Resistor_lot> lot;
   lot.push_back( Resistor_lot( 23, 1200, 36, 33 ) );
   lot.push_back( Resistor_lot( 448, 2000, 34, 33 ) );
   lot.push_back( Resistor_lot( 2, 148, 54, 2200 ) );
   lot.push_back( Resistor_lot( 505, 2450, 17, 15000 ) );
   lot.push_back( Resistor_lot( 201, 442, 19, 27000 ) );

   Resistor_lot_sorter sorter;

   cout << "ASCENDING ORDER BY LOT NUMBER\n";
   sort( lot.begin(), lot.end(), sorter );
   for_each( lot.begin(), lot.end(),
      mem_fun_ref( &Resistor_lot::print ) );

   cout << "\nDESCENDING ORDER BY NUMBER OF PIECES\n";
   sorter.field( Resistor_lot_sorter::pieces );
   sorter.ascending( false );
   sort( lot.begin(), lot.end(), sorter );
   for_each( lot.begin(), lot.end(),
      mem_fun_ref( &Resistor_lot::print ) );

   cout << "\nASCENDING ORDER BY RESISTANCE, THEN PRICE\n";
   sorter.field( Resistor_lot_sorter::resistance,
      Resistor_lot_sorter::price );
   sorter.ascending( true );
   sort( lot.begin(), lot.end(), sorter );
   for_each( lot.begin(), lot.end(),
      mem_fun_ref( &Resistor_lot::print ) );
}
```

The output is

```
ASCENDING ORDER BY LOT NUMBER
Lot #: 2     Resistance (ohms): 2200    Pieces: 148    Price/100: $54
Lot #: 23    Resistance (ohms): 33      Pieces: 1200   Price/100: $36
Lot #: 201   Resistance (ohms): 27000   Pieces: 442    Price/100: $19
Lot #: 448   Resistance (ohms): 33      Pieces: 2000   Price/100: $34
Lot #: 505   Resistance (ohms): 15000   Pieces: 2450   Price/100: $17
                                                                    →
```

```
DESCENDING ORDER BY NUMBER OF PIECES
Lot #: 505  Resistance (ohms): 15000  Pieces: 2450  Price/100: $17
Lot #: 448  Resistance (ohms): 33     Pieces: 2000  Price/100: $34
Lot #: 23   Resistance (ohms): 33     Pieces: 1200  Price/100: $36
Lot #: 201  Resistance (ohms): 27000  Pieces: 442   Price/100: $19
Lot #: 2    Resistance (ohms): 2200   Pieces: 148   Price/100: $54

ASCENDING ORDER BY RESISTANCE, THEN PRICE
Lot #: 448  Resistance (ohms): 33     Pieces: 2000  Price/100: $34
Lot #: 23   Resistance (ohms): 33     Pieces: 1200  Price/100: $36
Lot #: 2    Resistance (ohms): 2200   Pieces: 148   Price/100: $54
Lot #: 505  Resistance (ohms): 15000  Pieces: 2450  Price/100: $17
Lot #: 201  Resistance (ohms): 27000  Pieces: 442   Price/100: $19
```

Suppose your software needs to display information about electrical resistors stored in a vendor's warehouse. The resistors are in lots, and you know the lot number, number of resistors, resistor price and resistance. You'd like to sort on any of these fields and sort ties on a different field. In addition, you'd like to sort in ascending or descending order. The sample program demonstrates how to do all this.

The program starts by declaring a class to represent a resistor lot. Its constructor accepts the preceding information. There are accessor member functions to return those values and a member function to display the information about the lot.

To make the sorting criteria, the program declares another class designed to compare resistor lots. An enumeration in the class lets the user specify which value to sort on. The first field can be lot number, number of pieces, price, or resistance. The second field must be different than the first or can have the value "none." In this case, the order of tied elements is unspecified. The constructor accepts the values for the two fields and whether to sort in ascending or descending order. The class also has mutators to change those three values and an accessor to get the sorting direction.

The class also declares the call operator `operator()` that `sort` will use. The operator receives two arguments and passes them on to a private member function for comparison. That function returns `true` if its first argument is less than its second and `false` otherwise. If the resistor lots are to be sorted in ascending order, the call operator passes its arguments in the same order to the comparison function. If the sorting should be descending, the operator passes its arguments in reversed order. This essentially causes the comparison function make a greater-than decision and so sort in descending order.

The comparison function begins by getting the values specified by the first sorting field from the passed resistor lots, that is, the lot numbers, number of pieces, prices, or resistances. The function compares the two values and returns `true` if the first is less than the second and `false` if the second is less than the first. If they are equal and there's no sorting on the second field, the function returns `false`. If there is sorting on the second field, the function again compares the specified values and returns the result of the comparison. Although the logic in the comparison function and call operator is a little complicated, if you were to do the equivalent work by writing one global function for each sorting combination, you would need 32 such functions.

The main part of the program starts by declaring a vector and storing in it the resistor lots in the warehouse. The code then creates a resistor lot sorter with the default constructor, passes it to `sort`, and prints the sorted vector. The code does this by using `for_each` and calling the member function of the resistor lot class that displays the internal information. Tip 48 and Tip 59 give you more details on this technique. The first section of the output shows that the resistor lots are sorted in ascending lot number. This display would make it easy for a warehouse employee who might try to examine lots specified by lot number.

On the other hand, a salesman or warehouse manager might want to sell resistors from the lots that have the most pieces first. To accommodate him, the software changes the value of the first field in the sorter class to be the number of pieces and makes the sorting direction be descending. It sorts and displays the lots as before. The second section of the output shows the result.

Finally, a customer might want to browse through the available resistors and would likely do this by listing them by resistance. For resistors with the same resistance, he would like the cheapest ones listed first. The code accomplishes this by changing the two fields in the sorter, specifying an ascending sort, and then sorting and displaying the resistor lots. The last part of the output shows the result. Note that the first two lots have the same resistance, but the cheaper lot is listed first.

TIP 57   SORT WITHOUT COPYING

Applies to: Sort, vector, deque
See also: Tip 49, Tip 59

Quick Solution

```
bool less_than_iterator( const vector<Big_class>::iterator i,
    const vector<Big_class>::iterator j )
{  return *i < *j;   } // Big_class must define operator<
// ...

vector<Big_class> big;
// ...
```

```
// make a vector of iterators pointing to the big classes
   vector< vector<Big_class>::iterator > iterators( big.size() );

// set the iterators
   vector< vector<Big_class>::iterator >::iterator j =
iterators.begin();
      vector<Big_class>::iterator i = big.begin();
   while( i != big.end() )
      *j++ = i++;

   // sort iterators
sort( iterators.begin(), iterators.end(), less_than_iterator );
// ...
```

Detailed Solution

Sorting moves a container's elements around a lot by using the element's assignment operator and copy constructor. This implies that you should make those functions run fast. Actually, because copying is ubiquitous throughout the STL, any classes you write for use there should make these functions very efficient. Unfortunately, some classes may be difficult to move, even if you write them carefully. For example, they may simply use a lot of memory for data, which makes their copy constructors and assignment operators very time-consuming to run.

Here's a neat technique that alleviates this problem. This technique lets you access the elements in sorted order without having to copy or move them at all. The trick is to make a vector of iterators that point to the elements and then sort the iterators, which can be moved about very quickly. The program in Listing 9.11 demonstrates this idea.

LISTING 9.11   Sorting Without Copying

```cpp
// algorithm_sort_no_copy.cpp

#include <algorithm>
#include <functional>
#include <iostream>
#include <vector>

using namespace std;

class Experiment
{
   public:
   Experiment( int num_points = 0 );
```

```
        // num_points - number of data points in experiment

        bool operator<( const Experiment& rhs ) const;
        // return true if number of points in "this" is less than that in
        // rhs, return false otherwise

        int num_points() const;
        void print() const;

        private:
        vector<float> data_;
    };

    inline
    Experiment::Experiment( int num_points )
        : data_( num_points )    // simulate getting data
    {}    // empty

    inline
    bool Experiment::operator<( const Experiment& rhs ) const
    { return num_points() < rhs.num_points(); }

    inline
    int Experiment::num_points() const
    {   return static_cast<int>( data_.size() ); }

    inline
    void Experiment::print() const
    {   cout << "\nThis experiment has " << num_points()
        << " data points";
    }

    bool less_than_iterator( const vector<Experiment>::iterator i,
        const vector<Experiment>::iterator j );
    // evaluate *i < *j

    int main( )
    {
        vector<Experiment> experiments;

        const int num_experiments = 5;
        experiments.reserve( num_experiments );

        // create some experiments
```

```
experiments.push_back( Experiment( 30000 ) );
experiments.push_back( Experiment( 90000 ) );
experiments.push_back( Experiment( 5300 ) );
experiments.push_back( Experiment( 130000 ) );
experiments.push_back( Experiment( 2500 ) );

cout << "ORDER OF EXPERIMENTS BEFORE SORTING";
for_each( experiments.begin(), experiments.end(),
   mem_fun_ref( &Experiment::print ) );

// make a vector of iterators pointing to the experiments
vector< vector<Experiment>::iterator >
   iterators( experiments.size() );
vector< vector<Experiment>::iterator >::iterator j
   = iterators.begin();

vector<Experiment>::iterator i = experiments.begin();
vector<Experiment>::iterator experiments_end = experiments.end();
while( i != experiments_end )
   *j++ = i++;

sort( iterators.begin(), iterators.end(), less_than_iterator );

cout << "\n\nSORTED ITERATORS";
vector< vector<Experiment>::iterator >::iterator iterators_end
   = iterators.end();
for( j = iterators.begin(); j != iterators_end; ++j )
   (*j)->print();

// verify that order of experiments hasn't changed
cout << "\n\nORDER AFTER SORTING";
for_each( experiments.begin(), experiments.end(),
   mem_fun_ref( &Experiment::print ) );
}

bool less_than_iterator( const vector<Experiment>::iterator i,
   const vector<Experiment>::iterator j )
{  return *i < *j;   }
```

The output is

```
ORDER OF EXPERIMENTS BEFORE SORTING
This experiment has 30000 data points
This experiment has 90000 data points
This experiment has 5300 data points
This experiment has 130000 data points
This experiment has 2500 data points

SORTED ITERATORS
This experiment has 2500 data points
This experiment has 5300 data points
This experiment has 30000 data points
This experiment has 90000 data points
This experiment has 130000 data points

ORDER AFTER SORTING
This experiment has 30000 data points
This experiment has 90000 data points
This experiment has 5300 data points
This experiment has 130000 data points
This experiment has 2500 data points
```

The program starts by making a little class to represent an experiment. The class has a vector that holds data points. In the constructor, the user specifies the number of points to be gathered during the experiment. The amount of data can be quite large, so copying and assigning the experiment class could be slow. Nonetheless, the user may want to sort the vector, perhaps to analyze the smaller experiments first.

Execution begins by loading experiments of various sizes into a vector. Then the code uses the for_each STL algorithm (see Tip 59) and the print member function of the class (see Tip 49) to display the number of points in each element of the vector. The first section of the output shows the results, including the fact that the experiments are not ordered by number of data points.

Next, the program creates a vector of iterators that point to the elements in the vector of experiments. The program calls the STL algorithm sort and passes it a custom function that determines the ordering. This function accepts two iterators that point to instances of the Experiment class. The function dereferences the iterators and compares them using the class's less-than operator, which returns true if the number of data points in the first instance is less than that in the second instance. Otherwise, it returns false. The middle section of the output shows that the vector of pointers is now ordered by number of data points.

Finally, the program displays the elements in the original vector to demonstrate that their order has not changed.

TIP 58	**COPY IF A CONDITION IS MET**

Applies to: Standard containers
See also: Tip 5, Tip 7, Tip 16, Tip 50

Quick Solution

```
vector<int> v1;
// ...

// copy all numbers in v1 greater than 10 to v2
vector<int> v2;
remove_copy_if( v1.begin(), v1.end(), back_inserter( v2 ),
        not1( bind2nd( greater<int>(), 10 ) ) );
```

See the detailed solution for a better, though lengthier, method.

Detailed Solution

Suppose you want to copy all elements that meet a condition from one container to another. If you look through the STL algorithms, you'll find a bunch with "copy" in their names (there are actually 11 of them). You'll also find quite a few with "if" in their names. There are also a couple that have "copy_if" as part of their names. There isn't, however, a plain, old copy_if. It was accidentally left out of the Standard Library.

The program in Listing 9.12 shows you two ways of copying elements that satisfy a criterion. The first uses the STL algorithm remove_copy_if. The second uses a custom-written function, appropriately called copy_if. If you're going to be doing this sort of copying often (and it is a common task), you should just add copy_if to your toolbox and use it instead of remove_copy_if. It's clearer, better, and easier to use.

LISTING 9.12   Copying Elements if They Meet a Criterion

```
// algorithm_copy_if.cpp

#include <algorithm>
#include <functional>
#include <vector>

#include "tips.hpp"
```

```
using namespace std;

template<class InputIterator, class OutputIterator,
   class Predicate >
OutputIterator copy_if( InputIterator start, InputIterator stop,
   OutputIterator out, Predicate select  )
{
   while( start != stop )
   {
      if( select( *start ) )
         *out++ = *start;
      ++start;
   }
   return out;
}

int main( )
{
   const int numbers = 7;
   const int num[numbers] = { -5, 0, 13, 20, 10, 4, -1 };
   vector<int> v1( num, num+numbers );
   tips::print( v1, "Original numbers" );

   // put all numbers less than 10 in v2
   vector<int> v2;
   copy_if( v1.begin(), v1.end(), back_inserter( v2 ),
      bind2nd( less<int>(), 10 ) );
   tips::print( v2, "\nNumbers less than 10" );

   // put all numbers greater than 10 in v2
   v2.resize( v1.size() );
   vector<int>::const_iterator v2_copy_end =
      remove_copy_if( v1.begin(), v1.end(), v2.begin(),
         not1( bind2nd( greater<int>(), 10 ) ) );

   cout << "\nNumbers greater than 10: ";
   for( vector<int>::const_iterator i = v2.begin(); i != v2_copy_end;
      ++i )
      cout << *i << " ";
}
```

The output is

```
Original numbers: -5 0 13 20 10 4 -1

Numbers less than 10: -5 0 4 -1

Numbers greater than 10: 13 20
```

The top of the code shows the `copy_if` function. Like all the STL algorithms, this is a template. The first two function arguments specify the input range, the third argument is the start of the output range, and the fourth is the predicate that decides whether or not an element will be copied. (For more on predicates, see "Predefined Function Objects" in Chapter 2.) The predicate should have one argument with the same data type as that in the input range and should return `true` if a particular element is to be copied and `false` otherwise. `copy_if` returns an output iterator that marks the end of the elements that have been copied. The program demonstrates a use of this returned value.

As the beginning of Appendix A and Table A.1 explain, the names of the template parameters imply what kinds of data types the parameters should be. For example, the first parameter's name is `InputIterator` which means that whatever is passed to the first two arguments of the function must have the capabilities of an input iterator. This could (obviously) be an input iterator, but it could also be a forward, bidirectional, or random access iterator. Moreover, the input and output arguments of `copy_if` don't have to come from a container. You could make input iterators from an input stream like `cin` (see Tip 7) to copy only certain user inputs to an output container. Similarly, you could copy only certain elements of a container to the standard output stream, which is very close to what Tip 16 shows.

The code in `copy_if` that does the work is short and simple. A loop simply goes through the input range and copies any element that meets the passed criterion to the output range. That's it.

The main part of the program starts by loading some numbers into a vector, using the technique explained by Tip 5. The code then calls `copy_if` to copy all numbers less than 10 to the second vector. The code does this with the Standard Library `less` functor (see "Predefined Function Objects" in Chapter 2) and the second argument frozen at 10 (see Tip 50). Because the code doesn't know how many elements the function will copy to the output vector, it creates an empty vector and uses a back inserter to load the elements into the vector. ("Insert Iterators" in Chapter 2 explains inserters in more detail.) The first line of the output shows the original numbers and those less than ten.

The second half of the program shows alternatives to using a back inserter or `copy_if`. If you make the output vector large enough to hold the most elements it could possibly receive, you won't need a back inserter. For this program, that means the output vector has to be as large as the input vector, so the code calls the output vector's member function `resize` to set the appropriate length.

The remainder of the program demonstrates another way of copying elements that meet a condition. This technique uses the STL algorithm `remove_copy_if`, which copies elements for which the predicate is *not* true from the input to the output range. To get `remove_copy_if` to copy those elements that *do* make the predicate true just negate the condition using the STL functor `not1` as shown. The iterator that `remove_copy_if` returns is one past the last element that it wrote.

The program displays the second group of found numbers by looping from its beginning to the ending point that `remove_copy_if` returned. This will be different than the actual number of elements in the output vector if `remove_copy_if` didn't fill that container. The last line of the output shows the result.

You might wonder why you can't just make a `copy_if` function out of `remove_copy_if`. It would look something like this:

```
template<class InputIterator, class OutputIterator,
   class Predicate >
OutputIterator copy_if( InputIterator in, InputIterator stop,
   OutputIterator out, Predicate select  )
{
    return remove_copy_if( in, stop, out, not1( select ) );
}
```

The problem is that `not1` only operates on adaptable functions (see "Predefined Function Objects" in Chapter 2) and the passed predicate may or may not be adaptable. A common example of a non-adaptable functor is an ordinary function, which would prevent the preceding `copy_if` from even compiling.

TIP 59 OPERATE ON EACH ELEMENT OF A CONTAINER

Applies to: Standard containers, for_each, transform
See also: Tip 11, Tip 15, Tip 28, Tip 30, Tip 45, Tip 46, Tip 50, Tip 54,
                   Tip 57, Tip 90, Listing 13.4

Quick Solution

```
class Athlete
{
   public:
   // ...
   void print() const;
   int salary() const;
```

```
    // ...
};
// ...


vector<Athlete> team;
// ...

// print info about all team members
for_each( team.begin(), team.end(), mem_fun_ref( &Athlete::print ) );

// find team salary
vector<int> v( team.size() );
transform( team.begin(), team.end(), v.begin(),
    mem_fun_ref( &Athlete::salary ) );
cout << "Total team salary is " << accumulate( v.begin(), v.end(), 0 );
```

Detailed Solution

The STL provides two algorithms that allow you to perform an operation you specify on each element in a range: `for_each` and `transform`. The first operates on every element of an input range and has the signature

```
UnaryProcedure
for_each( InputIterator start, InputIterator stop,
    UnaryProcedure procedure )
```

The second algorithm, `transform`, operates on one or two input ranges and puts the result in an output range. `transform` has two versions, depending on whether there are one or two input ranges.

```
OutputIterator
transform( InputIterator start, InputIterator stop,
    OutputIterator startOut, UnaryOperation operation1 )

OutputIterator
transform( InputIterator start1, InputIterator stop1,
    InputIterator start2, OutputIterator startOut,
        BinaryOperation operation2 )
```

To help you decide which one to use, Table 9.4 compares the two algorithms.

Although Table 9.4 will help you decide which of the two algorithms to use, a bigger question is whether you should use either at all. As Tip 46 says, if there is a more specific algorithm available to do the job, use it. If you want to count, use `count`. If you want to replace, use `replace`.

TABLE 9.4 Differences Between `for_each` and `transform`

for_each	transform
One input range only	One or two input ranges
Can modify[a] or not modify input values	Can modify[b] or not modify input values
Has no output range	Must write to the output range
Returns a copy of the procedure	Returns an iterator marking the end of the output range
Argument passed by reference	Argument(s) passed by value
Slightly faster because procedure modifies argument directly	Slightly slower because returns and assigns result of procedure

a If the parameter in the function argument of for_each is passed by reference, the function argument can modify it. If it's passed by value or constant reference, the function argument can only read it.

b transform only passes parameters by value to its function argument. However, it can indirectly modify an input range by also using it as the output range.

Tip 11, Tip 28, Tip 45, and Tip 50 are examples of using transform. Chapter 7 and Chapter 11 also have many examples of this handy algorithm. Tip 15, Tip 30, Tip 54, Tip 57, Tip 90, and the program in Listing 9.13 demonstrate `for_each`.

LISTING 9.13 Operating on Each Element of a Container

```cpp
// algorithm_for_each.cpp

#include <algorithm>
#include <iostream>
#include <string>
#include <vector>

using namespace std;

class Base_counter
{
    public:
    Base_counter();
```

```
        void operator()( char base );
        // add base to internal count. base must be A, C, G, T or N

        int GC_clamping() const;
        // number of consecutive Gs and Cs at end of the sequence

        int num_A() const;
        int num_C() const;
        int num_G() const;
        int num_T() const;
        int num_unknown() const;
        // number of times a particular base is in the sequence

        int num_bases() const;
        // total number of bases in the sequence

        float percent_GC() const;
        // percentage of bases that are G or C (zero if no bases)

        void print() const;
        // display summary of data

        private:
        int GC_clamping_;
        int num_A_;
        int num_C_;
        int num_G_;
        int num_T_;
        int num_unknown_;
};

inline
Base_counter::Base_counter()
    :  GC_clamping_( 0 ), num_A_( 0 ), num_C_( 0 ), num_G_( 0 ),
       num_T_( 0 ), num_unknown_( 0 )
{} // empty

void Base_counter::operator()( char base )
{
    if( base == 'A' )
        ++num_A_;
    else if( base == 'C' )
        ++num_C_;
```

```
         else if( base == 'G' )
            ++num_G_;
         else if( base == 'T' )
            ++num_T_;
         else
            ++num_unknown_;

      if( base == 'C' || base == 'G' )
         GC_clamping_ = 0;

      if( base == 'C' || base == 'G' )
         ++GC_clamping_;
      else
         GC_clamping_ = 0;
}

inline
int Base_counter::GC_clamping() const
{  return GC_clamping_; }

inline
int Base_counter::num_A() const
{  return num_A_; }

inline
int Base_counter::num_C() const
{  return num_C_; }

inline
int Base_counter::num_G() const
{  return num_G_; }

inline
int Base_counter::num_T() const
{  return num_T_; }

inline
int Base_counter::num_unknown() const
{  return num_unknown_; }

inline
int Base_counter::num_bases() const
{  return num_A() + num_T() + num_C() + num_G() + num_unknown(); }
```

```cpp
inline
float Base_counter::percent_GC() const
{   return num_bases() == 0 ? 0 :
        100.0f * ( num_C()+num_G() ) / num_bases(); }

void Base_counter::print() const
{
    cout   << "A bases: " << num_A() << endl
           << "T bases: " << num_T() << endl
           << "G bases: " << num_G() << endl
           << "C bases: " << num_C() << endl
           << "Unknown bases: " << num_unknown() << endl
           << "Total bases: " << num_bases() << endl
           << "Percent GC: " << percent_GC() << endl
           << "GC clamping: " << GC_clamping() << endl;
}

int main( )
{
    string bee( "TTTACGCCCGATTCCCAACACGGTCGC" );
    Base_counter count = for_each( bee.begin(), bee.end(),
        Base_counter() );

    cout << "DNA ANALYSIS FOR BEE\n";
    count.print();

    string zebrafish( "GCTNGTAATGGGGTATACTGATTCAGCGTGGTGTTTCCCC" );
    count = for_each( zebrafish.begin(), zebrafish.end(),
        Base_counter() );

    cout << "\n\nDNA ANALYSIS FOR ZEBRAFISH\n";
    count.print();
}
```

```
DNA analysis for bee
A bases: 5
T bases: 6
G bases: 5
C bases: 11
Unknown bases: 0
Total bases: 27
Percent GC: 59.2593
GC clamping: 3
```

The output is

```
DNA analysis for zebrafish
A bases: 6
T bases: 13
G bases: 12
C bases: 8
Unknown bases: 1
Total bases: 40
Percent GC: 50
GC clamping: 4
```

The program demonstrates using `for_each` in a molecular biology application—a simple analysis of DNA. DNA, the blueprint of life, is made up of four different chemicals called bases. They are denoted by A, C, G, and T. Sometimes the kind of base hasn't been determined so a fifth symbol, N, is used to represent an unknown type of base.

It's useful to know how many of each kind of base there are in a strand of DNA. The percentage of the strand made up of Gs and Cs can also be important, and in some situations, the number of consecutive Gs or Cs at the end of the strand is of interest. This is called the amount of GC clamping. The idea behind the program is to make a class that can keep track of these numbers and use `for_each` to pass every base in a strand of DNA to the class so it can accumulate the statistics.

The class has five private variables to record the number of each of the bases it receives and has a sixth private integer that holds the amount of GC clamping. The constructor simply initializes all the variables to zero. `for_each` applies the class's call operator, which does two things. First, the call operator increments the counter corresponding to the base it receives. Second, it increments the GC clamping counter if the base is a G or a C or sets the counter to 0 for any other base. The resulting value is the number of consecutive G's and C's at the end of the sequence. The class also has seven accessors—five to get the number of times each of the five bases occurs, one for the total number of bases in the strand, and one for the percentage of G's and C's. Third, the print member function sends a little report to the standard output stream.

The main program starts by storing a little snippet of bee DNA in a string (you can find DNA sequences of many organisms at *http://www.ncbi.nlm.nih.gov*). Then it creates a temporary instance of the counting class and passes it as the third argument to `for_each`. That algorithm calls the class's call operator for each element of the string, that is, for each base in the DNA strand. String iterators aren't used that often, but this is a nice application of them.

When `for_each` finishes, it returns a copy of the class that was passed to it. (`for_each` is the only STL algorithm that does this.) Receiving a copy of the passed class is a very convenient feature because the copy can contain data about the sequence the algorithm ran over. That's the case for the base-counter class in the program. It now has information about the DNA sequence, which the program displays by calling the print member function. The result is the first section of the output that follows Listing 9.13.

The program finishes by analyzing DNA from a zebrafish the same way. Note that the program again creates a temporary instance of the class in the third argument to `for_each`. If you didn't want to create a new instance (for example, if each instance used a lot of resources) you could just pass it the old instance. However, you'd have to add a member function that would let you reset all the counters to zero. Otherwise, the numbers would accumulate with each run and would not reflect only the last piece of DNA analyzed. The second half of the output shows the analysis for the zebrafish.

10 Tips on Text Processing

C has always been weak in text processing. It manipulates lines of text, or text strings, through character arrays. Such an array, which this book will call a C-string, is simply an array of type char terminated by a zero.

There are two major problems with C-strings. The first is that their size is fixed. Once you declare or allocate the array, you can't make it bigger. This is a particularly annoying flaw because text lines vary widely in length. In practice, programmers have to do two things to handle this restriction. The first is to make the array long enough to hold the maximum number of text characters that would ever be put in it. The second is to constantly verify that text being stored in the array doesn't exceed that maximum.

The second problem is that pesky zero at the end of the array. Its presence is crucial because all the routines that use C-strings depend on it. For example, strlen, which computes the length of the string, starts at the beginning of the character array and counts array elements until it reaches an element that's zero. Then the routine stops and returns the count. If the zero is not there, you've got a problem. The routine will continue reading in memory until it comes across a value of zero that is there by chance or until it tries to access a protected region, at which point it will crash.

So one problem with the terminating zero is that you have to remember to put it there and be careful not to overwrite it with a nonzero value. Another problem is remembering to leave room in the array for the terminating zero. This means that if the array has *n* elements, it can only accept *n-1* characters because the last element needs to be zero. Put another way, if the maximum number of characters allowed in a particular line of text is *n*, the program must ensure that the text array is *n+1* elements long. This needs to be documented carefully and thoroughly and, well…you know what program documentation is like.

The C++ Standard Library comes to the rescue with a new class called string. (Let's refer to this class as a "string.") First, a string automatically expands to accept any text given to it. This process is invisible to the programmer—you don't have to worry about it. Second, it doesn't use a terminating zero (or more specifically, its programming interface doesn't use one), so you don't have to worry about that either.

string is in the standard namespace std. It integrates into C++ as well as a built-in data type. For example, it operates in streams, has operators such as + and +=, and generally behaves like a good C++ citizen.

string is very easy to use and you'll find it a joy and relief to work with it instead of C-strings. However, if you've been with C-strings for a while, you probably feel comfortable with the host of string manipulation functions that are available. Many of these functions have obvious analogies in strings. A number of them can also be carried out with the STL very easily, but it's certainly not obvious how. To ease your transition from C-style strings to C++ strings, this chapter gives you the Standard Library equivalent of many C-string functions. (Some of them, though common, are not officially part of the Standard Library.) Table 10.1 lists these functions alphabetically and tells you which tip has the Standard Library equivalent.

TABLE 10.1   Standard Library Equivalents of C-String Functions

Function	Standard Library	Description
sprintf	Tip 70	Formatted write to a string
sscanf	Tip 69	Formatted read from a string
strcat	Tip 61	Concatenate two strings
strchr	Tip 62	Find first occurrence of a given character
strcmp	Tip 65	Lexicographical comparison
strcpy	Tip 60	Copy one string to another
strcspn	Tip 62	Find first occurrence in one string of characters in another string
strdup	Tip 60	Duplicate a string
stricmp	Tip 67	Case insensitive string comparison
strlen	Tip 64	Length of string
strlwr	Tip 73	Convert to lower case
strncat	Tip 61	Append at most n characters
strncmp	Tip 65	Lexicographical comparison of first n characters of two strings
strncpy	Tip 60	Copy at most n characters
strnicmp	Tip 67	Case insensitive, lexicographical comparison of first n characters $\rightarrow$

Function	Standard Library	Description
strnset	Tip 63	Set the first *n* characters to a given character
strpbrk	Tip 62	Find first of a set of characters
strrchr	Tip 62	Find last occurrence of a given character
strrev	Tip 64	Reverse the characters in a string
strset	Tip 63	Set all characters to a given character
strspn	Tip 62	Find the first character not in a given set
strstr	Tip 62	Find first occurrence of a substring
strtok	Tip 75	Tokenize a string
strupr	Tip 73	Convert to upper case

The chapter also has tips on how to convert a C++ string to a C-string and how to strip leading and trailing whitespace from a string of text.

TIP 60 | ## COPY STRINGS AND SUBSTRINGS

Applies to: String

Quick Solution

```
string s1, s2;
//...
string s3( s1 ); // copy by construction
s2 = s1;         // copy by assignment

// copy substring of 8 characters starting at index 5
s3 = s1.substr( 5, 8 );
```

Detailed Solution

Table 10.2 shows three ways of copying C-strings and gives the equivalent functionality for C++ strings. The code in Listing 10.1 illustrates these techniques.

TABLE 10.2   Equivalents for Copying Strings

Function	Member Function	Description
strcpy	=	Copy one string to another
strdup	=	Duplicate a string
strncpy	=, substr	Copy at most *n* characters

LISTING 10.1   Copying Strings

```cpp
// string_copy.cpp

#include <iostream>
#include <string>

using namespace std;

int main( )
{
   string s1( "Jupiter Symphony" );
   string s1_copy;

   // equivalent of strcpy()
   s1_copy = s1;

   // equivalent of strdup()
   string s1_duplicate( s1 );
   cout << "String 1:             " << s1
        << "\nCopy of String 1:      " << s1_copy
        << "\nDuplicate of String1:  " << s1_duplicate;

   string s2( "Eroica Symphony" );
   cout << "\n\nString 2:  " << s2;

   // equivalent of strncpy()
   s1 = s2.substr( 0, 6 );
   cout << "\nCopying the first 6 letters of String 2 "
      "to String 1 gives:  " << s1;
}
```

The output is

```
String 1:              Jupiter Symphony
Copy of String 1:      Jupiter Symphony
Duplicate of String1:  Jupiter Symphony

String 2:  Eroica Symphony
Copying the first 6 letters of String 2 to String 1 gives:  Eroica
```

The program starts by declaring an initialized string and an empty string. It then assigns the first string to the empty one, thus making a copy of the former string. This is the equivalent of strcpy, and a nicer one at that.

The next line of code shows the equivalent for strdup, which is simply the copy constructor. This is not exactly the same as strdup because that function dynamically allocates memory and returns a pointer to the string. In C, this is useful for providing a copy of a string whose length is not known at compile time. Since C++ strings can dynamically change their size, having an exact equivalent of strdup is not very useful.

strncpy is in C to limit the number of characters moved to the destination string to prevent that string from overflowing. Again, because C++ strings automatically adjust their size, limiting the number of copied characters is not necessary. The clearest way to replace a string by the first *n* characters of another string is to set the former to a substring of the latter. The code for the equivalent of strncpy shows this. However, you can also use one of the many forms of the string's replace member function, specifically

```
s1.replace( p1, n1, s2, p2, n2 )
```

This replaces n1 characters of string s1 starting at index p1 with n2 characters of string s2 starting at index p2. For example, the substr call at the end of the code in Listing 10.1 would be

```
s1.replace( 0, s1.length(), s2, 0, 6 );
```

In other words, replace all of the characters of s1 with the first six characters of s2.

TIP 61   CONCATENATE STRINGS AND SUBSTRINGS

Applies to: Strings

Quick Solution

```
string s1, s2, s3;
//...

s1 += s3; // strcat
s2 += s3.substr( 0, 10 ); // strncat
```

Detailed Solution

C-strings provide a function to concatenate or append two strings. They have another function to concatenate an initial group of characters from one string to another. Table 10.3 shows that the C++ equivalents are done with the += operator using either full strings or substrings. The code in Listing 10.2 illustrates these methods.

TABLE 10.3 Equivalents for Concatenating Strings and Substrings

Function	Member Function	Description
strcat	+=	Concatenate two strings
strncat	+=, substr	Concatenate at most *n* characters

LISTING 10.2 CONCATENATING STRINGS

```
// string_concatenate.cpp

#include <iostream>
#include <string>

using namespace std;

int main( )
{
    string s1( "An apple a day " );
    string s1_original( s1 );  // save s1 for later
    string s2( "keeps the doctor away" );

    cout << "String 1:  " << s1 << endl << "String 2:  " << s2;

    // equivalent of strcat()
    s1 += s2;
    cout << "\nString 2 appended to String 1:  " << s1;
```

```
        s1 = s1_original;
        cout << "\n\nString 1:    " << s1 << "\nString 2:    " << s2;

        // equivalent of strncat()
        s1 += s2.substr( 0, 18 );
        cout
            << "\nAppending the first 16 letters of "
                "String 2 to String 1 gives:\n" << s1;
    }
```

The output is

```
String 1:  An apple a day
String 2:  keeps the doctor away
String 2 appended to String 1:  An apple a day keeps the doctor away

String 1:  An apple a day
String 2:  keeps the doctor away
Appending the first 16 letters of String 2 to String 1 gives:
An apple a day keeps the doctor
```

You can concatenate strings by using the += operator, as the code for the equivalent of strcat shows. You can also use the append member function, but the operator is common and makes sense, given its interpretation when used with numbers.

strncat is typically used in C to limit the number of characters moved to the destination string to prevent that string from overflowing. C++ strings automatically adjust their size, so limiting the number of copied characters is not necessary. However, the code shows that you can concatenate the first group of letters of a string by using the += operator as before but on the substring produced by the string's substr member function.

| TIP 62 | **SEARCH STRINGS** |

Applies to: Strings

Quick Solution

```
string s;
//...
```

```
// find first occurrence of a character
string::size_type index = s.find( 'u' );
if( index != string::npos )
   cout << "\nThe first \"u\" is at index " << index;
else
   cout << "\nThere is no \"u\" in the string";

// find last occurrence of a character
index = s.rfind( 'u' );
if( index != string::npos )
   cout << "\nThe last \"u\" is at index " << index;
else
   cout << "\nThere is no \"u\" in the string";

// find first occurrence of a string
index = s.find( "tub" );
// ...

// find last occurrence of a string
index = s.rfind( "tub" );
// ...

// find first occurrence of a character from a group of characters
index = s.find_first_of( "aeiou" );
//...

// find first occurrence of a character not in a group of characters
index = s.find_first_not_of( "aeiou" );
//...
```

Detailed Solution

There are a number of functions for searching in C-strings. C++ strings have equivalent member functions that are easy to use and have more descriptive names. Table 10.4 shows the C functions and their C++ equivalents. The program in Listing 10.3 demonstrates searching in strings.

TABLE 10.4 Equivalents for String Searches

Function	Member Function	Description
strchr	find	Find first occurrence of a given character
strcspn	find_first_of	Find first occurrence of characters in another string
strpbrk	find_first_of	Find first of a set of characters
strrchr	rfind	Find last occurrence of a given character
strspn	find_first_not_of	Find first character not in a given set
strstr	find	Find first occurrence of a substring

LISTING 10.3 Searching for Strings

```
// string_search.cpp

#include <iostream>
#include <string>

using namespace std;

int main( )
{
   string typing( "The quick, brown fox jumps over the lazy dog" );
   cout << "String:  " << typing << endl;

   // find first occurrence of a character - equivalent of strchr()
   string::size_type index = typing.find( 'u' );
   if( index != string::npos )
      cout << "\nThe first \"u\" is at index " << index;
   else
      cout << "\nThere is no \"u\" in the string";

   // find last occurrence of a character - equivalent of strrchr()
   index = typing.rfind( 'u' );
   if( index != string::npos )
      cout << "\nThe last \"u\" is at index " << index;
   else
      cout << "\nThere is no \"u\" in the string";

   // find first occurrence of a substring - equivalent of strstr()
   index = typing.find( "fox" );
```

```
        if( index != string::npos )
            cout << "\n\"fox\" first occurs at index " << index;
        else
            cout << "\n\"fox\" is not in the string";

        // find last occurrence of a substring - no C-string equivalent
        index = typing.rfind( "fox" );
        if( index != string::npos )
            cout << "\n\"fox\" last occurs at index " << index;
        else
            cout << "\n\"fox\" is not in the string";

        // equivalent of strcspn() and strpbrk()
        index = typing.find_first_of( "aeiou" );
        if( index != string::npos )
            cout << "\nThe first lower-case vowel is at index " << index;
        else
            cout << "\nThere is no lower-case vowel in the string";

        // equivalent of strspn()
        index = typing.find_first_not_of( "aeiou" );
        if( index != string::npos )
            cout << "\nThe first letter that is not a lower-case vowel "
                "is at index " << index;
        else
            cout << "\nAll letters in the string are lower-case vowels";
}
```

The output of this code is

```
String:  The quick, brown fox jumps over the lazy dog

The first "u" is at index 5
The last "u" is at index 22
"fox" first occurs at index 17
"fox" last occurs at index 17
The first lower-case vowel is at index 2
The first letter that is not a lower-case vowel is at index 0
```

The first search uses the `find` member function to locate the first occurrence of a character. This is the equivalent of `strchr`. If the character is present, `find` returns the zero-based index of the first occurrence of the character. If the character is not there, find returns string::npos. In general, you should always verify that a search member function found what it was looking for by making sure the return value is not string::npos. (In some idioms, though, this is not necessary.)

npos stands for "no position" and is a constant in the string scope. There are two ways of accessing npos. The first is to use it with the string scope, that is, string::npos. For example,

```
string canal( "Panama" );
if( canal.find( 'p' ) != string::npos )
{ //...
```

Alternatively, you can access npos as a public data member in a string variable, for example,

```
string canal( "Panama" );
if( canal.find( 'p' ) != canal.npos )
{ //...
```

The next search uses the string member function rfind (reverse find) to get the index of the last occurrence of a character. This is the equivalent of strrchr. This and other member functions that look in reverse return normal indexes, that is, zero-based with the first index being at the start of the string.

The next two searches are the same except that they look for substrings, not characters. The member function find with a string argument is the equivalent of strstr. Searching for the last occurrence of a substring is easy with rfind. There is no C equivalent for this.

strcspn and strpbrk are very similar. strcspn searches in a C-string until it finds any one of a specified set of characters, then returns the length of the initial segment that comprises characters that are *not* in the given set. strpbrk looks for the first occurrence of any character from a given set and returns a pointer to it. The find_first_of member function of a string acts similarly by returning the index of the first occurrence of any of a given group of characters. Finally, strspn returns the length of the initial segment of the C-string that is made up of characters only from a given set. Because the find_first_not_of member function returns the index of the first character not in a given set, these two values are equal.

TIP 63   **REPLACE CHARACTERS BY A GIVEN CHARACTER**

Applies to: Strings

Quick Solution

```
string s;
//...

// replace the 5 characters starting at index 4 with 10 asterisks
s.replace( 4, 5, 10, '*' );
s.assign( s.length(), '*' ); // replace all characters with asterisks
```

Detailed Solution

Table 10.5 shows that you can replace all characters in a C-string with one specific character by using strset. You can do the same thing for just an initial group of characters with strnset. The program in Listing 10.4 demonstrates how to do both of these things with C++ strings.

TABLE 10.5 Equivalents for Replacing Characters

Function	Member Function	Description
strnset	replace	Set the first *n* characters to a given character
strset	replace or assign	Set all characters to a given character

LISTING 10.4 Replacing Characters in Strings

```
// string_replace.cpp

#include <iostream>
#include <string>

using namespace std;

int main( )
{
    string credit_card( "4578 9906 512 6661" );
    cout << "Credit card number: " << credit_card;

    // equivalent of strnset()
    credit_card.replace( 0, credit_card.length()-4,
        credit_card.length()-4, '*' );
    cout << "\nSecure display of credit card number: " << credit_card;
```

```
          // equivalent of strset()
          credit_card.assign( credit_card.length(), '*' );
          cout << "\nMore secure display of credit card number: "
             << credit_card;
      }
```

The output is

```
Credit card number: 4578 9906 512 6661
Secure display of credit card number: **************6661
More secure display of credit card number: ******************
```

The program stores a credit card number as a string and displays the whole number. (This is a made-up number, so don't even think of using it.) A more secure and commonly used output is to just show the last four digits. The code does this by substituting an asterisk for all but the last four characters in the credit card number. It does this by calling one of the many forms of the string's `replace` member function, namely

```
replace( index, length, number, c )
```

where `index` is the index where the replacements will begin, `length` is the number of characters in the string that will be removed and `number` is the number of occurrences of the character `c` that will be inserted. (You can remove a different amount than what you put in.) The second line of the output shows the resulting string.

Finally, the `assign` member function replaces all characters with a given one, in this case an asterisk. The code could also have used the preceding form of `replace`, that is,

```
credit_card.replace( 0, credit_card.length(), credit_card.length(), '*' )
```

The last line of the output shows the result.

TIP 64 REVERSE STRINGS AND GET THEIR LENGTH

Applies to: Strings, reverse

Quick Solution
```
string s;
//...
```

```
cout << "String has " << s.length() << " characters";
reverse( s.begin(), s.end() ); // reverse characters
```

Detailed Solution

Finding the number of characters in a string (also called its length or size) is very common. Not as common is reversing the order of the characters. In either case, Table 10.6 provides the C++ equivalents, and the program in Listing 10.5 gives examples of using them.

TABLE 10.6   Equivalents for String Reversal and Length

Function	Member Function or Algorithm	Description
strlen	length or size	Length of string
strrev	reverse	Reverse the characters in a string

LISTING 10.5   Reversing a String and Finding its Length

```cpp
// string_reverse.cpp

#include <algorithm>
#include <iostream>
#include <string>

using namespace std;

int main( )
{
    string adage( "A bird in the hand is worth two in the bush" );
    cout << "String: " << adage;

    cout << "\nThe string has " << adage.length() << " letters";

    // equivalent of strrev()
    reverse( adage.begin(), adage.end() );
    cout << "\n\nReversed string: " << adage;
    cout << "\nThe reversed string has " << adage.length()
        << " letters";
}
```

The output is

```
String: A bird in the hand is worth two in the bush
The string has 43 letters

Reversed string: hsub eht ni owt htrow si dnah eht ni drib A
The reversed string has 43 letters
```

The program declares and initializes a string and prints the number of characters that it has. It gets this value by calling the member function `length`. (You can also use the member function `size`, which gives the identical result.) The `reverse` algorithm reverses the order of the characters. The output shows that the original and reversed strings still have the same length.

TIP 65	**COMPARE STRINGS WITH CASE-SENSITIVITY**

Applies to: Strings
See also: Tip 13, Tip 66, Tip 67, Tip 68

Quick Solution

```
string s1, s2;
//...

if( s1 < s2 ) // case-sensitive comparisons
    cout << s1 << " comes before " << s2;
else if( s1 > s2 )
    cout << s1 << " comes after " << s2;
else
    cout << s1 << " is the same as " << s2;
```

Detailed Solution

A *lexicographical comparison* is a fancy way of saying a "dictionary ordering." If one string comes before another in the dictionary, the first string is said to be less than the second. Similarly, if one string comes after another in the dictionary, it is greater than that string. Tip 13 provides the general definition of lexicographical comparison.

Table 10.7 shows that the function that compares C-strings is `strcmp`. It performs a lexicographical comparison on two C-strings and returns a negative value if the first is less than the second, a positive value if the first is greater than the second, and zero if they are the same.

All the comparisons are case-sensitive. This means that the results depend on whether the letters are in upper- or lower-case. For example, the two strings in the program in Listing 10.6 differ only by one letter—a capital "B" versus a small "b." The one with the capital letter is less than the other because in the ASCII character set, capital letters come before small letters. To learn how to make case-insensitive comparisons, see Tip 67. For making comparisons on substrings, see Tip 66 and Tip 68.

TABLE 10.7 Equivalents for Case-Sensitive String Comparison

Function	Member Function	Description
strcmp	compare, <, ==, >	Lexicographical comparison

LISTING 10.6 Case-Sensitive String Comparisons

```cpp
// string_case.cpp

#include <iostream>
#include <string>

using namespace std;

int main( )
{
   string saying1( "A bird in the hand is worth two in the bush" );
   string saying2( "A Bird in the hand is worth two in the bush" );

   cout << "USING compare()\n";

   // equivalent of strcmp()
   int result = saying1.compare( saying2 );
   if( result < 0 )
     cout << "\"" << saying1 << "\"\nis less than\n\""
        << saying2 << "\"";
   else if( result > 0 )
     cout << "\"" << saying1 << "\"\nis greater than\n\""
        << saying2 << "\"";
   else
     cout << "\"" << saying1 << "\"\nis equal to \n\""
        << saying2 << "\"";

   // now do again, using < and >

   cout << "\n\nUSING < AND >\n";
```

```
      // equivalent of strcmp()
      if( saying1 < saying2 )
         cout << "\"" << saying1 << "\"\nis less than\n\""
            << saying2 << "\"";
      else if( saying1 > saying2 )
         cout << "\"" << saying1 << "\"\nis greater than\n\""
            << saying2 << "\"";
      else
         cout << "\"" << saying1 << "\"\nis equal to\n\""
            << saying2 << "\"";
}
```

The output is

```
USING compare()

"A bird in the hand is worth two in the bush" is greater than
"A Bird in the hand is worth two in the bush"

USING < AND >
"A bird in the hand is worth two in the bush" is greater than
"A Bird in the hand is worth two in the bush"
```

The program creates two strings whose contents differ only by the capitalization of one letter (the "B" in "Bird"). The program first finds their order by using the compare member function. In its simplest form, the function accepts another string and returns an integer. The meaning is the same as in strcmp—if the value is less than zero, the string is less than the passed string, and so forth. The first line of the output shows that the string with the capital "B" is less than the string with the lowercase "b."

The second half of the program shows another way of comparing, which is by using the less-than (<) and greater-than (>) operators. This method is clearer because the meaning of those operators is obvious, and you don't have to remember the significance of any return values, as you do for compare.

The output shows that the results are the same.

TIP 66   COMPARE SUBSTRINGS WITH CASE-SENSITIVITY

Applies to: Strings
See also: Tip 65, Tip 67, Tip 68

Quick Solution

```
string s1, s2;
//...

if( s1.substr( 3, 7 ) < s2.substr( 3, 7 ) )
    cout << s1.substr( 3, 7 ) << " comes before " << s2.substr( 3, 7 );
else if( s1.substr( 3, 7 ) > s2.substr( 3, 7 ) )
    cout << s1.substr( 3, 7 ) << " comes after " << s2.substr( 3, 7 );
else
    cout << s1.substr( 3, 7 ) << " is the same as " << s2.substr( 3, 7 );
```

Detailed Solution

Tip 65 explained lexicographical comparisons and showed how to do such case-sensitive comparisons with C-strings and in C++. As Table 10.8 shows, to make a case-sensitive, lexicographical comparison of the first n characters of two C-strings, you use strncmp. Like strcmp, it returns a negative value if the first substring is less than the second, a positive value if the first substring is greater than the second, and zero if they are the same.

TABLE 10.8   Equivalents for Case-Sensitive Comparison of Substrings

Function	Member Function	Description
strncmp	compare, <, ==, >, substr	Lexicographical comparison of first n characters

The code in Listing 10.7 shows two ways of making case-sensitive, lexicographical comparisons of sections of C++ strings. Tip 65 explains how to do the same thing on whole strings. Tip 67 and Tip 68 provide the case-insensitive equivalents of these kinds of comparisons.

LISTING 10.7   Case-Sensitive Substring Comparison

```
// string_case_substring.cpp

#include <iostream>
#include <string>

using namespace std;
int main( )
{
    string saying1( "A Bird in the hand is worth two in the bush" );
```

```cpp
string saying2( "A bird in the hand is worth two in the bush" );

cout << "USING compare()\n";

// equivalent of strncmp()
int result = saying1.compare( 0, 6, saying2, 0, 6 );
if( result < 0 )
   cout << "\"" << saying1.substr( 0, 6 ) << "\" is less than \""
      << saying2.substr( 0, 6 ) << "\"";

else if( result > 0 )
   cout << "\"" << saying1.substr( 0, 6 ) << "\" is greater than \""
      << saying2.substr( 0, 6 ) << "\"";
else
   cout << "\"" << saying1.substr( 0, 6 ) << "\" is equal to \""
      << saying2.substr( 0, 6 ) << "\"";

// now do again, using < and >

cout << "\n\nUSING < and >\n";

// equivalent of strncmp()
if( saying1.substr( 0, 6 ) < saying2.substr( 0, 6 ) )
   cout << "\"" << saying1.substr( 0, 6 ) << "\" is less than \""
      << saying2.substr( 0, 6 ) << "\"";
else if( saying1.substr( 0, 6 ) > saying2.substr( 0, 6 ) )
   cout << "\"" << saying1.substr( 0, 6 ) << "\" is greater than \""
      << saying2.substr( 0, 6 ) << "\"";
else
   cout << "\"" << saying1.substr( 0, 6 ) << "\" is equal to \""
      << saying2.substr( 0, 6 ) << "\"";

// generalization of strncmp()
cout << "\n\nCOMPARE SUBSTRINGS OF DIFFERENT LENGTHS AND INDEXES\n";
if( saying1.substr( 2, 11 ) < saying2.substr( 14, 17 ) )
   cout << "\"" << saying1.substr( 2, 11 ) << "\" is less than \""
      << saying2.substr( 14, 17 ) << "\"";
else if( saying1.substr( 2, 11 ) > saying2.substr( 14, 17 ) )
   cout << "\"" << saying1.substr( 2, 11 )
      << "\" is greater than \"" << saying2.substr( 14, 17 ) << "\"";
else
   cout << "\"" << saying1.substr( 2, 11 ) << "\" is equal to \""
      << saying2.substr( 14, 17 ) << "\"";
}
```

The output is

```
USING compare()
"A Bird" is less than "A bird"

USING < and >
"A Bird" is less than "A bird"

COMPARE SUBSTRINGS OF DIFFERENT LENGTHS AND INDEXES
"Bird in the" is less than "hand is worth two"
```

The program starts by declaring two strings whose contents differ by the capitalization of two letters. The compare member function of a string then performs a lexicographical comparison on some initial substrings. The version of compare to use takes five arguments. The first two are the starting index and length of the substring in the current string. The third argument is the other string in the comparison. The fourth and fifth arguments are the starting index and length of the substring to use from the third argument.

The program uses starting indexes of zero and lengths that are the same to provide the equivalent functionality of strncmp. However, compare is clearly more powerful because the indexes can be different and nonzero and the substring lengths also need not be the same. The output shows that the first substring is less than the second because the only difference is a capital letter in the first. As Tip 65 explains, capital letters come before their lowercase equivalents in ASCII text.

The penultimate section of the code shows another way of comparing, which is by using the less-than (<) and greater-than (>) operators on substrings. This method is clearer because the meanings of those operators are obvious, and you don't have to remember the significance of any return values, as you do for compare. The substrings are easy to get via the substr member function. Its first argument is the starting index, and its second is the length. As before, this technique is more powerful than strncmp because the substrings can have different lengths and don't have to start at the beginning of the string. The last section of code and output demonstrates comparing substrings that start at different indexes and have different lengths.

It's worth noting that substr creates a new string and so is considerably slower than compare. If speed is not a problem in your application, use substr because it's clearer. Where performance is critical use the more complex member function compare.

| **TIP 67** | **COMPARE STRINGS WITHOUT CASE-SENSITIVITY** |

Applies to: String, lexicographical_compare, mismatch
See also: Tip 13, Tip 65, Tip 66, Tip 68

Quick Solution

See the detailed solution.

Detailed Solution

Making a lexicographical comparison of two strings is just determining their dictionary order. Tip 65 shows how easy it is to make a case-sensitive comparison. Doing the same thing while ignoring case is harder. Table 10.9 shows the STL algorithm that does the work; the code in Listing 10.8 and the discussion that accompanies it explain how.

TABLE 10.9   Equivalents for Case-Insensitive Comparison of Strings

Function	Algorithm	Description
stricmp	lexicographical_compare, mismatch	Case-insensitive string comparison

LISTING 10.8   Case-Insensitive String Comparison

```cpp
// string_caseless.cpp

#include <algorithm>
#include <cctype>
#include <iostream>
#include <string>

using namespace std;

// return true if c1 equals c2 (regardless of case), false otherwise
bool equal_to_insensitive( char c1, char c2 )
{
    return  tolower( static_cast<unsigned char>( c1 ) )
         == tolower( static_cast<unsigned char>( c2 ) );
}

// case-insensitive lexicographical comparison
// return < 0 if s1 < s2, return > 0 if s1 > s2,
// return 0 if s1 == s2
```

```
// either string can have any length
int case_insensitive_comparison( const string& s1, const string& s2 )
{
   string::const_iterator short_begin, short_end, long_begin, long_end;

   // set iterators to the beginning and end of the shorter and longer
   // strings
   if( s1.length() <= s2.length() )
   {
      short_begin = s1.begin();
      short_end = s1.end();
      long_begin = s2.begin();
      long_end = s2.end();
   }
   else
   {
      short_begin = s2.begin();
      short_end = s2.end();
      long_begin = s1.begin();
      long_end = s1.end();
   }

   // find the first spot where corresponding characters don't match,
   // ignoring case
   pair<string::const_iterator,string::const_iterator> spot =
      mismatch( short_begin, short_end, long_begin,
         equal_to_insensitive );

   int result;

   // if all characters of shorter string matched corresponding
   // characters of longer string...
   if( spot.first == short_end )

      // if at end of longer string both strings are same length so
      // both strings are the same
      if( spot.second == long_end )
         result = 0; // s1 == s2

      // not at end of longer string so shorter string is less than
      // longer one
      else
         result = -1; // s1 < s2
```

```
      // mismatch in short string - examine characters to decide result
      else
      {
         // convert characters to lower case
         int first =
            tolower( static_cast<unsigned char>( *spot.first  ) );
         int second =
            tolower( static_cast<unsigned char>( *spot.second ) );

         // result of routine based on case-insensitive character
         // comparison
         if( first < second )
            result = -1;
         else if( first > second )
            result = 1;
         else
            result = 0;
      }

      // if long string was first string passed, result is opposite of
      // that computed
      if( long_begin == s1.begin() )
         result *= -1;

      return result;
   }

   // return true if c1 < c2 (ignoring case), false otherwise
   bool less_than_insensitive( char c1, char c2 )
   {
      return  tolower( static_cast<unsigned char>( c1 ) )
            < tolower( static_cast<unsigned char>( c2 ) );
   }

   int main( )
   {
      string s1( "Fate casts its baleful eye" );
      string s2( "FATE CASTS ITS BALEFUL EYE" );
      string s3( "FaTe CaStS iTs BaLeFuL eYe On Ye" );

      cout << "COMPARE STRINGS IGNORING CASE\n\n";

      // equivalent of stricmp()
      int result = case_insensitive_comparison( s1, s2 );
```

```
    if( result < 0 )
        cout << "\"" << s1 << "\" is less than \"" << s2 << "\"";
    else if( result > 0 )
        cout << "\"" << s1 << "\" is greater than \"" << s2 << "\"";
    else
        cout << "\"" << s1 << "\" is equal to \"" << s2 << "\"";

    result = case_insensitive_comparison( s1, s3 );
    if( result < 0 )
        cout << "\n\"" << s1 << "\" is less than \"" << s3 << "\"";
    else if( result > 0 )
        cout << "\n\"" << s1 << "\" is greater than \"" << s3 << "\"";
    else
        cout << "\n\"" << s1 << "\" is equal to \"" << s3 << "\"";

    // case-insensitive determination of less-than
    if( s1.length() <= s2.length() )
        if( lexicographical_compare( s1.begin(), s1.end(),
                s2.begin(), s2.end(), less_than_insensitive ) )
            cout << "\n\"" << s1 << "\" is less than \"" << s2 << "\"";
        else
            cout << "\n\"" << s1 << "\" is not less than \"" << s2 << "\"";
    else
        if( lexicographical_compare( s2.begin(), s2.end(),
                s1.begin(), s1.end(), less_than_insensitive ) )
            cout << "\n\"" << s2 << "\" is less than \"" << s1 << "\"";
        else
            cout << "\n\"" << s2 << "\" is not less than \"" << s1 << "\"";
}
```

The output is

```
COMPARE STRINGS IGNORING CASE

"Fate casts its baleful eye" is equal to "FATE CASTS ITS BALEFUL EYE"
"Fate casts its baleful eye" is less than "FaTe CaStS iTs BaLeFuL eYe
On Ye"
"Fate casts its baleful eye" is not less than "FATE CASTS ITS BALEFUL
EYE"
```

The C++ Standard Library does not have a direct equivalent of stricmp, so you will have to use a custom function. Your initial thought might be to use the compare member function of strings (as in Tip 65 and Tip 66), but it only does case-sensitive comparisons. An alternative is to use the STL algorithm mismatch, which accepts a functor that specifies how each pair of elements should be compared.

The function to write will compare the strings lexicographically, but the actual case-insensitive comparison of a pair of characters will be done by another custom function, equal_to_insensitive, shown in the code. It does this by converting each character to lower case using tolower, which is in <cctype>. tolower takes an int argument, but the value of the int must be in the range of an unsigned char or have the special value EOF. Because a char can be signed or unsigned (this depends on your C++ implementation), the code explicitly casts to unsigned char to ensure that things work correctly.

Next, the program shows the custom-written function case_insensitive_comparison, which is the equivalent of stricmp. The routine starts by comparing the lengths of the two strings and storing the beginning and end iterators of the shorter string (or the first string if both are the same size) in a pair of local variables. The routine also stores the beginning and end iterators of the longer string. The function finds and maintains this information to specify the first range in the STL algorithm mismatch described later. This range must not be bigger than the second range used by that algorithm.

The next statement uses mismatch to do the bulk of the function's work. This STL algorithm in its basic form compares two ranges and returns a pair of iterators that marks the first place at which corresponding elements are not equal. In a more general version, the algorithm optionally accepts a predicate and returns a pair of iterators that point to the first pair of corresponding elements that make the predicate false. The code uses the home-grown function equal_to_insensitive, described previously, as the predicate. Using mismatch takes advantage of the seldom-used beginning and end iterators that a string has.

The function case_insensitive_comparison calls mismatch, which returns two iterators pointing to the first pair of corresponding elements that are not equal, ignoring case. The iterators are stored in a pair data structure that, as Tip 45 explains, has two public members, first and second. If first is equal to the first string's end iterator, mismatch determined that every character in the first range was equal to (ignoring case) the corresponding element in the second range. However, the second range could be the same size as the first or could be longer. The code handles these two cases by examining the second data member of the pair. If it's equal to the end of the longer sequence, both ranges are the same length and have the same corresponding characters, that is, the two strings are the same (ignoring case). The function returns zero to signal this relationship. If second is not equal to the end of the second range, that range is longer than the first and so, by the definition of lexicographical comparison (see Tip 13), the first string is shorter than the second. The function returns a negative value to report this fact.

If the iterator in `first` is not equal to the end of the first range, `mismatch` finds a pair of corresponding elements that are not equal, even after ignoring their capitalization. In this case, the result of comparing the function determines the relationship of the strings. `mismatch` converts both corresponding characters to lower case, compares them, and returns a negative value if the first character is less than (comes before than) the second, a positive value if the first comes after the second, or zero if the two are the same.

The results computed to this point in the function assume that the first string is shorter than or the same length as the second. If this is not true, the actual results are the opposite of what the routine calculated. The code checks this by seeing if the beginning iterator of the long string is the same as the beginning iterator of the first string. If this is true, the first string is actually the longer string, and the code multiplies the result by negative one to get the correct numbers. The first two comparisons in the output show the results of using `case_insensitive_comparison` to compare two strings.

Sometimes you may only need to know if one string is lexicographically less than the other and nothing else. That is, if it's not less, you don't care whether it is greater than or equal to the second string. In this case, you can call the STL algorithm `lexicographical_compare` with the function `less_than_insensitive`, as the code shows. Because the second range passed to the algorithm must be at least as large as the first, the program determines which string is longer and calls `lexicographical_compare` with the string ranges in the correct order.

Well, that's how to compare two strings regardless of their capitalization. If you want to do the same thing with substrings, see Tip 68. If you want to compare strings or substrings and account for capitalization, see Tip 65 and Tip 66.

One final note—the technique and code in this tip work on English text but may not, and most likely won't, work on words from other languages. Doing case-insensitive comparisons and sorting in a portable manner, that is, for various languages, is difficult. See the article by Matt Austern for details [Austern00]. If you have Scott Meyers' excellent book *Effective STL* [Meyers01], it has Austern's article in an appendix.

TIP 68   # COMPARE SUBSTRINGS WITHOUT CASE-SENSITIVITY

Applies to: Strings, mismatch
See also: Tip 65, Tip 66, Tip 67

Quick Solution

See the detailed solution.

Detailed Solution

Tip 67 shows how to compare two whole strings regardless of capitalization. This tip demonstrates the same thing for substrings. Table 10.10 lists the necessary Standard Library components, and the code in Listing 10.9 demonstrates how to use them. The technique is almost the same as that in Tip 67, so see the text there for a detailed explanation of both programs.

TABLE 10.10   Equivalents for Case-Insensitive Comparison of Substrings

Function	Member Function or Algorithm	Description
strnicmp	mismatch, substr	Case-insensitive, lexicographical comparison of first n characters

LISTING 10.9   Case-Insensitive Substring Comparison

```
// string_ caseless_substring.cpp

#include <algorithm>
#include <cctype>
#include <iostream>
#include <string>

using namespace std;

// return true if c1 equals c2 (regardless of case), false otherwise
bool equal_to_insensitive( char c1, char c2 )
{
    return  tolower( static_cast<unsigned char>( c1 ) )
         == tolower( static_cast<unsigned char>( c2 ) );
}

// case-insensitive lexicographical comparison of substrings
// compare first "length" characters of both strings
// length must be >=0, if greater than a string length
//     entire string is used
// return < 0 if substring of s1 < substring of s2
```

```cpp
// return > 0 if substring of s1 > substring of s2
// return 0 if substring of s1 == substring of s2
// either string can have any length
int case_insensitive_comparison( const string& string1,
   const string& string2, int length )
{
   // make substrings of specified length. If string is shorter, substr
   // returns entire string
   string s1 = string1.substr( 0, length );
   string s2 = string2.substr( 0, length );

   string::const_iterator short_begin, short_end, long_begin, long_end;

   // set iterators to the beginning and end of the shorter and longer
   // strings
   if( s1.length() <= s2.length() )
   {
      short_begin = s1.begin();
      short_end = s1.end();
      long_begin = s2.begin();
      long_end = s2.end();
   }
   else
   {
      short_begin = s2.begin();
      short_end = s2.end();
      long_begin = s1.begin();
      long_end = s1.end();
   }

   // find the first spot where corresponding characters don't match,
   // ignoring case
   pair<string::const_iterator,string::const_iterator> spot =
      mismatch( short_begin, short_end, long_begin,
         equal_to_insensitive );

   int result;

   // if all characters of shorter string matched corresponding
   // characters of longer string...
   if( spot.first == short_end )

      // if at end of longer string both strings are same length so
      // both strings are the same
```

```
         if( spot.second == long_end )
            result = 0; // s1 == s2

         // not at end of longer string so shorter string is less than
         // longer one
         else
            result = -1; // s1 < s2

      // mismatch in short string - examine characters to decide result
      else
      {
         // convert characters to lower case
         int first =
            tolower( static_cast<unsigned char>( *spot.first  ) );
         int second =
            tolower( static_cast<unsigned char>( *spot.second ) );

         // result of routine based on case-insensitive character
         // comparison
         if( first < second )
            result = -1;
         else if( first > second )
            result = 1;
         else
            result = 0;
      }

      // if long string was first string passed, result is opposite of
      // that computed
      if( long_begin == s1.begin() )
         result *= -1;

      return result;
}

int main( )
{
   string s1( "Fate casts its baleful eye" );
   string s2( "FATE CASTS ITS OMINOUS EYE" );

   const int comparisons = 2;
   const int lengths[comparisons] = { 10, 16 };
   int result;
   for( int i = 0; i < comparisons; ++i )
```

```
      {
         cout << "COMPARE (IGNORING CASE) THE FIRST " << lengths[i]
            << " CHARACTERS OF\n\"" << s1 << "\" and \"" << s2 <<
            "\"\n        ";

         // equivalent of strnicmp()
         result = case_insensitive_comparison( s1, s2, lengths[i] );

         cout << "\"" << s1.substr( 0, lengths[i] ) << "\" ";
         if( result < 0 )
            cout << "is less than";
         else if( result > 0 )
            cout << "is greater than";
         else
            cout << "is equal to";
         cout << " \"" << s2.substr( 0, lengths[i] ) << "\"\n\n";
      }

      const int s1_index = 1;
      const int s2_index = 6;
      const int length = 8;

      cout << "COMPARE (IGNORING CASE) THE FIRST " << length
         << " CHARACTERS OF\n\"" << s1 << "\" STARTING AT INDEX "
         << s1_index << " AND\n\"" << s2 << "\" STARTING AT INDEX "
         << s2_index << endl;

      // compare substrings of same length but different starting indexes
      result = case_insensitive_comparison( s1.substr( s1_index ),
         s2.substr( s2_index ), length );

      cout << "\"" << s1.substr( s1_index, length ) << "\" ";
      if( result < 0 )
         cout << "is less than";
      else if( result > 0 )
         cout << "is greater than";
      else
         cout << "is equal to";
      cout << " \"" << s2.substr( s2_index, length ) << "\"" << endl;
   }
```

The output is

```
COMPARE (IGNORING CASE) THE FIRST 10 CHARACTERS OF
"Fate casts its baleful eye" and "FATE CASTS ITS OMINOUS EYE"
    "Fate casts" is equal to "FATE CASTS"

COMPARE (IGNORING CASE) THE FIRST 16 CHARACTERS OF
"Fate casts its baleful eye" and "FATE CASTS ITS OMINOUS EYE"
    "Fate casts its b" is less than "FATE CASTS ITS O"

COMPARE (IGNORING CASE) THE FIRST 8 CHARACTERS OF
"Fate casts its baleful eye" STARTING AT INDEX 1 AND
"FATE CASTS ITS OMINOUS EYE" STARTING AT INDEX 6
"ate cast" is greater than "ASTS ITS"
```

The code in Listing 10.9 starts with two custom-written functions. The first, `equal_to_insensitive`, is identical to that in Tip 67. The second, `case_insensitive_comparison`, is almost the same as that in Tip 67, but it has an additional argument that specifies the length of the substrings to compare. This makes its signature the same as (or similar to) that of `strnicmp`.

The code in `case_insensitive_comparison` starts by extracting the substrings from the passed strings. It does this by using the string's member function `substr`. That function's first argument is the starting index of the substring, and its optional second argument is the number of characters to extract. If this is greater than the length of the string, `substr` just uses all of the characters. The remaining code in `case_insensitive_comparison` is identical to that in Tip 67, so see the text there for a detailed explanation of how the routine works.

The first call to `case_insensitive_comparison` simulates `strnicmp`, which compares the first *n* characters of a string without regard to capitalization. The first two sections of the output show the result of comparing the first 10 characters of each string and the first 16 characters of each string.

The last section of the code demonstrates comparing two substrings of the same length but starting at different indexes of the strings. To do this, the program passes the return from a call to the string member function `substr` when it is given the starting index. (There is no length passed, so `substr` uses the entire string from the index to the end.) The last section of the output shows the result.

This tip showed how to compare two substrings regardless of their capitalization. If you want to do the same thing with strings, see Tip 67. If you want to compare strings or substrings and account for capitalization, see Tip 65 and Tip 66.

TIP 69   READ FORMATTED STRINGS

Applies to: String, istringstream
See also: Tip 70

Quick Solution

```
string race( "800 Lubcek 2 10.56" );

// make an input string stream
istringstream information( race );

string runner;
int distance, minutes;
float seconds;

// read formatted string
information >> distance >> runner >> minutes >> seconds;
cout << runner << " won the " << distance << " meter run in " << minutes
     << " minutes and " << seconds << " seconds";
```

Detailed Solution

To read from a formatted C-string, you use sscanf. This function uses format specifiers, which have a number of drawbacks:

- You need to remember format specifiers, such as %d, %u, and %g.
- You have to make sure to have the same number of arguments as format specifiers.
- You have to make sure the arguments are in the right order.
- It's difficult to control how many characters are written to the output string, making it easy to overflow the string.

In addition, the arguments to sscanf are pointers, a fact that beginning programmers often forget.

C++ strings and string streams provide an easier way of reading formatted text. You simply make an input string stream from the string you want to read and then read it as if you were reading from cin. You can even use this technique to read values from a line in an input file stream. Table 10.11 shows the Standard Library component you need, and the program in Listing 10.10 demonstrates the procedure.

TABLE 10.11   Equivalent for Reading Formatted Strings

Function	Standard Library Component	Description
sscanf	istringstream	Formatted read from string

LISTING 10.10   Reading Formatted Strings

```cpp
// string_formatted_read.cpp

#include <iomanip>
#include <iostream>
#include <sstream>
#include <string>

using namespace std;

int main( )
{
   // start with a formatted string that you want to read
   string person( "Steinberg Saul 62 4 7" );

   // make an input string stream
   istringstream information( person );

   string first_name, last_name;
   int age, num_kids, num_grandkids;

   cout << "READ FROM STRING STREAM\n";
   information >> last_name >> first_name >> age >> num_kids
      >> num_grandkids;
   cout << first_name << " " << last_name << " is " << age
      << " and has " << num_kids << " kids and " << num_grandkids
      << " grandchildren";

   cout <<
      "\n\nTRY TO READ THREE NUMBERS FROM A STREAM WITH TWO NUMBERS\n";
   information.str( "123 456" );
   int num1, num2, num3;
   information >> num1 >> num2 >> num3;
   if( information )
      cout << "The three numbers are: " << num1 << " " << num2
         << " " << num3;
```

```
      else
         cout << "Couldn't read three numbers";

   cout << "\n\nCLEAR STREAM, THEN READ TWO NUMBERS\n";
   information.clear();
   information >> num1 >> num2;
   if( information )
      cout << "The two numbers are: " << num1 << " " << num2;
   else
      cout << "Couldn't read two numbers";
}
```

The output is

```
READ FROM STRING STREAM
Saul Steinberg is 62 and has 4 kids and 7 grandchildren

TRY TO READ THREE NUMBERS FROM A STREAM WITH TWO NUMBERS
Couldn't read three numbers

CLEAR STREAM, THEN READ TWO NUMBERS
The two numbers are: 123 456
```

The code provides an example of a formatted string, one that has a last name, first name, age, and two other numbers. First, the program creates an input string stream by passing the string to the constructor as shown. Then the program reads from the stream by using the extraction operator (>>), exactly as it would read from `cin`. The first two lines of output show the result.

A more sophisticated program would verify that the reading succeeded. It can do this by checking the status of the stream after reading, as the second section of the program demonstrates. The code stores the textual representation of two numbers in the input string stream by calling the stream's `str` member function. This overwrites the previous contents of the stream. The program then tries to read three numbers from a stream that has only two. It checks the result of reading by testing the stream as if it were a Boolean. If the result is `true`, the read was successful. If it is `false`, there is an error and you must clear the stream's state as shown before reading from it again.

If you're reading formatted strings, you're probably interested in writing them, too. Tip 70 tells you all about that.

TIP 70   WRITE FORMATTED STRINGS

Applies to: Strings, ostringstream
See also: Tip 69

Quick Solution

```
int port = 10;
int value = 0X24AEF;
string message( "Incomplete packet" );

ostringstream out;

// make a formatted string
out << "Error - " << message << "  Port - " << port << "  Value - "
    << hex << uppercase << showbase << value;
cout << out.str(); // simulate writing to message box
```

Detailed Solution

Creating formatted strings of text is not unusual. One common use is in error reporting. For example, a program might want to print information about an error into a string and then pass that string to another module to report the error. It might do this by logging the error string in a file or displaying it in a GUI dialog box.

To create a formatted C-string, you call `sprintf`. For example, this code

```
char text[100];
const int num_aliens = 20;
const char first_name[] = "John";
sprintf( text, "In the movie, all %d aliens were named \"%s\".",
    num_aliens, first_name );
```

produces the output

```
In the movie, all 20 aliens were named "John"
```

However, `sprintf` has several drawbacks. First, you have to make sure that you have the same number of arguments as format specifiers. Then you have to make sure the arguments are in the right order. Second, you need to remember all those format specifiers, such as %d, %u, and %g. And finally, it's difficult to control how many characters are written to the output string. It's easy to make the string overflow.

C++ strings and string streams provide an easier way of writing formatted text—you simply insert variables into an output stream. Although this is really a string output stream, the method of using it is the same as writing to cout. Data types know how to write themselves to streams, so there's no need for format specifiers that denote the data type. You can still control precision, width, and so on by using stream manipulators.

Table 10.12 tells what you need from the Standard Library to write formatted strings. The program in Listing 10.11 provides an example.

TABLE 10.12 Equivalent for Writing Formatted Strings

Function	Standard Library Component	Description
sprintf	ostringstream	Formatted write to string

LISTING 10.11 Writing Formatted Strings

```
// string_formatted_write.cpp

#include <iomanip>
#include <iostream>
#include <sstream>
#include <string>

using namespace std;

// primitive GUI display
void display_error( const string& message );

int main( )
{
   // simulate an error
   const int error_number = 37;
   const int chip_number = 4;
   const char error_message[] = "Unable to read from custom chip ";

   ostringstream out;

   // make the error message
   out << "Error number " << error_number << ": " << error_message
      << chip_number;

   // send it to the GUI for display
```

```
        display_error( out.str() );

        // display just the string
        cout << "FIRST TIME WRITING TO STREAM\n" << out.str() << endl;

        // write to stream
        out << "\nError number " << (error_number+2) << ": "
            << error_message << (chip_number+2);
        cout << "\nSECOND TIME WRITING TO STREAM\n" << out.str() << endl;

        // erase stream and write error message
        out.str( "" );
        out << "\nError number " << (error_number+2) << ": "
            << error_message << (chip_number+2);
        cout << "\nERASE AND THEN WRITE TO STREAM" << out.str() << endl;
    }

const string::size_type max_length = 60;
void display_error( const string& message )
{
    string::size_type length = min( max_length, message.length() );

    cout << setfill( '*' ) << setw( length+4 ) << '*' << endl
         << '*' << setfill( ' ' ) << setw( length+3 ) << '*' << endl
         << "* " << message.substr( 0, length+3 ) << " *" << endl
         << '*' << setw( length+3 ) << '*' << endl
         << setfill( '*' ) << setw( length+4 ) << '*' << endl << endl;
}
```

The output is

```
*****************************************************
*                                                   *
* Error number 37: Unable to read from custom chip 4 *
*                                                   *
*****************************************************


FIRST TIME WRITING TO STREAM
Error number 37: Unable to read from custom chip 4

SECOND TIME WRITING TO STREAM
Error number 37: Unable to read from custom chip 4
Error number 39: Unable to read from custom chip 6              →
```

```
ERASE AND THEN WRITE TO STREAM
Error number 39: Unable to read from custom chip 6
```

The first insertion into the output string stream shows how some numbers and text might be combined into a simple error message. The next line shows how to use the `str` member function of the stream to get a copy of its internal string. In this example, `display_error` simulates a GUI error. Note that the code declares the type of the constant variable `max_length` to be `string::size_type`. This is because `min` is a template with both arguments the same data type. If the two arguments were different, for example, `int` and `std::string::size_type`, the compiler would produce an error. This happened on two of the compilers the code was tested on. However, a third compiler was set up so that if the two arguments were different the compiler called a macro form of `min`. The macro accepted different data types so the compiler produced no error.

After displaying the error, the code prints the current contents of the string as a line of output and then writes to the stream again, using different numbers to distinguish the two writes. The output is surprising—both the first and second strings are still in the stream. That's a point to remember—repeated writes to an output string stream are concatenated.

To erase the contents of the stream, call its `str` member function with an empty string literal as shown. (The stream's `clear` member function clears error flags, not the contents of the stream.) Then write your line to the stream and it will be the only text present, as the output shows.

TIP 71 GET A C STRING FROM A C++ STRING

Applies to: String

Quick Solution

```
void print_title( const char* title );
// ...

string book_title( "The C++ Standard Library: Practical Tips" );

print_title( book_title.c_str() );
```

Detailed Solution

C++ strings are more powerful, easier to use, and more fun than C-strings. However, sometimes, especially for compatibility with old code, you need to use a C-string. Can you have your cake and eat it too?

The answer is, "Yes." You can get a C-string from a string, or more precisely, you can get a const pointer to a C-string. Do this by using the c_str member function of a string. For example, suppose for some crazy reason you wanted to use the old-fashioned printf function with a string. The program in Listing 10.12 shows how you could do it.

LISTING 10.12 Get a C-Style String from a C++ String

```cpp
// string_c_str.cpp

#include <cstdio>
#include <string>

using namespace std;

int main( )
{
    string boss( "Mr. Big" );
    // printf takes a const char* argument, so use c_str()
    printf( "%s is an important man.\n\n", boss.c_str() );

    // strupr() takes a char* argument, so make a copy first
    char man[50];
    strcpy( man, boss.c_str() );
    strupr( man );
    printf( "A big man should have big letters: %s\n", man );
}
```

The output is

```
Mr. Big is an important man.

A big man should have big letters: MR. BIG
```

The call to printf illustrates the use of a C++ string's c_str member function. Actually, many of the C-style string manipulation functions take constant pointers to string arrays, as printf does. Some, however, such as strlwr, strupr and strtok, change the string argument and so take nonconstant pointers. You can't get such a beast directly from a `string`. Instead, copy the string into a C-style string array, modify it, and then print the result, as in this tip's code.

TIP 72   STRIP WHITESPACE

TIP

Applies to: String, find_if
See also: Tip 15, Tip 47, Tip 49

Quick Solution

See detailed solution.

Detailed Solution

Whitespace is a sequence of characters that prints blank on paper, such as spaces, tabs, and carriage returns. It's often useful to be able to remove any whitespace that occurs at the beginning and end of a line of text. For example, in input files containing data, if the first character in the line is a particular character, such as a percent sign or a pound sign, the program might treat that line as a comment and ignore it. However, the person who created the data file may have accidentally put a space in front of the comment character. In this case, if your program checks only the first character of the line, it will not detect the initial comment character, so you need to remove any leading whitespace.

Another use for stripping whitespace is when you are counting the number of characters in a line. You don't want to count any leading or trailing whitespace, so you need to remove it. Of course, you would still keep any whitespace between alphanumeric characters, for example, spaces between words.

The code in Listing 10.13 shows you two ways of removing leading and trailing whitespace. Both methods assume the line is stored in a string. The first technique relies on the interesting fact that strings have iterators that can be used in STL algorithms.

LISTING 10.13   Stripping Whitespace in Strings

```
// string_whitespace.cpp

#include <algorithm>
#include <cctype>
#include <functional>
#include <iostream>
#include <string>
```

```
using namespace std;

void show_stripped( string& s );
void strip_whitespace1( string& s );
void strip_whitespace2( string& s );

int main( )
{
    string front_space( "  Space in front" );
    show_stripped( front_space );

    string back_space( "Space in back\t\t\t " );
    show_stripped( back_space );

    string front_and_back_space( "  Space in front and back\t\t" );
    show_stripped( front_and_back_space );

    string no_space( "ABCDEFGHIJKLMNOPQRSTUVWXYZ" );
    show_stripped( no_space );

    string all_space( "  \n\n\t\t" );
    show_stripped( all_space );
}

void strip_whitespace1( string& s )
{
    // find the first character that is not whitespace
    string::iterator first =
        find_if( s.begin(), s.end(), not1( ptr_fun( isspace ) ) );

    // erase from the beginning to just before that character
    s.erase( s.begin(), first );

    // find the last character that is not whitespace
    string::reverse_iterator last =
        find_if( s.rbegin(), s.rend(), not1( ptr_fun( isspace ) ) );

    // erase from after that character to the end
    s.erase( last.base(), s.end() );
}

void show_stripped( string& s )
{
    cout << "\n\"" << s <<  "\" has " << s.length() << " characters\n";
```

```cpp
      strip_whitespace1( s );

      cout << "After stripping, \"" << s <<  "\" has "
         << s.length() << " characters\n";
   }

   void strip_whitespace2( string& s )
   {
      const char whitespace[] = " \n\r\t\v";

      string::size_type spot = s.find_first_not_of( whitespace );

      // if it's all whitespace, delete all characters and return
      if( spot == string::npos )
      {
         s.erase();
         return;
      }

      // if there's leading whitespace, delete it
      else if( spot != 0 )
         s.erase( 0, spot );

      spot = s.find_last_not_of( whitespace );
      if( spot != s.length()-1 )
         s.erase( spot+1 );    // erase to end of string
   }
```

The output is

```
"  Space in front" has 16 characters
After stripping, "Space in front" has 14 characters

"Space in back          " has 17 characters
After stripping, "Space in back" has 13 characters

"  Space in front and back       " has 27 characters
After stripping, "Space in front and back" has 23 characters

"ABCDEFGHIJKLMNOPQRSTUVWXYZ" has 26 characters
After stripping, "ABCDEFGHIJKLMNOPQRSTUVWXYZ" has 26 characters

"            " has 6 characters
After stripping, "" has 0 characters
```

The first line of the function `strip_whitespace1` uses the `find_if` algorithm to start at the beginning of the string and look at each character until the algorithm finds one that is not a whitespace. The third argument of the algorithm determines whether a character is whitespace. `isspace` is in the header `<cctype>` and returns `true` (not equal to zero) if its argument is a space, tab, carriage return, newline, vertical tab, formfeed, or similar character. In essence, `isspace` defines what whitespace is.

`not1` is an adaptor functor that returns the logical negation of the output of `isspace` in order to find the first character that is not whitespace. `ptr_fun` is an adaptor that lets you use `not1` with a function, in this case, `isspace`. (See "Functors" in Chapter 2 or Tip 47 and Tip 49 for more information about using functions and adaptors in the STL algorithms.) The `erase` member function of the string removes all characters from the beginning of the string to just before the first nonwhitespace character. In other words, it erases the leading whitespace. If the entire line is whitespace, `find_if` returns the end iterator for the string, which makes `erase` delete all the characters. On the other hand, if there is no leading whitespace, `find_if` returns the beginning iterator. This makes the range passed to `erase` be empty, which responds by doing nothing.

The next occurrence of `find_if` does the same thing as the first, but it uses reverse iterators (see Tip 15 and "Reverse Iterators" in Chapter 2). They cause the algorithm to start at the end of the string and search towards the beginning for the first character that is not whitespace. The code then erases from after the last nonwhitespace character to the end of the string. Because string's `erase` member function takes a normal (not a reverse) iterator, the program uses the `base` member function of the reverse iterator to make the necessary conversion. "Reverse Iterators" in Chapter 2 discusses the conversion between forward and reverse iterators in more detail.

The function `show_stripped` is a simple test function that prints its string argument before and after stripping. The code calls this function for various strings, illustrating that the function that strips whitespace works for strings with whitespace that is leading, trailing, leading and trailing, or nonexistent. It also shows that a string that is all whitespace (such as a blank line in a file) has all of its characters removed.

An alternative to using the `find_if` algorithm is to perform the work using only member functions that belong to the string. The function `strip_whitespace2` in the code of Listing 10.13 shows how. One salient difference is in the first line, which defines what characters constitute whitespace, instead of using the definition in `isspace` as before. Although a custom-written definition is a little more work, it is also more flexible because it can precisely specify which characters constitute whitespace. The drawback, though, is that it is less portable—`isspace` will denote the whitespace on any system.

The second line of the function finds the first character in the string that is not whitespace. If there is no such character, the string is all whitespace (or empty) and the call of the `erase` member function gets rid of all characters. There's nothing left to do, so the function returns. If the code did find a character that is not whitespace, it deletes all characters up to that one. Note that in that call of `erase`, the first argument is the starting position and the second is the number of characters to erase.

Finally, the call to `find_last_not_of` returns the position of the last character that is not whitespace and the subsequent code deletes all characters after that. A nonwhitespace character must exist or the function would have returned already. The output of `strip_whitespace2` is the same as that for `strip_whitespace1`.

TIP 73   CONVERT TO UPPER OR LOWER CASE

Applies to: Strings, transform
See also: Tip 67, Tip 81

Quick Solution

See detailed solution.

Detailed Solution

Table 10.13 lists two handy functions that many C-strings come with for setting all letters to upper- or lowercase. Unfortunately, C++ strings don't have such a direct way of letting you do this. Actually, the topic of converting case is much more difficult than it appears and is still widely discussed in the C++ newsgroups. The program in Listing 10.14 shows a fairly easy way of changing case.

TABLE 10.13   Equivalents for Converting Case

Function	Algorithm	Description
strlwr	transform	Convert to lower case
strupr	transform	Convert to upper case

LISTING 10.14   Changing Case in Strings

```
// string_capitalization.cpp

#include <algorithm>
#include <cctype>
#include <iostream>
#include <string>
```

```
using namespace std;

inline
char my_tolower( char c )
{   return
    static_cast<char>( tolower( static_cast<unsigned char>( c ) ) );
}

inline
char my_toupper( char c )
{   return
    static_cast<char>( toupper( static_cast<unsigned char>( c ) ) );
}

int main( )
{
    string book( "The C++ Programming Language, 3rd Edition" );

    cout << "String:\t\t" << book << endl << endl;

    // equivalent of strupr()
    transform( book.begin(), book.end(), book.begin(), my_toupper );
    cout << "Big letters:\t" << book << endl << endl;

    // equivalent of strlwr()
    transform( book.begin(), book.end(), book.begin(), my_tolower );
    cout << "Small letters:\t" << book;
}
```

The output is

```
String:          The C++ Programming Language, 3rd Edition

Big letters:     THE C++ PROGRAMMING LANGUAGE, 3RD EDITION

Small letters:   the c++ programming language, 3rd edition
```

The code in Listing 10.14 is another example of using the iterators in a string. The basic idea is to have the STL algorithm transform pass each character of the string to either toupper or tolower, which sets its case. There are some nuances, though. For example, both toupper and tolower, which are part of the C++

Standard Library, expect their argument to be in the range of an `unsigned char`. However, the `char` data type can be signed or unsigned, depending on the implementation of the compiler. Thus, to ensure that the `char` elements of the string have the correct type, you should cast them to an `unsigned char` before passing them to `toupper` or `tolower`. This is what the custom functions `my_toupper` and `my_tolower` do. They also explicitly convert their return values back to `char`.

The way the program actually works is to use `transform`, but with the custom functions as the function argument. `transform` passes each input character to its conversion function and then stores the returned character in the output container. In this case, the input and output containers are the same, which is how the input string gets its capitalization changed.

For another example of `transform`, see Tip 81. As Tip 67 notes, this technique won't work for many languages other than English.

TIP 74   **EXTRACT WORDS DELIMITED BY WHITESPACE**

Applies to: String, copy
See also: Tip 7, Tip 75

Quick Solution

```
string preface;
// ...

istringstream stream( preface );
// make a vector with each word in the preface
vector< string > words( (istream_iterator<string>( stream )),
    istream_iterator<string>() );
```

Detailed Solution

Often, it's useful to be able to extract words from a string. A subsequent activity might be to count the number of words, find how many unique words there are, or sort the words. The program in Listing 10.15 shows a quick way of getting words that are separated by whitespace. The "words" could also include numerals and punctuation—actually, any symbols that are not whitespace. (If you want to extract words that are between characters that aren't whitespace, see Tip 75.)

TABLE 10.14   Equivalent for Tokenizing

Function	Component	Description
strtok	string	Tokenize text

LISTING 10.15   Extracting Words in Strings Delimited by Whitespace

```cpp
// string_extract_words.cpp

#include <iostream>
#include <iterator>
#include <sstream>
#include <string>
#include <vector>

#include "tips.hpp"

using namespace std;

int main( )
{
   string text( "How much wood would a woodchuck chuck?" );

   istringstream stream( text );

   // make a vector with each word of the text
   vector< string > words( (istream_iterator<string>( stream )),
        istream_iterator<string>() );

   // confirm by writing to output
   cout << "There are " << words.size() << " words in \"" << text
      << "\"\n\nTHE WORDS ARE\n";
   tips::print( words, 0, "\n" );
}
```

The output is

```
There are 7 words in "How much wood would a woodchuck chuck?"

THE WORDS ARE
How
much
wood
would
a
woodchuck
chuck?
```

After declaring a string variable, the code declares an input string stream and initializes it to the string that's stored in the string variable. Next, the code declares a vector using the form of the constructor that accepts a range. The code gets iterators from the range by making an input stream iterator (`istream_iterator`) from the input string stream. (See "Stream Iterators" in Chapter 2 for more information about the stream iterator adaptors.) Tip 7 does the same thing with the standard input stream instead of an input string stream. That tip explains the details of the technique, including the odd-looking but necessary parentheses around the first argument in the vector's constructor.

When the constructor reads from the input iterator, `istream_iterator<string>` translates this to a call to the input operator >>. This skips leading whitespace and reads characters until it finds more whitespace or gets to the end of the stream. In other words, it reads words and stores each one as an element in the array. The output shows the words and demonstrates that the size of the vector provides a word count.

TIP 75   EXTRACT TOKENS THAT ARE BETWEEN DELIMITERS

Applies to: Strings
See also: Tip 74

Quick Solution
See detailed solution.

Detailed Solution

Tip 74 illustrates a quick method of finding all the words in a text string. Although the example uses words of English, the "words" could include numbers, such as in a street address. However, a limitation of the technique is that the "words" be separated only by whitespace. Sometimes you have other characters that form the separation. One example is the group "/", ":", and "." in file names or URL addresses. Another example is a type of personal information in the United States called the Social Security number. It always has the form xxx-xx-xxx, where the x's are digits and the delimiter is the hyphen. This tip provides a generalization of the method in Tip 74 that will let you handle these cases.

The process of finding groups from one set of characters that are separated by characters from another set is called *tokenizing*. The groups of interest, the "words" in Tip 74, are known as tokens. The characters separating them are called *delimiters* or *separators*. C provides the function strtok that accepts text and any set of delimiters and tokenizes the text. Although powerful, it is clumsy to use.

C++ does not have an equivalent of strtok. However, the code in Listing 10.16 demonstrates a function (tokenize) that does the same thing and is easier to use.

LISTING 10.16   Tokenizing Strings

```cpp
// string_tokenize.cpp

#include <algorithm>
#include <iostream>
#include <iterator>
#include <string>
#include <vector>

#include "tips.hpp"

using namespace std;

vector<string> tokenize( const string& text, const char* delimiters );

int main( )
{
  const char file_delimiters[] = ":\\.";

  string file( "c:\\greg\\book\\code\\string_tokenize.cpp" );

  // find the parts of the file name
  vector<string> tokens = tokenize( file, file_delimiters );

  // display the tokens
  cout << "TOKENS IN " << file << endl;
  tips::print( tokens );

  // try a file with no delimiters
  file = "data";
```

```
        tokens = tokenize( file, file_delimiters );
        cout << "\nTOKENS IN " << file << endl;
        tips::print( tokens );

        // try a file that's all delimiters
        file = "..";
        tokens = tokenize( file, file_delimiters );
        cout << "\nTOKENS IN " << file << endl;
        tips::print( tokens );

        // try different delimiters by finding the numbers
        // in a Social Security number
        string social_security( "431-02-9495" );
        tokens = tokenize( social_security, "-" );
        cout << "\nTOKENS IN " << social_security << endl;
        tips::print( tokens );
    }

    vector<string> tokenize( const string& text, const char* delimiters )
    {
        vector<string> tokens;

        // can't use NULL pointer in find_first_of
        if( delimiters == 0   )
           return tokens;

        string::size_type start = 0;   // beginning index of token
        string::size_type finish;      // ending index of token
        while( true )
        {
           // find the next character that is not a delimiter
           start = text.find_first_not_of( delimiters, start );

           // if there is a character that is not a delimiter...
           if( start != string::npos )
           {
              // find the next character after it that is a delimiter
              finish = text.find_first_of( delimiters, start );

              // if there is such a delimiter, the token is all the
              // characters from the starting character to just before
              // the delimiter
              if( finish != string::npos )
              {
                 tokens.push_back( text.substr( start, finish-start ) );
```

```
            start = finish;    // use finish, not finish+1
        }
        // if there is not such a delimiter, the token is all the
        // characters from the starting character to the end of the
        // string. Bail out because there's no more text to look at
        else
        {
            tokens.push_back( text.substr( start,
                text.length()-start ) );
            break;
        }
    }

    // all remaining characters are delimiters
    else
        break;
    }
    return tokens;
}
```

The output is

```
TOKENS IN c:\greg\book\code\string_tokenize.cpp
c greg book code string_tokenize cpp

TOKENS IN data
data
TOKENS IN ..

TOKENS IN 431-02-9495
431 02 9495
```

Tokenizing is done by the custom function `tokenize`. Its algorithm is as follows:

■ Find the first token character and the first delimiter after that and take the token characters in between to be the first token.

■ Find the first token character after the first delimiter and the first delimiter after that and take the token characters in between to be the next token.

■ Keep doing this until there are no more delimiters.

The function starts out by verifying that the pointer `delimiters` is not NULL because `find_first_of` and `find_first_not_of` won't accept a NULL pointer. Then the function carries out the algorithm by repeatedly finding the index of the first character that is not a delimiter, that is, is a token character, finding the index of the first delimiter after that, and putting the substring in between in the output vector. Once the function has stored the substring, it stores the delimiter index as the new index to start the token search from. It might seem that the search should start one character later (because the delimiter is obviously not a token character), but if the string ends with a single delimiter, there is no subsequent character at all.

The first part of the main program demonstrates the use of `tokenize` in finding the parts of a file specification, such as the drive, the folders, the file name, and the extension. It uses the colon, backslash, and period as the delimiters. The output shows the results for a typical file specification in a Windows operating system, for a file specification with no delimiters and for one that's all delimiters.

The last part of the program is an example of extracting numbers separated by hyphens, as would be found in a Social Security number. In this case, the delimiters are just one character—the hyphen.

11 Tips on Numerical Processing

This chapter shows you how to use the C++ Standard Library for numerical processing, illustrates some common computations, such as calculating statistics, and demonstrates things you may not have heard of, such as computing the dot product of two vectors. The examples illustrate how some of the less common STL algorithms and capabilities are useful in numerical processing. Here are some of the things you'll learn:

- How to perform arithmetic on numbers in containers
- How to make sequences of consecutive or random numbers
- How to evaluate a one- or two-dimensional function
- How to compute statistics of data, including the minimum, maximum, mean, median, mode, variance, and percentiles
- How to work with complex numbers
- How to read and write a number in hexadecimal, octal, or binary format
- How to display leading or trailing zeros and a thousands' separator
- How to easily read a data set from or write one to a file

The techniques here are all practical and useful. However, they are not necessarily good for serious numerical work in which you need the utmost speed and must carefully control the accuracy of the computations. If this interests you, delve into the numerical-computation literature, which is extensive and sometimes quite arcane. One good book on the subject is *Numerical Recipes in C++* [Press02], which covers a lot of material and is actually fun to read.

TIP 76   PERFORM ARITHMETIC ON CONTAINERS

Applies to: Sequence containers, transform
See also: Tip 5, Tip 50, Tip 52, Listing 13.6, Listing 13.9

Quick Solution

```
vector<double> v1, v2;
// ... load numbers. v2 must be at least as long as v1

vector<double> result( v1.size() );

transform( v1.begin(), v1.end(), v2.begin(), result.begin(),
    plus<double>() ); // add corresponding elements

transform( v1.begin(), v1.end(), v2.begin(), result.begin(),
    minus<double>() ); // subtract corresponding elements

transform( v1.begin(), v1.end(), v2.begin(), result.begin(),
    multiplies<double>() ); // multiply corresponding elements

transform( v1.begin(), v1.end(), v2.begin(), result.begin(),
    divides<double>() ); // divide corresponding elements
```

Detailed Solution

If you have two containers, it would be reasonable to want to combine them element-by-element with arithmetic. That is, you would like to combine the first elements of the two containers by arithmetic and store them in the first element of an output container, combine the second elements of the two containers and store them in the second element of the output container, and so on. This type of operation is common in particular with vectors, both the mathematical kind and the STL variety.

Fortunately, it's easy to perform the arithmetic described. The Standard Library contains function objects for addition, subtraction, multiplication, division, and modulus. Each of these takes two arguments and returns its eponymous result. Table 11.1 lists the rather inconsistently named function objects. It also shows that there is a unary function object called `negate` that returns the negative of its argument.

TABLE 11.1 Arithmetic Function Objects in the STL

Function Object	Operation
plus	parameter1 + parameter2
minus	parameter1 − parameter2
multiplies	parameter1 * parameter2
divides	parameter1 / parameter2
modulus	parameter1 % parameter2
negate	−parameter1

By using these function objects with the STL algorithm `transform`, you can perform element-wise arithmetic. They are also useful in other STL algorithms, as the code in Tip 52 shows. The program Listing 11.1 is a useful demonstration of element-wise arithmetic.

LISTING 11.1   Performing Arithmetic on Containers

```cpp
// numeric_arithmetic.cpp

#include <algorithm>
#include <functional>
#include <iomanip>
#include <vector>

#include "tips.hpp"

using namespace std;

int main()
{
    const float data2003[] = { 55.43, 76.02, 89.90, 44.24, 79.87 };
    const float data2004[] = { 57.74, 82.68, 87.65, 44.89, 84.98 };

    // create and initialize vectors with above data
    vector<float> rates2004( data2004,
        data2004 + sizeof( data2004 ) / sizeof( data2004[0] ) );
    vector<float> rates2003( data2003,
        data2003 + sizeof( data2003 ) / sizeof( data2003[0] ) );

    vector<float> change( rates2004.size() );

    // compute the difference from 2003 to 2004
    transform( rates2004.begin(), rates2004.end(), rates2003.begin(),
        change.begin(), minus<float>() );

    // divide by the 2003 rates
    transform( change.begin(), change.end(), rates2003.begin(),
        change.begin(), divides<float>() );

    // multiply by 100 to get a percent
    transform( change.begin(), change.end(), change.begin(),
        bind2nd( multiplies<float>(), 100.0f ) );
```

```
    cout << fixed << setprecision( 1 );
    tips::print( change, "Percent change in rates" );
}
```

The output is

```
Percent change in rates: 4.2 8.8 -2.5 1.5 6.4
```

The program illustrates container arithmetic by computing the percent that programmer rates change over a year. The program starts by initializing two vectors with some made-up hourly programming rates, using the technique that Tip 5 explains. The vector `rates2004` contains the rates for five different programmers in 2004, and the vector `rates2003` has their corresponding rates a year earlier. Equation 11.1 gives the percent change:

$$\text{Percent change} = 100\% \times (\text{Rate}_{2004} - \text{Rate}_{2003}) / \text{Rate}_{2003} \qquad (11.1)$$

After initializing the vectors, the program declares a third vector to hold the percent change. It is the same size as the other two vectors. The first call to `transform` subtracts the 2003 rates from the 2004 rates and stores the difference in the change vector. The first two arguments to `transform` are the beginning and end of the first input range. The third argument is the beginning of the second input range, which is assumed to be at least as long as the first range. The fourth argument is the start of the output range and the last argument is a function object. The object takes two arguments, which come from the first and second input ranges. In this program, the function object is one that is built-in and performs subtraction. The code then calls `transform` again, this time to divide the differences by the 2003 rates. Note that the change vector is both an input and output, which is perfectly legitimate.

The last call to `transform` multiplies all elements in the change vector by 100. This form of transform only has one input, not two as the preceding calls to the algorithm have. The function object `multiplies` still takes two parameters, but the second one is "frozen" at 100 through the use of a binder, as Tip 50 explains.

TIP 77   COMPLEX NUMBERS

Applies to: Complex numbers

Quick Solution

```
complex<double> c1( 7.63, 9.88 ); // create from rectangular coordinates
```

```
complex<double> c2( polar( 10.04, 0.77 ) ); // from polar coordinates

complex<double> c3 = c1 + c2; // -, *, and / also available

cout << setprecision( 4 )
    << "Sum: " << c3 << "  Magnitude: " << abs( c3 )
    << "  Angle: " << arg( c3 ) << "  Norm: " << norm( c3 ) << endl
    << "Real: " << c3.real() << "  Imaginary: " << c3.imag()
    << "  Conjugate: " << conj( c3 ) << endl << "Square root: "
    << sqrt( c3 ) << "  Log: " << log( c3 ) << endl
    << "Sine: " << sin( c3 ) << "  Hyperbolic sine: " << sinh( c3 );
```

Detailed Solution

C++ finally has complex numbers. They come as a class template that can be parameterized by the floating-point data types `float`, `double` or `long double`. (The C++ Standard doesn't specify what happens if you use other data types.) Global functions or member functions let you perform the usual operations, for example, perform arithmetic, create a complex number in polar coordinates, find the norm, magnitude, argument (angle or phase), and conjugate, and get the real and imaginary parts. The class template defines the self-assignment arithmetic operators (+=, -=, *=, and /=) as well as the two comparison operators == and !=. These last two operations are not very useful with floating-point numbers, though. It's better to compare such numbers for equality by subtracting them, taking the absolute value, and seeing if that value is less than some small number.

Inequalities involving less-than or greater-than are not defined because they have no meaning for complex numbers. However, there are many transcendental functions for complex numbers, such as raising to a power, exponentiation, square root, natural and common log, and the trigonometric and hyperbolic functions. Finally, complex numbers can read themselves from and write themselves to streams.

Complex numbers are used in Fourier analysis, solving differential equations, and in electrical engineering. One application is circuit analysis. For example, Figure 11.1 shows a parallel RLC circuit, made up of a resistor of resistance R, an inductor of inductance L, and a capacitor of capacitance C. The goal is to compute the impedance Z of the network. The impedance is a complex number that is a generalization of resistance. Impedance describes how the network reacts to a sinusoidal input.

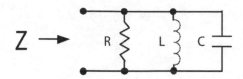

FIGURE 11.1 A parallel RLC circuit with impedance Z.

Equations 11.2 and 11.3 give the impedance Z:

$$Z = \frac{1}{\dfrac{1}{R} + \dfrac{1}{j\omega L} + j\omega C} \tag{11.2}$$

or

$$Z = \frac{1}{\dfrac{1}{R} + j\left(\omega C - \dfrac{1}{\omega L}\right)} \tag{11.3}$$

where $j = \sqrt{-1}$ and ω is the radian frequency of the sinusoid. One important fre-quency is $\omega = \sqrt{LC}$, called the resonant frequency. At this frequency, the imped-ance is a real number and, thus, has an imaginary part that is equal to zero.

The program in Listing 11.2 calculates the impedance of the parallel RLC circuit for the resonant frequency and several other ones.

LISTING 11.2 Computing an Impedance with Complex Numbers

```cpp
// numeric_complex.cpp

#include <complex>
#include <iomanip>
#include <iostream>
#include <cmath>

using namespace std;

// compute the complex impedance of a parallel RLC circuit
complex<double> parallel_RLC_impedance( double frequency,
    double resistance, double inductance, double capacitance );

int main( )
```

```
{
   const double R = 1000.0;   // R in ohms
   const double L = 0.2;      // L in henries
   const double C = 10.0e-9;  // C in farads
   double frequency;

   // set the resonant frequency
   frequency = 1.0 / sqrt( L * C );

   // compute the impedance at the resonant frequency
   complex<double> impedance =
      parallel_RLC_impedance( frequency, R, L, C );

   cout << setprecision( 2 ) << fixed
      << "AT RESONANT FREQUENCY\nImpedance = "
      << impedance << "   Magnitude = " << abs( impedance )
      << "   Phase = " << arg( impedance ) << endl;

   // compute the impedance at one tenth of the resonant frequency
   impedance = parallel_RLC_impedance( frequency / 10, R, L, C );

   cout << "\nAT ONE TENTH OF RESONANT FREQUENCY\nImpedance = "
      << impedance << "   Magnitude = " << abs( impedance )
      << "   Phase = " << arg( impedance ) << endl;

   // compute the impedance at ten times the resonant frequency
   impedance = parallel_RLC_impedance( frequency * 10, R, L, C );

   cout << "\nAT TEN TIMES THE RESONANT FREQUENCY\nImpedance = "
      << impedance << "   Magnitude = " << abs( impedance )
      << "   Phase = " << arg( impedance ) << endl;
}

inline
complex<double> parallel_RLC_impedance( double frequency,
   double resistance, double inductance, double capacitance )
{
   complex<double> impedance_inverse( 1.0 / resistance,
      frequency * capacitance - 1.0 / ( frequency * inductance ) );

   return 1.0 / impedance_inverse;
}
```

The output is

```
AT RESONANT FREQUENCY
Impedance = (1000.00,-0.00)   Magnitude = 1000.00   Phase = -0.00

AT ONE TENTH OF RESONANT FREQUENCY
Impedance = (169.48,375.17)   Magnitude = 411.68   Phase = 1.15

AT TEN TIMES THE RESONANT FREQUENCY
Impedance = (169.48,-375.17)   Magnitude = 411.68   Phase = -1.15
```

The first line of the function `parallel_RLC_impedance` shows a complex number being initialized on construction. The number is actually the denominator in Equation 11.3. The return is simply the inverse of the denominator, which the formula shows is the impedance. When taking the inverse of a complex number (as in the return statement of the function), you must include the decimal point on the numeral 1 because the complex template classes don't provide operators for dividing an integer by a complex number.

The first part of the output shows that the impedance is indeed real at the resonant frequency. Note that complex numbers write themselves to streams as a pair of numbers surrounded by parentheses. The remainder of the output shows complex impedances in rectangular coordinates (the numbers within parentheses) and polar coordinates (magnitude and phase).

TIP 78   DIFFERENCES BETWEEN A CONTAINER'S ELEMENTS

Applies to: Sequence containers, adjacent_difference
See also: Tip 7, Tip 16, Tip 76, Tip 97

Quick Solution

```
vector<int> v( 4, 3 ); // fill with 3s
v[1] = 5;
v[2] = v[3] = 15;

vector<int> difference( v.size() );
adjacent_difference( v.begin(), v.end(), difference.begin() );

// now difference has: 3, 2, 10, and 0
```

Detailed Solution

Sometimes the values of data are not as important as the changes in the values. For one thing, plots of changes can often let you see significant events in data more easily than charts of the data itself. For another, differences are often important in their own right. For example, the distance a car travels divided by the time it took to go that far is the car's speed, something that the police seem to be very interested in. Similarly, the change in a car's velocity divided by the time it takes to make that change is the vehicle's acceleration.

A third use of differences is to give data more meaning by putting the numbers in context, that is, making them relative to each other. For example, stock prices are often given in absolute terms (the closing price per share) and in relative terms (the percent change from the previous day's closing price). The former lets you know how much your fortune is worth, and the latter lets you compare daily changes in your hoard regardless of its actual size. The STL makes it easy to compute differences in values, as the code in Listing 11.3 shows.

LISTING 11.3 Differences Between a Container's Elements

```cpp
// numeric_difference.cpp

#include <algorithm>
#include <fstream>
#include <iomanip>
#include <iostream>
#include <iterator>
#include <numeric>
#include <vector>

using namespace std;

int main( )
{
   // open the file with the stock prices
   ifstream stock_file( "stock.txt" );
   if(!stock_file )
   {
      cout << "Couldn't open stock.txt\n";
      return 0;
   }

   // create a vector and initialize it with the stock prices
   vector<float> price( (istream_iterator<float>( stock_file )),
      istream_iterator<float>() );
```

```
        // compute the adjacent differences and store in a new vector
        vector<float> percent_change( price.size() );
        adjacent_difference( price.begin(), price.end(),
           percent_change.begin() );

        // divide by the previous day's stock price
        transform( percent_change.begin()+1, percent_change.end(),
           price.begin(), percent_change.begin()+1, divides<float>() );

        // multiply by 100 to get percent daily change
        transform( percent_change.begin()+1, percent_change.end(),
           percent_change.begin()+1, bind2nd( multiplies<float>(), 100 ) );

        // display the first five values
        cout << "First five stock prices:    "
           << fixed << setprecision( 2 );
        copy( price.begin(), price.begin()+5,
           ostream_iterator<float>( cout, "  " ) );
        cout << "\nFirst five percent changes: ";
        copy( percent_change.begin(), percent_change.begin()+5,
           ostream_iterator<float>( cout, "  " ) );
    }
```

The output is

```
First five stock prices:      18.84  18.85  19.23  19.01  17.39
First five percent changes: 18.84  0.05  2.02  -1.14  -8.52
```

The program is an example of computing the percent daily change in stock prices, and starts by opening a file with the daily closing prices of a stock during four months in the summer and fall. The program creates a vector and initializes it with the data the program reads in (see Tip 7 and Tip 97). Figure 11.2 is a plot of the prices in the file.

Next, the code makes a container that has enough elements to hold the data and then calls the STL algorithm adjacent_difference to insert new numbers. The function takes an input iterator range and writes the computed values starting at the given output iterator. The value at an output iterator is the difference between the corresponding input iterator value and the value preceding it. The first iterator has no preceding value, so adjacent_difference simply makes the first output value be the first input value. Storing the values this way also has the benefit that you can exactly reconstruct the original data from the `adjacent_difference` output by using the `partial_sum` STL algorithm.

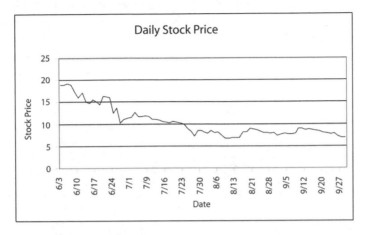

FIGURE 11.2 Some stock prices.

Equation 11.4 provides a more formal definition of `adjacent_difference`'s output. For an input container `in` and an output container `out`, the ith element of the output is

$$out[i] = \begin{cases} in[i] - in[i-1] & \text{for } i > 0 \\ in[0] & \text{for } i = 0 \end{cases} \tag{11.4}$$

After computing the adjacent difference, it uses `transform` to divide that difference by the preceding day's stock price to give the relative change. `transform` is a very powerful STL algorithm that allows you to combine two input ranges through a specified operation and place the result in an output range. Tip 76 explains in more detail how to do arithmetic with `transform`.

When the code calls `transform`, the first argument is the start of its input range, and this is element 1 of the vector, not element 0. Element 0 has no preceding-day price to divide by, so it must be ignored. The second argument is the end of the first input range. The third argument is the start of the second input range, which in the example is the actual stock price. The fourth argument is the start of the output range, and the fifth is the operation for combining the two inputs. In the code, the division functor specifies the operation.

The code shows that the output container is the same as one of the input containers, and this is a perfectly legitimate and common practice. Overall then, the call to `transform` divides all but the first element of `percent_change` by the preceding element in `price` and puts the results back into `percent_change`.

The next section of code calls `transform` again, but this variation of the algorithm contains only one input range. The call multiplies all elements of `percent_change` except the first by 100 to get a percent change in stock price instead of just the relative change. These are the numbers of interest, and Figure 11.3 shows them on a graph.

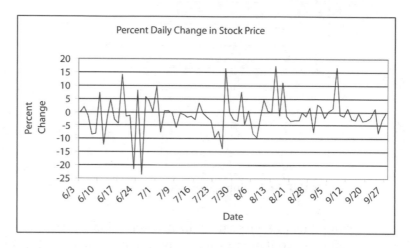

FIGURE 11.3   Percent changes in the stock prices.

The last part of the program displays the first five original stock prices and the first five numbers in the container of percent changes, using the method in Tip 16. Notice in the output that the first of these values is indeed the same as the first original value.

TIP 79   **MAKE CONSECUTIVE, EVENLY SPACED NUMBERS**

Applies to: Sequence containers, partial_sum
See also: Tip 4, Tip 55, Tip 81, Listing 13.11

Quick Solution

```
vector<int> n( 5, 1 ); // fill with 1s
partial_sum( n.begin(), n.end(), n.begin() ); // 1 2 3 4 5

n.assign( n.size(), 1 ); // fill with 1s
n[0] = 8;
partial_sum( n.begin(), n.end(), n.begin() ); // 8 9 10 11 12

n.assign( n.size(), 5 ); // fill with 5s
```

```
n[0] = 2;
partial_sum( n.begin(), n.end(), n.begin() ); // 2 7 12 17 22

n.assign( n.size(), -1 );
n[0] = 3;
partial_sum( n.begin(), n.end(), n.begin() ); // 3 2 1 0 -1
```

Detailed Solution

Sometimes it's useful to fill a container with evenly spaced numbers. One application of this is to use it to evaluate a (mathematical) function at a series of points, as Tip 81 shows. Another application is to use the numbers as the input of independent values (those usually appearing on the horizontal axis) to a graphing routine. The code in Listing 11.4 shows how to make evenly spaced numbers, starting on any number and with any spacing.

LISTING 11.4   Making Consecutive Numbers

```cpp
// numeric_consecutive.cpp

#include <iostream>
#include <numeric>
#include <vector>

#include "tips.hpp"

using namespace std;

int main( )
{
   vector<int> num1( 5, 1 );
   cout << "Consecutive numbers from " << num1[0]
      << " at intervals of " << num1[1] << ": ";
   partial_sum( num1.begin(), num1.end(), num1.begin() );
   tips::print( num1 );

   // intervals of 1 starting at 4
   num1.assign( num1.size(), 1 );
   num1[0] = 4;
   cout << "\nConsecutive numbers from " << num1[0]
      << " at intervals of " << num1[1] << ": ";
   partial_sum( num1.begin(), num1.end(), num1.begin() );
   tips::print( num1 );
```

```cpp
    // intervals of 3 starting at 2
    num1.assign( num1.size(), 3 );
    num1[0] = 2;
    cout << "\nConsecutive numbers from " << num1[0]
       << " at intervals of " << num1[1] << ": ";
    partial_sum( num1.begin(), num1.end(), num1.begin() );
    tips::print( num1 );

    // intervals of -1 starting at 5
    num1.assign( num1.size(), -1 );
    num1[0] = 5;
    cout << "\nConsecutive numbers from " << num1[0]
       << " at intervals of " << num1[1] << ": ";
    partial_sum( num1.begin(), num1.end(), num1.begin() );
    tips::print( num1 );

    // intervals of 0.5 starting at 3.2
    vector<float> num2( 5, 0.5 );
    num2[0] = 3.2;
    cout << "\nConsecutive numbers from " << num2[0]
       << " at intervals of " << num2[1] << ": ";
    partial_sum( num2.begin(), num2.end(), num2.begin() );
    tips::print( num2 );
}
```

The output is

```
Consecutive numbers from 1 at intervals of 1: 1 2 3 4 5

Consecutive numbers from 4 at intervals of 1: 4 5 6 7 8

Consecutive numbers from 2 at intervals of 3: 2 5 8 11 14

Consecutive numbers from 5 at intervals of -1: 5 4 3 2 1

Consecutive numbers from 3.2 at intervals of 0.5: 3.2 3.7 4.2 4.7 5.2
```

The first example in the code shows how to make consecutive integers starting at one. First, you construct a sequence container of integers filled with ones (see Tip 4). The code shows an example of a vector with five ones. Then, to construct the desired numbers, simply call the STL algorithm partial_sum with the beginning and end iterators of the container as inputs and the beginning iterator as the output. That's it.

partial_sum places the first element of the input in the first element of the output. Then it places the sum of the second and all previous elements of the input in the second element of the output, the sum of the third and all previous elements of the input in the third element of the output, and so on. This creates the desired sequence, as the output shows.

To create consecutive integers starting at a number other than 1, set all elements of the container to 1, set the first element to the starting number of the sequence, and then call `partial_sum` as before. The second paragraph of code and second line of output illustrate this.

To make consecutive integers separated by more than 1, fill the container with the number that you want to be the difference between any two consecutive elements, set the first element to the integer you want the sequence to start on, and call `partial_sum`. The code and corresponding output show an example of five integers starting at two and increasing by three. You can also make decreasing sequences, as the fourth paragraph of code and its output illustrate.

Finally, you can use the same techniques to make consecutive floating-point numbers separated by a fractional amount. The last paragraph of code and its output provide an example. For another example of using consecutive numbers, see Tip 55.

TIP 80   ## MAKE A SEQUENCE OF RANDOM NUMBERS

Applies to: Sequence container, generate
See also: Tip 50, Tip 76, Tip 99

Quick Solution

```
vector<int> v( 10 );

// fill with random numbers
generate( v.begin(), v.end(), rand ); // rand is in <cstdlib>
```

Detailed Solution

Occasionally, you may want to make a sequence of random numbers. You can do this very easily, as the example in Listing 11.5 shows.

LISTING 11.5 Making a Sequence of Random Numbers

```
// numeric_random.cpp

#include <algorithm>
#include <functional>
#include <cstdlib>
#include <vector>
```

```
#include "tips.hpp"

using namespace std;

int main( )
{
   vector<int> random( 8 );

   // fill the container with random numbers
   generate( random.begin(), random.end(), rand );
   tips::print( random, "Random numbers" );

   // make all random numbers go from 1 to 6
   transform( random.begin(), random.end(), random.begin(),
      bind2nd( modulus<int>(), 6 ) );
   transform( random.begin(), random.end(), random.begin(),
      bind2nd( plus<int>(), 1 ) );
   tips::print( random, "Random numbers from 1 to 6" );
}
```
The output is

```
Random numbers: 130 10982 1090 11656 7117 17595 6415 22948
Random numbers from 1 to 6: 5 3 5 5 2 4 2 5
```

The program creates a vector with space to hold some random numbers, in this case eight of them. Next, it fills the container with random numbers, all with one line of code. It accomplishes this feat by calling the STL algorithm generate. Its first two arguments are a range. Its third argument is a function or function object that accepts no parameters and returns a number. To get a random number, the program uses the Standard Library function rand, available in the <cstdlib> header. This produces uniformly distributed random integers in the range 0 to RAND_MAX, also defined in <cstdlib>. The first line of the output shows the resulting eight random numbers. Your numbers may be different because the implementation of rand varies.

The rest of the code shows how to make the numbers lie between two specified values. For example, if you wanted to simulate die rolls, you would make the numbers lie between 1 and 6, inclusive. The first step is to call transform to compute the remainder of each number when it is divided by 6, that is, to calculate the number modulo 6. Tip 76 explains this use of transform, and Tip 50 provides more details on using bind2nd to always pass the same argument to a function. After the call to transform, all elements of the vector lie between 0 and 5 inclusive. Adding 1 with a call to transform makes the random numbers fall in the inclusive range of 1 to 6.

The last line of the output shows the result. Again, your numbers may differ, but they should all be at least 1 and not greater than 6.

The program in Listing 11.5 will always produce the same sequence of random numbers. If you want to change the sequence, you can set the initial seed (starting number of the sequence) by calling srand in <cstdlib>. To always get a different sequence, initialize srand with the current system time, available from time in <ctime>.

The technique for limiting the range of random numbers by taking the modulus does not produce numbers that are as statistically random as those in the original sequence, but they are suitable for casual use. Good random number generators are actually pretty hard to make. To see some examples, and some generators that make nonuniform distributions, see [Press02] or the Boost library described in Tip 99.

TIP 81 EVALUATE A MATHEMATICAL FUNCTION

Applies to: Transform
See also: Tip 5, Tip 79, Listing 13.11

Quick Solution

```
float f1( float x );
float f2( float x, float y );
// ...

vector<float> v1, v2;
// ...

vector<float> z( v1.size() );

// evaluate function of one variable
transform( v1.begin(), v1.end(), z.begin(), f1 );

// evaluate function of two variables
transform( v1.begin(), v1.end(), v2.begin(), z.begin(), f2 );
```

Detailed Solution

The Standard Library makes it very easy to evaluate your own function using container elements as inputs. The function can have one or two arguments. The STL algorithm to use is transform. It has two signatures. The first form,

```
OutputIterator transform( InputIterator start, InputIterator stop,
    OutputIterator out, UnaryOperation unary_op )
```

takes an input range for the first two arguments, the start of an output range for the third argument and a function object as the fourth argument. It operates on each element of the input, and `transform` puts its result in the corresponding element of the output.

The second form is

```
OutputIterator transform( InputIterator1 start1, InputIterator1 stop1,
    InputIterator2 start2, OutputIterator out,
    BinaryOperation binary_op )
```

Its first two arguments specify the range of the first input, the third argument gives the start of the second input range, the fourth argument is the start of the output range, and the last argument is again a function object. This time the function object takes two arguments. The first comes from the first input range, and the second argument comes from the second input range. The output range must be at least the size of the first input range (unless you use a back inserter), but note, too, that the second input range must also be at least the size of the first.

The code in Listing 11.6 demonstrates the use of both of these forms to evaluate custom-written functions.

LISTING 11.6   Evaluating a Mathematical Function

```cpp
// numeric_function.cpp

#include <algorithm>
#include <numeric>
#include <vector>

#include "tips.hpp"

int factorial( int n );
int teams( int candidate_size, int team_size );

using namespace std;

int main( )
{
    // make a vector with 0, 1, 2, 3, 4, 5
    vector<int> numbers( 6, 1 );
    numbers[0] = 0;
    partial_sum( numbers.begin(), numbers.end(), numbers.begin() );

    // compute the factorial of each number
```

```
      vector<int> result( 6 );
      transform( numbers.begin(), numbers.end(), result.begin(),
         factorial );
      tips::print( result, "Factorials of 0-5" );

      // candidates available and team sizes for baseball, basketball,
      // football and soccer
      const int candidate_array[] = { 14, 11, 30, 17 };
      const int team_array[]      = {  9,  5, 22, 11 };
      const int array_length = sizeof( candidate_array )
         / sizeof( candidate_array[0] );

      vector<int> candidate( candidate_array,
         candidate_array + array_length );
      vector<int> team( team_array, team_array + array_length );
      result.resize( array_length );

      // compute the number of possible teams
      transform( candidate.begin(), candidate.end(), team.begin(),
         result.begin(), teams );

      cout << endl
      << "There are " << result[0] << " possible baseball teams\n"
      << "There are " << result[1] << " possible basketball teams\n"
      << "There are " << result[2] << " possible football teams\n"
      << "There are " << result[3] << " possible soccer teams";
   }

// n >= 0
int factorial( int n )
{
   int n_factorial = 1;
   for( int i = n; i > 1; --i )
      n_factorial *= i;

   return n_factorial;
}

// num_candidates >= 1,  1 <= team_size <= num_candidates
int teams( int num_candidates, int team_size )
{
   // use double to avoid integer overflow
   double permutations = 1;
```

```
    for( int i = num_candidates; i > num_candidates - team_size; --i )
        permutations *= i;

    for( int i = team_size; i > 1; --i )
        permutations /= i;

    return static_cast<int>( permutations );
}
```

The output is

```
Factorials of 0-5: 1 1 2 6 24 120

There are 2002 possible baseball teams
There are 462 possible basketball teams
There are 5852925 possible football teams
There are 12376 possible soccer teams
```

The program starts by making a vector containing the integers from 0 to 5. It does this using the technique in Tip 79. Then the program uses `transform` to compute the factorial of each of these integers. The factorial of a non-negative integer n is denoted $n!$. Equation 11.5 gives the formula for a factorial, namely,

$$n! = n \cdot (n-1) \cdot (n-2)\ldots 3 \cdot 2 \cdot 1 \tag{11.5}$$

The first line of the output shows the result.

The remainder of the program illustrates the evaluation of a two-parameter function. The function `teams` computes the number of different teams of a given size that could be made up from a pool of candidate team members. For example, how many different ways could a baseball team of 9 players be made from a pool of 14 potential team members? The other stored values compute the number of different teams that could be made up for basketball, football (an American game like rugby), and soccer, which is known in the rest of the world as football.

The code stores the data in initialized arrays and creates vectors with the same values using the technique of Tip 5. The code resizes the output vector to be the same length as the input vectors. (In this program, resizing is not actually necessary because the vector is already longer than it needs to be. However, resizing this way is good practice.) Finally, the code calls `transform` with the two input vectors. The last four lines of the output show the result.

TIP 82   COMPUTE THE DOT PRODUCT

Applies to: Inner_product
See also: Tip 8, Tip 76, Listing 13.13

Quick Solution

```
vector<double> x, y;
// ...

vector<double> z( x.size() );

// last argument must have decimal point
double dot_product = inner_product( x.begin(), x.end(), y.begin(), 0.0 );
```

Detailed Solution

The dot product of two vectors, also called the inner product, occurs frequently in fields where vectors are used. (Here, "vector" means the mathematical entity, not the C++ container.) In physics and engineering two- and three-dimensional vectors are common. In computer graphics, three- and four-dimensional vectors are often used. N-dimensional vectors, where N is much greater than four, occur often in pattern recognition.

To compute the dot product of two vectors, you multiply the first components of the two vectors, multiply the second components, and so forth, and add these products. (Both vectors must be the same size, that is, dimension.) In other words, for the two N-dimensional vectors

$$\mathbf{v} = (v_1, v_2, \cdots v_N) \qquad \mathbf{w} = (w_1, w_2, \cdots w_N)$$

Equation 11.6 defines the *dot product*, namely,

$$v \cdot w = \sum_{i=1}^{N} v_i w_i \qquad (11.6)$$

In computer graphics, the dot product can be used to calculate the distance of a point from the origin, the distance of a point from a plane and the intersection of a line and a circle. All of these are especially important in computer games. Another use, which the code in Listing 11.7 illustrates, is to calculate the angle between two vectors. This occurs in games when computing the angle at which one object bounces off another, for example, a hovercar rebounding from a wall or a pool ball caroming off a billiard table.

The formula for the angle θ between two vectors **v** and **w** is

$$\theta = \cos^{-1}\left(\frac{\mathbf{v} \cdot \mathbf{w}}{|\mathbf{v}\| \mathbf{w}|}\right) \tag{11.7}$$

where the absolute value (norm) of a vector is

$$|\mathbf{x}| = \sqrt{\mathbf{x} \cdot \mathbf{x}} = \sqrt{\sum_{i=1}^{N} x_i^2} \tag{11.8}$$

Equation 11.8 shows that the norm of a vector is the square root of the dot product of the vector with itself.

The code in Listing 11.7 calculates the angles in each pair of vectors in Figure 11.4.

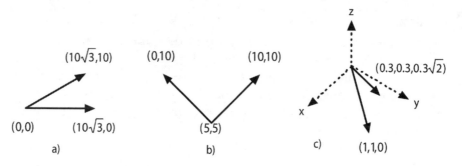

FIGURE 11.4   Pairs of vectors separated by different angles.

LISTING 11.7   Computing the Dot Product

```
// numeric_dot_product.cpp

#include <algorithm>
#include <cmath>
#include <iostream>
#include <numeric>
#include <vector>

using namespace std;

// compute angle (in degrees) between two vectors
double vector_angle( const vector<double>& v1,
    const vector<double>& v2 );
```

```cpp
int main( )
{
   vector<double> v( 2 ), w( 2 );

   // first pair of vectors
   v[0] = 10.0 * sqrt( 3.0 );    // v[1] = 0.0 from constructor
   w[0] = 10.0 * sqrt( 3.0 );
   w[1] = 10.0;
   cout << "There is a " << vector_angle( v, w ) <<
   " degree angle between the first pair of vectors\n";

   // second pair of vectors
   const double tail[2] = { 5.0, 5.0 };
   const double v_head[2] = { 10.0, 10.0 };
   const double w_head[2] = { 0.0, 10.0 };
   transform( v_head, v_head+2, tail, v.begin(), minus<double>() );
   transform( w_head, w_head+2, tail, w.begin(), minus<double>() );
   cout << "There is a " << vector_angle( v, w ) <<
   " degree angle between the second pair of vectors\n";

   // third pair of vectors
   const double v_3d[3] = { 1.0, 1.0, 0.0 };
   double w_3d[3] = { 0.3, 0.3, 0.3 };
   w_3d[2] *= sqrt( 2.0 );
   v.assign( v_3d, v_3d+3 );
   w.assign( w_3d, w_3d+3 );
   cout << "There is a " << vector_angle( v, w ) <<
   " degree angle between the third pair of vectors\n";
}

double vector_angle( const vector<double>& v1,
   const vector<double>& v2 )
{
   const double pi = 3.1415926535;

   // *** must put decimal point in constant at end of inner_product
   double norm1_squared =
      inner_product( v1.begin(), v1.end(), v1.begin(), 0.0 );
   double norm2_squared =
      inner_product( v2.begin(), v2.end(), v2.begin(), 0.0 );
   double dot_product =
      inner_product( v1.begin(), v1.end(), v2.begin(), 0.0 );

   // angle in radians
```

```
        double angle =
            acos( dot_product / sqrt( norm1_squared * norm2_squared ) );

        // convert to degrees
        angle *= 360.0 / ( 2 * pi );
        return angle;
    }
```

The output is

```
There is a 30 degree angle between the first pair of vectors
There is a 90 degree angle between the second pair of vectors
There is a 45 degree angle between the third pair of vectors
```

The first section of code sets up the vectors in Figure 11.4(a) and calls the custom-written function `vector_angle`, which computes the angle between the two vectors. The two vectors illustrated in Figure 11.4(b) don't meet at the origin, so the next section of the program subtracts the coordinates of the tails from the coordinates of the heads to get the vectors of interest. The code shows how to use the STL algorithm `transform` to do this easily. (Tip 76 gives details on performing arithmetic on a container's elements.) Finally, the last section shows the angle computation for the three-dimensional vectors in Figure 11.4(c). Note that the code transfers the data from the arrays to the vectors using the technique of Tip 8.

The function `vector_angle` computes the angle between the two vectors passed to it. It begins by calculating the square of the norm of the first vector by using Equations 11.6 and 11.8 and the STL algorithm `inner_product`. The fourth argument of that function is a constant to which each product of vector elements is added inside the `inner_product`. The constant must be 0 in this application, and if the vectors contain `doubles` or `floats`, as is the case, there must be a decimal point in the passed value, for example, `0.0` in the code. The reason is that the routine derives the data type of the returned value from whatever is passed as the fourth argument. If you pass an integer, the return type is an integer and the routine drops fractions in the dot product computation. Thus, for example, the norm of (0.3,0.3,0.3) will come out to be zero.

After computing the norms and the dot product, the routine calculates the angle using Equation 11.7. The denominator in the code shows the square root of the product of the squares of the norms. This is equivalent to the product of the square roots of the norms but saves the expense of calculating a second square root.

Finally, the routine converts the angle to degrees. It defines pi (π). Although not required to by the C++ standard, the header <cmath> often makes that constant available as M_PI. It may also contain additional common functions of pi, such as $\pi \times 2$, $\pi / 4$, and so forth.

TIP 83 FIND THE MINIMUM AND MAXIMUM IN A CONTAINER

Applies to: Min_element, max_element
See also: Tip 5, Tip 76, Tip 88, Listing 13.12

Quick Solution

```
vector<double> data;
// ...

vector<double>::iterator max_iterator
   = max_element( data.begin(), data.end() );
vector<double>::iterator min_iterator
   = min_element( data.begin(), data.end() );

cout << "Data max = " << *max_iterator
     << "   Data min = " << *min_iterator;
```

Detailed Solution

It's common to want to know the extremes of a data set. This tip demonstrates how easy it is to find the minimum and maximum of a collection of numbers. It applies these values to the practical problem of scaling a data set, that is, making it lie within a certain range. In this case, the program takes the input data set and makes it fall between 0 and 100 inclusive. The code in Listing 11.8 is parameterized, so it's easy to set any desired output range.

LISTING 11.8 Finding the Minimum and Maximum in a Container

```
// numeric_min_max.cpp

#include <algorithm>
#include <functional>
#include <iomanip>
#include <iostream>
#include <vector>

using namespace std;
```

```cpp
int main( )
{
   const float data_array[] = { 13.4, 27.6, 15.5, 44.3, 51.2,
      30.2, 18.0 };
   vector<float> data( data_array,
      data_array + sizeof( data_array ) / sizeof( data_array[0] ) );

   // find min and max
   float data_min = *min_element( data.begin(), data.end() );
   float data_max = *max_element( data.begin(), data.end() );
   cout << "Before scaling: Minimum = " << setw( 5 ) << data_min
      << "   Maximum = " << data_max;

   // make scale factor and additive offset
   const float desired_max = 100.0f;
   const float desired_min = 0.0f;
   const float m =
      ( desired_max - desired_min ) / ( data_max - data_min );
   const float b = desired_min - m * data_min;

   // scale the data
   transform( data.begin(), data.end(), data.begin(),
      bind2nd( multiplies<float>(), m ) );
   transform( data.begin(), data.end(), data.begin(),
      bind2nd( plus<float>(), b ) );

   cout << "\nAfter  scaling: Minimum = " << setw( 5 )
      << *min_element( data.begin(), data.end() )
      << "   Maximum = " << *max_element( data.begin(), data.end() );
}
```

The output is

```
Before scaling: Minimum =  13.4   Maximum = 51.2
After  scaling: Minimum =     0   Maximum = 100
```

The program starts by creating a vector and initializing with a given set of numbers, as Tip 5 explains. The code then finds the smallest and largest numbers by using `min_element` and `max_element`. These two algorithms find the extrema in a container, rather than the more common `min` and `max`, which just operate on two numbers. By default, `min_element` and `max_element` use whatever less-than operator is defined for the data elements of the container. However, you can use your own comparison method, as Tip 88 demonstrates.

Note that the two algorithms don't produce the minimum and maximum values. Instead, they return iterators, which mark the locations of those values. Thus, the results of the functions must be dereferenced as the sample program shows.

After finding the extrema, the software calculates a scaling factor and additive offset. If the data is first multiplied by the scaling factor and then has the offset added to it, the resulting numbers will have the desired minimum and maximum values. A more robust program would verify that the minimum and maximum of the data are not the same (which they would be if all numbers in the data set were equal) to avoid dividing by 0 when calculating the scaling factor.

Next, the code scales the data by calling transform twice. The first call multiplies all elements in the vector by the scaling factor. The second call adds the offset to all of the elements. Tip 76 describes using transform to do arithmetic on a container's elements. The output shows that the data has indeed been scaled so that its minimum is 0 and maximum is 100.

A final point to remember is that if you're sorting the elements in a container, perhaps to compute the mode as in Tip 88, you don't need to call min_element or max_element—just look at the first and last elements in the sorted container to get the values you want.

TIP 84 — MINIMUM AND MAXIMUM OF TWO VALUES USING CUSTOM CRITERION

Applies to: Min, max
See also: Tip 5, Tip 65

Quick Solution

```
bool my_less_than( const list<int>& lhs, const list<int>& rhs );
// custom definition of "less than".

list<int> a, b;
// ...

list<int> min_list = min( a, b, my_less_than );
list<int> max_list = max( a, b, my_less_than );
```

Detailed Solution

Using min and max to compute the minimum or maximum of two numbers is a common operation. Actually, these functions can also compare objects other than numbers, such as strings, classes or vectors. min and max compare two objects using the default less-than (<) operator, which may not always be appropriate.

Although it is not well-known, you can supply a custom comparison operator to both min and max. The function or functor should accept constant references to two arguments (the same ones supplied to min and max) and return true if the first argument is less than the second. Otherwise, it should return false.

The example in Listing 11.9 shows a custom comparison of vectors. The default less-than operator for vectors returns true if the first vector is lexicographically less than the second. (See Tip 65 for an explanation of lexicographical ordering.) Another way of comparing vectors is to compare their norms or magnitudes. The norm of a vector is the sum of the squares of its components; the magnitude is just the square root of the norm. The comparison function norm_less_than returns true if the norm of the first vector is less than that of the second and false otherwise.

LISTING 11.9   Using Custom Definitions of the Minimum and Maximum

```cpp
// numeric_custom_min_max.cpp

#include <numeric>
#include <vector>

#include "tips.hpp"

using namespace std;

bool norm_less_than( const vector<double>& a,
   const vector<double>& b );

int main( )
{
   const double data1[] = { 1.57, 3.32, -0.44 };
   const double data2[] = { -1.90, -2.01, 4.03 };

   vector<double> v1( data1, data1+sizeof( data1 )/sizeof( double ) );
   vector<double> v2( data2, data2+sizeof( data2 )/sizeof( double ) );

   const vector<double>& min_vector = min( v1, v2, norm_less_than );
   const vector<double>& max_vector = max( v1, v2, norm_less_than );

   tips::print( min_vector, "Vector with smallest norm" );
   tips::print( max_vector, "Vector with  largest norm" );
}
```

```
// returns true if the norm of a is < norm of b, false otherwise
inline
bool norm_less_than( const vector<double>& a,
   const vector<double>& b )
{
   return inner_product( a.begin(), a.end(), a.begin(), 0.0 )
         < inner_product( b.begin(), b.end(), b.begin(), 0.0 );
}
```

The output is

```
Vector with smallest norm: 1.57 3.32 -0.44
Vector with  largest norm: -1.9 -2.01 4.03
```

The program in Listing 11.9 starts by creating two vectors, each initialized with data from arrays. (Tip 5 explains this technique.) The code then finds the minimum and maximum of the pair, with the definition of the extrema provided by the custom function norm_less_than. A quick glance at the numbers shows that the second vector does indeed have the largest norm. If the program had used min and max without passing a comparison function, the second vector would have been the smallest because when compared lexicographically, its initial negative number would have made it come first.

The STL algorithm inner_product in the function norm_less_than makes it easy to compute the norm. inner_product multiplies each component of the first container to it by the corresponding component of the second container passed to it, sums the products, and adds the passed constant (the fourth argument, which is 0 in the preceding example). However, if the two containers are the same, the result is the sum of the squares of the elements.

By the way, using the norm instead of the magnitude for comparison is a nice little trick to remember. If the magnitude of one vector is less than the magnitude of another, the norm of the first is also less than the norm of the second. In other words, norms give the same ordering as magnitudes, but they don't compute the square root, which takes a lot of time.

TIP 85   MINIMUM AND MAXIMUM OF DATA TYPES

Applies to: All built-in data types
See also: Tip 4, Tip 9, Tip 76, Tip 79, Listing 13.6, Listing 13.8, Listing 13.11, Listing 13.12

Quick Solution

```
short a, b;
// ...

long int long_sum = static_cast<long int>( a ) + b;
short int short_sum;
if( long_sum > numeric_limits<short int>::max() )
    short_sum = numeric_limits<short int>::max();
else if( long_sum < numeric_limits<short int>::min() )
    short_sum = numeric_limits<short int>::min();
else
    short_sum = static_cast<short int>( long_sum );
```

Detailed Solution

You can easily get the minimum and maximum values of any built-in data type. This information is useful in situations where you need to guard against exceeding those values. Take digital images, for example. They are made up of pixels (picture elements), each of which is a numerical representation of the amount of light at the corresponding spot on the camera sensor. For black-and-white images, each pixel is typically an `unsigned char`, and for color images, a group of three `unsigned char`s. This data type usually has a range of 0 to 255 inclusive. Two images can be combined by adding their corresponding pixels. However, during this operation, it's easy for the sum to exceed the maximum value that an `unsigned char` can hold. If this happens, the value "wraps-around," so that it is interpreted as a much lower number.

The solution is to promote the `unsigned char` to a higher data type that can hold the sum without wrap-around (such as an `int`), replace the sum by the maximum value for an `unsigned char` if the sum exceeds that maximum amount, and then convert the result back to an `unsigned char`. You can use a similar procedure when subtracting images. In this case, test the difference to see if it is less than the minimum value for an `unsigned char`.

The code in Listing 11.10 demonstrates testing against the maximum value of an `unsigned char`.

LISTING 11.10   Finding the Minimum and Maximum of a Data Type

```
// numeric_data_type_min_max.cpp

#include <algorithm>
#include <limits>
#include <numeric>
#include <vector>
```

```cpp
#include "tips.hpp"

using namespace std;

unsigned char checked_sum( unsigned char num1, unsigned char num2 );

int main( )
{
   // create and display the first group of pixels
   const int n = 8;
   vector<unsigned char> pixels1( n, 250 );
   vector<int> int_pixels( pixels1.begin(), pixels1.end() );
   tips::print( int_pixels, "First  pixels" );

   // create and display the second group of pixels
   vector<unsigned char> pixels2( n, 1 );
   partial_sum( pixels2.begin(), pixels2.end(), pixels2.begin() );
   int_pixels.assign( pixels2.begin(), pixels2.end() );
   tips::print( int_pixels, "\nSecond pixels" );

   // perform and display sum with wrap-around
   vector<unsigned char> sum( n );
   transform( pixels1.begin(), pixels1.end(), pixels2.begin(),
      sum.begin(), plus<unsigned char>() );
   int_pixels.assign( sum.begin(), sum.end() );
   tips::print( int_pixels, "\nBad      sums" );

   // perform and display sum without wrap-around
   transform( pixels1.begin(), pixels1.end(), pixels2.begin(),
      sum.begin(), checked_sum );
   int_pixels.assign( sum.begin(), sum.end() );
   tips::print( int_pixels, "\nGood     sums" );
}

// add unsigned char's without wrap-around
inline
unsigned char checked_sum( unsigned char num1, unsigned char num2 )
{
   int sum = static_cast<int>( num1 ) + num2;
   int the_max = numeric_limits<unsigned char>::max();
   return static_cast<unsigned char>( sum <= the_max ? sum : the_max );
}
```

The output is

```
First   pixels: 250 250 250 250 250 250 250 250

Second pixels: 1 2 3 4 5 6 7 8

Bad        sums: 251 252 253 254 255 0 1 2

Good       sums: 251 252 253 254 255 255 255 255
```

The code starts out by creating a vector of eight unsigned chars (representing pixels), each with a value of 250. (See Tip 4 for more information on this constructor.) It then stores the values in a vector of ints (see Tip 9) before printing them on the screen. If it tried to print the unsigned chars directly on the screen, they would be interpreted as ASCII text and produce strange output.

Next, the program creates and displays another set of eight unsigned char pixels. It uses the partial_sum algorithm to create a sequence that goes from one to eight. (Tip 79 explains more about this handy technique.) Once the two containers are ready, the program adds the contents together and stores the results in a third container using the technique in Tip 76. The algorithm transform performs the addition using the functor plus for unsigned chars. This adds a pair of unsigned chars without converting them to a higher data type and thus produces wrap-around, as the third line of the output shows.

Finally, the code again adds the pixels, but this time passing the custom-written function checked_sum to perform the addition. The first line of that routine shows that one of the unsigned chars is cast to an int before being added to the other one. (C++ then automatically promotes the other to an int.) The return statement passes back the sum if it is not greater than the maximum value of an unsigned char or that maximum value otherwise.

The maximum and minimum values of each data type (along with a tremendous amount of other information) are available in the template class numeric_limits. This class is in the standard namespace, and you must include the header <numeric> to use it. Get the maximum value of a data type by using an expression like that shown in the code. Get the minimum the same way, except use min(). Note, however, that for floating types with denormalization (variable number of exponent bits), min returns the minimum *positive* normalized value.

The old C preprocessor limits are still available in C++. It's better to use the new ones, though, because they offer more type safety and you can easily supplement them for your own numeric data types.

| TIP 86 | **COMPUTE THE MEAN** |

Applies to: Accumulate
See also: Tip 5, Tip 90, Listing 13.4

Quick Solution

```
vector<int> v;
// ...

double mean = accumulate( v.begin(), v.end(), 0 )
    / static_cast<double>( v.size() );
```

Detailed Solution

The STL algorithm `accumulate` makes computing the mean (average) a snap. It returns the sum of all elements in a container. To get the mean you simply divide by the number of elements, which is the container's size. Listing 11.11 has a short example.

LISTING 11.11   Finding the Mean Value

```
// numeric_mean.cpp

#include <iomanip>
#include <iostream>
#include <numeric>
#include <vector>

using namespace std;

int main( )
{
    // miles per gallon for different cars in fleet
    const float mpg_data[] = { 21.4, 19.5, 8.8, 31.1, 20.2, 22.2,
        23.4 };

    // create a vector and initialize it with the above data
    vector<float> mpg( mpg_data,
        mpg_data + sizeof( mpg_data ) / sizeof( mpg_data[0] ) );

    // mean
    float fleet_average = accumulate( mpg.begin(), mpg.end(), 0.0 )
        / mpg.size();
```

```
    cout << "Fleet average miles per gallon: "
        << setprecision( 1 ) << fixed << fleet_average << endl;
}
```

The output is

```
Fleet average miles per gallon: 20.9
```

The program starts by creating a vector and initializing it with some data, as described in Tip 5. Next, it calls `accumulate`, which adds all elements in a range to a given value and returns the sum. The program passes the vector's starting and ending iterators as the first two arguments. The third argument is an initial value to which `accumulate` adds all of the elements in the input range. Be careful, because the third argument specifies the return type of the algorithm and the data type to which the input elements are converted during summation. If your container has floating-point numbers, make sure to make the initial value floating-point, too. If, for example, you were to make it an integer, each floating-point number would be converted to an integer when added to the variable within `accumulate` that is recording the sum. This could produce a substantially incorrect answer.

The program computes the average by dividing the sum of the elements returned from `accumulate` by the number of elements, that is, the vector size. More robust code would verify that the size is not 0 before dividing. The output shows the computed mean.

For those who like a little variety in their lives, Tip 90 demonstrates another method of computing the mean, as well as other statistics of data.

TIP 87 COMPUTE THE MEDIAN

Applies to: Nth_element
See also: Tip 5, Tip 88

Quick Solution

```
vector<int> v;
// ...

// midpoint is the median, assuming odd number of elements
nth_element( v.begin(), v.begin() + v.size() / 2, v.end() );
cout << "\nMedian value: " << v[v.size()/2];
```

Detailed Solution

One common statistic is the mean. Another useful characteristic of a data set is the median. The median is the middle number in a sorted data set. Half of the numbers are greater than or equal to the median, and half are less than or equal to it. The median is a common statistic of salary surveys because it is less sensitive to abnormally large numbers than the mean is. For example, the average salary in a survey of people working at software firms would be thrown off if a billionaire's earnings were included in the figures, but the median salary would most likely be unaffected by the high wages.

To find the median, it isn't necessary to sort the numbers. All that you really need to find is the number that falls in the middle of the set. Fortunately, the STL algorithm nth_element can separate numbers in exactly this way. The first argument to nth_element is the container's beginning iterator and the last argument is its ending iterator. The middle argument is an iterator that serves as a dividing point. After the call to nth_element, all elements in the container before the middle iterator will be less than or equal to the middle element and all elements after the middle iterator will be greater than or equal to that element. You can compute the median by letting the middle iterator point to the middle of the container. (If the array has an even number of elements, you adjust this procedure, for example, by taking the median to be the average of the two elements closest to the middle.) nth_element does not sort the numbers on either side of the middle iterator. However, that's unnecessary for computing the median and just makes the calculation slower.

The program in Listing 11.12 is an example of finding the median of some salaries.

LISTING 11.12   Finding the Median

```cpp
// numeric_median.cpp

#include <algorithm>
#include <vector>

#include "tips.hpp"

using namespace std;

int main( )
{
    // salaries
    const int num_salaries = 9;
    const int salary_array[num_salaries] = { 54200, 60100, 55500, 39000,
        44600, 43200, 58000, 180000000, 41300 };

    // create a vector and initialize it with the above data
```

```
vector<int> salaries( salary_array, salary_array+num_salaries );
tips::print( salaries, "Original salaries" );

// midpoint is the median
nth_element( salaries.begin(), salaries.begin()+num_salaries/2,
    salaries.end() );
tips::print( salaries, "\nAfter nth_element" );
cout << "\nMedian     salary: " << salaries[num_salaries/2];

// display sorted salaries for clarity
sort( salaries.begin(), salaries.end() );
tips::print( salaries, "\n\nAfter     sorting" );
}
```

The output is

```
Original salaries: 54200 60100 55500 39000 44600 43200 58000
180000000 41300

After nth_element: 41300 43200 44600 39000 54200 60100 58000
180000000 55500

Median     salary: 54200

After     sorting: 39000 41300 43200 44600 54200 55500 58000 60100
180000000
```

The program starts by making and initializing a vector with some salaries, using the technique of Tip 5. Next, the program calls nth_element to split the salaries in half, with the middle number being the median. The first line of the output shows the original order of the salaries and the second line shows the order after the partitioning. The median, 54200, is simply the middle element of the array. Notice that all the numbers to its left are smaller and all those to its right are larger. Neither of those two groups is sorted, though.

For interest, the program finishes by sorting and printing the array. This makes it easier to see that 54200 is indeed the middle number of the set. However, nth_element is faster than sort, and therefore a better choice for computing the median. On average, nth_element performs a number of operations that varies linearly with the number of elements in the input range, whereas the number of operations that sort performs is approximately the number of elements times the logarithm of that number.

If you have to sort all the numbers anyway—for example, to calculate the mode as described in Tip 88—don't call `nth_element`. Just select the middle element of the sorted container, and that will be the median.

TIP 88 COMPUTE THE MODE

Applies to: Map, vector, equal_range, sort
See also: Tip 5, Tip 35, Tip 83, Tip 87

Quick Solution

See detailed solution.

Detailed Solution

A useful data statistic is the mode, which is the number that occurs most often in a data set. If, for example, the data represents the identification numbers of parts that failed, you might want to redesign the part that fails most often first. Listing 11.13 has a program that computes the mode of some quiz grades two different ways.

LISTING 11.13 Computing the Median

```
// numeric_mode.cpp

#include <algorithm>
#include <iostream>
#include <map>
#include <vector>

#include "tips.hpp"

using namespace std;

inline
bool second_less( const pair<int,int> a, const pair<int,int> b )
{   return a.second < b.second;    }
// return true if second member of a is less than second member of b,
// otherwise false

int main( )
{
    const int num_grades = 15;
    const int grade_array[num_grades] =
```

```cpp
      { 9, 2, 3, 3, 7, 5, 7, 7, 4, 10, 5, 6, 7, 4, 7 };

   // create and initialize vector with above data
   vector<int> grades( grade_array, grade_array + num_grades );
   vector<int>::iterator grades_end = grades.end();
   tips::print( grades, "Original  grades" );

   // Method 1: increment entry in map each time a grade occurs
   map<int,int> frequency;
   for( vector<int>::iterator i = grades.begin(); i != grades_end;
      ++i )
      ++frequency[*i];

   // find the largest value in the map
   pair<int,int> mode_pair = *max_element( frequency.begin(),
      frequency.end(), second_less );

   // the corresponding key is the mode
   cout << "Mode by method 1: " << mode_pair.first;

   // Method 2: must sort grades first
   sort( grades.begin(), grades.end() );
   tips::print( grades, "\n\nSorted    grades" );

   // prepare for finding mode
   vector<int>::iterator start = grades.begin();
   int mode_range = 0;
   int mode_grade = 0;
   pair<vector<int>::iterator,vector<int>::iterator> range;

   // look for the largest range, which is the mode
   while( start != grades_end )
   {
      range = equal_range( start, grades_end, *start );
      if( range.second - range.first > mode_range )
      {
         mode_range = range.second - range.first;
         mode_grade = *start;
      }
      start = range.second;
   }
   cout  << "Mode by method 2: " << mode_grade
         << "\n\nMinimum: " << grades[0]
         << "  Maximum: " << grades[num_grades-1]
```

```
            << "  Median: " << grades[num_grades/2] << endl;
}
```

The output is

```
Original  grades: 9 2 3 3 7 5 7 7 4 10 5 6 7 4 7
Mode by method 1: 7

Sorted    grades: 2 3 3 4 4 5 5 6 7 7 7 7 7 9 10
Mode by method 2: 7

Minimum: 2  Maximum: 10  Median: 6
```

The program starts by creating a vector with some specific grades in it, using the technique of Tip 5. To start the first method of finding the mode, the code creates a map whose key and value are both integers. The map key will be the data value (in this program the grade), and the map value will be the frequency, that is, the number of times that the data value (grade) occurs. After creating the map, which is empty initially, the code goes through the entire vector with a simple for-loop that executes only one line. The line uses each vector element as an index into the map and increments the map value at that index. This creates a count of how often each grade is in the data set.

As Tip 35 explains, the map subscript operator has the curious property that if the key passed to it doesn't exist in the map, the operator creates a new element in the map with that key. The map value of that element is whatever is produced by the default constructor of the map value data type. For numeric data types, this is 0. Thus, if the map element for a grade doesn't exist, it is automatically created, its value is initialized to 0 and then incremented by 1. If the element does exist, its value is simply incremented. At the end of the loop, the map contains a count of how many times each grade occurs.

By definition, the mode is the value that occurs most often. To find it, use the STL algorithm max_element (as described in Tip 83) to look through the map and find the biggest map value. There's a small hitch, however—by default, the algorithm uses the less-than operator for the data type in the container. In this case, the data type is the STL pair and the less-than operator compares two pairs by using their first elements. These are the grades, not the frequencies of occurrence. To compare the second element of each pair, the code uses a simple function (second_less) that it passes as the third argument to max_element. This function compares the two arguments passed to it and returns true if the member second of the first argument is less than the member second of the second argument and false otherwise. `max_element` returns an iterator that points to the maximum element and the code dereferences this and stores the resulting pair. The first value in this pair is the grade that occurs most often, that is, the mode. The second line of the output shows the result.

The second method starts by sorting the grades with the STL algorithm `sort`. (The grades must be sorted in order to use the STL algorithm `equal_range`, which is described next.) The third line of the output shows the sorted grades. A grade of seven is the mode.

The part of the program that finds the mode is the `while` loop. It uses `equal_range`, which finds the range of elements that is equal to a given value (the third argument) and returns this range as a pair of iterators. The first member of the pair is the location of the first number in the vector equal to the specified number. The second pair member is one past the last location of that number. The loop calculates the range of each different number in the array. This range is equal to the number of times a number occurs, so by definition the largest of the ranges is the mode. Note that the vector must be sorted for `equal_range` to work properly.

The output shows the results of the computations. In addition, the last line of the output demonstrates that the minimum is the first element of the sorted vector, the maximum is the last element, and the median is the middle element. If you're finding the mode by using the second method, you get these other three free. If you don't need the mode, but would like these other data characteristics, see Tip 83 and Tip 87 for faster ways of computing these numbers.

Which method should you use? The advantages of the first method are that it's simpler and doesn't change the container with the original data. The benefits of the second method are that it only requires one container and you get the minimum, maximum and median of the data set as part of the computation. Use the one that's best for your application.

TIP 89   COMPUTE THE PERCENTILE

Applies to: Nth_element, partial_sort, sort
See also: Tip 5, Tip 16, Listing 13.5

Quick Solution

```
vector<int> v;
// ...

// find and display lowest 20th percentile unsorted
int percentile_20 = 0.2 * v.size();
nth_element( v.begin(), v.begin()+percentile_20-1, v.end() );
```

```
cout << "The lowest 20th percentile elements in unsorted order are: ";
copy( v.begin(), v.begin() + percentile_20,
   ostream_iterator<int>( cout, " " ) );

// find and display lowest 20th percentile sorted
partial_sort( v.begin(), v.begin()+percentile_20, v.end() );
cout << "\nThe lowest 20th percentile elements in sorted order are: ";
copy( v.begin(), v.begin()+percentile_20,
   ostream_iterator<int>( cout, " " ) );
```

Detailed Solution

Often in statistics or data analysis, you want to show a certain percentile of the data, such as the bottom 25th percentile or the top 5th percentile. Your first thought about how to do this might be to sort the numbers and then extract the appropriate set from the beginning or end of the sorted group. You can do this easily with C++, but it is inefficient. If you only want a top or bottom percentile, why bother sorting the entire set? Some STL algorithms can produce those numbers without sorting the whole thing. This can save a good bit of time. The program in Listing 11.14 shows you how.

LISTING 11.14 Finding a Percentile

```
// numeric_percentile.cpp

#include <algorithm>
#include <iostream>
#include <iterator>
#include <vector>

using namespace std;

int main( )
{
   const int grade_array[] = { 98, 7, 54, 69, 87, 88, 56, 92, 77,
      39, 22, 68, 80, 90, 93, 44, 75, 57, 98, 84, 82, 47, 34, 13, 78 };
   const int num_grades =
      sizeof( grade_array ) / sizeof( grade_array[0] );

   // make a vector of the grades to use for sorting
   const int percentile_20 = static_cast<int>( 0.2 * num_grades );
   vector<int> grades( grade_array, grade_array+num_grades );
```

```
// find and display grades in lowest 20th percentile
nth_element( grades.begin(), grades.begin()+percentile_20-1,
   grades.end() );
cout << "The lowest  20th percentile grades are: ";
copy( grades.begin(), grades.begin() + percentile_20,
   ostream_iterator<int>( cout, " " ) );

// find and display grades in highest 20th percentile
copy( grade_array, grade_array+num_grades, grades.begin() );
nth_element( grades.begin(), grades.begin()+percentile_20-1,
   grades.end(), greater<int>() );
cout << "\nThe highest 20th percentile grades are: ";
copy( grades.begin(), grades.begin() + percentile_20,
   ostream_iterator<int>( cout, " " ) );

// find and display sorted grades in lowest 20th percentile
copy( grade_array, grade_array+num_grades, grades.begin() );
partial_sort( grades.begin(), grades.begin()+percentile_20,
   grades.end() );
cout << "\n\nThe lowest  20th percentile sorted grades are: ";
copy( grades.begin(), grades.begin()+percentile_20,
   ostream_iterator<int>( cout, " " ) );

// find and display sorted grades in highest 20th percentile
copy( grade_array, grade_array+num_grades, grades.begin() );
partial_sort( grades.begin(), grades.begin()+percentile_20,
   grades.end(), greater<int>() );
cout << "\nThe highest 20th percentile sorted grades are: ";
copy( grades.begin(), grades.begin()+percentile_20,
   ostream_iterator<int>( cout, " " ) );

// sort and display all grades
copy( grade_array, grade_array+num_grades, grades.begin() );
sort( grades.begin(), grades.end() );
cout << "\n\nThe sorted grades are: ";
copy( grades.begin(), grades.begin()+9,
   ostream_iterator<int>( cout, " " ) );
cout << endl;
copy( grades.begin()+9, grades.end(),
   ostream_iterator<int>( cout, " " ) );
}
```

The output is

```
The lowest  20th percentile grades are: 13 7 22 34 39
The highest 20th percentile grades are: 98 93 98 92 90

The lowest  20th percentile sorted grades are: 7 13 22 34 39
The highest 20th percentile sorted grades are: 98 98 93 92 90

The sorted grades are: 7 13 22 34 39 44 47 54 56
57 68 69 75 77 78 80 82 84 87 88 90 92 93 98 98
```

The code shows a set of grades stored in a C array. It then creates a vector containing these numbers (see Tip 5) and calls nth_element to find the lowest 20th percentile. There are 25 elements, so the lowest five elements make up that percentile.

The first argument to nth_element is the container's beginning iterator and the last argument is its ending iterator. The middle argument is an iterator that serves as a dividing point. After the call to nth_element, all elements in the container before the middle iterator will be less than or equal to the middle element and all elements after the middle iterator will be greater than or equal to that element. In other words, each element in the first sequence is less than or equal to each element in the last sequence. Because the code is looking for the first five elements (the lowest 20th percentile) and numbering starts from zero, the middle argument is the beginning iterator plus the amount in the percentile minus one. The copy algorithm displays these five elements, using a technique explained in Tip 16. Note that the numbers are not sorted, but they are the five lowest, as the display of the complete sorted array at the end of the output shows.

The next section of the code illustrates finding the top 20th percentile. The code starts by copying the original data into the array (this is unnecessary but confirms that the starting input is the same as before) and then calling nth_element, this time with a fourth argument. By default, the algorithm partitions the numbers in ascending order. However, you can pass it a binary predicate (see "Predefined Function Objects" in Chapter 2) to control the partitioning. In this case, the fourth argument is the greater-than functor, which makes the highest numbers appear at the beginning of the container. Again, the numbers in the percentile are not sorted.

If you need the numbers in the percentile to be sorted, but you still don't want to sort the entire array, you can do that with partial_sort, which sorts the initial section of the numbers but not the second part. The first and third arguments are the beginning and ending iterators of the container. The middle argument is the ending iterator for a range that starts at the beginning iterator. As with all ranges, the ending iterator is actually one past the last element of interest. This is why the code does not subtract one from `percentile_20` as it does in the call to `nth_element`. Notice in the output that the numbers are indeed sorted.

The fourth section of code shows the call to `partial_sort` with the greater-than functor as the fourth argument. This forces the specified range to be sorted in descending order, as the output demonstrates.

Finally, the last few lines of code illustrate a full sort, using the appropriately named `sort` algorithm. If you need to find several percentiles, it may be better to just sort the whole set of numbers once and then extract the desired percentiles. The output shows the sorted array, which allows the previous answers to be confirmed.

Table 11.2 shows the complexities of the algorithms used in this example. The C++ Standard also provides additional information (such as worst-case behavior) for some of these algorithms.

TABLE 11.2 Complexities of Some STL Sorting and Partitioning Algorithms

Algorithm	Complexity
nth_element	On average, linear with number of elements
partial_sort	Approximately number of elements × log(number of sorted elements)
sort	On average, approximately number of elements × log(number of elements)

TIP 90 COMPUTE STATISTICS OF DATA

Applies to: For_each
See also: Tip 53, Tip 80, Tip 83, Tip 86, Tip 87, Tip 88, Tip 89

Quick Solution

See detailed solution.

Detailed Solution

In computing statistics of data, such as the mean and variance, each data value contributes to some fundamental quantities from which the statistics are computed. These quantities are the sum of the data values, the sum of the squares, and, for higher-order statistics, the sum of higher powers of the data. The process of going to each member of a set is an obvious application of the STL algorithm `for_each`. This general-purpose algorithm can go to every element of a container and perform some operation on that member. Listing 11.15 is a program that shows how to gather powers of the data values and then compute the mean and variance. You could easily enhance it to compute other statistics, such as the skewness or kurtosis.

LISTING 11.15   Computing Statistics

```cpp
// numeric_statistics.cpp

#include <algorithm>
#include <cstdlib>
#include <functional>
#include <iostream>
#include <list>

using namespace std;

class Statistics
{
   public:
   Statistics();
   void operator()( double value );
   double mean();
   double variance( );

   private:
   double x_, x_squared_;
   int count_;
};

inline
Statistics::Statistics()
: x_squared_(0), x_(0), count_(0)
{} // empty

inline
void Statistics::operator()( double value )
{
   ++count_;
   x_ += value;
   x_squared_ += value * value;
}

inline
double Statistics::mean( )
```

```cpp
{
   return x_ / count_;
}

inline double Statistics::variance( )
{
   return x_squared_ /count_ - mean() * mean();
}

int main( )
{
   list<int> data( 100000 );

   // create random numbers
   generate( data.begin(), data.end(), rand );

   // make them go from 0 to 200
   transform( data.begin(), data.end(), data.begin(),
      bind2nd( modulus<int>(), 201 ) );

   // make them go from -100 to 100
   transform( data.begin(), data.end(), data.begin(),
      bind2nd( minus<int>(), 100 ) );

   // gather the statistics
   Statistics stats = for_each( data.begin(), data.end(),
      Statistics() );

   // print the statistics
   cout << "Mean = " << stats.mean()
      << "\nVariance = " << stats.variance() << endl;
}
```

```
Mean = -0.15499
Variance = 3366.54
```

The output is

The idea behind the technique in this tip is to create a class that stores the sum of powers of the data. `for_each` will call the class on every member of a container and then return a copy of the class with the gathered information stored in it. Then the code will call class member functions to get the mean and variance.

The beginning of the code shows the class, called Statistics, that has private variables that store the sum of the values, the sum of the squares of the values, and the number of values. Statistics also has member functions that return the mean and the variance, which is equal to the mean of the squares minus the square of the mean. The most important member function is the call operator(), which for_each will use. for_each passes a number to the call operator, which adds the number and its square into the respective sums stored in the class, and also increments the counter in the class that records the number of data values processed. (See "Functors" in Chapter 2 for more information on the call operator.)

The program starts by making a large list and using the STL algorithm generate to fill it with random numbers (see Tip 80). Then the program uses transform and the modulus functor to make the numbers vary from 0 to 200 inclusive and calls transform again to subtract 100 from the numbers, which leaves a set of uniformly distributed random numbers that varies between −100 and +100 inclusively.

Next, the program calls for_each, passing the input data range and a temporary copy of the Statistics class Statistics. This contains the function operator that receives each element in the input range from for_each. Interestingly enough, for_each returns a copy of the function argument passed to it. Of all the STL algorithms, only for_each does this. The returned copy of the function argument may be different than the original. In this example, the class instance returned does differ from the original because it has stored the sums of powers of the data internally.

Once a copy of Statistics has been returned, the program uses it to display the mean and variance. The output shows the results, which are very close to the theoretical values of 0 and 3366.67.

There are other ways of calculating statistics using the C++ Standard Library. Tip 53 provides a method of finding the standard deviation, which is the square of the variance. Tip 86 shows you how to compute the mean. Tip 87 demonstrates finding the median. Tip 88 gives you to ways of calculating the mode, and Tip 89 delves into percentiles.

TIP 91   INPUT AND OUTPUT IN BINARY FORMAT

Applies to: Bitset
See also: Tip 44, Tip 92, Tip 93

Quick Solution

```
cout << "Enter a binary number: ";
bitset< numeric_limits<unsigned long>::digits > bits;
```

```
cin >> bits;
unsigned long decimal_equivalent = bits.to_ulong();

// write a decimal integer as a binary number
int num = 100;
cout  << "\nDecimal number: " << num << "\tBinary equivalent: "
   << bitset<8>(num);
```

Detailed Solution

By default, C++ reads and displays integers in base 10, that is, decimal. Unfortunately, the language doesn't provide direct support for reading and writing binary numbers. However, you can read and write them indirectly in binary format. The program in Listing 11.16 shows how.

LISTING 11.16   Making I/O in Binary Format

```
// numeric_binary.cpp

#include <bitset>
#include <iostream>
#include <limits>

using namespace std;

int main( )
{
   // Read a binary number into a bitset
   cout << "Enter a binary number: ";
   bitset< numeric_limits<unsigned long>::digits > bits;
   cin >> bits;
   unsigned long decimal_equivalent = bits.to_ulong();
   cout  << "Binary number: " << bits
         << "\nDecimal equivalent: " << decimal_equivalent;

   // write a decimal integer as a binary number
   int num = 100;
   cout  << "\n\nDecimal number: " << num
         << "\tBinary equivalent: " << bitset<8>(num) << endl;
}
```

The input and output are

```
Enter a binary number: 1101
Binary number: 00000000000000000000000000001101
Decimal equivalent: 13

Decimal number: 100   Binary equivalent: 01100100
```

You can accept a binary (base two) number from an input stream by using a bit-set. This class template, which is part of the Standard Library, allows you to easily manipulate groups of bits (see Tip 44 and "Miscellaneous Containers" in Chapter 2). In general, a bitset can have any number of bits. It can convert the bit pattern into an `unsigned long`, but the pattern must not have more bits than that data type does.

The program starts by creating a bitset. The code specifies the number of digits that the bitset will have by calling the `digits` member of the `numeric_limits` template class. In this example, the number of digits is that for an unsigned long integer. The program then inserts the bitset into the input stream to receive the user's binary number. A bitset reads until it has accepted as many bits as its creation size, until the user finishes entering digits (typically by pressing the Enter key), or until it finds a character that is not a zero or one. If the user enters fewer bits than the bitset can hold, the bitset fills its remaining bits with zeros.

The next line of code shows that to convert the binary number read in to a numeric variable, you call the bitset's `to_ulong` member function. This converts the bit pattern into an `unsigned long` that can then be used for other things such as arithmetic. (If there are too many bits to fit into an unsigned long integer, `to_ulong` throws an `overflow_error` exception.) For an input of "1101," the second line of the output shows the result of putting the bitset in the output stream. The pattern is correct but the bitset prints all its bits, resulting in a potentially cumbersome display. The text that follows explains how to mitigate this problem. The third line of the output shows the decimal value of the converted binary input.

If you have a variable in your program, you can display it in binary format as long as the variable is convertible to an unsigned integer. The last line of the program demonstrates that you can do this by making a temporary bitset variable from your number and inserting the bitset in the output stream. If you know that the binary value of the number will never occupy more than a certain number of bits, create the bitset with that number of bits. To illustrate this, the code makes a bitset with only eight bits. The bitset prints all its bits, so a smaller bitset produces a shorter, and most likely cleaner, display. Compare the two binary numbers displayed in the output following Listing 11.16 to see this.

If you're interested in base two I/O, you may also be interested in octal or hexadecimal I/O. If so, please see Tip 92 and Tip 93.

TIP 92   INPUT AND OUTPUT IN OCTAL FORMAT

Applies to: Oct, dec, resetiosflags, showbase, noshowbase
See also: Tip 91, Tip 93

Quick Solution

```
cout << "Enter an octal number: ";
int num;
cin >> oct >> num;
cout << "Octal: " << oct << num << "\tOctal with base: " << showbase
    << num;
```

Detailed Solution

By default, integers are displayed in base 10, that is, decimal. For some types of work, such as writing interfaces to hardware, it may be handy to have input and output in octal (base 8). Listing 11.17 demonstrates the ways to do this.

LISTING 11.17   Making I/O in Octal Format

```
// numeric_octal.cpp

#include <iomanip>
#include <iostream>

using namespace std;

int main( )
{
    // Read an octal number
    cout << "Enter an octal number: ";
    int num;
    cin >> oct >> num;

    // Display number in decimal and octal
    cout  << "Decimal: " << num << "\tOctal: " << oct << num
          << "\tOctal with base: " << showbase << num << endl;

    // Clear all numerical base flags for input stream
    cout << "\nEnter 77 and 077: ";
```

```
    int n77, n077;
    cin >> resetiosflags( ios::basefield ) >> n77 >> n077;

    cout << dec << "\nDecimal equivalents: 77 = " << n77
        << "\t077 = " << n077;
}
```

The input and output are

```
Enter an octal number: 61
Decimal: 49      Octal: 61        Octal with base: 061


Enter 77 and 077: 77 077


Decimal equivalents: 77 = 77     077 = 63
```

The program starts by prompting for an octal number. The code inserts the manipulator oct into the input stream before reading the number. The manipulator causes all subsequent integer inputs to be interpreted as octal numbers and, therefore, expects those numbers to have numerals only from 0 to 7 inclusive. The change to octal format stays in effect until you explicitly reset it.

Next, the program displays the number it read in. By default, the output is in decimal. The code writes the output in decimal, inserts the oct manipulator into the output stream, and writes the same number in octal. If the user entered 61 as shown, the second line of output shows the decimal equivalent (49) and the octal output, which is 61—the same as the octal input. The end of the output line demonstrates that C++ can put a prefix of "0" on octal outputs. This allows you to distinguish octal numbers from those in decimal or hexadecimal. To use this convenient feature, insert the showbase manipulator into the output stream. To stop displaying the base, insert the manipulator noshowbase into the output stream.

If you would like to enter numbers in different bases (octal, decimal or hexadecimal), there's a better way of accomplishing this than by constantly changing the base manipulators. What you can do is to set the input stream to have no default base by using the resetiosflags manipulator to clear all bases, as shown in the code. Then, if an input integer starts with 0, C++ assumes the number is octal; if it starts with 0x or 0X, it is taken to be hexadecimal; and otherwise, it is interpreted as a decimal integer. The last two lines of output demonstrate this behavior with a decimal and octal input.

To get back to the default input interpretation, that is, all integers are assumed to be decimal, insert the dec manipulator into the input stream. To work with numbers in binary format, see Tip 91. If hexadecimal I/O is important to you, see Tip 93.

TIP 93   INPUT AND OUTPUT IN HEXADECIMAL FORMAT

Applies to: Hex, showbase, noshowbase, uppercase, nouppercase
See also: Tip 91, Tip 92

Quick Solution

```
cout << "Enter a hexadecimal number: ";
int num;
cin >> hex >> num;

cout << "\nHexadecimal default: " << hex << num
    << "\nHexadecimal without base: " << noshowbase << num
    << "\nHexadecimal with uppercase base: "
      << showbase << uppercase << num
    << "\nHexadecimal with lowercase base: "
      << nouppercase << num;
```

Detailed Solution

By default, integers are read and written in base 10, that is, decimal. Sometimes it is convenient to work in hexadecimal (base 16). This might happen if you're writing software that interfaces with hardware. The code in Listing 11.18 shows how to get hexadecimal input and output.

LISTING 11.18   Making I/O in Hexadecimal Format

```
// numeric_hex.cpp

#include <iomanip>
#include <iostream>

using namespace std;

int main( )
{
    // Read a hexadecimal number
    cout << "Enter a hexadecimal number: ";
    int num;
    cin >> hex >> num;
```

```
// Display number in decimal and hexadecimal
cout  << "\nDecimal: " << num
      << "\nHexadecimal default: " << hex << num
      << "\nHexadecimal without base: " << noshowbase << num
      << "\nHexadecimal with uppercase base: "
         << showbase << uppercase << num
      << "\nHexadecimal with lowercase base: "
         << nouppercase << num;

// Clear all numerical base flags for input stream
cout << "\n\nEnter 77 and 0x77: ";
int n77, n077;
cin >> resetiosflags( ios::basefield ) >> n77 >> n077;

cout << dec << "\nDecimal equivalents: 77 = " << n77
   << "\t0x77 = " << n077;
}
```

The input and output are

```
Enter a hexadecimal number: 3a

Decimal: 58
Hexadecimal default: 3a
Hexadecimal without base: 3a
Hexadecimal with uppercase base: 0X3A
Hexadecimal with lowercase base: 0x3a

Enter 77 and 0x77: 77 0X77

Decimal equivalents: 77 = 77      0x77 = 119
```

The program starts by prompting for a hexadecimal number. It inserts the manipulator hex into the input stream before reading the number. The manipulator causes all subsequent integer inputs to be interpreted as hexadecimal numbers. C++ therefore expects those numbers to include only the 10 numerals, the letters "A" through "F" inclusive (in either upper or lower case), and possibly the prefixes "0x" or "0X." This change to hexadecimal format stays in effect until explicitly reset.

Next, the program displays the number it read in. By default, the output is in decimal. The code writes the output in decimal, inserts the hex manipulator into the output stream, and writes the same number in hexadecimal. If the user enters 3a as shown in the first line of the output, the program responds with the decimal equivalent (58) and the hexadecimal output 3a—the same as the hexadecimal input. These are in the second and third lines of the output.

By default, C++ does not show the base of the printed number. If the number contains only digits from 0 to 7 inclusive, it's hard to tell if it is in octal, decimal, or hexadecimal. You can alleviate this problem by having the output appear with the prefix "0x," in upper or lower case. To make the prefix be displayed, insert the show-base manipulator into the output stream. If you also insert the manipulator upper-case, it forces the hexadecimal digits that are letters (A–F) and the base (if any) to display in capital letters; otherwise, they appear in lower case. To produce a lower case prefix and letters, insert nouppercase. To stop displaying the base, insert noshowbase into the output stream.

If you would like to enter numbers in different bases (octal, decimal or hexadecimal), you can do so more easily than by constantly changing the base manipulators. First, set the input stream to have no default base by using the resetiosflags manipulator to clear all bases, as shown in the code. After that, if an input integer starts with 0, C++ assumes the number is octal; if it starts with 0x or 0X, it is taken to be hexadecimal, and otherwise it is interpreted as a decimal integer. The last two lines of output demonstrate this behavior with a decimal and hexadecimal input.

To get back to the default input interpretation, that is, all integers are assumed to be decimal, insert the dec manipulator into the input stream. To work with numbers in binary format, see Tip 91. If you work with octal numbers, see Tip 92.

TIP 94   DISPLAY LEADING ZEROS OF INTEGERS

TIP

Applies to: Setw, setfill

Quick Solution

```
int part, component;
// ...

// display part with 6 digits and component with 4. Use leading zeros
cout << setfill( '0' );
cout << "Part: " << setw( 6 ) << part << "   Component: "
     << setw( 4 ) << component;
```

Detailed Solution

In most circumstances when integers in base 10 are displayed, the leftmost digit shown is never a 0. In some situations, it is desirable to print leading 0s, which go on the left side of integers. In forms, for example, the month and day numbers often have to be written with two digits. If the number has only one digit, a leading 0 must be added. Moreover, sometimes only the last two digits of the year are shown, and this might require a leading 0, for example, 2003 written as 03.

Another use of showing integers with leading zeros is in displaying identification numbers. Usually an exact number of digits of the ID must be shown, and this might necessitate leading zeros. Unfortunately, you can't directly specify that C++ display leading zeros. However, it's easy to do, as the code in Listing 11.19 demonstrates, by using such zeros in dates and identification numbers.

LISTING 11.19   Displaying Leading Zeros

```cpp
// numeric_leading_zero.cpp

#include <iomanip>
#include <iostream>

using namespace std;

int main( )
{
   const int num_members = 6;
   const int id[num_members] = { 67809, 5492, 10000086, 8954,
      345, 2278 };
   const int month[num_members] = { 9, 1, 1, 12, 10, 4 };
   const int day[num_members] = { 2, 1, 13, 30, 31, 4 };
   const int year[num_members] = { 2000, 2003, 2004, 1998,
      2001, 2003 };

   // display data with leading zeros
   cout << setfill( '0' );
   for( int i = 0; i < num_members; ++i )
      cout << "Member " << setw( 8 ) << id[i]
         << " joined the club on " << setw( 2 ) << month[i] << "/"
         << setw( 2 ) << day[i] << "/" << setw( 2 )
         << year[i] % 100 << endl;
}
```

The output is

```
Member 00067809 joined the club on 09/02/00
Member 00005492 joined the club on 01/01/03
Member 10000086 joined the club on 01/13/04
Member 00008954 joined the club on 12/30/98
Member 00000345 joined the club on 10/31/01
Member 00002278 joined the club on 04/04/03
```

The program starts by making some arrays with information about the members of a club. The arrays store the members' identification numbers and the dates on which people joined. The remainder of the code illustrates the creation of output with leading zeros. The technique is to force the numbers that are written to occupy a certain number of characters in the output. The digits are right-justified, and if there aren't enough to occupy the required characters, C++ pads the output with a fill character. By default, this is a space, but by changing it to the numeral 0, you get a number with leading zeros.

The first thing the code does is to call setfill to make the fill character be "0." Once a program specifies the fill character with setfill, it remains that way until explicitly changed. Then the program uses the manipulator setw (set width) and passes it the number of characters that the output must take up. However, setting the width with setw only affects the next formatted output, so the code must call it before every number that it wants to be padded. The output shows member identifications and dates displayed with zeros in front of them. The dates are in the American format, that is, month, day, and year.

TIP 95   **DISPLAY PRECISION OF FLOATING-POINT NUMBERS**

Applies to: Setprecision, fixed, scientific, showpoint, noshowpoint

Quick Solution

```
double x = 0.39;
cout
    << "0.39, default, 1 decimal place:  " << setprecision( 1 ) << x
    << "\n0.39, fixed, 2 decimal places:  " << fixed
    << setprecision( 2 ) << x
    << "\n0.39, scientific, 3 decimal places: "  << scientific
    << setprecision( 3 ) << x;
```

Detailed Solution

In displays of scientific numbers, especially experimental data, it's important to show the precision of measurements, that is, to show a certain number of places after the decimal point. This may include trailing zeros if the precision warrants it. C++ allows you to show the precision of floating-point numbers, both in fixed-point and scientific notation. In the former, the decimal place is always between the one's and the one-tenth's digits. In the latter, the number is written as a number whose absolute value is at least 1 and less than 10 and is multiplied by 10 to an appropriate power. The program in Listing 11.20 illustrates how to set the displayed precision. (The precision of the data used in computation is independent of and unaffected by the displayed precision.)

LISTING 11.20   Displaying Precision of Numbers

```cpp
// numeric_trailing_zero.cpp

#include <iomanip>
#include <iostream>

using namespace std;

int main( )
{
   const double x = .39;
   const double y = 27;

   cout
      << ".39, fixed, 1 decimal place:  "
      << fixed << setprecision( 1 ) << x << endl

      << ".39, fixed, 2 decimal places: "
      << setprecision( 2 ) << x << endl

      << ".39, fixed, 3 decimal places: "
      << setprecision( 3 ) << x << endl << endl

      << ".39, scientific, 1 decimal place:   "
      << scientific << setprecision( 1 ) << x << endl

      << ".39, scientific, 2 decimal places: "
      << setprecision( 2 ) << x << endl

      << ".39, scientific, 3 decimal places: "
      << setprecision( 3 ) << x << endl << endl
```

```
                     // return to default floating-point output format
                     << resetiosflags( ios::fixed | ios::scientific )
                     << setprecision( 6 )

                     << ".39 and 27., default: "  << x << "    " << y << endl

                     << ".39 and 27., default, 1 decimal place:  "
                     << setprecision( 1 ) << x << "    " << y << endl

                     << ".39 and 27., default, 2 decimal places: "
                     << setprecision( 2 ) << x << "    " << y << endl

                     << ".39 and 27., default, 3 decimal places: "
                     << setprecision( 3 ) << x << "    " << y << endl << endl

                     << ".39 and 27., default, decimal point: "
                     << showpoint << x << "    " << y << endl

                     << ".39 and 27., default, decimal point, 1 decimal place:  "
                     << setprecision( 1 ) << x << "    " << y << endl

                     << ".39 and 27., default, decimal point, 2 decimal places: "
                     << setprecision( 2 ) << x << "    " << y << endl

                     << ".39 and 27., default, decimal point, 3 decimal places: "
                     << setprecision( 3 ) << x << "    " << y << endl;
}
```

The output is

```
.39, fixed, 1 decimal place:  0.4
.39, fixed, 2 decimal places: 0.39
.39, fixed, 3 decimal places: 0.390

.39, scientific, 1 decimal place:  3.9e-01
.39, scientific, 2 decimal places: 3.90e-01
.39, scientific, 3 decimal places: 3.900e-01

.39 and 27., default: 0.39    27
.39 and 27., default, 1 decimal place:  0.4    3e+01
.39 and 27., default, 2 decimal places: 0.39    27
.39 and 27., default, 3 decimal places: 0.39    27          →
```

```
.39 and 27., default, decimal point: 0.390    27.0
.39 and 27., default, decimal point, 1 decimal place:  0.4    3.e+01
.39 and 27., default, decimal point, 2 decimal places: 0.39   27.
.39 and 27., default, decimal point, 3 decimal places: 0.390  27.0
```

By default, C++ sometimes prints in fixed notation and sometimes in scientific notation. It's hard to set the precision in this mixed format, so the program uses easier formats first. The key is to always have the output of floating-point numbers appear in fixed-point notation or in scientific notation.

To make fixed-point output, insert the manipulator fixed into the stream. Then, to control the precision, insert setprecision with the desired number of decimal places into the stream also, as the code shows. This makes the output display the desired precision, as the first three lines of output indicate. They also show that numbers are rounded, not truncated, in the display of precision.

The next three pairs of code line produce similar output but in scientific notation. Again, note that the output shows exactly the desired number of decimal places.

The manipulators fixed, scientific, and setprecision affect all floating-point output after their insertion into the stream. They remain in effect until changed. The default precision is 6. To set the default display of floating-point numbers, use the resetiosflags manipulator as shown.

Left to its own devices, C++ prints floating-point numbers in either fixed or scientific notation, depending on the value of the number. The first set of four output lines labeled default show the result with the default number of decimal places and then one, two, and three decimal places. The result is confusing because the number of places after the decimal point is not always the same as the number specified in setprecision. If the number has an integer value, C++ omits the decimal point. To force it to always display a decimal point, use the manipulator showpoint. This remains in effect until you turn it off with the manipulator noshowpoint.

TIP 96   DISPLAY A THOUSANDS' SEPARATOR

Applies to: Locale, numpunct facet

Quick Solution

See detailed solution.

Detailed Solution

By default, C++ does not display digits' separators other than the decimal point. However, it's easier to read large numbers if their digits are broken into groups. In the United States and other countries, the digits are grouped into threes and a comma, called the thousands' separator, is inserted between each triplet. Thus, for example, one million is written as 1,000,000.

Other countries have different conventions. For example, in Germany, the thousands' separator is the period, not the comma. In Nepal, the groups are two and three digits long. The sample program in Listing 11.21 illustrates the case of dividing the digits into triplets and separating them by a comma.

LISTING 11.21   Displaying the Thousands' Separator

```cpp
// numeric_separator.cpp

#include <iomanip>
#include <iostream>
#include <locale>

using namespace std;

class Separator_facet: public numpunct<char>
{
   public:
   explicit Separator_facet( size_t refs = 0)
      : numpunct<char>( refs )
      {}

   protected:
   virtual string do_grouping() const
      { return "\3"; }
};

int main()
{
   const int million = 1000000;
   const double number = 1234.56789;
   cout << "Default format:        " << million
      << fixed << setprecision( 5 ) << "        " << number;

   // make a new locale and attach it to the standard output stream
   locale separator_locale( cout.getloc(), new Separator_facet );
   cout.imbue( separator_locale );
```

```
    cout << "\n\nThousands' separator: " << million << "      "
        << number << endl;
}
```

The output is

```
Default format:           1000000      1234.56789

Thousands' separator: 1,000,000      1,234.56789
```

Unfortunately, producing a thousands' separator is more complicated than what you would expect. To make this kind of formatting, you need to work with a *locale*, which is the way C++ encapsulates national formatting conventions. These conventions include the formatting for numbers, time, money, and text characters. The various aspects of the formatting are handled by classes called *facets*. For example, the class num_get handles numeric input, num_put produces numeric output, and numpunct contains the symbols used in numeric formatting. To use any of these, you must include the standard header <locale>.

Every stream contains a locale that does its formatting. However, once a locale is created, neither it nor its facets can be changed. The only way to modify a locale is to construct a new one from it, pass the alterations to the constructor, and replace it with the newly made locale. Specifically, in this tip, you have to replace the stream's locale with a new locale that has a numeric-punctuation facet with a thousands' separator in it.

The new facet will actually be a class that is derived from numpunct, the original facet. The top of the code shows this class definition. The important part is the overriding of the protected, virtual function do_grouping. The base class's function just returns an empty string, which makes the digits appear in their default format with no separators. The derived class instead returns a string whose one character has the numeric value 3. This produces output that is grouped by threes. The default thousands' separator is the comma, so that doesn't need to be changed.

The program starts by displaying an integer and floating-point number in the default format. The first line of the output shows that neither have thousands' separators. Next, the program creates a new locale based on the current output stream's locale. The first argument to the constructor is that locale, which you can obtain from the standard output stream by calling its member function getloc.

The second argument is a pointer to an instance of the derived class. If the facet is made with a constructor whose argument is explicitly or implicitly 0, and a pointer to it is passed to the locale, the locale takes ownership and becomes responsible for deleting the facet. This is why the code doesn't delete the facet.

The next line of code replaces the output stream's locale with the new one by passing it to the stream's `imbue` member function. Now all integer and floating-point values written to the standard output stream will display thousands' separators. The second line of the output shows what this looks like.

TIP 97 — ACCESS DATA IN A FILE

Applies to: Standard container , ostream_iterator, istream_iterator, copy
See also: Tip 5, Tip 7, Tip 16, Tip 80

Quick Solution

```
ifstream in( "numbers.txt" );

// read file with one number per row
vector<int> input_data( (istream_iterator<int>( in )),
    istream_iterator<int>() );
```

Detailed Solution

When working with data sets, it's often convenient to be able to quickly read a set of numbers from a file or write a set to a file. This tip shows you how to do that. One limitation in the technique, though, is that the data set must only have one data type. This isn't much of a problem because all elements in a container must also be the same type. Listing 11.22 demonstrates the technique.

LISTING 11.22 Accessing Data in a File

```cpp
// numeric_file_data.cpp

#include <algorithm>
#include <cstdlib>
#include <fstream>
#include <functional>
#include <iostream>
#include <iterator>
#include <vector>

#include "tips.hpp"

using namespace std;
```

```
int main( )
{
    // generate ten random numbers
    vector<int> output_data( 10 );
    generate( output_data.begin(), output_data.end(), rand );

    // turn them into numbers that go from 0 to 9
    transform( output_data.begin(), output_data.end(),
        output_data.begin(), bind2nd( modulus<int>(), 10 ) );

    // open a file
    ofstream out( "data.txt" );
    if( !out )
    {
        cout << "Couldn't open output file\n";
        return 0;
    }

    // write data to the file and close it
    copy( output_data.begin(), output_data.end(),
        ostream_iterator<int>( out, "\n" ) );
    out.close();

    // open the file to read from it
    ifstream in( "data.txt" );
    if( !in )
    {
        cout << "Couldn't open input file\n";
        return 0;
    }

    // read the data and close the file
    vector<int> input_data( (istream_iterator<int>( in )),
        istream_iterator<int>() );
    in.close();

    // display the input and output data
    tips::print( output_data, "Output data" );
    tips::print( input_data, "Input  data" );
}
```

The output is

```
Output data: 0 2 0 6 7 5 5 8 6 4
Input  data: 0 2 0 6 7 5 5 8 6 4
```

and the text file the program creates (data.txt) is

```
0
2
0
6
7
5
5
8
6
4
```

The program starts by using the STL algorithm generate to create some random numbers in a vector and make them lie in the range of zero to nine inclusive. (See Tip 80 for more details on making sequences of random numbers.) Next, the code creates an output stream connected to a data file and verifies that the creation succeeded. Then, in one call to an algorithm, the code writes the entire data set in the list to the file by using copy. The typical use of this function is to copy one container to another. However, the destination is actually an output iterator, and it doesn't necessarily have to point to a container.

The first two arguments are the usual suspects, input iterators to the beginning and end of the container. For the last argument, the code constructs an output iterator from a file output stream. "Stream Iterators" in Chapter 2 explains this technique. In fact, you can use almost identical code to write the standard output stream, as Tip 16 shows. And if you wanted to, you could omit the closing of the file that the program shows to make the code more analogous to that in Tip 16. However, it is good practice to close a file stream when you're done with it.

To read from a file, you first make an input file stream that is connected to that file. Then, to read the data into a container, you use the form of the container's constructor that accepts an iterator range. (Tip 5 explains this constructor.) The first argument shows how to make an input iterator that points to the beginning of an input stream. The second argument, which is the default constructor for istream_iterator, creates an end-of-stream iterator, equivalent to end() in a container. It marks the end of the file, as "Stream Iterators" in Chapter 2 explains. The code passes these two iterators to the vector's constructor. Tip 7 illustrates that you can use the same technique to fill a container from the standard input stream. It also explains why the parentheses around the first argument are necessary.

The output shows that the code read the same numbers from the file that it stored there.

12 Final Tips

T his chapter has some final suggestions on ways to get more out of the C++
Standard Library, and especially out of the Standard Template Library. These
tips are general in nature and aren't about coding per se. Actually, they don't
have any programs with them. However, in the long run, they can be just as valuable as coding techniques. This chapter will show you the following:

- Where to get a free, portable version of the STL
- Where to get free, high quality code that uses the STL
- How to let great C++ Standard Library tips you've discovered help others

---

TIP 98   **GET A FREE, PORTABLE STL**

Applies to: Standard Template Library on many platforms and compilers

Quick Solution

A free, highly portable, STL is available from *www.stlport.org*.

Detailed Solution

Sometimes a small project starts out well and just keeps getting bigger and better.
A good example is Boris Fomitchev's STLport, a portable version of the STL. In
1997, after the first release of SGI's STL, he made a quick port of the STL for internal use at his workplace. He also started distributing it on his own Web page. People found the ported code very useful and many volunteered to help him write
versions for other platforms. Now (September 2004), the code runs on about 20
different platforms and usually on a number of versions of each compiler. Here are
some interesting points about this library:

- It's available for free, even on commercial projects. There are no royalties to pay.
- It comes with extensions to the official version of the STL, such as hash tables, singly linked lists and ropes (strings designed to handle large amounts of text).
- It's the only current version of the STL that has built-in debugging help. It provides checks on the validity, ownership, and dereferenceability of iterators and on the preconditions of the STL algorithms. This is very useful because STL code can be quite hard to debug.
- The developers make bug fixes available immediately.
- You can get information from and have discussions with other users online.
- The development team has professional consultants available, though there is a charge for that.

If you're going to be moving your code among platforms, you may want to consider using STLport. The library and more information are available for free at *www.stlport.org*.

TIP 99   GET FREE, HIGH-QUALITY STL CODE

Applies to: Applications that use the STL

Quick Solution

Get free, powerful, high-quality, STL code from *www.boost.org*.

Detailed Solution

Want some great STL libraries? For free? They're yours for the taking. The Boost libraries, at *www.boost.org*, are a tremendous resource. The organization's Web site provides C++ source libraries. The code is free (under terms of a license), it's portable, and it's peer-reviewed. This last item means that other programmers scrutinize the code and approve it before it is made available to the public. This really increases the libraries' quality. Thousands of programmers use the libraries and there are newsgroups and mailing lists for developers, users, and specific projects.

Besides providing software libraries, Boost serves as a test bed for code that may become part of the C++ Standard Library. As of September 2004, 10 Boost libraries were included in a report to the C++ Standards Committee recommending their addition to the C++ Standard. By using these libraries, you can gain experience with code that may become an official part of the language.

Here's a partial list of what was available on September 2004:

String and Text Processing: Conversion of arbitrary data types to and from text, including better numerical conversions than currently available, recursive-descent parser generator framework, tokenizer, regular expression matching (wildcards)

Containers: Arrays of constant size, runtime-sized bitsets, graph components and algorithms, multidimensional arrays

Iterators: Iterator construction framework

Function objects and higher-order programming: Generalized binders, function object wrappers for deferred calls or callbacks, enhanced function object adaptors, lambda abstractions (unnamed functions)

Math and numerics: Greatest common divisor and least common multiple, quaternions and octonions, special functions such as the hyperbolic arctangent (atanh) and the sine cardinal (sinc), random number generation, rational numbers, linear algebra

Miscellaneous: Cyclic redundancy codes; dates and times; portable paths, directory iteration and other file system operations; timers

One of the most exciting prospects is the lambda abstraction library, which lets you define small, unnamed functions directly in the call of an STL algorithm. To illustrate, suppose you want to construct a container filled with ones but don't know the simple way to do this that Tip 4 shows. First, you write a little function that accepts a reference and sets that passed value to one. Then you use for_each with the container and function, for example,

```
void initialize( int& n )
{    n = 1;    }
// ...

list<int> bid( 100 );
for_each( bid.begin(), bid.end(), initialize );
```

This works, but you've had to create a whole function to do something very simple. This is extra work and extra maintenance for a function that you might never use again. With lambda abstractions you can simply write

```
list<int> bid( 100 );
for_each( bid.begin(), bid.end(), _1 = 1 );
```

The expression _1 = 1 creates a lambda functor that assigns a value of one to the variable _1. for_each calls the functor for every element, replacing the _1 with the element. It then executes the expression (the "body" of the functor), which sets the element to 1. The result is that all elements of the list are set to 1. In effect, the lambda expression behaves the same as a custom-written function but entails less work. Lambda functors make the STL algorithms more convenient to use and much more powerful. Let's hope they make it into the standard soon.

TIP 100   SHARE THE WEALTH—CONTRIBUTE YOUR FAVORITE TIP

Applies to: All C++ programmers

Quick Solution

Send in your tips and show other programmers the cool things you've discovered.

Detailed Solution

The preceding 99 tips in this book can make your C++ Standard Library code better, faster, and cleaner. I figured some of them out while writing lots and lots of software. However, many of them came from reading books and magazines, having technical discussions with colleagues, and studying other people's code. Programmers have a long and strong tradition of sharing their work so that the entire community can be more productive and make higher quality software. Here's another chance to participate.

Is there an STL trick that you've found immensely helpful? Do you have a Standard Library code snippet of unrivaled elegance? Is there a technique that's saved you lots of time? Let others know about it and make life easier for everyone. Drop me an email at Greg.Reese@ieee.org, and I can add your little masterpiece to our collection of tips.

13 Image Processing

This chapter is an example of using this book's tips in realistic code. The software here performs some basic digital image processing. A *digital image* is a picture that is stored in a computer and whose colors or shades of gray have been converted to numbers. *Digital image processing*, or simply *image processing*, is computationally manipulating digital images to better extract information from them. In some cases of image processing, you want the computer to explicitly take measurements in the image, such as the size of the object, the distance between two points in the image, or the brightness of various points of light in the image. These may, for example, be pictures of stars. In other cases, you just want to make the image look better so that a person can see things in it more easily. You might want to blur the image to get rid of speckling, make the contrast larger to let objects in the image be more distinguishable, or bring out edges so that items in the image can be seen more easily.

Figure 13.1 shows the basic sequence of events in image processing. Light falls on a scene and is reflected to a digital camera that focuses it onto a two-dimensional grid of light receptors. Each receptor measures the amount of light that falls on it and converts that value into a number. Low numbers represent small amounts of light (dark areas), and high numbers represent large amounts of light (bright areas). The array of numbers is moved to a computer on which the image can be processed. The computer then displays the image for a person to examine, stores it, or sends it along to other software that can process it further and automatically extract information.

There are many variations to this sequence of events:

- What enters the camera from the scene does not have to be visible light—it can be sound (medical ultrasound images), invisible light (infrared or X-ray images), or other forms of electromagnetic radiation (radar or radio wave images).
- Light can come from the scene itself, such as stars or fireworks.
- You can create images on the computer so that no camera is needed. Artificial images are common in research settings and for testing software.

- Instead of just capturing the strength of the light, the camera can measure the strength at different wavelengths (colors). Consumer digital cameras measure the strength in three colors—red, green, and blue. Satellites often take *hyperspectral images* in which they measure the strength in many wavelength bands, including ones that are not visible.
- The images can be three-dimensional, such as CT scans or MRI images. Currently, however, these 3D pictures are made up of two-dimensional images that are stacked to simulate three dimensions.

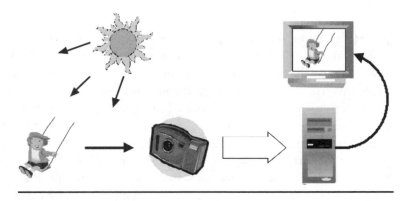

FIGURE 13.1 Sequence of events in image processing.

When the measurement from a light receptor is stored as a number in an image, it is known as a *pixel* or *pel*, meaning a picture element. When you look at a digital image, you can't see the individual pixels because they are displayed closely together, as Figure 13.2(a) demonstrates. However, if you enlarge the image enough, you will be able to see the pixels. They look like squares of solid shades of gray or color (if the image is a color image). Figure 13.2(b) is an enlargement of the part of the image in the white square of Figure 13.2(a).

This chapter will only cover simple forms of image creation and image enhancement and will only deal with *gray-level images*, that is, digital images that have no colors, only shades of gray. These are analogous to black-and-white photographs. The chapter also assumes that each pixel takes up one byte whose values run from 0 to 255 inclusive. In C++, an unsigned char usually has that size and range.

The coding style for the software in this chapter is more realistic than that for the tips. Functions and classes are well-documented and have descriptions of their inputs, outputs, and the requirements that the user must uphold to call the software. Also, the code does not have any using statements and, in particular, does not contain the using namespace std; statement that the tips have. You'll see that, in

this application, explicitly writing the standard namespace scope operator `std::`
actually causes very little clutter.

 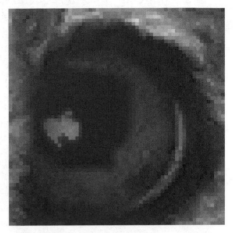

FIGURE 13.2(a) A digital image.   **FIGURE 13.2(b)** Enlarged view of the
white square in (a).

IMAGE CLASS

Before creating images or processing them, it's necessary to have a class that represents the image. The first question about this class is how it will store a two-dimensional (2D) image. C++ stores native two-dimensional arrays, for example,
`unsigned char image[128][64]`, row by row in a one-dimensional array. The image
class can't use a native C++ 2D array because its size is fixed at compile time and the
image class should be able to resize at runtime. (Images also tend to be much larger
than what should be declared locally, that is, on the stack.) Although there are various ways of storing a 2D array, the image class will use a method similar to how
C++ stores a 2D array.

The image class will store the pixels in a one-dimensional vector. The first (top)
row of pixels comes first in the vector, followed by the second row, the third row,
and so on. Figure 13.3 shows this arrangement for an image with R rows and C
columns.

The fact that the class actually stores the image in a one-dimensional vector is
an implementation detail that is invisible to the user, who always specifies a particular pixel by giving its row and column. The class must convert this to an index in
the vector. The formula for this is

$$i = r \times C + c \qquad\qquad (13.1)$$

where *r* is the row number of the pixel, *c* is its column number, *C* is the number of columns in the image and *i* is the resulting index in the vector. The number of rows doesn't enter into the equation. The image class has a private member function called `convert` that performs the conversion in Equation 13.1.

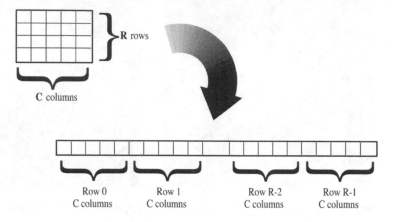

FIGURE 13.3 Two-dimensional image in a one-dimensional vector.

Another common procedure with images is to read all the pixels or write to all of them. For example, to find the minimum and maximum pixels in the image, you have to examine all the pixels. If you want to make the entire image brighter by the same amount, you can add a constant to all the pixels. Because operating on all pixels is common and useful, the image class has the member functions `begin` and `end`, which provide an STL range that covers the entire image. The class specifies the range with iterators so you can use it in the STL algorithms.

A third common procedure is to iterate over a section of columns in one row or all columns in one row. To make this easier to do, the image class provides the member functions `row_begin` and `row_end` to return the requested stretch of columns as an STL iterator range. The class doesn't provide analogous functions for iterating over the rows of a column because that is rarely done in image processing.

Listing 13.1 shows the code for the image class, called `Image`. Although it is the longest piece of code in this book, `Image` isn't very complicated. For example, all but one of the member functions are simple enough to be inlined.

LISTING 13.1 The Image Class

```
1    // ip_image.hpp
2
3    template<class T>
```

```
4    class Image
5    {
6    public:
7
8    // iterators and references
9    typedef typename std::vector<T>::iterator iterator;
10   typedef typename std::vector<T>::const_iterator const_iterator;
11   typedef typename std::vector<T>::reference reference;
12   typedef typename std::vector<T>::const_reference const_reference;
13
14   // constructors
15   Image();
16   // make empty image
17
18   Image( int rows, int columns, T initial_value = T() );
19   // make image of specified size and filled with given value
20   // REQUIRE: rows > 0, columns > 0,
21   //          initial_value in range of T (see NOTE of operator=)
22   // NOTE:    to make an empty image use the default constructor
23
24    // assignment operator and destructor
25    // use compiler's default versions
26
27   // operators
28   reference operator()( int row, int column );
29   const_reference operator()( int row, int column ) const;
30   // read and write pixel at specified location, e.g., im(3,17)
31   // REQUIRE: 0 <= row < rows(), 0 <= column < columns()
32   // NOTE: in all coordinates in this class, row zero is the top
33   //       row, row rows()-1 is the bottom row, column zero is the
34   //       left column, column columns()-1 is the right column
35
36   void operator=( T value );
37   // fill image with specified value
38   // NOTE: passed value may have data type other than T as long as
39   //       it is convertible to T. If so, passed value should lie
40   //       in range of T to avoid problems with conversion, e.g.,
41   //       Image<unsigned char> im;
42   //       im = 100; <- constant interpreted as int but must lie
43   //                    in range of unsigned char to avoid conversion
44   //                    error
45
46   // iterator functions
47   iterator begin();
```

```
48     const_iterator begin() const;
49     iterator end();
50     const_iterator end() const;
51
52     // read or write all pixels
53     iterator row_begin( int row );
54     const_iterator row_begin( int row ) const;
55     iterator row_end( int row );
56     const_iterator row_end( int row ) const;
57     // returns beginning and end of a single row for reading and
58     // writing all pixels in a row. Refer to this as a
59     // "row iterator"
60     // REQUIRE: 0 <= row < rows(), when used as range, row in
61     //          row_begin and row_end must be the same
62     // PROMISE: iterators mark half open ranges so can be used in
63     //          STL algorithms. End iterators should not be
64     //          dereferenced
65
66     iterator row_begin( int row, int column );
67     const_iterator row_begin( int row, int column ) const;
68     iterator row_end( int row, int column );
69     const_iterator row_end( int row, int column ) const;
70     // row iterators for reading and writing between specified
71     // columns of a single row
72     // REQUIRE: 0 <= row < rows(), 0 <= column < columns()
73     //          when used as range, row in row_begin
74     //          and row_end must be the same and column in row_begin
75     //          must be <= column in row_end
76     // PROMISE: iterators mark half open ranges so can be used in
77     //          STL algorithms. End iterators should not be
78     //          dereferenced
79     // NOTE:    the columns specified are inclusive, i.e., the
80     //          returned range includes both the column in row_begin
81     //          AND the column in row_end. row_end actually returns
82     //          one column past the column specified so that the
83     //          range can be used in STL algorithms. For example,
84     //
85     //          copy( image.row_begin( 3, 5 ),
86     //              image.row_end( 3, 8 ), v.begin() );
87     //
88     //          copies the pixels in columns 5, 6, 7, AND 8 to
89     //          v.begin()
90
91     void clear();
```

```
 92    // make the image be empty, i.e., have zero rows and columns
 93
 94    int columns() const;
 95    // number of columns in image
 96    // PROMISE: columns() >= 0
 97
 98    bool empty() const;
 99    // returns true if the image has zero rows and columns,
100    // otherwise false
101
102    void resize( int rows, int columns );
103    // change the size of the image
104    // REQUIRE: rows > 0, columns > 0
105    // PROMISE: if rows and columns are the same as the current
106    //          values, does nothing. If not, gets rid of the old
107    //          image and makes a new one of the specified size
108    //          filled with zeros.
109
110    int rows() const;
111    // number of rows in image
112    // PROMISE: rows() >= 0
113
114    private:
115
116    typename std::vector<T>::size_type convert( int row, int column )
       const;
117    // convert from a 2D pixel location to 1D index in pixels_
118    // REQUIRE: 0 <= row < rows(), 0 <= column < columns
119
120    int columns_;
121    int rows_;
122    std::vector<T> pixels_;
123 };
124
125 // constructors
126
127 template<class T>
128 inline
129 Image<T>::Image()
130    : columns_( 0 ), rows_( 0 ), pixels_()
131 {} // empty
132
133 template<class T>
134 inline
```

```
135  Image<T>::Image( int rows, int columns, T initial_value )
136    : columns_( columns ), rows_( rows ),
137      pixels_( rows * columns, initial_value )
138  {} // empty
139
140  // image fill and pixel read/write
141  template<class T>
142  inline void Image<T>::operator=( T value )
143  { pixels_.assign( pixels_.size(), value ); }
144
145
146  template<class T>
147  inline typename Image<T>::reference Image<T>::operator()( int row,
148    int column )
149  { return pixels_[convert( row, column )]; }
150
151  template<class T>
152  inline typename Image<T>::const_reference
153  Image<T>::operator()( int row, int column ) const
154  { return pixels_[convert( row, column )]; }
155
156  // iterator functions
157  template<class T>
158  inline typename Image<T>::iterator Image<T>::begin()
159  { return pixels_.begin(); }
160
161  template<class T>
162  inline typename Image<T>::const_iterator Image<T>::begin() const
163  { return pixels_.begin(); }
164
165  template<class T>
166  inline typename Image<T>::iterator Image<T>::end()
167  { return pixels_.end(); }
168
169  template<class T>
170  inline typename Image<T>::const_iterator Image<T>::end() const
171  { return pixels_.end(); }
172
173  template<class T>
174  inline typename Image<T>::iterator Image<T>::row_begin( int row )
175  { return pixels_.begin() + row * columns(); }
176
177  template<class T>
178  inline typename Image<T>::const_iterator
```

```
179 Image<T>::row_begin( int row ) const
180 { return pixels_.begin() + row * columns(); }
181
182
183 template<class T>
184 inline typename Image<T>::iterator Image<T>::row_end( int row )
185 { return row_begin( row + 1); }
186
187 template<class T>
188 inline typename Image<T>::const_iterator
189 Image<T>::row_end( int row ) const
190 { return row_begin( row + 1 ); }
191
192 template<class T>
193 inline typename Image<T>::iterator
194 Image<T>::row_begin( int row, int column )
195 { return row_begin( row ) + column; }
196
197 template<class T>
198 inline typename Image<T>::const_iterator
199 Image<T>::row_begin( int row, int column ) const
200 { return row_begin( row ) + column; }
201
202 template<class T>
203 inline typename Image<T>::iterator
204 Image<T>::row_end( int row, int column )
205 { return row_begin( row, column ) + 1; }
206
207 template<class T>
208 inline typename Image<T>::const_iterator
209 Image<T>::row_end( int row, int column ) const
210 { return row_begin( row, column ) + 1; }
211
212
213 // other functions in alphabetical order
214
215 template<class T>
216 inline void Image<T>::clear()
217 {
218     pixels_.clear();
219     rows_ = 0;
220     columns_ = 0;
221 }
222
```

```
223 template<class T>
224 inline int Image<T>::columns() const
225 { return columns_; }
226
227 template<class T>
228 inline typename std::vector<T>::size_type
229 Image<T>::convert( int row, int column ) const
230 { return row * columns() + column; }
231
232 template<class T>
233 inline bool Image<T>::empty() const
234 { return pixels_.empty(); }
235
236 template<class T>
237 void Image<T>::resize( int the_rows, int the_columns )
238 {
239     if( the_rows == rows() && the_columns == columns() )
240         return;
241
242     // clear first because resize won't change values of undeleted
243     // pixels
244     pixels_.clear();
245     pixels_.resize( the_rows * the_columns ); // fills with T()
246     rows_ = the_rows;
247     columns_ = the_columns;
248 }
249
250 template<class T>
251 inline int Image<T>::rows() const
252 { return rows_; }
253
```

Although this chapter will only deal with gray-level images, it's easy to make the image class be a class template. That will let you work with images of other data types, such as unsigned short, float, or a class for color pixels.

The template for Image starts by declaring some type definitions (typedef) for iterators, references, and their constant versions in lines 9–12. Then Image declares two constructors. The first, in line 15, is the default constructor and makes an empty image, that is, one with no rows and no columns. The second constructor (line 18) lets the user make an image of the specified dimensions and, optionally, filled with a given constant. (The expression T() in line 18 is the default constructor of the image's data type. For numerical data types, this produces a value of 0.)

The compiler will create a default assignment operator and destructor, and these will work fine for the template classes.

Lines 28–29 define `operator()` to take two values, the row and column of a pixel. The call operator returns a reference or constant reference to that pixel. This operator allows convenient access to individual pixels. For example,

```
Image<unsigned char> image( 256, 256 );
// ...

if( image( 10, 20 ) > image( 10, 40 ) )
    image( 10, 20 ) = 100;
```

shows individual pixels being read from and written to. Note that you can't access pixels using double brackets as you do for 2D C++ arrays; for example, `image[10][20]` is not allowed.

Line 36 defines an assignment operator that accepts a value and sets all pixels equal to that value, for example, `image = 50` makes all pixels in `image` be 50. Be aware that when using an `unsigned char` image and assigning it an integer constant, you may get a warning from the compiler about losing precision or significant digits. This is because C++ assumes the constant is an `int` and you're trying to assign it to an `unsigned char`. As long as the value of the constant is within the range of an `unsigned char` (typically 0–255 inclusive), you'll be all right.

Next comes a slew of member functions that return iterators or row iterators. They can all be used in STL algorithms that require forward iterators. (It turns out that they are actually random iterators, but because none of the code in this application requires that an iterator be that versatile , being a forward iterator is sufficient.) When specifying the end column for the `row_end` member functions in lines 68–69, the user should make the column number inclusive, that is, that column is to be included in a range. (Image processing users typically think in closed ranges, not the half-open ranges of the STL.) The `row_end` member functions will actually return an iterator to one pixel past that column, which enables you to use `row_begin` and `row_end` with STL algorithms.

Finally, the class template declares a few additional member functions. These let you get the number of rows and columns in the image, determine whether the image is empty, and resize the image. The last function, declared on line 102, deletes the pixels in the current image and replaces them by an image of the specified dimensions filled with pixels that are 0. If, however, the number of rows and number of columns are the same as those in the image, the function does nothing.

The rest of `Image` is declared private. It contains variables for the pixels and the number of rows and columns. A member function (`convert`) converts a two-dimensional pixel location to an index into the pixel vector using Equation 13.1.

The member function definitions start on line 127. Most are straightforward. On line 143, the operator that sets each pixel to the specified value uses the vector's `assign` member function. The first argument is the number of elements in the vector that are to be assigned, and the second argument is the assigned value. By using the total number of elements in the vector as the first argument, the code changes all elements. Tip 47, Tip 50, and Tip 79 demonstrate this technique more fully.

Line 151 is the start of the iterator function definitions. `Image`'s beginning and end iterators are simply those of its vector data member. Line 175 illustrates that the beginning iterator for a row is an iterator pointing to column 0 of that row. The pixel vector's iterators are random iterators; Tip 20 explains that you can add integers to them. Thus, the returned iterator is the sum of the vector's beginning iterator and the number of elements to the first column of the desired row. The end iterator is just the start of the next row, as line 185 shows. Note that the element for the end iterator of the last row doesn't exist. This is why `Image` specifies that its end iterators can't be dereferenced.

The `clear` member function starts on line 215. It calls the pixel vector's `clear` function and takes the necessary step of setting the dimensions of the image to 0. Another member function, `resize`, starts on line 236. The routine first checks the desired dimensions; if they're the same as the current ones, the routine returns without doing anything. If the dimensions aren't the same, the code clears the vector, resizes it (which automatically fills the vector with zeros), and sets the new dimensions. The function clears the vector because if it is resized to a smaller size, the vector won't set all the elements to 0. (An alternative would be to skip the clearing and set all elements to 0 after resizing.)

The remainder of this chapter demonstrates various image processing techniques and how they use the tips in this book. Most of the code is made up of global functions, though there are some member functions, too. Many of the routines are template functions, but sometimes it's more practical to make them only run on `unsigned char` images.

IMAGE CREATION

Not all images are captured by cameras—some are created on the computer. These artificial images are useful for a variety of reasons:

- To test image processing software. If the images are simple, you can compute the output of a process by hand and compare it to the results of the software.
- To make images for vision research. Because it can be easier than making a physical object to view, the pixel values in the artificial image can be set more precisely, or the object may not exist (random patterns of bright and dark).

■ To make images of objects that are infeasible for most people to photograph, for example, planes in flight.

Block

The first image to create is a block, that is, a rectangle of one pixel value. Blocks are useful for providing uniform backgrounds for other objects, for testing other image enhancement code such as edge enhancement, and even for research in human vision, including illusions. For example, which of the blocks in the middle of Figure 13.4(a) and Figure 13.4(b) is lighter?

The code in Listing 13.2 produces a uniform, rectangular block anywhere in an image.

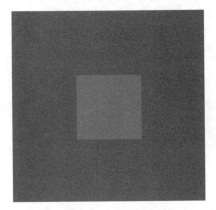

FIGURE 13.4(a)   One block.

FIGURE 13.4(b)   Another block.

LISTING 13.2   Make a Block

```
// ip_block.hpp

template<class T>
void block( Image<T>& image, int top, int left, int bottom, int right,
   T value )
// draw a rectangle of one value in the image
// INPUT:   top - top row of block         left - left column of block
//          bottom - bottom row of block  right - right column of block
// REQUIRE: both rows and columns must be in the image and
//          top <= bottom,   left <= right
{
   for( int i = top; i <= bottom; ++i )
      std::fill( image.row_begin( i, left ), image.row_end( i, right ),
```

```
                value );
   }

   inline
   void block( Image<unsigned char>& image, int top, int left, int bottom,
     int right, int value )
   // REQUIRE: same as above but value must be in range of unsigned char
   {  block( image, top, left, bottom, right,
       static_cast<unsigned char>( value ) );
   }
```

The function operates by looping over all the rows in the block and, for each row, filling in all the columns with the passed pixel value. The STL algorithm `fill` does this by setting each element in its input range to the specified value. The code in `block` demonstrates the generality of the STL algorithms by operating on custom iterators.

The code to make the images in Figure 13.4 is

```
Image<unsigned char> image( 600, 600 );
int width_third = image.rows() / 3;
int top = width_third;
int bottom = image.rows() - width_third;
int left = width_third;
int right = image.columns() - width_third;

image = 100;
block( image, top, left, bottom, right, 127 ); // left figure
image = 154;
block( image, top, left, bottom, right, 127 ); // right figure
```

This code snippet also tells you which block is lighter.

In the preceding snippet, `image` is an instance of the `Image<unsigned char>` class. In the remainder of this chapter `image`, `image1`, `image2`, and `out` will also be instances of that class.

Vertical Bars

Another simple pattern is a set of vertical bars. Bars are useful for testing monitor displays, for debugging image processing code such as edge enhancement, and sometimes for research in human vision, including illusions. Figure 13.5 shows some vertical bars, and Listing 13.3 is the code that makes them.

FIGURE 13.5 Vertical bars.

LISTING 13.3 Make Bars

```
// ip_bars.cpp

#include <algorithm>
#include <limits>

#include "ip_all.hpp"

void bars( Image<unsigned char>& image, unsigned char start,
    unsigned char increment, int width )
// draw an image of vertical bars. Each bar has the same width and
// the pixel value of the bars increases by a fixed amount.
// INPUT:   image - image in which to draw
//          start - pixel value in left bar
//          increment - increase in pixel value between a bar and the
//          one on its left
//          width - width in pixels of each bar
// REQUIRE: 0 < width < image.rows()
// NOTE:    1) The right bar may be narrower than the others if the
//          number of columns in the image is not a multiple of width.
//          2) Whenever the pixel value exceeds the maximum value of
//          an unsigned char it is set back to start.
//          3) If the image is empty the function does nothing.

{
    if( image.empty() )
        return;
```

```
int value = static_cast<int>( start ) - increment;

// make the first row
for( int i = 0; i < image.columns(); ++i )
{
   if( i % width == 0 )
   {
      value += increment;
      if( value > std::numeric_limits<unsigned char>::max() )
         value = start;
   }
   image( 0, i ) = static_cast<unsigned char>( value );
}

// copy the top row into all the others
for( int i = 1; i < image.rows(); ++i )
   std::copy( image.row_begin( 0 ), image.row_end( 0 ),
      image.row_begin( i ) );
}
```

The first thing the function does is to check if the image is empty and, if so, the function returns. Next, the function creates the first row by looping through each pixel of that row, computing the value of the bar there, and setting the pixel to that value. Because the remaining rows are the same as the first, the function avoids more of the bar calculations by using the STL algorithm copy to copy the first row to the remaining rows. Note the use of custom iterators in the STL algorithm.

The code to make the image in Figure 13.5 is

```
Image<unsigned char> im( 600, 600 );
const int start = 0;
const int increment = 24;
const int width = 64;
bars( image, start, increment, width );
```

If you look carefully at the bars, especially in the right side of the image, you may see a very narrow dark stripe on the left side of a bar's edge and a very narrow bright stripe on the right side of that edge. However, as you can tell from the code in Listing 13.3, those stripes aren't in the image. These illusory stripes are known as Mach bands.

IMAGE MAGNIFICATION

One advantage of digital images is that you can easily write code to zoom in on or magnify an image. Similarly, you can have the computer digitally shrink the image. Current consumer digital cameras can even do this in real time.

Shrinking

Sometimes it's useful to shrink an image. The obvious application is to make images small enough to fit in a document, for example, an image catalog, or to match the size of other images. Another use that occurs frequently is in GUIs where, for example, the operating system or programs may show thumbnails (small versions of images) of files in a directory.

Figure 13.6 illustrates one technique for shrinking an image. The method is simple and fast, but it does restrict you to constricting the dimensions by integer amounts, for example, $1/2$ the length and width, $1/3$ the length and width, and so on. In the technique, each pixel in the output is the average of a block of pixels in the input. Each block is a square n pixels on a side, where n is the factor by which to shrink the image. For $n = 3$, Pixel A' in the output is the average of the pixels marked A in the input, Pixel B' is the average of the pixels marked B', and so forth. Figure 13.6 also shows that if the number of rows or columns is not an exact multiple of the factor by which you shrink the image, there may be some leftover columns on the right or rows on the bottom. The shrinking technique ignores them. Figure 13.7(a) shows an original image. Figure 13.7(b) is the result of applying the shrinking technique.

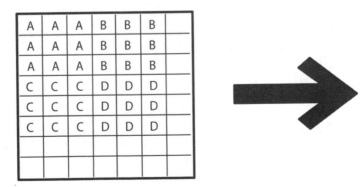

FIGURE 13.6 Shrinking an image.

FIGURE 13.7(a) An image.

FIGURE 13.7(b) A shrunken version.

Listing 13.4 shows the code for shrinking an image.

LISTING 13.4 Shrinking an Image

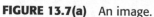

```cpp
// ip_shrink.cpp

#include <algorithm>
#include <numeric>

#include "ip_all.hpp"

void shrink( const Image<unsigned char>& in, int amount,
    Image<unsigned char>& out )
// shrink image by the specified amount. Each dimension is shrunk by
// the same factor (given by amount), e.g., amount=2 makes length and
// width half the size of the original
// INPUT:   in - original image
//          amount - factor by which to shrink
// OUTPUT:  out - shrunk image
// REQUIRE: amount >= 1
// NOTE:    1) if input image is empty or amount is greater than the
//             number of rows or columns, the function clears the output
//             image and does nothing.
//          2) if amount is 1, the function copies the input to the
//             output
//          3) if the number of rows or number of columns is not an
//             exact multiple of amount, the function ignores the excess
//             columns on the right or rows on the bottom of the input
```

```
{
    if( in.empty() || in.rows() / amount == 0
        || in.columns() / amount == 0 )
    {
        out.clear();
        return;
    }
    else if( amount == 1 )
    {
        out = in;
        return;
    }

    out.resize( in.rows() / amount, in.columns() / amount );

    // number of input pixels to be averaged
    int divisor = amount * amount;

    int in_row = 0;

    // for each output row...
    for( int i = 0; i < out.rows(); ++i, in_row += amount )
    {
        int in_col = 0;

        // for each output column...
        for( int j = 0; j < out.columns(); ++j, in_col += amount )
        {
            int sum = 0;

            // for each input row...
            for( int k = in_row; k < in_row + amount; ++k )

                // sum over input columns in current input row
                sum += std::accumulate( in.row_begin( k, in_col ),
                        in.row_end( k, in_col + amount - 1 ), 0 );

            out(i,j) = static_cast<unsigned char>( sum / divisor );
        }
    }
}
```

The code in Listing 13.4 starts by checking if the image is empty or if the number of rows or columns is less than the amount being shrunk. If so, the routine clears the output image and returns. The second alternative is to assign the input image to the output if the amount of shrinkage is one. The true work starts if the amount of shrinkage is greater than one.

First, the code computes the number of output rows and columns and resizes the output image accordingly. Then the code follows with a nested loop that traverses every pixel of the output image. For each such pixel, the loop computes the average of the corresponding input pixels by calling the STL algorithm `accumulate` for each row of the input block and dividing the sum of these calls by the number of pixels in the block. Tip 86 explains `accumulate` in detail. Tip 48, Tip 49, Tip 53, and Tip 59 provide additional examples of its use.

The code to make the image in Figure 13.7(b) is

```
const int shrinkage = 2;
shrink( image, shrinkage, out );
```

Expanding

It can be useful to expand or enlarge an image. Actually, often you want to zoom in on just a section of the image. The obvious application is to see more detail in the image, but you might also want to enlarge the image for aesthetic reasons.

The expansion method the code uses is primitive but fast—it simply duplicates pixels. Figure 13.8 illustrates the technique. The method replicates by the specified amount and in both directions each pixel in the input image. In other words, to enlarge an image section by a factor of n for each input pixel, the method places an $n \times n$ block of pixels of the same value in the corresponding spot in the output image. For example, suppose the user wants to expand the small section of the image on the left in Figure 13.8 by a factor of three. The right side of the figure shows that Pixel A in the input becomes a 3×3 block of pixels, each equal to A, in the output. The other three input pixels are replicated in the same way. Note that the output image consists only of pixels in the selected region of the input. The code ignores input pixels that aren't in that area. Figure 13.9(a) is an original image with a section marked, and Figure 13.9(b) shows that area enlarged by a factor of 3.

Although the technique is fast, it does have some disadvantages. One is that the image section can only be enlarged by integer amounts. A more serious drawback is that the magnified image can easily appear "blocky," that is, composed of squares with no shading in them. Figure 13.10(a) and Figure 13.10(b), made by the code in Listing 13.5, illustrate the blocky appearance at high magnification. Other methods (called interpolation techniques) are more complicated and slower than replication but are much less blocky.

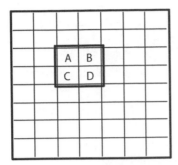

FIGURE 13.8 Enlarging a section of an image.

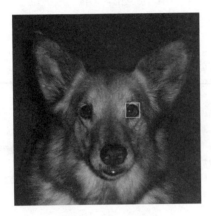

FIGURE 13.9(a) An image.

FIGURE 13.9(b) The section in (a) magnified by three.

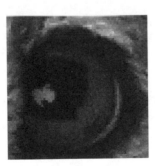

FIGURE 13.10(a) The section in Figure 13.9(a) magnified by seven.

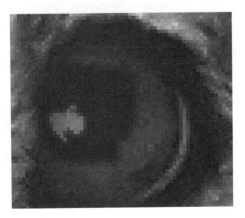

Figure 13.10(b) Magnified by 11.

LISTING 13.5 Expanding an Image

```cpp
// ip_expand.cpp

#include <algorithm>

#include "ip_all.hpp"

void expand( const Image<unsigned char>& in, int top, int left,
    int bottom, int right, int zoom, Image<unsigned char>& out )
// expand a block in an image by the specified amount. Each dimension
// is expanded by the same factor (given by zoom),
// e.g., zoom=2 makes length and width double the original size
// INPUT:    in - original image
//           zoom - factor by which to expand
//           top - top row of block          left - left column of block
//           bottom - bottom row of block  right - right column of block
// OUTPUT:   out - expanded block
// REQUIRE: zoom >= 1
//           both rows and columns must be in the image and
//           top <= bottom,   left <= right
// NOTE:     1) if input image is empty the function clears the output
//           image and does nothing more
//           2) if zoom is 1, the function copies the input block
//           to the output image

{
   if( in.empty() )
   {
      out.clear();
      return;
   }

   out.resize( (bottom - top + 1) * zoom, (right - left + 1) * zoom );

   // for every input row...
   for( int i = top, out_row = 0; i <= bottom; ++i, out_row += zoom )
   {
      // and every pixel of this input row...
      for( int j = left, out_col = 0; j <= right;
         ++j, out_col += zoom )

         // replicate the pixel in the output image
         std::fill_n( out.row_begin( out_row, out_col ), zoom,
```

```
        in(i,j) );

    // copy the above row to complete replication of the input row
    for( int k = 1; k < zoom; ++k )
        std::copy( out.row_begin( out_row ), out.row_end( out_row ),
            out.row_begin( out_row + k ) );
  }
}
```

The code in Listing 13.5 starts by checking whether the image is empty. If so, the routine clears the output image and exits. Otherwise, the routine makes the dimensions of the output image be that of the input section multiplied by the magnification factor. The heart of the routine is a nested loop that traverses every pixel of the input image section. For each such pixel, the loop calls the STL algorithm fill_n to replicate that pixel in the output row a number of times equal to the magnification factor (zoom). (The algorithm shows the use of a custom iterator and the unusual occurrence in an STL algorithm of one iterator and a length to specify an input range.) Once the routine fills in that output row, it uses the STL algorithm copy to copy that row into the following rows until the current input row has been replicated in the output zoom times. Many of the tips in the book, including Tip 16 and Tip 89, use copy.

The code to make the image in Figure 13.9(b) is

```
const int width = 65;
const int left = 490;
const int top = 390;
const int right = left + width - 1;
const int bottom = top + width - 1;

int expansion = 3;
expand( image, top, left, bottom, right, expansion, out );
```

The code for the images in Figure 13.10 is the same except for a different value of expansion.

IMAGE ARITHMETIC

Another series of techniques in image enhancement is to combine images pixel by pixel. Assuming the images have the same dimensions, the first pixel in one image is combined with the first pixel in the other image to yield the first pixel in the output image. Next, the second pixels are combined to give the second output pixel, and so on. The operation for combining two pixels is general, but often turns out to be arithmetic. The text that follows describes image subtraction. Adding images is typically used as part of computing their average. Multiplication is not very common, but you can use it to superimpose texture on an object. Division can sometimes compensate for different amounts of lighting on a scene. Astronomers apply it to some types of images to show details of stars obscured by interstellar dust and to make young stars more visible.

Another set of techniques for combining pixels is logical operators, such as AND, OR, EXCLUSIVE OR, and so on. These operations are more commonly applied to binary images (those containing only two shades of gray—black and white) than to gray-level images.

By using the STL algorithm `transform` and passing it different operations, you can combine images with any form of arithmetic. As Listing 13.6 shows, the code is very simple and short, but it demonstrates the power of the C++ Standard Library.

LISTING 13.6   Combining Images

```
// ip_combine.hpp

template<class Operation>
inline
void combine( const Image<unsigned char>& in1,
   const Image<unsigned char>& in2,
   Image<unsigned char>& out, Operation operation )
// combine two images pixel by pixel
// INPUT:   in1, in2 - two input images. Can be the same
//          operation - a function argument that specifies how a pixel
//          from one input image is to be combined with the
//          corresponding pixel from the other. operation must be able
//          to be used in std::transform. operation accepts two
//          unsigned char inputs (the pair of pixels) and returns an
//          unsigned char for the output pixel
// OUTPUT:  out - the output image. Can be the same as an input image
// REQUIRE: the dimensions of the two images must be the same
{
   // resize only if output dimensions not same as input dimensions
   if( out.rows() != in1.rows() || out.columns() != in1.columns() )
      out.resize( in1.rows(), in1.columns() );
   std::transform( in1.begin(), in1.end(), in2.begin(), out.begin(),
      operation );
}

inline
```

```
unsigned char clip( int value )
// if value is higher than the max unsigned char, return that max
// if value is lower than the min unsigned char, return that min
// otherwise return value. All returns are unsigned char
{
   unsigned char result;
   if( value > std::numeric_limits<unsigned char>::max() )
      result = std::numeric_limits<unsigned char>::max();
   else if( value < std::numeric_limits<unsigned char>::min() )
      result = std::numeric_limits<unsigned char>::min();
   else
      result = static_cast<unsigned char>( value );
   return result;
}


inline
unsigned char minus_safe( unsigned char a, unsigned char b )
// if a-b is less than zero, return zero, otherwise return a-b
// NOTE: this function is particularly useful as an operation in the
//       function called combine

{ return a >= b ? a - b : 0; }


inline
unsigned char plus_safe( unsigned char a, unsigned char b )
{ return static_cast<int>( a ) + b
   > std::numeric_limits<unsigned char>::max()
   ? std::numeric_limits<unsigned char>::max() : a + b;
}
// if a+b is higher than the max unsigned char, return that max
// otherwise return a+b
// NOTE: this function is particularly useful as an operation in the
//       function called combine


inline
void subtract( const Image<unsigned char>& in1,
   const Image<unsigned char>& in2, Image<unsigned char>& out )
// subtract two images pixel by pixel
// INPUT:   in1, in2 - two input images
// OUTPUT:  out - the output image, in1 - in2
// REQUIRE: the dimensions of the two images must be the same
// SEE:     combine(), minus_safe()
// NOTE:    differences are clipped to the minimum of an unsigned char
{ combine( in1, in2, out, minus_safe ); }
```

The template function `combine` does the work. It has two input images and one output image as parameters and an operation that specifies how each pair of pixels should be combined. If the dimensions of the output image are not the same as those of an input image, the function resizes the output image to the input image dimensions. This avoids reallocation of memory and, more importantly, lets the user pass the same image for input and output, thus saving memory. `combine` then uses `transform`, the ranges of both input images, and the passed operation to combine the images. Tip 76 and "Predefined Function Objects" in Chapter 2 explain `transform` in detail. In essence, one call to an STL algorithm lets you add two entire digital images, subtract them, and so forth. This is truly powerful.

A major problem with performing arithmetic on pixels represented by `unsigned char`s is that the range of that data type (typically 0–255 inclusive) is too small to contain the result of the arithmetic. For example, the sum of two `unsigned char` pixels can easily exceed 255; the difference of two `unsigned char` pixels can easily be negative; multiplication can produce numbers far out of bounds, and division can yield fractions. When you write code to do the arithmetic, for example, add or subtract two `unsigned char`s, if the result exceeds the range of the data type, there is no error. The program simply interprets the resulting bit pattern as an `unsigned char`, but its value is not correct and can't be used in computations.

One way to handle the addition and subtraction of `unsigned char` pixels is to *clip* the result. This means that if the result is greater than the maximum of an `unsigned char`, the clipped result is that maximum value. Similarly, if the result is less than the minimum of an `unsigned char`, the clipped result is that minimum. Otherwise, the clipped result is the same as the result because it is in the range of an `unsigned char`. The software must store the `unsigned char`s in a data type with a larger range before doing the actual addition or subtraction. The code assumes this data type can be a `short int` or an `int`. This is usually true, though, strictly speaking, it doesn't have to be.

The function `clip` in Listing 13.6 clips the value of an `int` to the range of an `unsigned char` in the manner previously discussed. The function obtains the minimum and maximum values of an `unsigned char` by using the technique of Tip 85. If you know the operation that is being performed on two pixels, a hand-coded safe version is faster than `clip`. For example, the function `minus_safe` subtracts two `unsigned char`s. This difference can never exceed the maximum of an `unsigned char`, so the code doesn't need to check for that condition. Similarly, `plus_safe` avoids checking for a negative sum.

The last function in Listing 13.6 demonstrates what the user actually calls to combine a pair of images. This function, `subtract`, simply calls combine with `minus_safe` as an argument.

Subtraction

You can use subtraction to remove backgrounds and to aid in making images appear sharper. However, the main use of image subtraction is to bring out differences between images. These differences can arise for a variety of reasons:

- Objects in the scene are not aligned exactly, for example, a label on a can that is stuck on at an angle compared to another label.
- Objects in one scene may be missing in another, for example, a missing chip in a circuit board caused by a manufacturing defect.
- Objects in the two scenes may be slightly different. For example, X-ray images from special cameras can indicate the composition of materials by vertical lines. Faint, additional lines are present in a material with trace compounds.
- Objects in a scene may have moved between images.

The last case is particularly interesting because if you measure the amount the object moved and you know the time between images, you can compute the object's velocity. Figure 13.11(a) is an image of a scene. The scene in Figure 13.11(b) has a slight change, and the difference may be hard to notice. By subtracting one image from the other, the change stands out clearly, as Figure 13.12 shows.

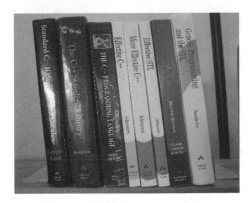

FIGURE 13.11(a)   Image.

FIGURE 13.11(b)   Changed image.

FIGURE 13.12 Difference of images in Figure 13.11.

The code to create the image in Figure 13.12 is

```
subtract( image2, image1, out );
contrast_stretch( out );
```

The function constrast_stretch is explained later in this chapter. It expands the contrast in the image and can make objects stand out more. Figure 13.12 shows that the brightest region, which is where the biggest change between the images is, occurs where there is a lamppost in one image but not in the other. Everything else is the same in the two images.

IMAGE ENHANCEMENT

Image enhancement is the process of improving an image so that you can get more information from it. You can enhance an image in many ways:

- Blur the image to get rid of speckling
- Remove patterns imposed on the image from electronic interference
- Remove geometric distortion due to lens imperfections
- Make the contrast larger so objects in the image become more distinguishable
- Bring out edges so that things in the image can be seen more easily
- Remove irrelevant parts of the image

Some enhancements that you perform are for the benefit of people, that is, they make it easier for a person to see things in the image. Other enhancements make it easier for computerized image processing to extract information. Techniques that help the computers can make the images look worse to people and vice versa.

The rest of this chapter demonstrates some basic kinds of image enhancements. The sections that follow, "Clipping" and "Look-Up Tables," are examples of point operations. A *point operation* is a technique in which the value of the output pixel depends only on the value of the corresponding input pixel. The last section, "Convolution," demonstrates a different enhancement in which the value of an output pixel depends on the value of the corresponding input pixel and on other input pixels around it.

Clipping

Clipping is setting all pixels that are above some gray level to one value, or all pixels below some gray level to one value. Clipping can make it easier for people to concentrate on certain shades in the image. For example, if you know that the object you're interested in can never appear dark, it may be helpful to set all dark pixels to 0, that is, complete black. This helps prevent you from being distracted by dark shapes and helps image processing software avoid finding objects in dark regions.

Clipping High or Low

Figure 13.13(a) is an X-ray image of a real tooth in a model jaw. (People studying to be dental hygienists practice taking X-rays on these models.) A thin, black frame added around the image shows that the top and bottom right corners are bright white, perhaps from an exposure problem. These high pixel values can invalidate some types of image enhancement, such as the contrast stretching described later . No part of the tooth is anywhere near this bright, so it is safe to change very bright pixels to black so you can ignore them. Figure 13.13(b) shows the image when all pixels greater than 200 have been set to zero. Although there is still a faint white curve, almost all the bright white is gone, and the rest of the image, especially the tooth, is untouched. The code in Listing 13.7 lets you clip an image.

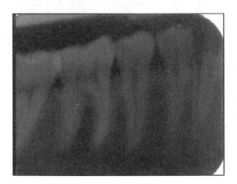

FIGURE 13.13(a)   Original.

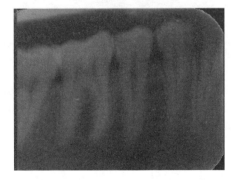

FIGURE 13.13(b)   All values greater than 200 set to zero.

LISTING 13.7   Clipping High or Low

```cpp
// ip_clip.hpp

template<class T>
inline
void clip_high( Image<T>& image, T threshold, T replacement )
// changes all pixels > a number to the same value
// INPUT: image - image to be clipped
//        threshold - set all values > threshold to replacement
// OUTPUT: image - original but with values clipped
// REQUIRE: T must define >
{
   std::replace_if( image.begin(), image.end(),
      std::bind2nd( std::greater<T>(), threshold ), replacement );
}

template<class T>
inline
void clip_low( Image<T>& image, T threshold, T replacement )
// changes all pixels <= a number to the same value
// INPUT: image - image to be clipped
//        threshold - set all values <= threshold to replacement
// OUTPUT: image - original but with values clipped
// REQUIRE: T must define >
{
   std::replace_if( image.begin(), image.end(),
      std::bind2nd( std::less_equal<T>(), threshold ), replacement );
}

inline
void clip_high( Image<unsigned char>& image, int threshold,
   int replacement )
// same as above clip_high. Lets threshold and replacement be integers
// without making a compiler warning
// REQUIRE: threshold and replacement must be in range of unsigned char
{
   clip_high<unsigned char>( image,
      static_cast<unsigned char>( threshold ),
      static_cast<unsigned char>( replacement ) );
}

inline
void clip_low( Image<unsigned char>& image, int threshold,
```

```
    int replacement )
// same as above clip_low. Lets threshold and replacement be integers
// without making a compiler warning
// REQUIRE: threshold and replacement must be in range of unsigned char
{
    clip_low<unsigned char>( image,
        static_cast<unsigned char>( threshold ),
        static_cast<unsigned char>( replacement ) );
}
```

The first function in Listing 13.7 is `clip_high`, which replaces all pixels in the passed image that are above (greater than) the threshold with the replacement value. The impressive thing is that it does this with one call to the STL algorithm `replace_if`. Its first two arguments are the range of pixels provided by the image. The third is a function argument that is the replacement criterion. The code passes the predefined functor `greater` with its second argument frozen at the specified threshold value. (Tip 50 explains more about binding arguments to functors. Tip 53 and Tip 56 have examples of using `greater` with a bound argument.) The last argument is the replacement value.

The next function in Listing 13.7, `clip_low`, replaces all pixels in the image that are less than or equal to a specified threshold with a given value. This function operates the same way as `clip_high` does, except that `clip_low` uses `less_equal` as the replacement criterion. Finally, the last two functions are wrappers that permit `clip_high` and `clip_low` to be called when the image data type is `unsigned char` but the other two arguments are `int`s. This is the case if the arguments that are passed are integer constants because C++ considers those constants to be `int`s.

The code to clip the image in Figure 13.13(a) is

```
const int threshold =200;
const int replacement = 0;
clip_high( image, threshold, replacement );
```

Making a Binary Image

Making a *binary image*, that is, an image with only two pixel values, is an important special case of clipping. For eight-bit images such as those in this chapter, the two values are typically 0 (complete black) and 255 (complete white). Conversion to a binary image often follows a chain of image enhancements designed to bring out pixels of a certain type, such as those on vertical edges or those on horizontal lines. For example, if the user is looking for vertical lines in the image, he first does some processing to make these lines show up (see Figure 13.24(b) later in this chapter). Each pixel in the resulting image is a measure of how likely it is that the pixel is on a vertical line. The user chooses a value in the range of an `unsigned char` as the threshold. This means that he considers all pixel values above the threshold to be on a vertical line and all pixels less than or equal to the threshold to not be on such a line. Once the user has thresholded the pixels, he can compute properties of the objects in the binary image, such as their area, perimeter, length, and so forth.

Usually, most of the binary pixels do not meet the criterion, resulting in an image that is mainly black. To save ink or make a monitor display more understandable, the values are commonly reversed before they are displayed or printed. In this case, black pixels are those of interest, and white pixels are not.

Occasionally, you may get an original image that is already almost binary. In this case, you can just convert the image with various gray levels to a binary image, which looks very similar to the original. For example, Figure 13.14(a) shows an original image of a Russian-style church in Alaska. Figure 13.14(b) is the result of converting to a binary image by thresholding at 90.

FIGURE 13.14(a)   Original image.   **FIGURE 13.14(b)**   Binary version.

The code in Listing 13.8 shows how simple the function to make a binary image is. The code calls `clip_high` (discussed previously) and passes a replacement value that is the maximum for the instantiated data type. Then the code calls `clip_low`, passing the minimum value. Tip 85 explains how to get properties of a data type, such as the maximum and minimum.

LISTING 13.8   Making a Binary Image

```
template<class T>
inline
void binary( Image<T>& image, T threshold )
// convert to a binary (two-valued) image
```

```
// INPUT: image - image to be turned binary
//        threshold - set all values > threshold to maximum value of T
//                    set all values <= threshold to minimum value of T
// OUTPUT: image - has only two values in it
// REQUIRE: T must define >
{
   clip_high( image, threshold, std::numeric_limits<T>::max() );
   clip_low(  image, threshold, std::numeric_limits<T>::min() );
}


inline
void binary( Image<unsigned char>& image, int threshold )
// same as above binarize. Lets threshold be an integer without
// making a compiler warning
// REQUIRE: threshold must be in range of unsigned char
{
   binary<unsigned char>( image,
      static_cast<unsigned char>( threshold ) );
}
```

The code to convert the image in Figure 13.14(a) to a binary image is

```
const int threshold =90;
binary( image, threshold );
```

Making a Negative

Another image enhancement is to invert the pixels in a gray-level image. To do this, you replace each pixel by the maximum of an unsigned char minus that pixel. The effect is that of making a photographic negative. There are various uses of such a negative:

- If you have a lot of black in a binary image that you want to print, you can save ink by making a negative, thus reversing the black and white.
- In some fields that use X-rays, low densities (such as air) appear dark and high densities (such as bone) are bright. Other fields have the opposite convention. You can convert between the two by making a negative.
- Some monitors may be able to display bright regions better than dark ones or vice versa. If you're interested in one of these regions, making a negative can let the monitor display the image better.
- Sometimes people can see (perceive) things in a negative that they can't in the original image and vice versa.

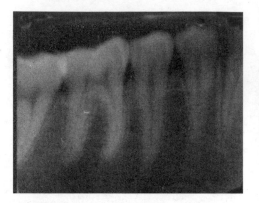 

FIGURE 13.15(a) Original image.   **FIGURE 13.15(b)** Negative.

Figure 13.15(a) shows an original image and Figure 13.15(b) is its negative. Listing 13.9 has the code to do this processing.

LISTING 13.9   Making a Negative

```
// ip_negative.cpp

#include <algorithm>
#include <functional>
#include <limits>

#include "ip_all.hpp"

void negative( Image<unsigned char>& image )
// replace each pixel by the maximum of an unsigned char minus pixel
{
   std::transform( image.begin(), image.end(), image.begin(),
      std::bind1st( std::minus<unsigned char>(),
         std::numeric_limits<unsigned char>::max() ) );
}
```

The code in Listing 13.9 demonstrates again how powerful the STL can be by taking only one statement to make the negative of an image. This also provides a good example of performing arithmetic on each element of a container, the subject of Tip 76. The STL algorithm transform does the work. Its first two arguments are the input range, and its third argument is the start of the output range. In this case, the input and output ranges are the same. The last argument is the predefined functor minus, which takes two numbers and returns their difference. However, the code freezes or binds the first number (see Tip 50) to be the maximum of an `unsigned char`, typically, 255. Thus, the net effect of the algorithm is to replace every pixel in the image by 255 minus the pixel, that is, to make the negative of the image.

The code to make the negative of the image in Figure 13.15(a) is

```
negative( image );
```

Look-Up Tables

A *look-up table* (LUT) is a mapping from any possible input value to an output value. It's a powerful enhancement tool for eight-bit images and is practical for integer-valued pixels of even 10 or 12 bits. The big advantage of a LUT is that it lets you compute the output for each of the 256 possible inputs of an eight-bit image just once. After you've done that, getting any pixel's output is simply a matter of indexing, not computation. This can be a great time saver, especially if you have large images or complicated output calculations.

Figure 13.16 illustrates the mechanics of a LUT. Initially, you compute the output for each possible input value, say, 0–255 inclusive. Next, you store the results in a container that can be indexed. (A vector works well for this.) In the container, which will become the LUT, store the output for an input value of 0 in element 0, the output for an input of 1 in element 1, and so on. Then, to use the LUT on an image, run through each of the input image's pixels, using the value of the pixel as an index into the LUT that yields the output value. For example, in Figure 13.16 an input value of 1 denotes element 1 of the LUT. This has a value of 41, which is what the output pixel is set to. Similarly, an input pixel value of 254 becomes an output

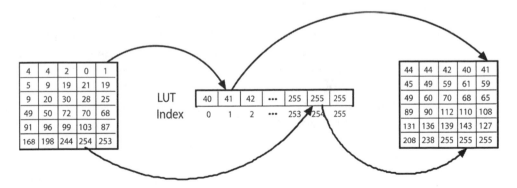

FIGURE 13.16 A look-up table (LUT).

value of 255. Notice that when using a LUT, you can use the same image for the input and the output. This is because an output pixel depends only on the value of its corresponding input pixel. The body of the for-loop in the code of Listing 13.10 explicitly shows the replacement of each input pixel by a value in the LUT.

LISTING 13.10   Making the Output with a LUT

```
// ip_lut.hpp

template< class ForwardIterator, class RandomIterator >
void lut( ForwardIterator start, ForwardIterator stop,
    RandomIterator lookup_table )
// run every element in the range through the look-up table (LUT)
// INPUT:    start - beginning of range
//           stop - end of range
//           lookup_table - iterator pointing to the start of the LUT
// REQUIRE: 1) all iterators must only point to unsigned char
//          2) lookup_table must be a random iterator and has at least
//             as many elements as there are values in an unsigned char
{
   for( ; start != stop; ++start )
     *start = lookup_table[*start];
}
```

The code in Listing 13.10 shows the function that converts a range of pixels with a given LUT. This function template accepts a range, given by forward iterators and the start of a LUT, given by a random iterator. The function loops through the range using the value of each pixel as an index with the random iterator. The loop replaces each pixel with the corresponding value found in the LUT.

The function lut is a template so that it can accept any forward iterator that points to an unsigned char. This allows the function to be used with Image<unsigned char> regardless of the specific iterator returned by that class. For example, if the class maintained the pixels internally in a list, and so returned iterators into a list instead of a vector, lut would still work.

Adding a Constant

The first application of an LUT is to add a (positive) constant to each pixel of an image. This is helpful if the objects you're interested in are dark and you're not interested in bright areas. Adding the constant can easily saturate the bright areas as "Image Arithmetic," earlier in this chapter, explains. However, because bright regions aren't of interest in this example, that saturation isn't detrimental.

Figure 13.17 shows an original and a version brightened by adding a constant to it. The code sets the constant to be the number that will raise the maximum pixel in the image up to the maximum value of an `unsigned char`. Listing 13.11 shows the code for adding a constant to an image.

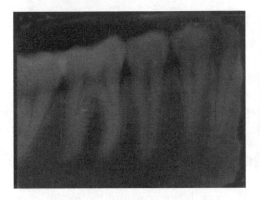

FIGURE 13.17(a)   Original image.

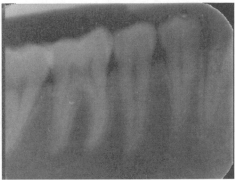

FIGURE 13.17(b)   A constant added.

LISTING 13.11   Adding a Constant to an Image

```cpp
// ip_plus_equals.cpp

#include <algorithm>
#include <limits>
#include <numeric>

#include "ip_all.hpp"

void operator+=( Image<unsigned char>& image, int value )
// add a constant to each pixel in the image. If a pixel exceeds the
// maximum of an unsigned char it is set to that maximum
// INPUT:    image - the image
//           value - number to add to each pixel
// REQUIRE:  value must be in range of unsigned char
{
    std::vector<unsigned char>
        lookup_table( std::numeric_limits<unsigned char>::max() + 1, 1 );

    // put 0,1,2,...,255 into the look-up table (LUT)
    lookup_table[0] = 0;
    std::partial_sum( lookup_table.begin(), lookup_table.end(),
        lookup_table.begin() );
```

```
    // compute the LUT
    std::transform( lookup_table.begin(), lookup_table.end(),
      lookup_table.begin(),
      std::bind2nd( std::ptr_fun( plus_safe ),
      static_cast<unsigned char>( value ) ) );

    // apply the LUT to the image
    lut( image.begin(), image.end(), lookup_table.begin() );
}
```

The software adds a constant to every pixel by making a += operator for an image of unsigned chars. The code declares a vector with enough elements to hold all the possible values of an unsigned char. This length is 1 plus the maximum value of that data type, which (as Tip 85 explains) is available from the predefined numeric_limits template. The function then uses the technique of Tip 79 to fill the LUT with the numbers 0, 1, 2, . . . 255. To compute the numbers in the LUT, the code uses the STL algorithm transform with the custom function plus_safe. (Tip 81 demonstrates the same technique, and Tip 47 and Tip 50 explain why ptr_fun and bind2nd are necessary.) Finally, the code calls the function lut to apply the LUT to the image.

To get Figure 13.17(b) from Figure 13.17(a), the code adds the number that will make the image have the maximum value of an unsigned char. This is the difference between that maximum and the maximum of the image, for example,

```
unsigned char image_max = *max_element( image.begin(), image.end() );
image += numeric_limits<unsigned char>::max() - image_max;
```

Contrast Stretch

The intuitive meaning of *contrast* in a (gray) image is the range of gray levels. If the image has just a few shades of gray, it has low contrast. If it has many shades of gray, its contrast is high. A *contrast stretch* is a more complex and more powerful image enhancement than is adding a constant to an image. This technique spreads out the gray levels in an image so that they occupy the full eight-bit range. The number of gray levels remains the same, as does their relative order. This means that if one gray level is less than another in the original image, its stretched value will also be less than the stretched value of the other gray level.

The formula for a contrast stretch that takes the gray-level range $[I_{Min}, I_{Max}]$ and changes it to the range $[0, O_{Max}]$ is

$$O = \begin{cases} \dfrac{O_{Max}}{\left(I_{Max} - I_{Min}\right)} x \left(I - I_{Min}\right) & \text{for } I_{Max} \neq I_{Min} \\[2em] I & \text{for } I_{Max} = I_{Min} \end{cases} \tag{13.2}$$

where I is an input pixel value and O is the corresponding output value. For the eight-bit images in this chapter, O_{Max} is 255.

You can perform a contrast stretch via an LUT, as Figure 13.18(a) and Figure 13.18(b) show. Listing 13.12 shows the code that stretches the contrast in an image.

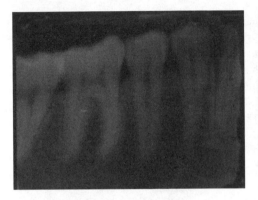

FIGURE 13.18(a)   Original image.

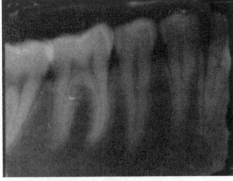

FIGURE 13.18(b)   Image after contrast stretch.

LISTING 13.12   Performing a Contrast Stretch

```
// ip_contrast_stretch.cpp

#include <algorithm>
#include <functional>
#include <limits>

#include "ip_all.hpp"

void contrast_stretch( Image<unsigned char>& image )
// stretch gray levels so that they occupy the entire 8-bit range
// NOTE:   if image has only one pixel value or is empty
//         function does nothing
{
   if( image.empty() )
      return;

   unsigned char image_max
      = *std::max_element( image.begin(), image.end() );
   unsigned char image_min
      = *std::min_element( image.begin(), image.end() );
```

```
        // one shade only in image so nothing to do. Return to avoid
        // dividing by zero below
        if( image_max == image_min )
           return;

        std::vector<unsigned char>
           lookup_table( std::numeric_limits<unsigned char>::max() + 1 );

        float scale = static_cast<float>(
           std::numeric_limits<unsigned char>::max() )
           / ( image_max - image_min );

        // make the lookup table
        for( int i = 0; i < std::numeric_limits<unsigned char>::max(); ++i )
           lookup_table[i] = static_cast<unsigned char>(
              scale * ( i - image_min ) );

        lut( image.begin(), image.end(), lookup_table.begin() );
     }
```

After verifying that the image is not empty, the function `contrast_stretch` in the code of Listing 13.12 finds the minimum and maximum values in the image, using the STL functions that Tip 83 describes. If they are the same, the image has only one shade of gray. In this case, stretching the range has no meaning (and would lead to a division by 0 if the first part of Equation 13.2 were used), so the function returns without doing anything to the image. If there is more than one pixel value, the code computes the scaling coefficient in Equation 13.2. Tip 85 explains how to get the maximum value of an `unsigned char`. Once it has the scaling coefficient, the code constructs the LUT by using Equation 13.2 to compute the output for every possible input value. Finally, the code applies the LUT to the image using the function `lut`, described previously.

Figure 13.18 shows an original image and the result of contrast stretching. The code to stretch the image contrast is simply

```
        contrast_stretch( image );
```

Convolution

Another general category of image enhancement techniques is the *neighborhood operation*. In a neighborhood operation, the output at a given pixel depends on the corresponding input pixel and on the pixels in a little region or neighborhood around that input pixel. One good example of a neighborhood operation is convolution.

Convolution is a powerful and general image enhancement technique. You can use it to blur an image, enhance lines or edges running in various directions, and increase the sharpness of images. The most important part of convolution is the *kernel* or *mask*. This is a rectangular array of numbers. The array is usually small and square. This chapter assumes that the kernel is a square with an odd number of pixels on each side. The data type of the kernel is int, and the numbers can be positive, negative, or zero. The mechanics of convolution are the same regardless of the numbers, so one routine will handle any convolution. The values of the numbers are what create the different kinds of enhancements.

Figure 13.19 shows how convolution works. The input and output images are the same dimensions. To get the output at any pixel, imagine centering the kernel above the corresponding input pixel. You then multiply each element of the kernel by the input pixel beneath it, and add up these products. To get the output at the next pixel (the one to the right of the current output pixel), you slide the kernel to the right one pixel and repeat the multiplication and summation process. Once you do this for an entire row, you move the kernel down one row and compute the outputs for that row. The process is over when you have computed the convolution for all rows.

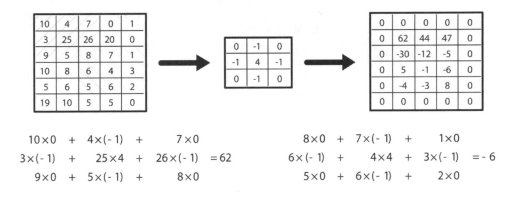

$$10 \times 0 \;+\; 4 \times (-1) \;+\; 7 \times 0$$
$$3 \times (-1) \;+\; 25 \times 4 \;+\; 26 \times (-1) \;=\; 62$$
$$9 \times 0 \;+\; 5 \times (-1) \;+\; 8 \times 0$$

$$8 \times 0 \;+\; 7 \times (-1) \;+\; 1 \times 0$$
$$6 \times (-1) \;+\; 4 \times 4 \;+\; 3 \times (-1) \;=\; -6$$
$$5 \times 0 \;+\; 6 \times (-1) \;+\; 2 \times 0$$

FIGURE 13.19 How convolution works.

There are a few details to note before proceeding to the code. The first is that typically the user provides a divisor and offset to the convolution routine. In this case, the code divides the sum of products at each pixel by the divisor and adds the offset. The second is that the function stores the sum of the products in an int and assumes that the sum doesn't exceed the range of that data type. This is rarely a problem because the numbers in the kernel are typically small, that is, single digits. A third issue is what to do when the kernel hangs over the edge of the input image. For example, if you use a 3×3 kernel, Figure 13.19 shows that whenever the kernel is centered on the outer edge of the image, that is, the top or bottom rows, or the left or right columns, part of the kernel will not fall on the input image. There are various ways of handling this problem. The routine in Listing 13.13 computes the convolution only for input pixels in which the kernel is entirely on the image and simply sets the other pixels to the passed offset value.

LISTING 13.13   Convolving

```
// ip_convolve.cpp

#include "ip_all.hpp"

void convolve( const Image<unsigned char>& in, const int kernel[],
   Image<unsigned char>& out, int width, int divisor, int offset )
// convolve an image with the given square kernel
// INPUT:   in - input image
//          kernel - array with kernel elements, arranged row-by-row
//          width - width of square kernel (default = 3)
//          divisor - number by which to divide sum of products
//             (default = 1)
//          offset - number to add to product sum divided by divisor
//             (default = 0)
// OUTPUT:  out - input image convolved with kernel. Has same
//                dimensions as input image
// REQUIRE: 1) width must be odd and greater than one
//          2) divisor must not be zero
//          3) kernel must have at least width*width elements with
//             the top row of the kernel first, the second row second,
//             etc.
// NOTE:    1) if the width is greater than the number of input rows
//             or columns the function does nothing
//          2) the function does not process a border of size width/2
//             pixels. Instead, it sets those pixels to the clipped
//             value of the offset.
{
   // if any dimension of the kernel is bigger than the corresponding
   // dimension of the input image, bail out
   if( in.rows() < width || in.columns() < width )
      return;

   out.resize( in.rows(), in.columns() );

   int border_width = width / 2;

   // for every input row except the top and bottom borders
```

```
for( int i = border_width; i < in.rows() - border_width; ++i )
{
    // for every input column except the left and right borders
    for( int j = border_width; j < in.columns() - border_width; ++j )
    {
        const int* p = kernel;
        int sum = 0;

        // for every kernel row
        for( int k = i - border_width; k <= i + border_width; ++k,
            p += width )

            // compute and accumulate the sum of products in the row
            sum += std::inner_product(
                in.row_begin( k, j - border_width ),
                in.row_end( k, j + border_width ), p, 0 );

        sum = sum / divisor + offset;
        out(i,j) = clip( sum );
    }
}

// fill the borders
frame( out, border_width, clip( offset ) );
}
```

The function first verifies that the image is at least as large as the kernel and
exits if not. If the image is at least as large as the kernel, the code resizes the output
image to have the same dimensions as the input image, computes the width of the
border, and enters the processing loop. This nested loop covers every pixel inside
the border. Before proceeding to the innermost loop, the function initializes two
variables. One is an `int` that stores the sum of the products, and the other is a
pointer set to the start of the kernel array. At every input pixel, the function computes the sum of the products for each row of the kernel.

This calculation (the sum of products) is common in science and engineering
and is called the inner product or dot product. Fortunately, the STL has an algorithm that is specifically designed to compute it—`inner_product`. Tip 82 explains
this algorithm in detail, and Tip 53 provides another example of its use. The algorithm takes two ranges, multiplies their corresponding elements, and returns the
sum of those products. The first two arguments to `inner_product` are the range of
columns in the input image row. (This demonstrates the use of a custom iterator in
an STL algorithm.) The third argument is an iterator that points to the start of the
second range. Note that what is passed is actually a pointer, but Tip 3 explains that

a pointer in a C-style array can be used as an iterator into that array. The last argument is the value to which `inner_product` initializes the internal variable that holds the sum of products. The type of the variable is the same as the type of the last argument. Because that argument is an integer constant, C++ makes the data type be an `int`. Thus, each product is the multiplication of an `int` by an `unsigned char`, and this prevents the product from overflowing. If both data types were `unsigned char`, the product would easily exceed the range of that data type and make the resulting number useless.

When the loop finishes, `sum` contains the sum of the inner products of each processed row. This is equal to the convolution of the kernel with the image when the kernel is centered on the current pixel. The code finishes by dividing the sum by the divisor, adding the offset, clipping the result to lie in the range of an `unsigned char`, and setting the output pixel to that value. Although Listing 13.13 doesn't show it, the function declaration for `convolve` provides default values of 3 for the kernel width, 1 for the divisor, and 0 for the offset.

The function `frame`, which is called at the end of Listing 13.13, is an auxiliary function that draws a frame (an unfilled rectangle) in an image. The preceding text explains how the convolution code of Listing 13.13 uses it. However, `frame` is also convenient for highlighting regions in images (see Figure 13.2(a)) or the entire image itself, as in Figure 13.13(a). The code in Listing 13.14 first draws the top and bottom of the frame by getting an iterator range from the image for each section of a row. The code then passes the range to the STL algorithm `fill`, which copies the specified frame value to those columns of the row. The function finishes by filling in the left and right sides of the frame using the STL algorithm `fill_n`. This algorithm sets to a given value the specified number of elements, starting at the beginning of a range. Although it would be easy to use `fill` again, `fill_n` is particularly useful in this case because the code is given the number of elements, that is, the thickness of the frame. Listing 13.14 concludes with two overloaded variations of the `frame` function that make using it more convenient.

LISTING 13.14   Drawing a Frame in an Image

```
// ip_frame.hpp

template<class T>
void frame( Image<T>& image, int top, int left, int bottom, int right,
    int thickness, T value )
// draw a frame in an image
// INPUT:   image - input image
//          top - top row of block        left - left column of block
//          bottom - bottom row of block  right - right column of block
//          thickness - thickness of frame in pixels
```

```
//          value - pixel value to use for frame
// REQUIRE: both rows and columns must be in the image and
//          top <= bottom,   left <= right
//          thickness <= 2*image.rows(), thickness <= 2*image.columns()
{
  // draw top and bottom
  for( int i = 0; i < thickness; ++i )
  {
    std::fill( image.row_begin( top+i, left ),
       image.row_end( top+i, right ), value );
    std::fill( image.row_begin( bottom-i, left ),
       image.row_end( bottom-i, right ), value );
  }

  // draw left and right
  for( int i = top + thickness; i <= bottom - thickness; ++i )
  {
    std::fill_n( image.row_begin( i, left ), thickness, value );
    std::fill_n( image.row_begin( i, right-thickness+1 ), thickness,
       value );
  }
}

inline
void frame( Image<unsigned char>& image, int top, int left, int bottom,
   int right, int thickness, int value )
// REQUIRE: same as above but value must be in range of unsigned char
{
  frame( image, top, left, bottom, right, thickness,
     static_cast<unsigned char>( value ) );
}

inline
void frame( Image<unsigned char>& image, int thickness, int value )
// draw frame around entire image
// REQUIRE: same as above
{ frame( image, 0, 0, image.rows()-1, image.columns()-1, thickness,
   static_cast<unsigned char>( value ) );
}
```

The convolution code in Listing 13.13 is independent of the kernel values. By simply changing the kernel and using the same function, you can get many different image enhancements. Here are some examples.

Averaging

If an image has a lot of speckling in it, you can mitigate its effects by blurring the image. To do this, you let each output pixel be the average in a square neighborhood centered about the corresponding input pixel. You can compute this average with convolution by using a square kernel filled with ones, a divisor equal to the sum of the kernel elements, and an offset of zero. For example, a 3×3 kernel with a divisor of nine, an offset of zero, and centered on a 3×3 section of the image

$$\begin{bmatrix} a\ b\ c \\ d\ e\ f \\ g\ h\ i \end{bmatrix}$$ produces the value

$$\frac{1}{9}\begin{bmatrix} 1\ 1\ 1 \\ 1\ 1\ 1 \\ 1\ 1\ 1 \end{bmatrix} * \begin{bmatrix} a\ b\ c \\ d\ e\ f \\ g\ h\ i \end{bmatrix} + 0$$

$$= \frac{1}{9}\left(1\cdot a + 1\cdot b + 1\cdot c + 1\cdot d + 1\cdot e + 1\cdot f + 1\cdot g + 1\cdot h + 1\right)$$

$$= \frac{a+b+c+d+e+f+g+h+i}{9}$$

which is just the average of the nine input pixels. (In the preceding equation, the asterisk denotes convolution.) Figure 13.20(a) shows a highly speckled image of a small block on a background, similar to Figure 13.4. Figure 13.20(b) shows the result of blurring with the 3x3 kernel. The code in Listing 13.15 makes the blurred image.

LISTING 13.15   Blurring an Image

```
const int width = 3;
const int divisor = width * width;
const vector<int> kernel( divisor, 1 );
convolve( image, &kernel[0], out, width, divisor );
```

The code parameterizes the width of the kernel and then sets the divisor, which is the square of the width. Then the code creates a vector filled with that number of ones by using the technique of Tip 4. Finally, the code passes those elements to con-volve as a C-style array by using the method explained in Tip 25.

FIGURE 13.20(a)   Original image.   **FIGURE 13.20(b)**   Blur with 3×3 kernel.

Blurring can make it easier to see objects in the image by reducing the amount of speckling, but blurring also gets rid of some details. You can adjust the amount of blurring by changing the size of the averaging kernel. The code to do this is the same as in Listing 13.15, except the value of width changes. Figure 13.21(a) shows the result of blurring with a 7×7 kernel. Figure 13.21(b) uses an 11×11 kernel.

FIGURE 13.21(a)   Blur with 7×7 kernel.   **FIGURE 13.21(b)**   Blur with 11×11 kernel.

Sharpening

You can also sharpen an image using convolution. Details can show up better, but speckling is also amplified. Figure 13.22(a) is a micrograph (a very magnified picture) of the grains in a material. Figure 13.22(b) shows a sharpened version of the image. The kernel and code to do this are

```
const int kernel[] = { 0, -1,  0,
                      -1,  5, -1,
                       0, -1,  0 };
convolve( image, kernel, out );
```

The call does not specify the last three arguments to convolve, so the function uses its default values of 3 for the kernel width, 1 for the divisor, and 0 for the offset.

 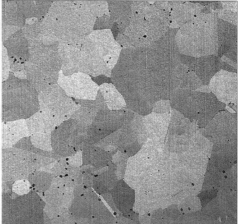

FIGURE 13.22(a)   Original image.   **FIGURE 13.22(b)**   Sharpened version.

Edge enhancement

The final demonstrations of convolution show its use in enhancing edges in images. By using various kernels, you can bring out horizontal or vertical edges, edges running at different angles, or edges running in any direction.

Figure 13.23(a) shows an image of a Russian-style church in Alaska. You can make the horizontal edges stand out, as in Figure 13.23(b), with the code

```
const int width = 3;
const int divisor = 3;
const int threshold = 25;
const int kernel[] = { -1, -1, -1,
                        0,  0,  0,
                        1,  1,  1 };
convolve( image, kernel, out, width, divisor );
binarize( out, threshold );
negative( out );
```

FIGURE 13.23(a) Original image.

FIGURE 13.23(b) Horizontal edges enhanced.

The code thresholds the convolved image, setting all pixels greater than 25 to 255 (white) and all other pixels to 0 (black). In essence, this defines what a horizontal edge is in this image. To make the printed image appear better, the last line in the code snippet makes a negative of the image, which in this case simply reverses black and white.

The kernel makes horizontal edges come out strongly and enhances edges in other directions, but the further the edges are from the horizontal, the less the kernel brings them out. The enhancement of horizontal lines is apparent in a number of ways. Notice that the horizontal bars in the window panes are present, but not the vertical bars. Similarly, the horizontal bar of the cross on the steeple is fully visible, but the vertical bar has disappeared. The telephone wires stand out even though they're about 45° from the horizontal because they are very strong edges, that is, they jump from the bright white of the clouds to the dark black of the wires. This makes the kernel bring them out more than would be expected.

Figure 13.24(a) shows the church again. The code to make the vertical edges stand out, as in Figure 13.24(b), is

```
const int width = 3;
const int divisor = 3;
const int threshold = 25;
const int kernel[] = { -1, 0, 1,
                       -1, 0, 1,
                       -1, 0, 1 };
convolve( image, kernel, out, width, divisor );
binarize( out, threshold );
negative( out );
```

FIGURE 13.24(a)   Original image.

FIGURE 13.24(b)   Vertical edges enhanced.

As before, the code thresholds the convolved image to create a binary image and reverses black and white to make the printed image appear better. Note now that the vertical bar of the cross and vertical bars on the window panes appear.

FIGURE 13.25(a)   Original image.

FIGURE 13.25(b)   Northeast edges enhanced.

Figure 13.25(a) is again the original image of the church. As an example of en-hancing an edge at an angle, consider a northeast edge, that is, one such that move-ment in the northeast direction crosses the edge. The telephone wires are good examples of this. The code to make northeast edges stand out, as in Figure 13.25(b), is

```
const int width = 3;
const int divisor = 3;
const int threshold = 25;
const int kernel[] = { 0,   1,  1,
                      -1,   0,  1,
                      -1,  -1,  0 };
convolve( image, kernel, out, width, divisor );
binarize( out, threshold );
negative( out );
```

As before, the code thresholds the convolved image to create a binary image and reverses black and white to make the printed image appear better. The telephone wires and the right edge of the roof now come out strongly. The left edge of the roof and the top of the stair railings, which are southwest edges, disappear completely.

FIGURE 13.26(a) Original image.

FIGURE 13.26(b) All edges enhanced.

The last example of convolution demonstrates the enhancement of edges that run in any direction. Figure 13.26 shows that both horizontal and vertical edges, for example, the cross and the window pane bars, and diagonal edges, for example, the rooftop and telephone wires, come out strongly in the processed image. The code to make all edges stand out is

```
const int width = 3;
const int divisor = 1;
const int threshold = 25;
const int kernel[] = { 0, -1,  0,
```

```
                        -1,  4, -1,
                         0, -1,  0 };
convolve( image, kernel, out, width, divisor );
binarize( out, threshold );
negative( out );
```

This kernel is known as the Laplacian.

Appendix A

More Information on STL Algorithms

This appendix provides more information on the STL algorithms used in this book. Not all the algorithms in the library are here, nor is every version of the algorithms. Check an STL reference book such as Matthew Austern's *Generic Programming and the STL* [Austern00] or Nicolai Josuttis's *The C++ Standard Library* [Josuttis99], or the C++ Standard itself [ISO98] for the complete list. The descriptions in the appendix are concise but still helpful. If you want additional information—for example, on errors that can be thrown or on the complexity of the algorithm—check one of the aforementioned sources.

All the algorithms are template functions. For clarity, this list uses the names of the function parameters to represent the requirements of the parameter data type. For example,

```
OutputIterator adjacent_difference( InputIterator first,
    InputIterator last, OutputIterator out )
```

means that the actual function declaration is

```
template <class InputIterator, class OutputIterator>
OutputIterator adjacent_difference( InputIterator first,
    InputIterator last, OutputIterator out);
```

Table A.1 describes the terminology used in the rest of the appendix.

TABLE A.1 Abbreviations of Data Types Used in Appendix A

Term	Data Type
BidirectionalIterator BidirectionalIterator1 BidirectionalIterator2	Bidirectional iterator. $\rightarrow$

Term	Data Type
BinaryOperation	Binary operation. A functor or function that has two arguments and returns a value that can be assigned to an element in the output range.
BinaryPredicate	Binary predicate. A functor or function that has two arguments and returns a value that can be tested for being true or false. The first argument always comes from the first input range, and the second always comes from the second input range. The algorithm dereferences the iterators and passes them to the predicate.
Compare	A functor or function that returns `true` if the first argument is less than the second and `false` otherwise.
ForwardIterator ForwardIterator1 ForwardIterator2	Forward iterator.
Generator	A functor or pointer to a function that takes no arguments and returns a value that is convertible to the data type of the output range.
InputIterator InputIterator1 InputIterator2	Input iterator.
OutputIterator OutputIterator1 OutputIterator2	Output iterator.
RandomAccessIterator RandomAccessIterator1 RandomAccessIterator2	Random access iterator.
T	Data type.
UnaryOperation	Unary operation. A functor or function pointer that has one argument and returns a value that can be assigned to an element in the output range.
UnaryPredicate	Unary predicate. A functor or function pointer that has one argument and returns a value that can be tested for being true or false.
UnaryProcedure	Unary procedure. A functor or function pointer that has one argument and can read the argument or modify it. In the latter case, the argument is passed by reference. The procedure shouldn't return a value.

The STL algorithms that this book uses are, in alphabetical order, the following:

```
T accumulate( InputIterator stop, InputIterator stop, T init )
```

The output of this algorithm is the sum of the initial value and all the values in the input range. For example, if there are five values in the input range, a_1 through a_5, the outputs are

$$init + a_1 + a_2 + a_3 + a_4 + a_5$$

However, internally, the algorithm computes the result differently. The algorithm declares a variable of type T (say, total) that's initialized to init. Then the algorithm computes total = total + *i for every i in the input range. Note that the assignment converts the result of every addition to the data type of total, which is the same as the data type of init. This can cause problems, for example, if the range has floating-point numbers but the initial value is an integer. See Tip 86 for more information.

```
OutputIterator adjacent_difference( InputIterator start,
    InputIterator stop, OutputIterator out )
```

This algorithm assigns the first input element to the first output element. For every input element after that, it assigns the difference of that element and the previous one to the corresponding element in the output. The input and output ranges may be the same. The algorithm returns the position of the first element in the output range that it didn't overwrite.

```
OutputIterator copy( InputIterator start, InputIterator stop,
    OutputIterator out )
```

This algorithm copies each element in the input range to the output range and returns the position of the first element in the output range that it didn't overwrite.

```
iterator_traits<InputIterator>::difference_type
    count_if( InputIterator start, InputIterator stop,
        UnaryPredicate predicate )
```

This algorithm returns the number of iterators i in the input range for which the predicate is true.

```
bool equal( InputIterator1 start1, InputIterator1 stop1,
    InputIterator2 start2 )
```

The algorithm returns `true` if every element in the first input range is equal to (==) the corresponding element in the second input range. Otherwise, the algorithm returns `false`.

```
bool fill( ForwardIterator start, ForwardIterator stop,
    const T& value )
bool fill_n( OutputIterator start, Size n, const T& value )
```

The first algorithm assigns the specified value to each element in the range [start,stop). The second algorithm does the same for the range [start,start+n).

```
InputIterator find( InputIterator start, InputIterator stop,
    const T& value )
```

The algorithm finds the first iterator `i` in the input range whose value is the same as that specified. If `find` doesn't locate one, the algorithm returns `stop`.

```
InputIterator find_if( InputIterator start, InputIterator stop,
    UnaryPredicate predicate )
```

The algorithm finds the first iterator `i` in the input range that makes the predicate true. If `find` doesn't locate one, the algorithm returns `stop`.

```
UnaryProcedure for_each(InputIterator start, InputIterator stop,
    UnaryProcedure f)
```

This algorithm applies the unary procedure to every element in the input range in order, that is, starting with `start` and going up to but not including `stop`. The procedure can just read the element or modify it. In the latter case, the algorithm passes in the value by reference. The algorithm ignores any value that the procedure returns. `for_each`, however, returns a copy of the procedure.

```
void generate( ForwardIterator start, ForwardIterator stop,
    Generator generator )
```

This algorithm calls `generator` once for each element in the input range and assigns the result of the call to the element.

```
T inner_product( InputIterator1 start1, InputIterator1 stop1,
    InputIterator2 start2, T init)
```

This algorithm computes the sum of the products of the corresponding elements in the two input ranges. For example, if the five values in the input ranges are a_1 through a_5 and b_1 through b_5, the output is

$$output = init + a_1 \times b_1 + a_2 \times b_2 + a_3 \times b_3 + a_4 \times b_4 + a_5 \times b_5$$

The algorithm actually computes the output by setting some internal variable `total` of data type `T` to `init` and then calculating `total = total + ( *i1 ) X ( *i2 )` for every pair of corresponding elements `i1` and `i2` in the input ranges. This means that each time the total is updated, the value being added is converted to data type `T`. See Tip 86 for an example of the problems this can cause.

```
bool lexicographical_compare( InputIterator1 start1,
    InputIterator1 stop1, InputIterator2 start2, InputIterator2 stop2 )

bool lexicographical_compare( InputIterator1 start1,
    InputIterator1 stop1, InputIterator2 start2, InputIterator2 stop2,
    Compare compare )
```

These algorithms return `true` if the sequence of elements in the first range is lexicographically less than the sequence in the second range. Otherwise, they return `false`. The first form uses the less-than operator (<) to compare two elements. The second form uses an operator supplied by the user. When making the lexicographical comparison, the following rules hold:

- If two sequences are the same, that is, they have the same number of elements and the corresponding elements are equivalent, neither sequence is lexicographically less than the other.
- Suppose one sequence has *N* elements and is shorter than the other. If the first *N* elements of the long sequence are the same as in the short sequence, the short sequence is lexicographically less than the longer one.
- Otherwise, the result of the lexicographical comparison is the same as the result of the comparison of the first pair of corresponding elements that aren't equivalent.

```
const T& max( const T& a, const T& b )
const T& max( const T& a, const T& b, Compare compare )
```

The first form of this algorithm returns the larger value. The second form returns `b` if `compare( a, b )` is true, otherwise it returns `false`. If the two arguments are equivalent, the algorithm returns the first one.

```
ForwardIterator max_element( ForwardIterator start,
    ForwardIterator stop )
```

```
ForwardIterator max_element( ForwardIterator start,
    ForwardIterator stop, Compare comp)
```

This algorithm returns the location of the element with the maximum value. If there is more than one such element, the iterator points to the first one.

```
OutputIterator merge( InputIterator1 start1, InputIterator1 stop1,
    InputIterator2 start2, InputIterator2 stop2, OutputIterator out )
```

This algorithm merges two sorted ranges together to produce a third sorted range. The output range can't overlap either of the two input ranges. The input ranges should be sorted by the less-than operator (<) because that's how the algorithm sorts the merged elements. The sorted output is stable, that is, for equivalent elements in the two input ranges, the element from the first range always precedes the element from the second. The algorithm returns the position of the first element in the output range that it didn't overwrite.

```
pair<InputIterator1, InputIterator2>
mismatch(InputIterator1 first1, InputIterator1 last1,
    InputIterator2 first2, BinaryPredicate pred)
```

This algorithm returns an iterator i and its corresponding iterator j such that j is the same distance (number of elements) from first2 as i is from first1. i is the first iterator in the range [first1, last1) for which pred(*i, *j) is false. If no such i exists, the algorithm returns the pair last1 and its corresponding iterator.

```
const T& min( const T& a, const T& b )
```

```
const T& min( const T& a, const T& b, Compare comp )
```

The first form of this algorithm returns the smaller value. The second form returns b if compare(b, a) is true, otherwise it returns a false. If the two arguments are equivalent, the algorithm returns the first one.

```
ForwardIterator min_element( ForwardIterator start,
    ForwardIterator stop )
```

This algorithm returns the location of the element with the minimum value. If there is more than one such element, the iterator points to the first one.

```
void nth_element( RandomAccessIterator start, RandomAccessIterator nth,
    RandomAccessIterator stop )

void nth_element( RandomAccessIterator start, RandomAccessIterator nth,
    RandomAccessIterator stop, Compare comp)
```

After this algorithm finishes, the element in the position marked by nth is the element that would be there if the whole range were sorted. All elements that precede that element are less than or equal to it. All elements that follow that element are greater than or equal to it. In the second form, for any iterator i that comes before nth and any iterator j that comes at or after nth, comp(*j, *i) is false.

```
void partial_sort( RandomAccessIterator start,
    RandomAccessIterator middle, RandomAccessIterator stop )

void partial_sort( RandomAccessIterator start,
    RandomAccessIterator middle, RandomAccessIterator stop, Compare
    comp))
```

These algorithms place the first middle – first elements in sorted order in the range [start, middle). The order of the remaining elements in [middle, stop) is unspecified.

```
OutputIterator partial_sum( InputIterator start, InputIterator stop,
    OutputIterator out )
```

For each element in the input range, this algorithm computes the sum of that element and all preceding elements. Then the algorithm assigns the sum to the corresponding element of the output range. The input and output ranges can be the same. The algorithm returns the position of the first element in the output range that it didn't overwrite.

```
OutputIterator remove_copy( InputIterator start, InputIterator stop,
    OutputIterator out, const T& value )
```

This algorithm copies all the elements from the input range to the output range except those that equal the passed value. The input and output ranges can't overlap. The relative order of the elements in the output range is the same as that in the input range. The algorithm returns the position of the first element in the output range that it didn't overwrite.

```
OutputIterator remove_copy_if( InputIterator start, InputIterator stop,
    OutputIterator out, UnaryPredicate predicate )
```

This algorithm copies all the elements from the input range to the output range except those for which the predicate is true. The input and output ranges can't overlap. The relative order of the elements in the output range is the same as that in the input range. The algorithm returns the position of the first element in the output range that it didn't overwrite.

```
ForwardIterator remove_if( ForwardIterator start, ForwardIterator stop,
    UnaryPredicate predicate )
```

This algorithm eliminates all elements in the range for which the predicate is true. The algorithm returns the end of the resulting range. The order of the remaining elements is stable, that is, they are in the same relative order as they were originally.

```
void replace_copy( ForwardIterator start, ForwardIterator stop,
    OutputIterator out, const T& old_value, const T& new_value )
```

This algorithm copies the input range to the output, replacing any elements equal to old_value with new_value.

```
void replace_if( ForwardIterator start, ForwardIterator stop,
    UnaryPredicate predicate, const T& new_value )
```

This algorithm replaces each element in the range that makes the predicate true with new_value.

```
void reverse( BidirectionalIterator start, BidirectionalIterator stop )
```

This algorithm reverses the order of elements in the given range.

```
OutputIterator set_difference( InputIterator1 start1,
    InputIterator1 stop1, InputIterator2 start2, InputIterator2 stop2,
    OutputIterator out )
```

This algorithm takes the elements of the first range that are not in the second range and copies them to the output. The output range can't overlap either of the input ranges. The input ranges must be sorted, and the output will be sorted. The algorithm returns the end of the output range that it made.

```
OutputIterator set_intersection( InputIterator1 start1,
    InputIterator1 stop1, InputIterator2 start2, InputIterator2 stop2,
    OutputIterator out )
```

This algorithm takes the elements that are in both containers and copies them to the output. If there are multiple occurrences of an element in either range, the routine copies the smaller of the number of occurrences in both ranges to the output. The output range can't overlap either of the input ranges. The input ranges must be sorted, and the output will be sorted. The algorithm returns the end of the output range that it made.

```
OutputIterator set_symmetric_difference( InputIterator1 start1,
    InputIterator1 stop1, InputIterator2 start2, InputIterator2 stop2,
    OutputIterator out )
```

This algorithm takes the elements of the first range that are not in the second range and the elements of the second range that are not in the first and copies them to the output. The output range can't overlap either of the input ranges. The input ranges must be sorted, and the output will be sorted. The algorithm returns the end of the output range that it made. A "set symmetric difference" is also known as an "exclusive OR."

```
OutputIterator set_union( InputIterator1 start1, InputIterator1 stop1,
    InputIterator2 start2, InputIterator2 stop2, OutputIterator out )
```

This algorithm copies the elements that are in one or both ranges to the output. If there are multiple occurrences of an element in either range, the routine copies the larger of the number of occurrences in both ranges to the output. The output range can't overlap either of the input ranges. The input ranges must be sorted, and the output will be sorted. The algorithm returns the end of the output range that it made.

```
void sort( RandomAccessIterator start, RandomAccessIterator stop )

void sort( RandomAccessIterator start, RandomAccessIterator stop,
    Compare compare )
```

This algorithm sorts the elements in the specified range. The first form uses the less-than operator (<). The second uses the comparison operation supplied by the user.

```
ForwardIterator2 swap_ranges(ForwardIterator1 start1,
    ForwardIterator1 stop1, ForwardIterator2 start 2)
```

This algorithm exchanges corresponding elements in the two ranges, which cannot overlap. It returns the first position in the second range that it didn't exchange.

```
OutputIterator transform( InputIterator start, InputIterator stop,
    OutputIterator out, UnaryOperation unary_op )
```

```
OutputIterator transform( InputIterator1 start1, InputIterator1 stop1,
    InputIterator2 start2, OutputIterator out, BinaryOperation
    binary_op )
```

The first form of this algorithm applies the unary operator to each element in the input range and assigns the result to the corresponding element in the output range. The output range can be the same as the input range. The second form applies the binary operator to pairs of corresponding elements in the input ranges and assigns the result to the corresponding element in the output range. The element from the first input range is the first argument to the operator and the element from the second input range.

```
ForwardIterator unique ( ForwardIterator start, ForwardIterator stop )
```

This algorithm removes all but the first element from every group of consecutive, equal (==) elements and returns the end of the resulting range.

Appendix B

About the CD-ROM

CONTENTS

The CD-ROM included with the book contains all the source code files shown in the book. They are in two folders—TIPS and IMAGE_PROCESSING. In addition, the FIGURES folder has electronic versions of the book's figures. TIPS has the source code files listed in the tips. There are 95 source files (cpp), one header file (hpp), and one data file (txt). All files can be used with any C++ compiler that conforms to the C++ standard.

IMAGE_PROCESSING has eight source files, nine header files, and a makefile. These carry out all the processing in Chapter 13. The file `ip_test.cpp` contains a driver program that performs some simple tests on each routine in that chapter. `ip_test.cpp` displays the routine function and whether the code passed the test. The software does not have any provisions for reading and writing images. If you want to do this, you can get code on the Internet to work with the various file formats, such as *http://www.libtiff.org/* for TIFF files, *http://www.libpng.org/* for PNG files, or *http://www.ijg.org/* for JPEG files.

The folder BOOST has the code for the Boost library, version 1.32.0. The code is independent of platform. There are three files, each compressed a different way and each containing the entire library. For more information on Boost or the latest version of the software, go to *www.boost.org*.

All the files and folders are from Borland's C++ Builder Personal Edition except for the following: `filelist.txt`, `about_the_CD_ROM.rtf`, and `Publisher-ReadMe.rtf` (in the main folder) and the subfolders TIPS, IMAGE_PROCESSING, BOOST, and FIGURES.

Here's how some compilers perform on the source code for the tips and image processing:

Borland C++ 5.6.4 (in Borland Builder 6): compiles all

Comeau 4.3.3 for Windows XP: compiles all except `algorithm_sort_sets.cpp` (known bug)

MinGW 3.2.0 (which uses GCC 3.4.2): compiles all but `string_whitespace.cpp`, which compiles if you replace `isspace` by `::isspace`

Microsoft C++ Compiler 14.00.50215.44 (Visual C++ 2005 Express Edition Beta 2): compiles 77 of the 95 tip files and all the image-processing files

The file `filelist.txt` in the main folder of the CD-ROM gives the names of all the files in TIPS, IMAGE_PROCESSING, and BOOST.

SYSTEM REQUIREMENTS

There are no special system requirements or software frameworks needed for the tip and image processing code. All you need is a standard-conforming C++ compiler. Similarly, the Boost library is independent of platform. There are, however, precompiled versions for some platforms that make installation of the library easier. See *www.boost.org*.

The minimum system requirements for Borland's C++ Builder Personal Edition are the following:

- Intel Pentium II/400 MHz or compatible
- Microsoft Windows 98, 2000 (SP2), or XP
- 128 MB RAM (256 MB recommended)
- 550 MB hard disk space (full install)
- CD-ROM drive
- SVGA or higher resolution monitor (800x600, 256 color)
- Mouse or other pointing device

INSTALLATION

You don't need to run any installation software for the tip or image processing files. Just copy them to a folder for compiling. The file `installation.html` contains the instructions for installing the Boost library. The file is in each of the three Boost compressed files.

To install the Borland C++ Builder Personal Edition:

1. Go to *http://www.borland.com/products/downloads/download_cbuilder.html#*, scroll to the bottom and select the Personal link.

2. Select the New User button and answer the registration questions. You will have to enter a valid email address. Borland will send the serial number and authorization key to that address.

3. Insert the CD-ROM that comes with this book into your CD-ROM drive. After a few seconds, you should see an installation dialog box. Follow the instructions in the dialog box to install the program. If you don't get a dialog box, press the Windows' Start button, select Run, type D:\install, where D is the letter of your CD-ROM drive, and press the OK button. Then follow the instructions.

References

[Austern00] Austern, Matthew. *Generic Programming and the STL*. Addison-Wesley, 1999.

[Basketball04] National Basketball Association. "Basketball statistics." *http://www.nba.com/*

[Billionaire04] Forbes.com. "The World's Richest People." *http://www.forbes.com/lists/2003/02/26/billionaireland.html*

[Cities04] United States Census Bureau. "IDB—Rank countries by Publication." *http://www.census.gov/ipc/www/idbrank.html*

[Cline99] Cline, Marshall, Lomow, Greg A., and Girou, Mike. *C++ FAQS*. 2nd ed. Addison-Wesley, 1999.

[Countries04] GeoHive. "Largest agglomerations in the world." *http://www.xist.org/charts/city_agg1950_2015.php*, attributes all estimates and projections to the Population Division of the United Nations.

[Dog04] The Westminster Kennel Club. "Best in Show Winners." *http://www.westminsterkennelclub.org/history/biswinners.html*

[Horse04] Dulay, Cindy Pierson. "Historical data and results for the Triple Crown races." *http://www.horse-races.net/library*

[Horstmann04] Horstmann, Cay. "Safe STL." *http://www.horstmann.com/safestl.html*

[ISO98] ISO. *Information Technology—Programming Language—C++*. Document Number ISO/IEC 14882-1998. ISO/IEC, 1998.

[Jarvi02] Jarvi, Jaakko. *Proposal for adding tuple types into the standard library*. 2002. Available at *http://www.open-std.org/jtc1/sc22/wg21/docs/papers/2002/n1403.pdf*

[Josuttis99] Josuttis, Nicolai M. *The C++ Standard Library*. Addison-Wesley, 1999.

[LoRusso97] Lo Russo, Graziano. "Intervista a Alexander Stepanov." *Computer Programming*. No. 60, July/August 1997. Available in English at *http://www.stlport.org/resources/StepanovUSA.html*

[Meyers01] Meyers, Scott. *Effective STL*. Addison-Wesley, 2001.

[Musser01] Musser, David R., Derge, Gillmer J., and Saini, Atul. *STL Tutorial and Reference Guide.* 2nd ed. Addison-Wesley, 2001.

[Press02] Press, William H. et al., eds. *Numerical Recipes in C++: The Art of Scientific Computing.* 2nd ed. Cambridge University Press, 2002.

[Soccer04] SoccerAge.com. "Beckham Tops List of Highest Paid Players." *http://www.soccerage.com/en/13/u7713.html*

[Stevens95] Stevens, Al. "Al Stevens Interviews Alex Stepanov." *Dr. Dobb's Journal.* March 1995.

[STLport04] STLport.org. *http://www.stlport.org*

[Stroustrup94] Stroustrup, Bjarne. *The Design and Evolution of C++.* Addison-Wesley, 1994.

[Stroustrup97] Stroustrup, Bjarne. *The C++ Programming Language.* 3rd ed. Addison-Wesley, 1997.

Bibliography

BOOKS

The C++ Standard Library and the STL

Austern, Matthew. *Generic Programming and the STL*. Addison-Wesley, 1999.

Breymann, Ulrich. *Designing Components with the C++ STL*. Revised edition. Addison-Wesley, 2000.

Cline, Marshall, Lomow, Greg A., and Girou, Mike. *C++ FAQS*. 2nd ed. Addison-Wesley, 1999.

ISO. *Information Technology—Programming Language—C++*. Document Number ISO/IEC 14882-1998. ISO/IEC, 1998.

Josuttis, Nicolai M. *The C++ Standard Library*. Addison-Wesley, 1999.

Langer, Angelika, and Kreft, Klaus. *Standard C++ IOStreams and Locales*. Addison-Wesley Longman, 2000.

Meyers, Scott. *Effective STL*. Addison-Wesley, 2001.

Musser, David R., Derge, Gillmer J. and Saini, Atul. *STL Tutorial and Reference Guide*. 2nd ed. Addison-Wesley, 2001.

Robson, Robert. *Using the STL*. 2nd ed. Springer-Verlag, 2000.

Schildt, Herbert. *STL Programming from the Ground Up*. Osborne/McGraw Hill, 1999.

General C++

Alexandrescu, Andrei. *Modern C++ Design: Generic Programming and Design Patterns Applied*. Addison-Wesley, 2001.

Meyers, Scott. *Effective C++*. Addison-Wesley, 1992.

Meyers, Scott. *More Effective C++*. Addison-Wesley, 1996.

Stroustrup, Bjarne. *The C++ Programming Language*. 3rd ed. Addison-Wesley, 1997.

Stroustrup, Bjarne. *The Design and Evolution of C++*. Addison-Wesley, 1994.

Sutter, Herb. *Exceptional C++*. Addison-Wesley, 2000.

Vandevoorde, David, and Josuttis, Nicolai. *C++ Templates: The Complete Guide*. Addison-Wesley, 2003.

MAGAZINE ARTICLES

Ablavsky, Vitaly, Stevens, Mark R., and Pollak, Joshua B. "Data-Structure-Independent Algorithms for Image Processing." *C/C++ Users Journal*. November 2003.

Batov, Vladimir. "The Same STL Algorithms—Only Better." *C/C++ Users Journal*. September 2003.

Carrato, Michael. "Space Efficient Sets and Maps." *C/C++ Users Journal*. July 2003.

Dibling, John. "Extending the STL." *C/C++ Users Journal*. February 2005.

Hyslop, Jim, and Sutter, Herb. "Im-Paired Programming." *C/C++ Users Journal*. March 2004.

Lo Russo, Graziano. "Intervista a Alexander Stepanov," *Computer Programming*. No. 60, July/August 1997. Available in English at *http://www.stlport.org/resources/StepanovUSA.html*

McCallum, Ethan. "Custom Containers & Iterators for STL-Friendly Code." *C/C++ Users Journal*. March 2005.

Ruud, Brian. "Building a Mutable Set." *C/C++ Users Journal*. June 2003.

Smith, Mark L. "An STL-based N-way Set." *C/C++ Users Journal*. March 2000.

Sobczak, Maciej. "STL Sequences & the View Concept." *C/C++ Users Journal*. April 2004.

Stevens, Al. "Al Stevens Interviews Alex Stepanov." *Dr. Dobb's Journal*. March 1995.

Sutter, Herb, and Hyslop, Jim. "Typedefs and Iterators: If You've Got 'Em, Use 'Em." *C/C++ Users Journal*. September 2004.

Sutter, Herb, and Hyslop, Jim. "Order, Order." *C/C++ Users Journal*. February 2005.

Taglienti, Claudio. "STL Member Function Adaptors." *C/C++ Users Journal*. January 2004.

Wilson, Matthew. "Adapting Win32 Enumeration APIs to STL Iterator Concepts." *Windows::Developer Magazine*. March 2003.

Zolman, Leor. "Thinking in STL: You Know It Don't Come Easy." *C/C++ Users Journal.* January 2003.

WEB SITES

ANSI. "ANSI Electronic Standard Store." *http://webstore.ansi.org/ansidoc-store/default.asp*

Barry, Chris. "Still Trying to Learn the STL." *http://echellon.hybd.net/issues/5/articles/stl/part1.html*

Boost.org. "Welcome to Boost.org." *http://www.boost.org/*

Clarke, Allan. "C++ Tips: STL." *http://cpptips.hyperformix.com/Stl.html*

DevX.com. "DevX Tip Bank - STL." *http://www.devx.com/tips/vtBrowser/20528?node=1714*

Dinkumware. "Dinkum C++ Library." *http://www.dinkumware.com/manuals/reader.aspx?lib=cpp*

Doederlein, Osvaldo Pinali . "Crash Course on STL." *http://www.geocities.com/ResearchTriangle/Node/2005/stl.htm*

Forschungszentrum Julich. "WWW C++ Information." *http://www.fz-juelich.de/zam/cxx/extern.html*

Horstmann, Cay. "Safe STL." *http://www.horstmann.com/safestl.html*

Kirman, Jak. "A Modest STL Tutorial." *http://www.cs.brown.edu/people/jak/programming/stl-tutorial/tutorial.html*

Kremer, Rob. "Standard Template Library Overview." *http://pages.cpsc.ucalgary.ca/~kremer/STL/monitor/index.html*

Langer, Angelika. "Angelika Langer's Home Page." *http://www.langer.camelot.de/Welcome.html*

Microsoft. "The Standard C++ Library." *http://msdn.microsoft.com/library/default.asp?url=/library/en-us/vclang98/HTML/INDEX.asp*

Moreno, Carlos. "An Introduction to the Standard Template Library (STL)." *http://www.mochima.com/tutorials/STL.html*

Musser, David. "STL Tutorial Resources at Rensselaer."*http://www.cs.rpi.edu/~musser/stl-book/*

Myers, Nathan. "(Draft) Standard C++ and C++ Library Architecture." *http://www.cantrip.org/cpp.html*

Open Standards. "C++ Standards Committee Papers." *http://www.open-std.org/jtc1/sc22/wg21/docs/papers/*

Ottewell, Phil. "Phil Ottewell's STL Tutorial." *http://www.yrl.co.uk/phil/stl/stl.htmlx*

Rogue Wave Software. "Standard C++ Library User Guide." *http://www.ccd.bnl.gov/bcf/cluster/pgi/pgC++_lib/stdlibug/ug1.htm*

SGI. "Standard Template Library Programmer's Guide." *http://www.sgi.com/
tech/stl/index.html*

STLsoft. "STLsoft Home." *www.stlsoft.org*

Stroustrup, Bjarne. "Welcome to Bjarne Stroustrup's homepage!" *http://www.
research.att.com/~bs/homepage.html*

STLport.org. "Welcome! STLport." *http://www.stlport.org*

Weidl, Johannes. "The Standard Template Library Tutorial." *http://www.in-
fosys.tuwien.ac.at/Research/Component/tutorial/*

Wiki Wiki Web. "STL sucks." *http://c2.com/cgi/wiki?StlSucks*

Zolman, Leor. "STLFlit: An STL Error Message Decryptor for C++."
http://www.bdsoft.com/tools/stlfilt.html

INTERNET USENET GROUPS

alt.comp.lang.learn.c-c++
comp.lang.c++
comp.lang.c++.moderated
comp.std.c++

Index

A

accessing memory, see memory
accumulate algorithm, 77, 423–424, 515
activate_minicam_port, 15–16
Ada Generic Library, 29
adaptors
    container, 56–58
    overview, 28, 241
adding vectors, 64
address operator (&), 148
adjacent_difference algorithm, 77, 398–402, 515
adjacent_find algorithm, 72
advance function, 182
algorithms, 70–77, 513–522
    binary, 77
    class member functions in, 271–276
    described, 70–71
    errors, avoiding, 79
    freezing arguments to function objects, 66–67, 283–286
    functions in, 62–63, 264–276
    header support, 10, 71
    heap, 76
    in-place vs. copying versions, 70–71
    member function alternatives to, 263
    modifying, 71, 73
    multipass, 35
    mutating, 10, 71, 73–74
    nonmodifying, 10, 71, 72
    numeric, 71, 76–77
    overview, 4, 27–28
    pointers to class member functions, 276–283
    for searching, 10, 72, 74–76
    single-pass, 33
    for sorting, 10, 71, 74–76
    using most specific, 261–263
allocators, 28
amicable pair, 264–270
angles between vectors, 411–415

appending
    characters to strings, 343–345
    containers, 104–106
appliances, 207–218
argument-dependent lookup, 22
arguments
    function, 63
    in headers, 5, 6
arithmetic operations
    on images, 483–488
    predefined functions, 63–64
    See also numerical processing
arrays
    C-style, from vectors, 147–149
    C-style and beginning/ending iterators, 90–93, 95, 96
    header support, 11
    indexing, 128–131
assert header, 7
assert macro, 7
assign function, 101, 104
assigning container elements, 87–90
assignment operators, 87, 136–140
associative containers
    described, 53–56
    hash maps, 187
    header support, 9
    initialize with specified values, 189–193, 196
    maps, 55, 85–87, 207–218, 222–233
    maps/multimaps as dictionaries, 193–197
    member functions, 263
    multimaps, 55–56, 85–87, 207–218, 222–233
    multisets, 54, 85–87, 197–207, 218–222, 233–239
    sets, 54, 85–87, 197–207, 218–222, 233–239
    sorting, 187–189
at function, 144–145
auction items, 153–156
Austern, Matthew, 29, 364, 513
averages

image processing, 506–507
numerical processing, 423–424

B

back function, 140, 156, 162
back inserters, 45–46, 192–193, 264–270
base for numbers, see numerical processing
basketball players, 164–169
beginning iterators, 37, 90–93, 95, 96
bibliography, 529–532
bidirectional iterators, 32, 35
billionaires, 256–260
binary algorithms, 75, 77
binary function objects, 66–67, 283–286
binary images, 491–493
binary_function, 70
binders, 66–67, 271–276, 283–286
bitset header, 9, 58
bitsets, 58–59, 252–256, 437–440
blocks, creating, 473–474
blurring images, 506–507
Boehm, Hans, 29
boolalpha, 111
Booleans
    bitsets, 252–256
    comparison of, 253
    deque of, 156–160
    vector of, 64, 149–151
Boost libraries, 458, 523
buffers
    I/O header support, 12
    priority queues, 248–252
    queues, 57, 244–248

C

"c" prefix for headers, 5, 24
C++ language
    extensible languages, 60
    support, overview, 4, 5–6
C++ Standard (ISO98), 71, 513
C++ Standard Library
    components of, 3

exception handling, 18–20, 78
headers, 4–5
introduction and history, 1–3
overview, 3–12
See also Standard Template Library (STL)
C++ Standard Library, The (Josuttie), 513
calculations, see numerical processing
call operators, 60–62
car models, 189–193
card game, 140–144
carwash, 244–248
case-insensitive comparisons
    of strings, 359–364
    of substrings, 364–369
case-sensitive comparisons
    of strings, 353–355
    of substrings, 355–358
catch blocks, 15–17
CD-ROM (included with book), 523–525
changing, see modifying
characters, header support, 8, 12
clashes, name, 21
classes
    with call operator, 61
    image class, 463–472
clipping
    described, 489
    high/low, 489–491
    making binary images, 491–493
    making negatives, 493–495
club membership, 444–446
code tips, see tips
collisions, name, 21
combining images, 484–486
commit-or-rollback action, 78, 86
comparing
    case-insensitive comparison of strings, 359–364
    case-insensitive comparison of substrings, 364–369
    case-sensitive comparison of strings, 353–355
    case-sensitive comparison of substrings, 355–358
    containers for equality, 114–116
    dictionary ordering (lexicographical comparison), 72, 111–113, 353, 359–364
comparison functions, 64–65
comparison operators, 112, 189, 215, 417–419
complement, logical, 67

complex header, 11
complex numbers, 394–398
concatenating strings, 343–345
consecutive, evenly spaced numbers, 402–405
constructors, 90, 136–140
containers, 49–60
    adapters, 56–58, 241
    appending, 104–106
    associative containers, 9, 53–56
    bitsets, 9, 58–59, 252–256
    changes in elements, 398–402
    changing types, 96–98
    choosing correct, 85–87
    constructing, from another, 96–98
    constructing from standard input, 98–100
    copying if condition is met, 327–330
    C-style arrays, 90–93, 95, 96, 129
    deques as, 52
    described, 49
    displaying elements of, 82–85
    displaying on standard output, 120–122
    elements, requirements on, 87–88
    equal, 114–116
    errors, avoiding, 79
    exchanging, 106–109
    filled with identical elements, 93–94
    filled with specified elements, 94–96, 100–102
    header support, 9
    heterogeneous, 59
    homogeneous, 49
    invariants, 78
    lexicographical comparison, 111–113, 353, 359–364
    lists as, 51–52
    maximum size, 109–111
    numerical processing, see numerical processing
    operating on each element of, 330–337
    overview, 4, 27–28
    pair, 59–60
    performing arithmetic on, 391–394
    priority queues, 57–58, 248–252
    queues, 57, 244–248
    replacing with contents from another, 102–104
    reverse access, 116–120
    sequence, see sequence containers

    size of, 49, 109–111
    stacks, 14–15, 56, 140–144, 241–244
    standard, described, 49
    vectors as, 50–51
    See also iterator adaptors; iterators; specific containers
contrast, 498
contrast stretch, 498–500
convolutions, 500–505
copying
    algorithms capable of, 70–71
    copy algorithm, 43, 47, 49, 73, 93, 515
    copyable elements, 87
    if condition is met, 327–330
    remove_copy algorithm, 45, 73
    replace_copy algorithm, 45, 73
    sorting without, 322–327
    strings and substrings, 341–343
core languages, 18
count algorithms, 72, 515
creating container elements, 88–90
credit card numbers, 349–351
criteria for sorting, see sorting
cstdef header, 5
C-strings, 7–8
customers and sales contacts, 156–160

D

data types, 513–514
date functions, 6, 7
decimal numbers, 440–442
decrement (- -) operator and iterations, 39
delimiters, 386–390
deque header, 9
deques
    alternative to vector of Booleans, 156–160
    choosing as container, 85–87
    converting between iterators and indexes, 131–133
    described, 52, 153
    features of, 253
    filled from standard input, 98–100
    indexing, 128–131
    operations at front, 153–156
    sorting on one of many fields, 310–314
    sorting without copying, 322–327
dereferencing iterators, 32, 79
destroyable elements, 88
destroying container elements, 88–90
destructors, 90, 136–140

diagnostics
    header support, 6–7
    overview, 4
dictionaries
    lexicographical comparison, 72, 111–113, 353, 359–364
    maps/multimaps as, 188, 193–197
differences between values, 398–402
digit separators, displaying, 449–452
digital images, 461. See also image processing
divides function, 64
DNA analysis, 330–337
dog breed and weights, 128–131
dog show winners, 197–207
domain_error, 19–20
duplicates, removing, 182–185
duplicating, see copying

E
edge enhancement for images, 508–512
Effective STL, 364
elements
    appending containers, 104–106
    assignable, 87
    copyable, 87
    creating, assigning, and destroying, 88–90
    destroyable, 88
    displaying container, 82–85
    erasing matching, 297–302
    exchanging containers, 106–109
    finding/erasing matching, 287–294
    identical, filling container with, 93–94
    matching, 287–302
    modifying or removing, in sets/multisets, 218–222
    operating on each, 330–337
    removing from sequence containers, 294–302
    requirements on container, 87–88
    reserve space for, 123–125
    specified, filling container with, 94–96, 100–102
    storing contents of one container in another, 102–104
    See also specific containers
empty function, 110–111
empty ranges, 36
end iterators, 37, 90–93, 95, 96, 216
enhancements, image, 488–489
equal algorithm, 72, 116, 515
equal containers, 114–116

equal_range algorithm, 75, 427–430
equal_range function, 197, 205, 216, 231
equal_to function, 65
equality operator (= =), 88, 115
equality vs. equivalence, 188–189
equivalence vs. equality, 188–189
erase function, 90, 182, 231–233, 287
error handling
    exception handling, 13–18
    overview, 12–13, 77–78
    tips for avoiding errors, 78–79
    See also exception handling
error messages, 373–376
error numbers, header support, 7
errors, logic vs. runtime, 19, 78
examples, see tips
exception class, 18
exception handling
    C++ Standard Library, guarantee for, 78
    catch blocks, 15–17
    handler, described, 15
    header, 5, 6
    hierarchy of exceptions, 19
    out_of_range, 19–20, 145–147
    slicing, 17
    stack unwinding, 14–15
    in standard library, 18–20
    system, overview, 13–18
    throwing exceptions, 14
    try blocks, 15–17
    unexpected calls, 18
    used by core languages, 18
exception specifications, 17–18
exceptions
    exception header, 5, 6
    hierarchy of, 19
    stdexcept header, 7
    See also exception handling
exit routines, 6
experiments and data points, 322–327

F
facets, 451
factorials, 407–410
FIFO (first-in, first-out) order, 244–248
filenames and headers, 5, 24
files, accessing data, 452–455
fill algorithms, 73, 516
find algorithms
    described, 72, 187, 516
    searching sets/multisets, 197–218

strip whitespace from strings, 378–382
find function, 217, 222, 231, 232, 345–349
first-in, first-out (FIFO) order, 244–248
fixed manipulator, 446–449
flip function, 151
float header, 5, 6
floating-point numbers, 446–449
Fomitchev, Boris, 457
for_each algorithm
    alternatives to, 261–263
    compared to transform algorithm, 332
    computing statistics of data, 434–437
    described, 62, 72, 73, 516
    operating on each element of containers, 330–337
for-loop, 233
formatted strings
    reading, 370–372
    writing, 373–376
forward iterators, 32, 34–35
frames, drawing in images, 504–505
front function, 154, 162
front inserters, 45–46
function object, 63
functional header, 7
function-like object, 63
functions
    in algorithms, 264–270
    alternatives to algorithms, 263
    class member, in algorithms, 271–276
    evaluating mathematical functions, 407–410
    freezing arguments to function objects, 66–67, 283–286
    polymorphism, 276–283
    pure virtual, 282
functors
    adapting functions, 68
    arithmetic operations, 63–64
    binders, 66–67
    call operators, 60–62
    comparison functions, 64–65
    function arguments, 63
    logic operations, 65–66
    negators, 66–67
    overview, 28, 60
    predefined function objects, 63–70
    predicates, 67

using functions in algorithms, 62–63, 264–270

G

general inserter, 45–46
generate algorithms, 73, 405–407, 516
generic programming, 27
Generic Programming and the STL (Austern), 513
global namespace, 22, 24
grades of students, 218–222, 427–434
graduating students, 161–164
graphical user interfaces (GUIs), 184–185
gray-level images, 462
greater function, 65
greater_equal function, 65
GUIs (graphical user interfaces), 184–185

H

.h filename extension, 5, 24
half-open ranges, 36
hash maps, 187
headers
    language support, 4–5
    naming conventions, 5, 24
heap algorithms, 76
hexadecimal I/O, 442–444
high/low clipping, 489–491
horse races, 233–239
Horstmann, Cay, 78
hyper-spectral images, 462

I

if tests and algorithms, 70–71
image processing
    averaging, 506–507
    binary images, 491–493
    blocks, creating, 473–474
    blurring, 506–507
    clipping, 489–495
    combining images, 484–486
    constants, adding to images, 496–498
    contrast, 498
    contrast stretch, 498–500
    convolutions, 500–505
    creating images, 472–476
    digital images, 461
    drawing frames in images, 504–505
    edge enhancement, 508–512
    enhancements, 488–489
    expanding images, 480–483

gray-level images, 462
high/low clipping, 489–491
hyper-spectral images, 462
image arithmetic, 483–488
image class, 463–472
index formula, 463–464
kernel, 501
look-up tables (LUTs), 495–500
masks, 501
negative images, 493–495
neighborhood operations, 500
overview, 461–462
pixels, 462
sharpening, 507–508
shrinking images, 477–480
subtraction of images, 487–488
vertical bars, creating, 474–476
impedance, 394–398
implementation properties, headers, 5, 6
includes algorithm, 75
income of soccer players, 271–276
increment (++) operator and iterators, 31, 32, 38
indexes
    converting between iterators and, 131–133
    index formula for images, 463–464
    for maps, 187–188
    for multimaps, 231
    vectors, 128–131, 144–147
inequality operator (!=), 116
information, typeinfo header, 5, 6
inner_product algorithm, 77, 411–415, 516–517
inplace_merge algorithm, 75
input iterators, 32, 33. See also I/O (input/output)
input stream iterators
    constructing containers from standard input, 98–100
    data file access, 452–455
    described, 48–49
    extracting words delimited by whitespace, 384–386
insert containers, 104–106
insert iterators
    back inserters, 45–46
    front inserters, 45–46
    general inserter, 45–46
    prepending elements, 45–46
inserter, see insert iterators
inspection of car parts, 302–310
installation directions, 524–525
integers and leading zeroes, 444–446
international support, 8

Internet groups, 532
invalid iterators, 134–136
invalid_argument, 19–20
invariants, 78
I/O (input/output)
    in binary format, 437–440. See also bitsets
    header support, 11–12
    in hexadecimal format, 442–444
    in octal format, 440–442
    overview, 4
iostream header, 84
istream_iterator, 48–49, 98–100, 384–386, 452–455
istringstream, 370–372, 384–386
iter_swap algorithm, 77
iterator adaptors, 38–49
    insert iterators, 44–46
    reverse iterators, 38–44
    stream iterators, 43, 47–49
    See also iterators
iterator header, 38
iterators, 30–38
    beginning/end, 37, 90–93, 95, 96
    bidirectional, 32, 35
    container, 37–38
    converting between indexes and, 131–133
    C-style arrays, 90–93, 95, 96
    dereferencing, 32, 79
    described, 30
    forward, 32, 34–35
    header support, 9–10
    incrementing (++), 31, 32, 38
    input, 32, 33
    invalid, 131, 134–136
    for multipass algorithms, 35
    output, 32, 33–34
    overview, 4, 27–28
    pointers vs., 30
    random access, 32, 35–36
    ranges for, 36–38
    regular, from reverse, 222–233
    from regular to reverse, 42–43
    from reverse to regular, 43–44
    searching maps/multimaps, 207–218
    searching sets/multisets, 205–206
    sequences, moving through, 30–31
    for single-pass algorithms, 33
    types of, 30–33
    See also iterator adaptors

J

Josuttis, Nicolai, 513
judging competitions, 169–176

jumps, setting, 5, 6

K

kernel and images, 501
keys, 55, 207–218, 222–233
Koenig, Andrew, 29
Koenig lookups, 22

L

lambda abstraction library, 459–460
Laplacian kernel, 512
last-in, first-out order (LIFO), 56, 140, 242
"Law of the Big Three, The", 88
Lee, Meng, 29
length function, 109, 351–353
length_error, 19–20
less function, 65
less_equal function, 65
lexicographical_compare algorithm
    comparing containers, 111–113
    comparing strings, 353, 359–364
    described, 72, 517
libraries, 1, 457–460. See also C++
    Standard Library
LIFO (last-in, first-out) order, 56, 140, 242
lighting control, 252–256
limits header, 5, 6
list header, 9
lists
    appending containers, 104–106
    assigning front and back, 161–164, 175
    choosing as container, 85–87
    constructing lists/vectors from, 96–98
    described, 51–52, 161
    exchanging containers, 106–109
    filled with specified elements, 94–96
    iterations through, 31
    member functions, 263
    merging, 176–182
    nodes, 51
    removing duplicates, 182–185
    size information, 109–111
    sorting, 164–169, 176, 181
    splice, 169–176
    storing contents in another container, 102–104
locales, 4, 8, 451
logic errors, 19, 78
logic operations, 65–67
logical algorithms, 160
look-up tables (LUTs)

adding constants, 496–498
    contrast stretch, 498–500
    described, 495–496
lookups
    argument-dependent, 22
    Koenig lookups, 22
loops
    for-loop, 233
    ranges, 36–38
    searching maps/multimaps, 207–218
    searching sets/multisets, 205
lower_bound algorithm, 75, 187
lowercase/uppercase conversion, 382–384

M

macros, 6
magazine articles, 530–531
make_heap algorithm, 76
make_pair function
    described, 59–60
    mentioned, 164, 185, 193, 197
    using for same or different data types, 256–260
manipulators, 12
map header, 9
maps
    choosing as container, 85–87
    described, 55
    as dictionaries, 193–197
    member functions, 263
    mode value, 427–430
    modifying or removing elements, 222–233
    searching, 207–218
    See also associative containers
masks and images, 501
math header, 11
matrix, sparse, 188
max algorithm, 77, 417–419, 517
max_element algorithm, 72, 131, 415–417
maximum
    in containers, 415–417
    of data types, 419–422
    size of containers, 109–111
    using custom criterion, 417–419
means, computing, 423–424, 434–437
median, computing, 424–427
mem_fun function, 68
mem_fun_ref function, 68–69, 271–276
memory
    checked/unchecked vector access, 144–147

deques, accessing, 52
    lists, accessing, 51–52
    remove excess, 125–128
    reserve space for elements, 123–125
    vectors, accessing, 50–51
    See also containers
memory management
    memory header, 7
    new header, 5, 6
merge algorithm, 75, 233–239, 518
merging
    lists, 176–182
    sets/multisets, 233–239
Meyers, Scott, 100, 364
min algorithm, 77, 417–419, 518
min_element algorithm, 72, 415–417, 518–519
minicam example, 14–16
minimum
    in containers, 415–417
    of data types, 419–422
    using custom criterion, 417–419
minus function, 64
mismatch algorithm, 72, 359–364, 518
modes, computing, 427–430
modifying
    algorithms, 71
    container types, 96–98
    elements in maps/multimaps, 222–233
    elements in sets/multisets, 218–222
modifying algorithms, 73
modulus function, 64
multimaps
    choosing as container, 85–87
    described, 55–56
    as dictionaries, 193–197
    member functions, 263
    modifying or removing elements, 222–233
    searching, 207–218
    See also associative containers
multiplies function, 64
multisets
    choosing as container, 85–87
    described, 54
    member functions, 263
    modifying or removing elements, 218–222
    searching, 197–207
    sorted range algorithms, 233–239
    See also associative containers
Musser, Dave, 29
mutating algorithms, 10, 71, 73–74

N

name collision/clash, 21
names and ages, 131–133
namespace, 5, 21–25
   argument-dependent lookup, 22
   global, 22, 24
   header naming conventions, 5, 24
   Koenig lookups, 22
   qualifying members, 21–22
   scope operator (::), 21, 22
   std namespace, 24–25
   using-declaration, 23–24
   using-directive, 24
NDEBUG macro, 145–147
negate function, 64
negative images, 493–495
negators, 66–67
neighborhood operations, 500
new header, 5, 6
next_permutation algorithm, 74
nonmodifying algorithms, 10, 71, 72
norm of vectors, 417–419
noshowbase manipulator, 440–442
noshowpoint manipulator, 446–449
not_equal_to function, 65
not1, not2 (function objects), 66–67
nouppercase manipulator, 442–444
nth_element algorithm, 74, 424–427,
   430–434, 519
numerical processing
   arithmetic operations, 63–64
   complex numbers, 394–398
   consecutive, evenly spaced numbers, 402–405
   data file access, 452–455
   differences between values,
   398–402
   digit separators, displaying,
   449–452
   dot product of vectors, 411–415
   evaluating mathematical functions, 407–410
   header support, 10–11
   input/output in binary format,
   437–440
   input/output in hexadecimal
   format, 442–444
   input/output in octal format,
   440–442
   integers and leading zeroes,
   444–446
   mean (average) value, 423–424,
   434–437
   median value, 424–427

minimum/maximum in containers, 415–417
minimum/maximum of data
   types, 419–422
minimum/maximum using custom criterion, 417–419
mode value, 427–430
overview, 4, 391
percentiles, 430–434
performing arithmetic on containers, 391–394
precision of floating-point numbers, 446–449
random number sequence,
   405–407
statistics of data, 434–437
variance, 434–437

O

octal I/O, 440–442
operators
   arithmetic, 63–64
   comparison, 112
   logic, 65–67
   See also functors
ostream_iterator, 47–48, 120–122,
   452–455
ostringstream, 373–376
out_of_range, 19–20, 145–147
outliers, 297–302
output iterators, 32, 33–34
output stream iterators
   data file access, 452–455
   described, 47–48
   displaying container on standard
   output, 120–122
output/input, see I/O (input/output)
overflow_error, 19–20

P

pair data structure
   described, 28
   make_pair function, 59–60
   using for same or different data
   types, 256–260
partial_sort algorithms, 74, 430–434,
   519
partial_sum algorithm, 77, 149,
   402–405, 519
partitioning, 74
percent changes, 398–402
percentiles, 430–434
percents, 391–394, 398–402
perfect numbers, 264–270

pixels, 419–422, 462
plus function, 64
pointers
   to class member functions in
   algorithms, 276–283
   vs. iterators, 30
pollution, global-namespace, 24
polymorphism, 276–283
pop_back function, 140, 144, 162, 176
pop_front function, 154, 162, 164, 176
pop_heap algorithm, 76
population rankings, 222–233
predefined function objects, 63–70,
   264
predicates, 67
prepended elements and front inserters, 45–46
prev_permutation algorithm, 74
prices, sorting, 310–314
prices, stock, 398–402
prime numbers, 294–302
print function, 169
priority queues, 57–58, 248–252
programming
   generic, 27
   tips, see tips
ptr_fun function, 67–68, 206, 264–270
publications, 287–294
push_back function, 136, 139, 141,
   162, 185
push_front function, 144, 154, 156,
   162
push_heap algorithm, 76

Q

qualifying namespace members, 21–22
queue header, 9, 57, 58
queues
   as containers, 57
   FIFO and buffering, 244–248
   priority queues, 57–58, 248–252

R

random access
   of containers, 49–60
   iterators, 32, 35–36
random number sequence, 405–407
random_shuffle algorithm, 74
ranges, 36–38
   empty, 36
   equal_range algorithm, 75, 197
   errors, avoiding, 79
   half-open, 36
   out_of_range, 19–20, 145–147

partitioning, 74
range_error, 19–20
sorted range algorithms, 75–76, 233–239
swap_ranges, 106–109
validity of, 37
rational numbers, 60
reading formatted strings, 370–372
references, 527–528
remove algorithms, 45, 73, 294–302, 327–330, 519–520
removing
    duplicates from lists, 182–185
    elements from priority queue, 248–252
    elements from sequence containers, 294–302
    elements in maps/multimaps, 222–233
    elements in sets/multisets, 218–222
    excess memory from vectors, 125–128
replace algorithms, 45, 73, 520
replacing string characters with given characters, 349–351
reserve memory, 123–125
resetiosflags manipulator, 440–442
resistor stock, 314–322
resize function, 139
reverse access to containers, 116–120
reverse algorithms, 74, 116, 520
reverse iterators, 38–44, 117
    from, to regular, 43–44, 222–233
    from regular iterators to, 42–43
reversing strings, 351–353
rotate algorithms, 74
runtime errors, 19, 78
runtime support headers, 5, 6

S
safe STL, 78
salaries, 424–427
salespeople and districts, 176–182
scientific manipulator, 446–449
scope operator (::), 21, 22
searching
    algorithms for, 10, 72, 74–76
    errors, avoiding, 79
    maps/multimaps, 207–218
    sequence containers, 287–294
    sets/multisets, 197–207
    speed of, 217–218
security messages, 248–252
separators
    numerical processing, 449–452

text processing, 386–390
sequence containers
    appending, 104–106
    described, 49–52
    differences between values, 398–402
    elements, requirement on, 88
    erasing all matching elements, 297–302
    filled from standard input, 98–100
    filled with identical elements, 93–94
    finding/erasing first or last matching elements, 287–294
    header support, 9
    performing arithmetic on, 391–394
    removing elements from, 294–302
    sorting before set operations, 302–310
    sorting with multiple criteria, 314–322
sequences and iterators, 30–31
set algorithms, 75–76, 233–239, 302–310, 520–521
set header, 9
setfill manipulator, 444–446
setjmp header, 5, 6
setprecision manipulator, 446–449
sets
    choosing as container, 85–87
    described, 54
    member functions, 263
    modifying or removing elements, 218–222
    searching, 197–207
    sorted range algorithms, 233–239
    See also associative containers
setw manipulator, 444–446
shapes, 276–283
sharpening images, 507–508
ships and cargo, 144–147
shots and pets, 149–151
showbase manipulator, 440–444
showpoint manipulator, 446–449
shrinking images, 477–480
signal header, 5, 6
size of containers, 49, 109–111
sizeof operator, 93
slicing, 17
sort algorithm, 75, 427–434, 521
sorting
    accessing containers in reverse, 116–120
    algorithms for, 10, 71, 74–76, 233–239

associative containers, 187–189
    for computing modes, 427–430
    for computing percentiles, 430–434
    lists, 164–169, 176, 181
    with multiple criteria, 314–322
    on one of many fields, 310–314
    sequence containers before set operations, 302–310
    sorted range algorithms and sets/multisets, 233–239
    without copying, 322–327
sparse matrix, 188
splicing lists, 169–176
stable_partition algorithm, 75
stable_sort algorithm, 75
stack header, 9, 56
stacks
    as containers, 56
    fast access at back of vectors, 140–144
    unwinding, 14–15
    using, 241–244
Standard C Library, 2, 3
standard containers, 49. See also containers
standard libraries, 1. See also C++ Standard Library
Standard Template Library (STL)
    components of, 27–28
    free, portable versions, 457–458
    history of, 29–30
    overview, 3–4
start and termination header, 5, 6
statistics, see numerical processing
std namespace, 24–25
stdarg header, 5, 6
stddef header, 6
stdlib header, 5, 6, 8, 11, 12
Stepanov, Alexander, 27, 29
STL (Standard Template Library), see Standard Template Library (STL)
STL port, 457–458
stream iterators
    input stream iterators, 48–49, 98–100, 384–386, 452–455
    output stream iterators, 47–48, 120–122, 452–455
    using copy, 43, 47, 49, 120–122, 452–455
streams
    input string streams, 384–386
    I/O header support, 12
    reading formatted strings, 370–372
    writing formatted strings, 373–376
strings

appending characters, 343–345
appending containers, 104–106
C++ Standard Library equivalents of C-string functions, 340–341
case-insensitive comparison of, 359–364
case-sensitive comparison of, 353–355
concatenating, 343–345
container size information, 109–111
converting between iterators and indexes, 131–133
copying strings and substrings, 341–343
C-style string from C++, 376–378
delimiters, 386–390
displaying container on standard output, 120–122
exchanging containers, 106–109
extract words delimited by whitespace, 384–386
filling container from standard input, 98–100
filling container with identical values, 93–94
filling container with specified values, 94–96, 100–102
header support, 7–8
length of, 351–353
overview, 4, 339–340
reading formatted, 370–372
replacing characters with given character, 349–351
reverse, 351–353
searching, 345–349
strip whitespace, 378–382
tokenizing text, 384–390
uppercase/lowercase conversion, 382–384
writing formatted, 373–376
strip whitespace in strings, 378–382
Stroustrup, Bjarne, 24, 29
substrings
    case-insensitive comparison of, 364–369
    case-sensitive comparison of, 355–358
    concatenating, 341–343
    copying, 341–343
    See also strings
subtraction of images, 487–488
sum of proper divisors, 264–270
swap_ranges algorithm, 106–109, 522
swapping
    containers, 77, 106–109
    iter_swap, 77
    vectors, 125–128, 134
system requirements, 524

T
take_pictures, 15–16
teams, number of possible, 407–410
temporary variable, unnamed, 48, 62, 128
text processing, see strings
throwing exceptions, 14
time header, 5, 6, 7
tips
    for avoiding STL errors, 78–79
    contributing, 460

displaying elements of containers, 82–85
overview, 81–82
Tip 0, 82–85
Tip 1, 85–87
Tip 2, 87–90
Tip 3, 90–93
Tip 4, 93–94
Tip 5, 94–96
Tip 6, 96–98
Tip 7, 98–100
Tip 8, 100–102
Tip 9, 102–104
Tip 10, 104–106
Tip 11, 106–109
Tip 12, 109–111
Tip 13, 111–113
Tip 14, 114–116
Tip 15, 116–120
Tip 16, 120–122
Tip 17, 123–125
Tip 18, 125–128
Tip 19, 128–131
Tip 20, 131–133
Tip 21, 134–136
Tip 22, 136–140
Tip 23, 140–144
Tip 24, 144–147
Tip 25, 147–149
Tip 26, 149–151
Tip 27, 153–156
Tip 28, 156–160
Tip 29, 161–164
Tip 30, 164–169
Tip 31, 169–176
Tip 32, 176–182
Tip 33, 182–185
Tip 34, 189–193
Tip 35, 193–197
Tip 36, 197–207
Tip 37, 197–207
Tip 38, 218–222
Tip 39, 222–233
Tip 40, 233–239
Tip 41, 241–244
Tip 42, 244–248
Tip 43, 248–252
Tip 44, 252–256
Tip 45, 256–260
Tip 46, 261–263
Tip 47, 264–270
Tip 48, 271–276
Tip 49, 276–283
Tip 50, 283–286
Tip 51, 287–294
Tip 52, 294–302
Tip 53, 297–302

Tip 54, 302–310
Tip 55, 310–314
Tip 56, 314–322
Tip 57, 322–327
Tip 58, 327–330
Tip 59, 330–337
Tip 60, 341–343
Tip 61, 343–345
Tip 62, 345–349
Tip 63, 349–351
Tip 64, 351–353
Tip 65, 353–355
Tip 66, 355–358
Tip 67, 359–364
Tip 68, 364–369
Tip 69, 370–372
Tip 70, 373–376
Tip 71, 376–378
Tip 72, 378–382
Tip 73, 382–384
Tip 74, 384–386
Tip 75, 386–390
Tip 76, 391–394
Tip 77, 394–398
Tip 78, 398–402
Tip 79, 402–405
Tip 80, 405–407
Tip 81, 407–410
Tip 82, 411–415
Tip 83, 415–417
Tip 84, 417–419
Tip 85, 419–422
Tip 86, 423–424
Tip 87, 424–427
Tip 88, 427–430
Tip 89, 430–434
Tip 90, 434–437
Tip 91, 437–440
Tip 92, 440–442
Tip 93, 442–444
Tip 94, 444–446
Tip 95, 446–449
Tip 96, 449–452
Tip 97, 452–455
Tip 98, 457–458
Tip 99, 458–460
Tip 100, 460
tokenizing text, 384–390
transaction safe action, 78
transform algorithm
    compared to for_each algorithm, 332
    described, 73, 522
    evaluating mathematical functions, 407–410
    operating on each element of containers, 330–337
    performing arithmetic on containers, 391–394
    uppercase/lowercase conversion, 382–384

trucks and cargo, 241–244
try blocks, 15–17
tuples, 59
type identification header, 5, 6
typeinfo header, 5, 6
types, header, 5, 6, 8

U
unary_function, 70
underflow_error, 19–20
unexpected calls, 18
unique algorithms, 76, 183–185, 233–239, 522
unnamed, temporary variable, 48, 62, 128
upper_bound algorithm, 76
uppercase manipulator, 442–444
uppercase/lowercase conversion, 382–384
using-declaration, 23–24
using-directive, 24
utilities, general, 4, 7
utility header, 7

V
valarray header, 11
variables, unnamed temporary, 48, 62, 128
variance, 434–437
vector header, 9
vectors
    adding, 64
    appending containers, 104–106
    assignment operators, 136–140
    of Booleans, 64, 149–151, 253
    checked and unchecked access, 144–147
    choosing as container, 85–87
    constructing from lists, 96–98
    constructors, 136–140
    as containers, 50–51
    converting between iterators and indexes, 131–133
    C-style arrays from, 147–149
    destructors, 136–140
    displaying, on standard output, 120–122
    dot product, 411–415
    exchanging containers, 106–109
    fast access at back, 140–144
    filled with identical elements, 93–94
    filled with specified elements, 100–102
    indexing, 128–131, 144–147
    invalid iterators, 131, 134–136
    mode value, 427–430
    norms, 417–419
    overview, 123
    remove excess memory, 125–128
    reserve space for elements, 123–125
    reverse access, 116–120
    size information, 109–111
    sorting on one of many fields, 310–314
    sorting without copying, 322–327

storing contents in another container, 102–104
swapping, 125–128, 134
vertical bars, creating, 474–476
vowels, 283–286

W
Web sites, 336, 457, 458, 523, 531–532
Westminster Kennel Club competition, 204
whitespace
extract words delimited by, 384–386
stripping in strings, 378–382
writing formatted strings, 373–376

Z
zeros, show leading, 444–446